# Computational Social Networks

T0137989

Ajith Abraham
Editor

# Computational Social Networks

Mining and Visualization

 Springer

*Editor*
Ajith Abraham
Machine Intelligence Research Labs
    (MIR Labs)
Scientific Network for Innovation
    and Research Excellence
Auburn, Washington, USA

ISBN 978-1-4471-6237-7        ISBN 978-1-4471-4054-2 (eBook)
DOI 10.1007/978-1-4471-4054-2
Springer London Heidelberg New York Dordrecht

Printed on acid-free paper

Springer is part of Springer Science+Business Media (www.springer.com)

# Preface

Computational Social Network is a new emerging field that has overlapping regions from Mathematics, Psychology, Computer Sciences, Sociology, and Management. Emails, blogs, instant messages, social network services, wikis, social bookmarking, and other instances of what is often called social software illustrate ideas from social computing.

Social network analysis is the study of relationships among social entities. Very often, all the necessary information is distributed over a number of Web sites and servers, which brings several research challenges from a data mining perspective. Real-world social networks are very dynamic and constantly evolving. Sometimes, it is much harder for us to comprehend how users in a network are connected and how influential some connections are. Visualization helps us with a better understanding of how networks function. This volume is a collection of chapters authored by world-class experts illustrating the concept of social networks from a computational point of view, with a focus on knowledge discovery (mining) and visualization of complex networks, and open avenues for further research. The authors present some of the latest advances of computational social networks and illustrate how organizations can gain competitive advantages by a better understanding of real-world complex social networks. Experience reports, survey articles, and intelligence techniques and theories with specific networks technology problems are depicted. We hope that this book will be useful for researchers, scholars, postgraduate students, and developers who are interested in social networks research and related issues. In particular, the book will be a valuable companion and comprehensive reference for both postgraduate and senior undergraduate students who are taking a course in Computational Social Networks. The book contains fourteen Chapters, which are divided into two Parts and all chapters are self-contained to provide greatest reading flexibility.

Part I comprises of nine chapters (including an introductory chapter) and deals with the modeling aspects and various computational tools used for better understanding and knowledge discovery in complex networks.

In Chap. 1, Ghali et al. introduce the concept of mining and visualization in social networks. This chapter bridges the gap by combining social network analysis methods and information visualization technology to help a user visually identify the occurrence of a possible relationship among the members in a social network.

Panda et al. in Chap. 2 introduce clustering analysis to analyze social networks. The authors' approach is intended to address the users of social network, which will not only help an organization to understand their external and internal associations but is also highly necessary for the enhancement of collaboration, innovation, and dissemination of knowledge.

In Chap. 3, Bojic et al. provide a useful insight into the differences between the human social networks based on human-to-human (H2H) interactions and the machine social networks based on machine-to-machine interactions (M2M). The authors illustrate how to analyze social networks by connecting ethological approaches to social behavior in animals and M2M interactions.

Mirkovic et al. in Chap. 4 propose approaches to understand georeferenced community-contributed multimedia data that enable users to answer many questions regarding human behavior, since they are able to discover new trends in who (user), what (content), when (time), and where (place).

In Chap. 5, Liu et al. focus on the problem of correlation mining in news retrieval. The authors present a framework of multimodal multicorrelation news retrieval, which integrates news event correlation, news entity correlation, and event-entity correlation simultaneously by exploring both text and image information. The proposed framework enables a more vivid and informative news browsing by providing two views of result presentation, namely a query-oriented multicorrelation map and a ranking list of news items with necessary descriptions including news image, title, central entities, and relevant events.

Liao et al. in Chap. 6 investigate how micromessaging technologies such as Twitter messages can be harnessed to obtain valuable information. The authors provide some of the potential applications of the micromessaging services and then discuss some insight into different challenges faced by data mining applications. Finally, microblogging services are illustrated by three different case studies.

In Chap. 7, Liu and Yang propose a time-sensitive network by using timestamp to enhance edge representation, and then provide a methodology based on the framework of business intelligence platform to support dynamic network modeling, analysis, and data mining. A proposed framework is illustrated using a nice case study.

Ben Abdesslem et al. in Chap. 8 provide a detailed review about social network data collection and user behavior. The authors highlight the shortcomings in the past research works, and introduce a novel methodology based on the experience sampling method.

In Chap. 9, Guidi et al. focus on Twitter social network features and well known, user's behavior. The authors used the contents that previously Senator and then President Barack Obama has shared in Twitter during a course of three years, and applied text-analysis. The study reveals that the discovered data clusters could be interpreted as a mirror of his political strategy.

Part II deals with usage of social network tools and frameworks for visualization and consists of five chapters.

Reinhardt et al. in Chap. 10 propagate that Artifact-Actor-Networks (AANs) serve well for modeling, storing, and mining the social interactions around digital learning resources originating from various learning services. The authors illustrate the concept by the analysis of six networks.

In Chap. 11, Hung et al. present hypergraph-based clustering method, which utilizes 3D user usage and traversal pattern information to capture user access patterns. The authors introduce a storage solution called object-oriented hypergraph-based clustering approach, which employs hidden hinting among objects in virtual environments.

Catanese et al. in Chap. 12 analyze Facebook by acquiring the necessary information directly from the front-end of the Web site, in order to reconstruct a subgraph representing anonymous interconnections among a significant subset of users. The authors describe a privacy-compliant crawler for Facebook data extraction and two different graph-mining techniques: breadth-first search and rejection sampling to analyze the structural properties of samples consisting of millions of nodes.

Yu and Ramaswamy in Chap. 13 analyze the relationship between human–computer interaction and social networking. A framework is outlined for representing and measuring online social networks, especially those formed through Web 2.0 applications and is illustrated using a case study performed on Wikipedia.

In the last chapter, Sulaiman et al. analyze Web cache server data using social network analysis (SNA) and make a number of statistic measurements to reveal the hidden information in a real-world E-learning environment. The log dataset is displayed as a connected graph and is clustered based on the similarity of characteristics, and the analysis reveal interesting results.

I am very much grateful to the authors of this volume and to the reviewers for their tremendous service by critically reviewing the chapters. Most of the authors of chapters included in this book also served as referees for chapters written by other authors. Thanks go to all those who provided constructive and comprehensive reviews. I would like to thank Wayne Wheeler and Simon Rees of Springer Verlag, London, for the editorial assistance and excellent cooperative collaboration to produce this important scientific work. Finally, I hope that the reader will share our excitement to present this volume on social networks and will find it useful.

Machine Intelligence Research Labs (MIR Labs)          Prof. (Dr.) Ajith Abraham
Scientific Network for Innovation and Research
   Excellence (SNIRE)
P.O. Box 2259, Auburn, WA 98071, USA
http://www.mirlabs.org
Email: ajith.abraham@ieee.org
Personal WWW: http://www.softcomputing.net

# Contents

# Contributors

**Ajith Abraham** Machine Intelligence Research Labs (MIR Labs), Scientific Network for Innovation and Research Excellence, Auburn, WA, USA

**Timothy Baldwin** Department of Computer Science and Software Engineering, The University of Melbourne, Melbourne, VIC, Australia

**Fehmi Ben Abdesslem** School of Computer Science, University of St Andrews, St Andrews, UK

**Iva Bojic** Faculty of Electrical Engineering and Computing, University of Zagreb, Zagreb, Croatia

**Izaskun Canga-Sanchez** Sapienza Università di Roma, Rome, Italy

**Salvatore Catanese** Department of Physics, Informatics Section, University of Messina, Messina, Italy

**Jung Tzung Chen** Department of Applied Game Technology, WuFeng University, Chiayi, Taiwan

**Chih-Ming Chiu** Department of Computer Science and Information Engineering, National Chung Cheng University, Chiayi, Taiwan

**Vladimir Crnojevic** Faculty of Technical Sciences, University of Novi Sad, Novi Sad, Serbia

**Dubravko Culibrk** Faculty of Technical Sciences, University of Novi Sad, Novi Sad, Serbia

**Pasquale De Meo** Department of Physics, Informatics Section, University of Messina, Messina, Italy

**Sachidananda Dehuri** Department of Computer and Information Technology, F.M. University, Balasore, India

**Hendrik Drachsler** Centre for Learning Sciences and Technologies, Open University of the Netherlands, Heerlen, The Netherlands

**Emilio Ferrara** Department of Mathematics, University of Messina, Messina, Italy

**Giacomo Fiumara** Department of Physics, Informatics Section, University of Messina, Messina, Italy

**Tsou Tsun Fu** Department of Applied Digital Media, WuFeng University, Chiayi, Taiwan

**Neveen Ghali** Faculty of Science, Al-Azhar University, Cairo, Egypt

**Marco Guidi** Department of Pedagogical, Psychological and Teaching Sciences, Università del Salento, Lecce, Italy

**Bo Han** Department of Computer Science and Software Engineering, The University of Melbourne, Melbourne, VIC, Australia

**Aaron Harwood** Department of Computer Science and Software Engineering, The University of Melbourne, Melbourne, VIC, Australia

**Aboul Ella Hassanien** Faculty of Computers and Information, Cairo University, Cairo, Egypt

**Tristan Henderson** School of Computer Science, University of St Andrews, St Andrews, UK

**Shao-Shin Hung** Department of Computer Science and Information Engineering, WuFeng University, Taiwan, China

**Shanika Karunasekera** Department of Computer Science and Software Engineering, The University of Melbourne, Melbourne, VIC, Australia

**Ramamohanarao Kotagiri** Department of Computer Science and Software Engineering, The University of Melbourne, Melbourne, VIC, Australia

**Zechao Li** Institute of Automation, Chinese Academy of Sciences, Beijing, China

**Yang Liao** Department of Computer Science and Software Engineering, The University of Melbourne, Melbourne, VIC, Australia

**Tomislav Lipic** Centre for Informatics and Computing, Rudjer Boskovic Institute, Zagreb, Croatia

**Jing Liu** Institute of Automation, Chinese Academy of Sciences, Beijing, China

**Xiao Liu** College of Economics, Jinan University, Guangzhou, China

**Hanqing Lu** Institute of Automation, Chinese Academy of Sciences, Beijing, China

**Milan Mirkovic** Faculty of Technical Sciences, University of Novi Sad, Novi Sad, Serbia

**Matthias Moi** Faculty of Mechanical Engineering, Computer Application and Integration in Design and Planning, University of Paderborn, Pohlweg, Paderborn, Germany

**Masud Moshtaghi** Department of Computer Science and Software Engineering, The University of Melbourne, Melbourne, VIC, Australia

**Mrutyunjaya Panda** Department of ECE, Gandhi Institute for Technological Advancement (GITA), Bhubaneswar, Odisha, India

**Iain Parris** School of Computer Science, University of St Andrews, St Andrews, UK

**Manas Ranjan Patra** Department of Computer Science, Berhampur University, Ganjam, India

**Philippa Pattison** Faculty of Medicine, Dentistry and Health Sciences Psychological Sciences, The University of Melbourne, Melbourne, VIC, Australia

**Vedran Podobnik** Faculty of Electrical Engineering and Computing, University of Zagreb, Zagreb, Croatia

**Alessandro Provetti** Department of Physics, Informatics Section, University of Messina, Messina, Italy

Oxford-Man Institute, University of Oxford, Oxford, UK

**Srini Ramaswamy** Industrial Software Systems, ABB Corporate Research Center, Bangalore, India

**Wolfgang Reinhardt** Department of Computer Science, Computer Science Education Group, University of Paderborn, Paderborn, Germany

**Igor Ruiz-Agundez** DeustoTech, Deusto Institute of Technology, University of Deusto, Basque Country, Spain

**Siti Mariyam Shamsuddin** Soft Computing Research Group, Faculty of Computer Science and Information Systems, K-Economy Research Alliance, Universiti Teknologi Malaysia, Johor, Malaysia

**Peter Sloep** Centre for Learning Sciences and Technologies, Open University of the Netherlands, Heerlen, The Netherlands

**Vaclav Snasel** Faculty of Electrical Engineering and Computer Science, VSB – Technical University of Ostrava, Ostrava – Poruba, Czech Republic

**Sarina Sulaiman** Soft Computing Research Group, Faculty of Computer Science and Information Systems, K-Economy Research Alliance, Universiti Teknologi Malaysia, Johor, Malaysia

**Jyh-Jong Tsay** Department of Computer Science and Information Engineering, National Chung Cheng University, Chiayi, Taiwan

**Adrian Wilke** Department of Computer Science, Computer Science Education Group, University of Paderborn, Paderborn, Germany

**Jianmei Yang** School of Business Administration, South China University of Technology, Guangzhou, China

**Liguo Yu** Computer Science and Informatics, Indiana University South Bend, South Bend, IN, USA

# Part I
# Mining

# Chapter 1
# Social Networks Analysis: Tools, Measures and Visualization

**Neveen Ghali, Mrutyunjaya Panda, Aboul Ella Hassanien, Ajith Abraham, and Vaclav Snasel**

**Abstract** Social Network Analysis (SNA) is becoming an important tool for investigators, but all the necessary information is often available in a distributed environment. Currently there is no information system that helps managers and team leaders monitor the status of a social network. This chapter presents an overview of the basic concepts of social networks in data analysis including social network analysis metrics and performances. Different problems in social networks are discussed such as uncertainty, missing data and finding the shortest path in a social network. Community structure, detection and visualization in social network analysis is also illustrated. This chapter bridges the gap among the users by combining social network analysis methods and information visualization technology to help a user visually identify the occurrence of a possible relationship amongst the members in a social network. The chapter illustrates an online visualization method for a DBLP

N. Ghali (✉)
Faculty of Science, Al-Azhar University, Cairo, Egypt
e-mail: nev_ghali@yahoo.com

M. Panda
Department of ECE, Gandhi Institute for Technological Advancement (GITA),
Bhubaneswar, Odisha, India
e-mail: mrutyunjaya74@gmail.com

A.E. Hassanien
Faculty of Computers and Information, Cairo University, Cairo, Egypt
e-mail: aboitcairo@gmail.com

A. Abraham
Machine Intelligence Research Labs (MIR Labs), Scientific Network for Innovation
and Research Excellence, Auburn, WA, USA
e-mail: ajith.abraham@ieee.org

V. Snasel
Faculty of Electrical Engineering and Computer Science, VSB – Technical University
of Ostrava, Ostrava – Poruba, Czech Republic
e-mail: vaclav.snasel@vsb.cz

A. Abraham (ed.), *Computational Social Networks: Mining and Visualization*,
DOI 10.1007/978-1-4471-4054-2_1, © Springer-Verlag London 2012

(Digital Bibliography & Library Project) dataset of publications from the field of computer science, which is focused on the co-authorship relationship based on the intensity and topic of joint publications. Challenges to be addressed and future directions of research are presented and an extensive bibliography is also included.

## Introduction

Social media brings people together in many creative ways, for example users are playing, tagging, working, and socializing online, demonstrating new forms of collaboration and communication that were hardly imaginable just a short time ago. Moreover, social networks play a crucial role in the entrepreneurial process and also help reshape business models and emotions, and open up numerous possibilities to study human interaction and collective behaviour on an unparalleled scale [4, 22, 48, 49].

Nowadays, the Internet plays an increasingly important role and it has gradually infiltrated into every aspect of our lives because of its rich and varied resources. More and more people would like to spend their time on the Internet especially in order to build some kind of large social entertainment community and then try to communicate with each other as frequently as practicable to enable the relationship between them to become closer. Hence, Social Network Analysis (SNA) has become a widely applied method in research and business for inquiring into the web of relationships on the individual, organizational and societal level. With ready access to computing power, the popularity of social networking websites such as Facebook, Twitter, Netlog etc., and automated data collection techniques, the demand for solid expertise in SNA has recently exploded. This interdisciplinary subject is presented herein and introduces the readers to the basic concepts and analysis techniques in SNA to help them understand how to identify key individuals and groups in social systems, to detect and generate fundamental network structures, and then finally to design model growth and diffusion processes in networks. After this introduction to SNA, the readers will be able to design and execute network analysis projects including collecting data and considering ethical and legal implications, to perform systematic and informed analyses of network data for personal, commercial and scholarly use, and to critically review SNA projects conducted by others. It may be concluded that the social network approach for the study of behaviour involves two main themes: (a) the use of formal theory organized in mathematical terms, (b) followed by the systematic analysis of empirical data. The study of social networks really began to take off as an interdisciplinary specialty only after 1970, when modern discrete combinatorics (particularly graph theory) experienced rapid development and relatively powerful computers became readily available. Since then, it has found important applications in organizational behaviour, interorganizational relations, the spread of contagious diseases, mental health, social support, the diffusion of information and animal social organization [44]. Choudhury and Pentland [6] explained how sensors proliferate and how an increasing volume of data is generated from the sensors that contain information about social groupings among sensed individuals. Understanding these groups can be of much importance for a variety of reasons. For example, the DARPA CALO (Cognitive Assistant that Learns and Observes) project [30] exploits knowledge of social groups to anticipate user needs and scheduling conflicts. Physical security and safety applications can then use the knowledge obtained about the social groups to identify unusual, dangerous or threatening behaviour. The MERL (Mitsubishi Electric Research Lab) dataset [54] is an excellent example of the result of daily use of large numbers of sensors in an office environment. This is a dataset of activations of motion sensors distributed through the MERL environment, recorded during the course of 1 year. The sensors generate a high volume of data each day, resulting in a dataset that is difficult to process exhaustively in a short amount of time. The situation is further complicated when one wishes to examine n-way social networks inherent in such a dataset. Jenson and Neville [22] used the Internet Movie Database (IMDb) (www.imdb.com) and the Hollywood Stock Exchange (HSX) (www.hsx.com), an artificial market where players trade in stocks that track the relative popularity of movie actors, both of which are publicly available datasets for research and other non-commercial purposes. The dataset consists of over 300,000 movies, 650,000 persons, and 11,000 studios and the objects are connected by over 2.3 million acted-in links, 300,000 directed links, and 200,000 produced links. The available data on movies vary widely, as not all movies have releases, and HSX data are only available for a small percentage of actors in IMDb. However, the data is more complete for more recent movies and persons.

This chapter is organized in the following way. Section "Social Network Analysis: Basics" provides an explanation of some basic related concepts including social networks versus computer networks and describes some of the social network sites (SNSs). Section "Social Networks: Analysis Metrics and Performance" briefly describes the different performance measures that are encountered during any network analysis. Section "Different Problems in Social Networks" discusses different problems in social networks including uncertainty, missing data in the social network and finding the shortest path. Section "Community Structure and Detection" discusses community structure and detection. Section "Social Network Visualization" discusses visualization in the social networks and briefly illustrates an online analysis tool called FORCOA.net, which is built over the DBLP dataset of scholarly publications in the field of computer science. Finally, conclusions are provided in section "Social Network Concepts to Visualize Terrorist Networks".

## Social Network Analysis: Basics

### *Social Network Versus Computer Networks*

Networks can be categorized according to the topology, which is the geometric arrangement of a computer system. Common topologies include a bus, star, and ring, protocol which defines a common set of rules and signals that computers on the network follow. Network architectures can be broadly classified as either a peer-to-peer or client/server architecture. Computers on a network are sometimes called nodes. Computers and devices that allocate resources for a network are called servers. It is argued that social networks differ from most other types of networks, including technological and biological networks, in two important ways. First, they have non-trivial clustering or network transitivity and second, they show positive correlations between the degrees of adjacent vertices. Social networks are often divided into groups or communities, and it has recently been suggested that this division could account for the observed clustering. Furthermore, group structure in networks can also account for degree correlations. Hence, assortative mixing in such networks with a variation in the sizes of the groups provides the predicted level and compares well with that observed in real-world networks.

## *Social Network Sites*

Social network sites are web sites that allow users to register, create their own profile page containing information about themselves (real or virtual), to establish public 'Friend' connections with other members and to communicate with other members [4]. Communication typically takes the form of private emails, public comments written on each others' profile pages, blog or pictures, or instant messaging. SNSs like Facebook and MySpace are amongst the ten most popular web sites in the world. SNSs are very popular in many countries and include Orkut (Brazil), Cyworld (Korea), and Mixi (Japan).

The growth of SNSs seems to have been driven by the youth, with Facebook originating as a college site [4] and MySpace having an average age of 21 for members in early 2008 [48]. However, an increasing proportion of older members are also using these sites. The key motivating factor for using SNSs is sociability, however, this suggests that some types of people may never use social network sites extensively [49]. Moreover, it seems that extraversion is beneficial in SNSs [42] and that female MySpace users seem to be more extraverted and more willing to self-disclose than male users [40], which suggests they may be more effective communicators in this environment.

SNSs are very interesting because they support public conversations between friends and acquaintances. Walther et al. [51] mentioned that SNS profiles are known as venues for identity expression of members and since public comments appear in these profiles, they may also be composed or interpreted from the perspective of identity expression rather than simply performing a purely communicative function. At the same time, such public conversations are interesting because the web now contains millions of informal public messages that researchers can access and analyze. The availability of demographic information about the sender and recipient in their profile pages makes it more interesting and useful but certain ethical issue might arise (unlike standard interview or questionnaire protocols). However, if the data has been placed in the most public place online as found though Google then its use does not constitute any kind of invasion of privacy [31]. An ethical issue only arises if feedback is given to the text authors or if contact is established. The data mining research on MySpace was more commercially oriented rather than for social science goals, but then an IBM study demonstrated how to generate rankings of musicians based upon opinions mined from MySpace comments [14], and a Microsoft team developed a league table system for movies by extracting lists from MySpace profiles, without explicit sentiment analysis [41].

## Social Networks: Analysis Metrics and Performance

This section illustrates the different performance measures that are encountered during any network analysis in order to understand the fundamental concepts. The four most important concepts used in network analysis are closeness, network density, centrality, betweenness and centralization. In addition to these, there are four other measures of network performance that include: robustness, efficiency, effectiveness and diversity. The first set of measures concern structure, whereas the second set concern dynamics and thus depend on a theory explaining why certain agents do certain things in order to access the information.

### *Social Networks Analysis Metrics*

#### Closeness

This refers to the degree with which an individual is nearer to all others in a network either directly or indirectly [20]. Further, it reflects the ability to access information through the "grapevine" of network members. In this way, closeness is considered to be the inverse of the sum of the shortest distance (sometimes called geodesic distance) between each individual and all others available in the network. For a network with $n$ number of nodes, the closeness is represented mathematically as:

$$c_c(n_j) = \frac{n-1}{\sum_{k=i,j=k}^{n} d(n_i, n_j)} \tag{1.1}$$

where $C_c n_k$ defines the standardized closeness centrality of node $j$ and $d(n_i, n_j)$ denotes the geodesic distance between $j$ and $k$.

#### Network Density

Network density is a measure of the connectedness in a network. Density is defined as the actual number of ties in a network, expressed as a proportion of the maximum possible number of ties. It is a number that varies between 0 and 1.0. When density is close to 1.0, the network is said to be dense, otherwise it is sparse. When dealing with directed ties, the maximum possible number of pairs is used instead. The problem with the measure of density is that it is sensitive to the number of network nodes; therefore, it cannot be used for comparisons across networks that vary significantly in size [20].

## Centrality: Local and Global

The concept of centrality comprises two levels: local and global. A node is said to have local centrality, when it has a higher number of ties with other nodes, otherwise it is referred to as a global centrality. Whereas local centrality considers only direct ties (the ties directly connected to that node), global centrality also considers indirect ties (which are not directly connected to that node). For example, in a network with a "star" structure, in which, all nodes have ties with one central node, local centrality of the central node is equal to 1.0. Whereas local centrality measures are expressed in terms of the number of nodes to which a node is connected, global centrality is expressed in terms of the distances among the various nodes. Two nodes are connected by a path if there is a sequence of distinct ties connecting them, and the length of the path is simply the number of ties that make it up. The shortest distance between two points on the surface of the earth lies along the geodesic that connects them, and, by analogy, the shortest path between any particular pair of nodes in a network is termed a geodesic. A node is globally central if it lies at a short distance from many other nodes. Such a node is said to be "close" to many of the other nodes in the network, sometimes global centrality is also called closeness centrality. Local and global centrality depends mostly on the size of the network, and therefore they cannot be compared when networks differ significantly in size [20].

## Betweenness

Betweenness [20] is defined as the extent to which a node lies between other nodes in the network. Here, the connectivity of the node's neighbours is taken into account in order to provide a higher value for nodes which bridge clusters. This metric reflects the number of people who are connecting indirectly through direct links. The betweenness of a node measures the extent to which an agent (represented by a node) can play the part of a broker or gatekeeper with a potential for control over others. Methodologically, betweenness is the most complex of the measures of centrality to calculate and also suffers from the same disadvantages as local and global centrality. The betweenness of the nodes in a network can be defined as:

$$c_b(n_j) = \frac{x\,x}{\dfrac{(n-2)(n-1)}{2}} \tag{1.2}$$

$$xx = \sum_{k<i,j=k,j=t} \frac{g_{kt}(n_j)}{g_{kt}} \tag{1.3}$$

where $c_b(n_j)$ denotes the standardized betweenness centrality of node $j$, $g_{kt}(n_j)$ represents the number of geodesics linking $k$ and $I$ that contain $j$ in between.

## Centralization

Centralization is calculated as the ratio between the numbers of links for each node divided by the maximum possible sum of differences [20]. Centralization provides a measure of the extent to which a whole network has a centralized structure. Whereas centralization describes the extent to which this connectedness is organized around particular focal nodes; density describes the general level of connectedness in a network. Centralization and density, therefore, are important complementary pair measures. While a centralized network will have many of its links dispersed around one or a few nodes, the decentralized network is one in which there is little variation between the number of links each node possesses. The general procedure involved in any measure of network centralization is to look at the differences between centrality scores of the most central node and those of all other nodes. Basically, centralization can be graphed in three ways – one for each of the three centrality measures: local, global and betweenness. All three centralization measures vary from 0 to 1.0. Zero corresponds to a network in which all the nodes are connected to all other nodes whereas a value of 1.0 is achieved on all three measures for "star" networks. However, the majority of real networks lie between these two extremes. Methodologically, the choices of one of these three centralization measures depends on which specific structural features the researcher wants to focus upon. For example, while a betweenness-based measure is sensitive to the chaining of nodes, a local centrality-based measure of network centralization seems to be particularly less sensitive to the local dominance of nodes [20]. It is measured as:

$$R = \frac{\sum_{j=1}^{g}\{\max(D_i) - D_i\}}{(g-1)^2} \tag{1.4}$$

where $D_i$ represents the number of actors in the network that are directly linked to the actor $j$ and $g$ is denoted as the total number of actors present in the network.

## *Social Network Performance*

Once the network analysis is completed, the network dynamics predict the performance of the network which can be evaluated as a combination of: (1) the network's robustness to the removal of ties and/or nodes, (2) network efficiency in terms of the distance to traverse from one node to another and its non-redundant size,

(3) effectiveness of the network in terms of information benefits allocated to central nodes and finally, (4) network diversity in terms of the history of each of the nodes [20].

## *Robustness*

Social network analysts have highlighted the importance of network structure with relation to the network's robustness. The robustness can be evaluated based on how it becomes fragmented when an increasing fraction of nodes is removed. Robustness is measured as an estimate of the tendency of individuals in networks to form local groups or clusters of individuals with whom they share similar characteristics, i.e., clustering. For example, if individuals X, Y, and Z are all computer experts and if $X$ knows $Y$ and $Y$ knows $Z$, then it is highly likely that $X$ knows $Z$ using the so-called chain rule. If the measure of the clustering of individuals is high for a given network, then the robustness of that network increases – within a cluster/group [20].

## *Efficiency*

Network efficiency can be measured by considering the number of nodes that can instantly access a large number of different nodes – sources of knowledge, status, etc., through a relatively small number of ties. These nodes are treated as non-redundant contacts. For example, with two networks of equal size, the one with more non-redundant contacts provides more benefits than the others. Also, it is quite evident that the gain from a new contact redundant with existing contacts will be minimal. However, it is wise to consume time and energy in cultivating a new contact to un-reached people. Hence, social network analysts measure efficiency by the number of non-redundant contacts and the average number of ties an ego has to traverse to reach any alter, this number is referred to as the average path length. The shorter the average path length relative to the size of the network and the lower the number of redundant contacts, the more efficient is the network [20].

## *Effectiveness*

Effectiveness targets the cluster of nodes that can be reached through non-redundant contacts. In contrast, efficiency aims at the reduction of the time and energy spent on redundant contacts. Each cluster of contacts is an independent source of information. One cluster around this non-redundant node, no matter how numerous its members are, is only one source of information, because people connected to one another tend to know about the same things at about the same time. For example, a network is more effective when the information benefit provided by multiple clusters of contacts is broader, providing better assurance that the central node will be informed. Moreover, because non-redundant contacts are only connected through the central node, the central node is assured of being the first to see new opportunities created by needs in one group that could be served by skills in another group [20].

## *Diversity*

While efficiency is about getting a large number of (non-redundant) nodes, a node's diversity, conversely suggests a critical performance point of view where those nodes are diverse in nature, i.e., the history of each individual node within the network is important. It is particularly this aspect that can be explored through case studies, which is a matter of intense discussion among social network analysts. It seems to suggest that social scientists should prefer and use network analysis according to the first strand of thought developed by social network analysts instead of actor-attribute-oriented accounts based on the diversity of each the nodes [20].

## Different Problems in Social Networks

## *Uncertainty in a Social Network*

The uncertainty in digital evidence is not being evaluated at present, thus making it difficult to assess the reliability of evidence stored on and transmitted using computer networks [38]. Uncertainty occurs when the actors are confronted with too many interpretations, causing confusion. In an ambiguous situation there is no lack of information, no gap that could be filled with a better scanning of available information, rather there are at least two (and often more) different interpretations of the situation [2]. Many research works tackled the problem that the data collected through automated sensors, anonymized communication data, and self-reporting logging on Internet-scale networks as a proxy for real relationships and interactions causes some uncertainty.

Gutirrez-Muñoz and Kandel [15] introduced a methodology that incorporates into the social interaction activity records of the uncertainty and time sensitiveness of the events through Fuzzy Social Networks Analysis (FSNA). Also, they investigated an approach based on the analysis of current flows in electrical networks for the extraction of primary routes of interaction among key actors in a social network. They proposed that the ability to capture the influence of all nodes involved in a network over a particular path represents a promising avenue for the extraction of characteristics of the social network assuming that uncertainty and time sensitiveness are parameters of the information stored on activity logs that cannot be ignored and must be accounted for. In Yang et al. [55] an adaptive group Fuzzy analytic network process group decision support system under uncertainty is put forth which makes up for some deficiencies in the conventional analytic network process. In the first step fuzzy judgments are used when it is difficult to characterize the uncertainty by point-valued judgments due to partially known information, and a bipartite graph is formulated to model the problem of group decision making under uncertainty. Then, a Fuzzy prioritization method is proposed to derive the local priorities from missing or inconsistent Fuzzy pairwise comparison judgments. As a result of the unlikeliness for all the decision makers to evaluate all elements under uncertainty, an original aggregation method is developed to cope with the situation where some of the local priorities are missing. Finally, an evaluation of petroleum-contaminated site remedial countermeasures using the proposed group fuzzy analytic network process, indicates that the presented group decision support system can effectively handle uncertainty and support group decision making with high level of user satisfaction. Authors in [16] observed that the characteristics of social systems are poorly modelled with crisp attributes. A concrete agent-based system illustrates the analysis of the evolution of values in a society enhanced with fuzzy logic to improve agent models that get closer to reality. This has been explored in five aspects: relationships among agents, some variable attributes that determine agent states, functions of similarity, evolution of agent states, and inheritance. Vindigni and Janssen [50] proposed a new approach to combine survey data with multi-agent simulation models of consumer behaviour to study the diffusion process of organic food consumption. This methodology is based on rough set theory, which is able to translate survey data into behavioural rules. However, the peculiarity of the rough set approach is that the inconsistencies in a data set about consumer behaviour are not aggregated or corrected since lower and upper approximations are computed. Also rough set data analysis provides a suitable link between survey data and multi-agent models since it is designed to extract decision rules from large quantitative and qualitative data sets.

## Missing Data in a Social Network

The inherent problem with much of the data is that it is noisy and incomplete, and at the wrong level of fidelity and abstraction for meaningful data analysis. Thus, there is a need for methods that extract and infer "clean" annotated networks from noisy observational network data. This involves inferring missing attribute values (attribute prediction), adding missing links and removing spurious links between the nodes (link prediction), and eliminating duplicate nodes (entity resolution).

Moustafa et al. [32] identified a set of primitives to support the extraction and inference of a network from observational data, and describe a framework that enables a network analyst to easily implement and combine new extraction and analysis techniques, and efficiently apply them to large observation networks. Perez et al. [36] proposed linguistic decision analysis to solve decision making problems involving linguistic information by using ordinal fuzzy linguistic modelling. In such situations, experts are forced to provide incomplete fuzzy linguistic preference relations. So an additive consistency based estimation process of missing values to deal with incomplete Fuzzy Linguistic preference relations was developed.

## *Finding the Shortest Path*

The problem of finding the shortest path is finding the path with minimum distance or cost from a starting node to an ending node. It is one of the most fundamental network optimization problems. The shortest path problem also has a deep connection to the minimum cost flow problem, which is an abstraction for various shipping and distribution problems, the minimum weight perfect matching, and the minimum mean-cycle problem. Computing shortest paths in graphs is one of the most well-studied problems in combinatorial optimization [33, 46]. The ant colony optimization algorithm is a very efficient machine learning technique for finding the shortest path. The ants, during the activity of finding food and bringing it back to the nest, manage not only to explore a vast area, but also to indicate to their peers the location of the food while bringing it back to the nest. Most of the time, they will find the shortest path and adapt to ground changes, hence proving the great efficiency with which they carry out this difficult task. The authors of [29] proposed the SEMANT algorithm based on ant colony optimization. The proposed algorithm finds the shortest path from every querying peer to one or more appropriate answering peers that possess resources for the given query. An unstructured peer-to-peer network is designed that consists of carefully selected constituents of the ant colony system, AntNet, and AntHocNet, which were combined and adapted for the purposes of the application. Lertsuwanakul and Unger [27] applied the ant colony optimization system where a messenger distributes its pheromone, the long-link details, in the surrounding area. The subsequent forwarding decision has more options to move to, select among local neighbours or send to a node that has a long link closer to its target. They introduced a novel approach for routing in a social network. The authors showed that with additional information, the existence of a shortcut in the surrounding area, they were able to find a shorter path than using the greedy algorithm. Perumbuduru and Dhar [35] proposed the AntNet algorithm by using ant colony optimization. The authors in [26] proposed the Open Shortest Path First protocol by using a genetic algorithm. They implemented a genetic algorithm to find the set of optimal routes to send the traffic from source to destination. A genetic algorithm is well suited for routing problems as it explores solution space in multiple directions at once with less chances to attain a local optimum. The proposed algorithm works on an initial population created by another module, assesses fitness, generates a new population using genetic operators and converges after meeting a specified termination condition.

A hybridization between the ant colony optimization algorithm and genetic algorithm was presented by Cauvery et al. [5] for routing in packet switched data networks. The ant algorithm is found to reduce the size of the routing table. The genetic algorithm cannot use the global information of the network. Hence a combination of these two algorithms, which allows the packets to explore the network independently, helps in finding a path between pairs of nodes effectively. White et al. [52] applied the Ant System with Genetic Algorithm (ASGA) system to the problem of path finding in networks, demonstrating by experimentation that the hybrid algorithm exhibits improved performance when compared to the basic ant system. They demonstrated that the ant system can be used to solve hard combinatorial optimization problems as represented by Steiner vertex identification and shortest cycle determination. The authors in [3] proposed a new neural network to solve the shortest path problem for inter-network routing. The proposed solution extends the traditional single-layer recurrent Hopfield architecture introducing a two-layer architecture that automatically guarantees an entire set of constraints held by any valid solution to of the shortest path problem. This solution aims to achieve an increase in succeeded and valid convergence which is one of the main limitations of previous solutions based on neural networks. Additionally, in general, it requires less neurons. Sang and YI [39] applied a Pulse Coupled Neural Network (PCNN) model called Dual Source PCNN (DSPCNN), which can improve the computational efficiency of pulse coupled neural networks for shortest path problems. Deng and Tong [9] proposed a new algorithm by using a particle swarm optimization algorithm with a priority-based encoding scheme based on a fluid neural network to search for the shortest path in stochastic traffic networks.

## Community Structure and Detection

Community structure is one of the key properties of complex networks and detecting communities is a problem of considerable interest. Community structure in the context of networks, refers to the occurrence of groups of nodes in a network that are more densely connected internally than with the rest of the network. This inhomogeneity of connections suggests that the network has certain natural divisions within it. Note that communities are often defined in terms of the partition of the set of vertices, that is each node is put into one and only one community. This is a useful simplification but may not be appropriate in many cases [18]. Identifying meaningful community structure in social networks is inherently a hard problem. Extremely large network size or sparse networks compound the difficulty of the task. Moreover, their scalability is limited to at most a few thousand nodes and execution becomes intractable for very large networks [11]. Among many different community detection approaches, there are two main ones [10]: (1) the graph structure of the network which is named the topology-based community detection approach, and (2) the textual information of the network nodes under consideration which is named the topic-based community detection approach. The detection of the community structure is a promising field of research with many open research challenges. Detecting communities is of great importance in many fields including sociology, biology and computer science, disciplines where systems are often represented as graphs. This problem is very hard and has not yet been satisfactorily solved, despite the huge effort of the large interdisciplinary community of scientists that have been working on it over the past few years.

Community detection in social network analysis is usually considered as a single-objective optimization problem, in which different heuristics or approximate algorithms are employed to optimize an objective function that captures the notion of community. Because of the inadequacy of those single-objective solutions, Shi et al. [43] formulated a multi-objective framework for community detection and presented a multi-objective community detection system (called MOCD) for finding efficient solutions under the framework. The system includes two stages: (1) the community detection stage, and (2) the community selection stage. In the first stage, MOCD simultaneously optimizes two conflicting objective functions with an evolutionary algorithm (EA) and returns a set of solutions, which are optimal in terms of optimization objectives. In order to help decision makers in selecting proper community partitions, in the second stage, two selection approaches are proposed to select one recommendation solution from the solution set returned by the first stage. Through extensive experiments on both simulated and real networks, Shi et al. [43] demonstrated that a combination of two negatively correlated objectives under the multi-objective framework usually leads to remarkably better performance compared with either of the original single objectives, including even many popular algorithms.

## Social Network Visualization

Visualizing social networks is of immense help for social network researchers in understanding new ways to present and manage data and to effectively convert the data into meaningful information [47]. A number of visualization tools have been proposed for effective visualization of social networks including Pajek [12], NetVis, Krackplot, IKnow, InFlow, Visone, JUNG and Prefuse, to name a few. Another source of online collaboration has also been visualized to better understand interactions that are provided in a discussion form [8]. Visualizing tasks for better collaboration during software development are proposed in [8] to address issues of co-ordination and geographical distribution of developer teams. Visualizing social networks using query interfaces for wikis and blogs [28] are used to provide end-users with more user-friendly alternatives.

## *FORCOA.net: An Interactive Tool for Exploring the Significance of Authorship Networks in DBLP Data*

To illustrate the importance of visualization, we use the FORCOA.net [19] online tool which provides a nice visualization scheme for Computer Science authors who have publications in selected journals and conferences as registered in DBLP [21]. During the analysis of authors involved in the scholarly publication of articles over

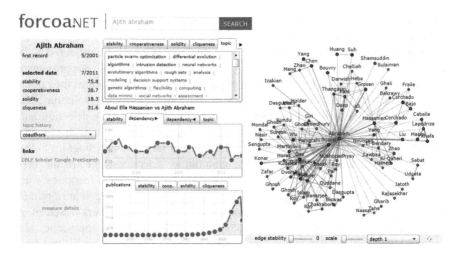

Fig. 1.1 Illustration of Ajith Abraham and Aboul ella Hassanien as a co-author network (01/2012) [19]

a long period of time, the actuality and clarity of the author's collaboration network is often lost. A key requirement was the need for the visualization of an author and his/her academic network in the context of their publication activities. The online tool is built over the DBLP dataset and the dataset contains information about 913,534 authors from the field of computer science and 5,192,020 interactions between these authors [17].

Authors used the stability measure based on the forgetting curve [17, 19]. The stability measure characterizes the behaviour of an author in the network (if the author publishes regularly and over a long term). The online tool is focused on the analysis and visualization of the co-authorship relationship based on the intensity and topic of joint publications. The visualization of co-authorship networks allows one to describe the author and his/her current surroundings, while still incorporating the historical aspects. The analysis is based on using the forgetting function to hold the information relevant to the selected date. Several measures, which can describe different aspects of user behaviour from the scientific social network point of view [17] are also illustrated in the network. In comparison to classical SNA measures (such as centrality, clustering coefficient, etc.) [17, 19] focuses on the usage of edge and vertex stability.

Figure 1.1 illustrates a screenshot of the author Ajith Abraham using the online tool. In the left part of the interface, is a panel containing author details, such as first record in the network and values of several metrics with respect to selected date. This panel also contains a detailed illustration of co-authors and direct links pointing to details about other co-authors [19].

The right part of the interface contains the visualization of the authors social network with current author highlighted. The network can be filtered using some minimum edge weight (see below) or can be switched to a different network view. The default network view contains co-authors to depth 1. The view can be switched

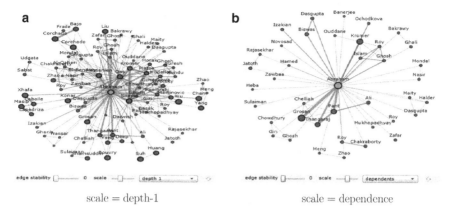

scale = depth-1                                    scale = dependence

**Fig. 1.2** Illustration of Ajith Abraham network with edge stability = 0 and depth = 1 [19]

to depth 2, but also to the so-called dependency or independency network (showing only dependent or independent co-authors).

The middle part contains three groups of panels. The first group contain values of author measures (such as stability, cooperativeness, topics, etc.) over the time period. If you select an edge with a co-author, the second group of panels will appear. These panels contains values of relation measures (stability of the relation, dependency between authors and the topics of the relation). By clicking somewhere in the timeline you can switch the view to a different point in time. The third group of panels contains global values of the whole dataset (such as number of publications, distribution of particular measures over the authors). Figure 1.2 depicts Ajith Abraham's network with a different scale.

## Social Network Concepts to Visualize Terrorist Networks

After the 9/11 attacks, much effort was put into developing effective methods for anti-terrorism strategies. Visualization is a very important part of analyzing such a network since it can quickly provide good insight into the network's structure, major members, and their properties [12]. Analyzing huge networks is not an easy task and there is a need to reduce the complexity of these networks, which is usually depicted in the form of huge matrices. The Matrix Factorization Method is a well-established approach and Semi-Discrete Decomposition is highly suitable for dealing with huge networks. Empirical results using the 9–11 network data illustrate the efficiency of the proposed approach [45]. The analysis of general complex networks, link prediction etc. are well illustrated in [1, 7, 13, 23, 24, 34, 37, 53].

The obtained experiment is based on the dataset involving 9/11 attacks from [25]. A binary incidence matrix of involved persons was created and then the rank for Semi-Discrete Decomposition (SDD) factorization was computed and this reduced

**Fig. 1.3** Terrorist network with highlighted link suggestions using SDD reduction (rank 10)

matrix was compared with the original one [45]. A change from zero to one in the reduced matrix can be in a wider sense considered as a link suggestion. In different fields, the suggestion can have different meanings. In the terrorist network, we can consider them as suggestions for investigation to determine whether the link truly exists in reality; for more detail the reader may refer to [45]. The results for a rank parameter setting equal to 10 are illustrated in Fig. 1.3. Same colouring is used as in the original paper [25] by Krebs. Green triangles represent flight AA #11, which crashed into WTC North, full red squares represent flight AA #77 which crashed into the Pentagon, empty blue squares represent flight UA #93 which crashed in Pennsylvania, and full purple diamonds represent flight UA #175 which crashed into WTC South.

Edges drawn in bold red are suggestions obtained by the mentioned reduction. As is evident, the suggested links are in the group of Zacarias Moussaoui, Abu Qatada, David Courtaillier, Jerome Courtaillier, Abu Walid, Kamel Daoudi and Djamal Beghal. This group is also connected using several subgroups in the original data, therefore the proposed method suggests their stronger interconnection. The same holds for the suggested link between Ramzi bin al-Shibh and Lofti Raissi as it connects two different groups of individuals. Remaining suggestions can be explored in a similar way.

Results obtained using a rank parameter setting equal to 20 (that means a lower ratio of reduction) are shown in the right part of Fig. 1.4. Less reduction in this case means less suggestions, but the suggestions obtained for rank 20 are not a subset

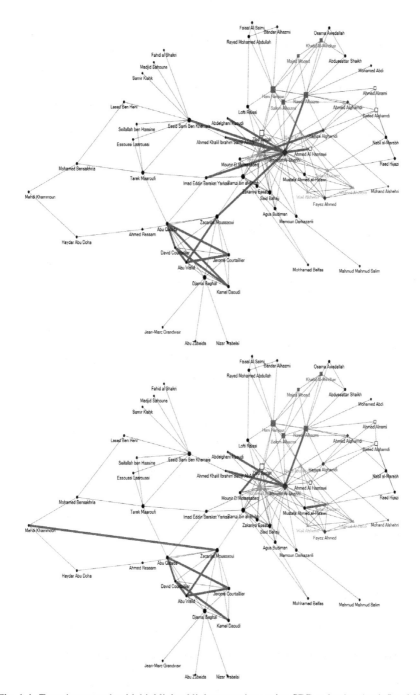

**Fig. 1.4** Terrorist network with highlighted link suggestions using SDD reduction (rank 5 and 20)

of suggestions for rank 10. As SDD always tries to minimize the error function, the reduction process is not straightforward – for example the links between Mehdi Khammoun and Zacarias Moussaoui, Mustafa Ahmed al-Hisawi and Satam Suqami as well as the link between Marwan Al-Shehhi and Nawaf Alhazmi are present at rank 20, but disappear at rank 10. The remaining links are still present at rank 10. A similar situation occurs with the setting $k = 5$ (left part of Fig. 1.4), which gives us 16 suggestions – using stronger reduction we have obtained more suggestions, but not all suggestions from rank 10 are present.

## Conclusions

The popularity and ease of use of social networking services have excited institutions with their potential in a variety of areas. However, effective use of social networking services poses a number of challenges for institutions including long-term sustainability of the services; user concerns over use of social tools in a work or study context; a variety of technical issues and legal issues such as copyright, privacy, accessibility; etc. Institutions would be advised to consider carefully the implications before promoting significant use of such services. Clear understanding of the structural properties of a criminal network may help analysts target critical network members for removal or surveillance, and locate network vulnerabilities where disruptive actions can be effective. Appropriate network analysis techniques, therefore, are needed to mine criminal networks and gain insight into these problems.

Social Network Analysis (SNA) is becoming an important tool for investigators, but all the necessary information is often distributed over a number of Web servers. Currently there is no information system that helps managers and team leaders to monitor the status of a social network. This Chapter presented an overview of the basic concepts of social networks in data analysis including social network analysis metrics and performances. Different problems in social networks are discussed such as uncertainty, missing data and finding the shortest path in a social network. Community structure, detection and visualization in social network analysis were also discussed.

## References

1. Abadie, A., Gardeazabal, J.: Terrorism and the world economy. Eur. Econ. Rev. **52**(1), 1–27 (2008)
2. Antheunis, M.L., Valkenburg, P.M., Peter, J.: Getting acquainted through social network sites: testing a model of online uncertainty reduction and social attraction. Comput. Hum. Behav. **26**, 100–109 (2010)
3. Araujo, F., Ribeiro, B., Rodrigues, L.: A neural network for shortest path computation. IEEE Trans. Neural Netw. **12**(5), 1067–1073 (2001)

4. Boyd, D., Ellison, N.: Social network sites: definition, history and scholarship. J. Comput. Mediat. Commun. **13**(1), 210–230 (2007)
5. Cauvery, N., Viswanatha, K.V.: Routing in dynamic network using ants genetic algorithm. IJCSNS Int. J. Comput. Sci. Netw. Secur. **9**(3), 194–200 (2009)
6. Choudhuri, T., Pentland, A.: Sensing and modelling human networks using the sociometer. In: Proceedings of 7th IEEE Symposium on Wearable Computing, New York (2003)
7. Czinkota, M.R., Knight, G.A., Liesch, P.W., Steen, J.: Positioning terrorism in management and marketing: research propositions. J. Int. Manag. **11**(4), 581–604 (2005)
8. De Nooy, W., AMrvar, A., Batagelig, V.: Exploring SNA with pajek. Cambridge University Press, Cambridge/New York (2004)
9. Deng, Y., Tong, H.: Dynamic shortest path algorithm in stochastic traffic networks using PSO based on fluid neural network. J. Intell. Learn. Syst. Appl. **3**, 11–16 (2011)
10. Ding, Y.: Community detection: topological vs. topical. J. Informetr. **5**(4), 498–514 (2011)
11. Fortunato, S.: Community detection in graphs. Phys. Rep. **486**(3–5), 75–174 (2010)
12. Freeman, L.: Visualizing social network. J. Soc. Struct. **1**(1) (2000)
13. Frey, B.S.: How can business cope with terrorism? J. Policy Model. **31**(5), 779–787 (2009)
14. Grace, J., Gruhl, D., et al.: Artist ranking through analysis of on-line community comments. IBM Research technical report (2007)
15. Gutirrez-Muñoz, A., Kandel, A.: Current flows in electrical networks for fuzzy social network analysis (FSNA). Department of Computer Science and Engineering, University of South Florida (2009)
16. Hassan, S., Garmendia, L., Pavon, J.: Introducing uncertainty into social simulation: using fuzzy logic for agent-based modelling. Int. J. Reason. Based Intell. Syst. **2**(2), 118–124 (2010)
17. Horak, Z., Kudelka, M., Snasel, V., Abraham, A., Rezankova, H.: Forcoa.NET: an interactive tool for exploring the significance of authorship networks in DBLP Data. In: Third International Conference on Computational Aspects of Social Networks (CASoN 2011), Salamanca, pp. 261–266. IEEE (2011). ISBN: 978-1-4577-1131-2
18. http://en.wikipedia.org/wiki/Community_structure. Accessed on March 2012
19. http://www.FORCOA.net. Accessed on 07 Jan 2012
20. http://en.wikipedia.org/wiki/Betweenness. Accessed on 07 Jan 2012
21. http://www.informatik.uni-trier.de/ley/db/. Accessed on 07 Jan 2012
22. Jenson, D., Neville, J.: Data mining in networks. In: Symposium on Dynamic Social Network Modelling and Analysis, National Academy of Sciences. National Academy Press, Washington (2002)
23. Koh, W.T.H.: Terrorism and its impact on economic growth and technological innovation. Technol. Forecast. Soc. Change **74**(2), 129–138 (2007)
24. Kollias, C., Messis, P., Mylonidis, N., Paleologou, S.: Terrorism and the effectiveness of security spending in Greece: policy implications of some empirical findings. J. Policy Model. **31**(5), 788–802 (2009)
25. Krebs, V.E.: Uncloaking terrorist networks. First Monday **7** (2002)
26. Kumar, R., Kumar, M.: Exploring genetic algorithm for shortest path optimization in data networks. Glob. J. Comput. Sci. Technol. (GJCST 2010) **10**(11), 8–12 (2010)
27. Lertsuwanakul, L., Unger, H.: An improved greedy routing algorithm for grid using pheromone-based landmark. World Acad. Sci. Eng. Technol. **59**, 172–176 (2009)
28. Matsuo, Y., et al.: Polyphonet: an advanced social network extraction system from the web. In: www 06, Proceedings of International Conference on World Wide Web, New York, pp. 397–406 (2006)
29. Michlmayr, E.: Ant algorithms for self-organization in social networks. Ph.D. thesis, Vienna University of Technology, Faculty of Informatics (2007)
30. Mitchell, T., wang, S., Huang, Y., Cheyer, A.: Extracting knowledge about users activities from raw workstation contents. In: Proceedings of 21st National confefernce on Artificial Intelligence, AAAI-2006, Boston (2006)
31. Moor, J.H.: Towards a theory of privacy for the information age. In: Spinello, R.A., Tavani, H.T. (eds.) Readings in CyberEthics, 2nd edn., pp. 407–417. Sudbury, MA: Jones and Bartlett (2004)

32. Moustafa, W., Deshpande, A., Namata, G., Getoor, L.: Declarative analysis of noisy information networks. In: Proceedings of IEEE 27th International Conference on Department of Computer Science, Data Engineering Workshops (ICDEW), Hannover, pp. 106–111 (2011)
33. Mukhef, H.A., Farhan, E.M., Jassim, M.R.: Generalized shortest path problem in uncertain environment based on PSO. J. Comput. Sci. **4**(4), 349–352 (2008)
34. Paraskevas, A., Arendell, B.: A strategic framework for terrorism prevention and mitigation in tourism destinations. Tour. Manag. **28**(6), 1560–1573 (2007)
35. Perumbuduru, S., Dhar, J.: Performance evaluation of different network topologies based on ant colony optimization. Int. J. Wirel. Mob. Netw. (IJWMN) **2**(4), 141–157 (2010)
36. Prez, I.J., Alonso, S., Cabrerizo, F.J., Herrera-Viedma, E.: A fuzzy linguistic decision support system to aid users in e-commerce activities. In: Proceedings of the 2010 World Congress in Computer Science, Computer Engineering, and Applied Computing (WORLDCOMP 2010). The 2010 International Conference on Artificial Intelligence (ICAI 2010), Las Vegas, 12–15 July 2010
37. Reid, E.F., Chen, H.: Mapping the contemporary terrorism research domain. Int. J. Hum. Comput. Stud. **65**(1), 42–56 (2007)
38. Saint-Charles, J., Mongeau, P.: Different relationships for coping with ambiguity and uncertainty in organizations. Soc. Netw. **31**, 33–39 (2009)
39. Sang, Y., YI, Z.: A modified pulse coupled neural network for shortest path computation. J. Comput. Inf. Syst. **6**(9), 3095–3102 (2010)
40. Schrock, A., Examining social media usage: technology clusters and social network relationships. First Monday **14**(1–5), January (2009)
41. Shani, G., Chickering, M., Meek, C.: Mining recommendations from the web. In: Proceedings of 2008 ACM Conference on Recommender System, Lausanne, pp. 35–42 (2008)
42. Sheldon, P.: The relationship between unwillingness to communicate and students Facebook use. J. Media Psychol. Theor. Method Appl. **20**(2), 67–75 (2008)
43. Shi, C., Yan, Z., Cai, Y., Wu, B.: Multi-objective community detection in complex networks. Appl. Soft Comput. **12**(2), 850–859 (2012)
44. Snasel, V., Harak, Z., Abraham, A.: Understanding social networks using formal concept analysis. In: Web Intelligence and Intelligent Agent Technology, 2008, WI-IAT '08, Sydney, 390–393 (2008)
45. Snasel, V., Horak, Z., Abraham, A.: Link suggestions in terrorists networks using semi discrete decomposition. In: Sixth International Conference on Information Assurance and Security (IAS), pp. 337–339. IEEE (2010). ISBN 978-1-4244-7408-0
46. Sommer, C.: Approximate shortest path and distance queries in network. Ph.D. thesis, Department of Computer Science Graduate School of Information Science and Technology, The University of Tokyo (2010)
47. Tantipathananandh, C., Breger-wolf, T., Kempe, D.: A framework for community identification in dynamic social network, In: Proceedings of KDD 2007, pp. 717–726. San Jose, California, USA (2007)
48. Thellwal, M.: Social networks, gender and friending, analysis of Myspace profiles. J. Am. Soc. Inf. Sci. Technol. **591**(8), 1321–1330 (2008)
49. Tufekci, Z.: Groming, gossip Facebook and Myspace: what can we learn about these sites from those who wont assimilate? Inf. Commun. Soc. **11**(4), 544–564 (2008)
50. Vindigni, G., Janssen, M.A.: Organic food consumption a multi-theoretical framework of consumer decision making, The current issue and full text archive of this journal is available at http://www.emeraldinsight.com/0007070X.hm. Accessed on 20 Mar 2012 (2002)
51. Walther, J., Ander Heide, B., Kim, S. Westerman, D., Tang, S.T.: The role of friends appearance and behaviour on evaluations of individuals on facebook: are we known by the company we keep? Hum. Commun. Res. **34**, 28–49 (2008)
52. White, T., Pagurek, B., Oppacher, F.: ASGA: improving the ant system by integration with genetic algorithms. In: Proceedings of the Third Annual Conference, University of Wisconsin, Madison, pp. 610–617 (1999)

53. Wolf, Y., Frankel, O.: Terrorism: toward an overarched account and prevention with a special reference to pendulum interplay between both parties. Aggress. Violent Behav. **12**(3), 259–279 (2007)
54. Wren, C.R., Ivanov, Y.A., Leign, D., Westhues, J.: The MERL motion detector datasets: 2007 Workshop on Massive Datasets. Mitsubishi electric research laboratories tech report, TR-2007-069
55. Yang, W.Z., Ge, Y.H., He, J.J., Liu, B.: Designing a group decision support system under uncertainty using group Fuzzy analytic network process (ANP). Afr. J. Bus. Manag. **4**(12), 2571–2585 (2010)

# Chapter 2
# Performance Evaluation of Social Network Using Data Mining Techniques

**Mrutyunjaya Panda, Ajith Abraham, Sachidananda Dehuri, and Manas Ranjan Patra**

**Abstract** Social network research relies on a variety of data sources, depending on the problem scenario and the questions, which the research is trying to answer or inform. Social networks are very popular nowadays and the understanding of their inner structure seems to be promising area. Cluster analysis has also been an increasingly interesting topic in the area of computational intelligence and found suitable in social network analysis in its social network structure. In this chapter, we use k-cluster analysis with various performance measures to analyse some of the data sources obtained for social network analysis. Our proposed approach is intended to address the users of social network, that will not only help an organization to understand their external and internal associations but also highly necessary for the enhancement of collaboration, innovation and dissemination of knowledge.

M. Panda (✉)
Department of ECE, Gandhi Institute for Technological Advancement (GITA), Bhubaneswar, Odisha, India
e-mail: mrutyunjaya74@gmail.com

A. Abraham
Machine Intelligence Research Labs (MIR labs), Scientific Network for Innovation and Research Excellence, Auburn, WA, USA
e-mail: ajith.abraham@ieee.org

S. Dehuri
Department of Computer and Information Technology, F.M. University, Balasore, India
e-mail: sachilapa@gmail.com

M.R. Patra
Department of Computer Science, Berhampur University, Ganjam, India
e-mail: mrpatra12@gmail.com

A. Abraham (ed.), *Computational Social Networks: Mining and Visualization*,
DOI 10.1007/978-1-4471-4054-2_2, © Springer-Verlag London 2012

# Introduction

A social network is an umbrella with nodes of individuals, groups, organizations and related systems that tie in one or more types of interdependencies. Social network data analysis is intended to understand the social structure, which subsists amongst entities in an organization [1–3]. Social network analysis is focused on uncovering the patterning of people's interaction. Network analysis is based on the intuition that these patterns are important features of the lives of the individuals who display them. Further, the social network approach has primarily involved in two important aspects such as: (1) it is guided by formal theory organized in mathematical terms, and; (2) it is grounded in the systematic analysis of empirical data.

Fining et al. [4] used a similar wave that is imminent under the generic banner of data mining tools that may stem from reality mining [5] and its link with social networking relationships.

With the proliferation of social media and online communities in networked world, large gamut of data have been collected and stored in databases. The rate at which such data is stored is growing at a phenomenal rate. As a result the classical method of data analysis is of rare interest. This chapter presents a study about the effectiveness of the data mining methods in analysing the social network data collected from various social network sites and UCI machine learning database. Our integrated framework leads to a term swam based data mining to address the users of social network, that will not only help an organization to understand their external and internal associations but also highly necessary for the enhancement of collaboration, innovation and dissemination of knowledge.

The rest of the chapter is organized as follows. A brief overview on the related research in this field is outlined in section "Related Research", followed by overview on social network analysis in section "Preliminaries". Section "Social Network Data" introduces the dataset obtained for our analysis, with the proposed methodology in section "Methodology and Experimental Setup". Section "Results and Discussion" discusses some results with discussion. Finally, we conclude the chapter in section "Conclusion" with a light on future direction of research.

# Related Research

Boyd and Ellison [6] used social network sites (SNSs) that allow users to register, create their own profile page containing information about themselves which may either be real or virtual, in order to establish the public connections with the other members and to communicate with them. SNS like Facebook and MySpace are amongst the ten most popular websites in the world including Orkut, Cyworld and Mixi. Tufekci [7] emphasized the motivation behind the use of SNS as its sociability with a suggestion to consider that some types of people may never use Social network sites extensively [8]. Data mining emotion in social network communication with MySpace is proposed in [9], where the authors confirm that MySpace is an emotion-rich environment and therefore suitable for the development of specialist sentiment analysis techniques. Apart from this, it is observed that using both age and gender in the emotion strategies for classification points to the difficulty in making accurate classifications and poses several challenges to the automatic classification with the existing methodologies. Zhou et al. [10] build up an social network mining solution to discover the social network, users' relationship, key figures and impaction to the organization on BBS website in order to understand the internal and external association of an organization so as to enhance the collaboration and disseminating knowledge. Kaufman et al. [11] introduce a new social network dataset site Facebook.com with findings to exemplify the scientific and pedagogical potential of this new network resource with a future prospect in this area of research. Since social network research embodies a range of expertise from anthropology to Computer Sciences, it is quite difficult to find the benchmarks for social networks [12]. Further, social networks have been measured on various dataset including online social networks [13] to sexual transmission networks [14]. The authors propose a method by using formal concept analysis in understanding the social networks with ease in analysis and visualizing the networks and propose to use bigger networks in future [15]. Social data mining is used to improve bioinspired intelligent systems with swarm optimization, ant colony and cultural algorithms are discussed in [16]. Research on social network analysis in the data mining community includes following areas: clustering analysis in [17] and [18], classification [19], link prediction [20] and [21]. Other achievements include PageRank [22, 23] and Hub-Authority [24] in web search engine. An experimental study on important set of "small world" problem is discussed by Milgram in [25] and [26], which gives an insight about the network structure rather than reconstructing the actual networks. In this, the authors tries to probe the distribution of path lengths in an acquaintance network by passing a letter to one of their first name acquaintance to an assigned target individual in an attempt. while doing this, many letters got missed while only six people could successfully targeted and passed on average through their hands, which subsequently led to the of the "six degrees of separation", coined by Guare [27].A review of the issues regarding controlling the possible sources of inconsistency in social network data gathered directly by using questionnaires and interviews, has been discussed in [28], citing the reason for which the researchers tried to adopt other possible methods for probing social network. One source of copious and relatively reliable data is collaboration networks. These are typically affiliation networks in which participants collaborate in groups of one kind or another, and links between pairs of individuals are established by common group membership. Examples of such a network include: collaboration network of film actors, which has been well documented online in Internet Movie Database[29], where actors collaborate in films and two actors are considered connected if they have worked in a film together, the statistical properties of this type of networks can be understood from the research done in [30, 31]; networks of co-authorships amongst academicians, where individuals are linked if they have coauthored in one or more papers as explained in [32, 33] and networks of board of directors in which two directors are linked if they belong to the same board of directors at least in any one company, as discussed in [34, 35] to name a few. Aiello et al. [36, 37] have analysed a network of telephone calls made over the AT&T long-distance network on a single day. The vertices of this network represent telephone numbers and the directed edges calls from one number to another. Ebel et al. [38] have reconstructed the pattern of email communications between 5,000 students at Kiel University from logs maintained by email servers. In this network the vertices represent email addresses and directed edges represent a message passing from one address to another. Abraham et al. [39] addressed the computational complexity of social networks analysis and clarity of their visualization that uses combination of Formal Concept Analysis and well-known matrix factorization methods. The goal is to reduce the dimension of social network data and to measure the amount of information which is lost during the reduction. Singular value decomposition has already been used in the field of social network data [40] to determine the position of nodes in the network graph. The research made in [41] by Bulkley et al. examines hypotheses about the efficient and strategic uses of social networks by a specific group of white collar workers, in which they examined two existing theories relating network structure and tie strength to performance and put forward a new hypothesis. They used a unique data set containing email patterns and accounting records for several dozen executive recruiters and found statistically significant differences related to network (1) structure (2) flow and (3) age. Abraham et al. [42] try to consider a Web page as information with social aspects. Each Web page is the result of invisible social interaction. For the description of the social aspects of Web pages, they used the term MicroGenre with fundamental concepts of MicroGenre with an illustration to the experiments for the detection and usage of MicroGenres. Social Network Analysis (SNA) that is based on the data are collected from the students at the Faculty of Organization and Informatics, University of Zagreb is presented in [43], where they conclude firstly, that the position in a social network cannot be forecast only by academic success and, secondly, that part-time students tend to form separate groups that are poorly connected with full-time students.

## Preliminaries

### *Social Network Analysis (SNA)*

Social network analysis is used to understand the social structure, which exists amongst entities in an organization. The defining feature of social network analysis (SNA) is its focus on the structure of relationships, ranging from causal acquaintance to close bonds. This is in contrast with other areas of the social sciences where the focus is often on the attributes of agents rather than on the relations between them. SNA maps and measures the formal and informal relationships to understand what facilitates or impedes the knowledge flows that bind the interacting units i.e. who knows whom and who shares what information and how. Social network analysis is focused on uncovering the patterning of people's interaction. SNA is based on the intuition that these patterns are important features of the lives of the individuals who display them. The network analysts believe that how an individual lives depends in large part on how that individual is tied into larger web of social connections. Moreover, many believe that the success or failure of societies and organizations often depends on the patterning of their internal structure, which is guided by formal concept analysis, which is grounded in systematic analysis of the empirical data. With the availability of powerful computers and discrete combinatorics (especially graph theory) after 1970, the study of SNA take off as an interdisciplinary speciality, the applications are found many folds that include: organizational behaviour, inter-organizational relations, the spread of contagious diseases, mental health, social support, and the diffusion of information and animal social organization [17].

## SNA Basics

The two basic elements of SNA are links and nodes. Links are connections, or ties, between individuals or groups and nodes are the individuals or groups involved in the network. A nodes importance in a social network refers to its centrality. Central nodes have the potential to exert influence over less central nodes. A network that possesses just a few or perhaps even one node with high centrality is a centralized network. In this type of network all nodes are directly connected to each other. Subordinate nodes direct information to the central node and the central node distributes it to all other nodes. Centralized networks are susceptible to disruption because they have few central nodes and damage to a central node could be devastating to the entire network. A simple social network is shown in Fig. 2.1.

Decentralized networks are those that do not possess one central hub; but rather possess several important hubs. Each node is indirectly tied to all others and therefore the network has more elasticity. Consequently, these networks are more difficult to disrupt due to their loose connections and ability to replace damaged nodes. Consequently, terror networks choose this type of structure whenever possible.

Social network analysts use the term degrees in reference to the number of direct connections that a node enjoys. The node that possesses the largest number of connections is the hub of the network. The term betweenness refers to the number of groups that a node is indirectly tied to through the direct links that it possesses. Therefore, nodes with high a degree of betweenness act as liaisons or bridges to other nodes in the structure. These nodes are known as "brokers" because of the power that they wield. However, these "brokers" represent a single point of failure because if their communication flows is disrupted than they will be cut off to the nodes that it connects. Closeness measures the trail that a node would take in order to reach all other nodes in a network. A node with high closeness does not necessarily have the most direct connections; but because they are "close" to many members they maintain rapid access to most other nodes through both direct and indirect ties.

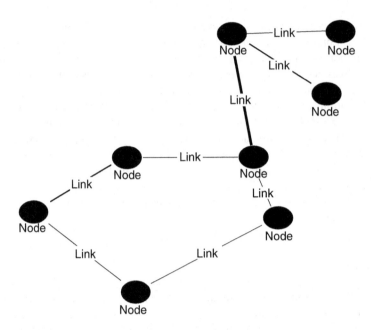

**Fig. 2.1** Social network diagram

**Strengths**

- Provides visual representations. Social network analysis allows the researcher to visualize the structure of an organization through the use of link charts. It, also, allows researchers to identify previously unknown links. The knowledge gained through this type of analysis permits analysts to forecast activities of an actor/ organization and outline a possible attack strategy on criminal or terrorist organizations by focusing resources on important actors in the hopes of weakening the entire network.
- Provides data that is useful for analysis. SNA software, also, provides the researcher with data that can be analysed to determine the centrality, betweenness, degree, and closeness of each node.

**Weaknesses**

- Analysis is dependent upon data. Like any other software, SNA software will only analyse the data it is given. Therefore, if the data is incomplete or incorrect than the final product will be inaccurate. Furthermore, it will only provide a complete overview of a network unless ALL factors have been researched and entered, which is almost impossible. Consequently, it should be used as a tool only and not relied upon to provide an absolute depiction of a network.

- Time consuming. It takes a great deal of time to research a topic in order to find the appropriate information. A first time user of social network analysis will not only have to research the target vigorously; but, also become familiar with SNA which is a daunting task.
- Various resources are needed. A computer with an Internet connection is essential in conducting social network analysis. Specialized software is, also, needed to perform SNA.

## Applications

With regard to purposes of knowledge management, social network analysis may help to evaluate availability and distribution of critical knowledge and thus facilitates:

- Strategic development of organizational knowledge,
- Transfer and sustainable conservation of implicit knowledge,
- Development of core competencies (like leadership development),
- Creation of opportunities to improve communication processes,
- Identification and support of communities of practice,
- Harmonization of knowledge networks (after mergers and acquisitions),
- Sustainable management of external relationships.

## Step-by-Step Procedure

We provided a basic step-by-step procedure on how to design a social network model as below:

**Step 1:** The researcher must first identify a suitable target.

**Step 2:** Thoroughly research the subject matter. The researcher must explore who knows whom and how well do they know each other? They must, also, discover how does the information or resources flow within a network? Researchers should also analyse how members of a network know each other? Although these are not the only factors to consider they provide a good starting point. The actual factors will vary from project to project.

**Step 3:** The information gathered must be placed into a database. The most commonly used matrix is a node-by-node matrix. This type of matrix uses as many rows and columns as there are nodes in a network. The simplest method of data entry is done by placing O's or 1's into a spreadsheet. The O's represent no connection and 1's signify a link. A sample is shown in Fig. 2.2 below.

This is a binary matrix. A signed matrix assigns a nodes relationship with another with +1 (positive relationship), 0 (no relationship) and −1 (negative relationship). However, an ordinal matrix allows the researcher to assign a strength rating to each connection. In other words if a strong connections exists than instead of placing a

**Fig. 2.2** Relation matrix

|   | A | B | C |
|---|---|---|---|
| A | 0 | 1 | 1 |
| B | 0 | 0 | 0 |
| C | 1 | 0 | 0 |

1 in the spreadsheet, the researcher would place a number that signifies strength such as a 5 or a 10. Once the spreadsheet is complete the SNA software is able to generate, using various mathematical equations, interpretable data

**Step 4:** A researcher must investigate the basics of SNA before he/her can begin to analyse the compiled data. There are numerous articles, books, and websites available to the novice social network analyst that will provide everything from basic knowledge to expert advice. When the researcher purchases the appropriate SNA software many will come with tutorials that will explain basic social network theories. The tutorial should, also, provide the researcher with directions as to how to use the software itself; however, an equally effective way to learn this type of software is trial and error. In other words the researcher can simply "plays around" with the software functions and use the tutorial to interpret the results.

**Step 5:** The last step is to perform the actual analysis. The basic knowledge of SNA and of the specialized software that the researcher gained should make the actual analysis much less difficult. The analysed data may then be used to identify possible tactics to disrupt or improve a networks communications or resources.

## Data Mining

There has been extensive research work on clustering in data mining. Traditional clustering algorithms [44] divide objects into classes based on their similarity. Objects in a class are similar to each other and are very dissimilar from objects in different classes. Social network clustering analysis, which is different from traditional clustering problem, divides objects into classes based on their links as well as their attributes. The biggest challenge of social network clustering analysis is how to divide objects into classes based on objects' links, thus we need find algorithms that can meet this challenge. A k-clustering scheme is used with $k = 5$ with Tabu search to build the SNA. Tabu search is a numerical method for finding the best division of actors into a given number of partitions on the basis of approximate automorphic equivalence. In using this method, it is important to explore a range of possible numbers of partitions unless one has a prior theory about this, to determine how many partitions are useful. Having selected a number of partitions, it is useful to re-run the algorithm a number of times to insure that a global, rather than local minimum has been found. The method begins by randomly allocating nodes to partitions. A measure of badness of fit is constructed by calculating the sums of squares for each row and each column within each block, and calculating the variance of these sums of squares. These variances are then summed across the blocks to construct a measure of badness of fit. Search continues to find an allocation of actors to partitions that minimizes this badness of fit statistic. The Tabu search algorithm is provided below:

The Tabu Search Algorithm has traditionally been used on combinatorial optimization problems related to feature selection and has been frequently applied to many integer programming, routing and scheduling, traveling salesman and related problems. The basic concept of Tabu Search is presented by Glover [45] who described it as a meta-heuristic superimposed on another heuristic. It explores the solution space by moving from a solution to the solution with the best objective function value in its neighbourhood at each iteration even in the case that this might cause the deterioration of the objective. (In this sense, "moves" are defined as the sequences that lead from one trial solution to another.) To avoid cycling, solutions that were recently examined are declared forbidden or "Tabu" for a certain number of iterations and associated attributes with the Tabu solutions are also stored. The Tabu status of a solution might be overridden if it corresponds to a new best solution, which is called "aspiration". The Tabu lists are historical in nature and form the Tabu search memory. The role of the memory can change as the algorithm proceeds. For initializations at each iteration, the objective is to make a coarse examination of the solution space, known as "diversification", but as locations of the candidate solutions are identified, the search is more focused to produce local optimal solutions in a process of "intensification". Intensification and diversification are fundamental cornerstones of longer term memory in Tabu search. In many cases, various implementation models of the Tabu Search method can be achieved by changing the size, variability, and adaptability of the Tabu memory to a particular problem domain. In all, Tabu Search Algorithm is an intelligent search technique that hierarchically explores one or more local search procedures in order to search quickly for the global optimum. As one of the advanced heuristic methods, Tabu Search is generally regarded as a method that can provide a near-optimal or at least local optimal solution within a reasonable time domain.

What is being minimized is a function of the dissimilarity of the variance of scores within partitions. That is, the algorithm seeks to group together actors who have similar amounts of variability in their row and column scores within blocks. Actors who have similar variability probably have similar profiles of ties sent and received within, and across blocks – though they do not necessarily have the same ties to the same other actors. Unlike the other methods mentioned here, the Tabu search produces a partitioned matrix, rather than a matrix of dissimilarities. It also provides an overall badness of fit statistic. Both of these would seem to recommend the approach, perhaps combined with other methods.

## Social Network Data

### *Dataset Used*

We use Terrorist data available in UCINET [46] and Netlog Data [47] for building our social network analysis.

**Terrorist Dataset**

In this, we use terrorist dataset with their name and their relationships to each other. In this, 64 terrorist names from different terrorist organization are taken into consideration for the study of their social network with 0 for no relationship and 1 for having some kind of relationship. Their names include Hani Hanjour, Abu Walid, Madjid Sahoune, and Faisal Al Salmi etc. A sample of the terrorist network dataset is shown in Table 2.1 in terms of relation matrix.

**Netlog Dataset**

Netlog is an online platform where users can keep in touch with and extend their social network. It is an online social portal, specifically targeted at the European Youth. It is developed by Netlog NV, based in Ghent, Belgium. Netlog is currently available in 37 languages and has more than 72 million members throughout the Europe, and this number is increasing day by day.

On Netlog, One can create its own webpage with a blog, picture, videos, events and much more to share with their own needs. It is thus the ultimate tool for the young people to connect and communicate with their social network. Netlog NV has developed a unique localization technology ensuring that all content is geotargeted and personalized to each member's profile.

**Table 2.1** Relation matrix for a sample of Terrorist Network dataset in 2-mode

|                     | HH | MM | NA | SA* | KAM | MA | WA | WA | SS |
|---------------------|----|----|----|-----|-----|----|----|----|----|
| Hani Hanjour        | 0  | 1  | 1  | 1   | 1   | 1  | 0  | 0  | 0  |
| Majed Moqed         | 1  | 0  | 1  | 1   | 1   | 0  | 0  | 0  | 0  |
| Nawaf Alhazmi       | 1  | 1  | 0  | 1   | 1   | 1  | 0  | 0  | 0  |
| Salem Alhazmi*      | 1  | 1  | 1  | 0   | 1   | 0  | 0  | 0  | 0  |
| Khalid Al-Mihdhar   | 1  | 1  | 1  | 1   | 0   | 0  | 0  | 0  | 0  |
| Mohamed Atta        | 1  | 0  | 1  | 0   | 0   | 0  | 0  | 1  | 1  |
| Waleed Alshehri     | 0  | 0  | 0  | 0   | 0   | 0  | 0  | 1  | 1  |
| Wail Alshehri       | 0  | 0  | 0  | 0   | 0   | 1  | 1  | 0  | 1  |
| Satam Suqami        | 0  | 0  | 0  | 0   | 0   | 1  | 1  | 1  | 0  |

Netlog collect the following types of personal data to publish the information intended to be made public by the people, under the conditions specified in their privacy settings.

- *Public information uploaded by the person*

  - Information in individual profile, blog, shouts, pictures, videos, events, music, links
  - Messages sent to other users, as well as ratings, shouts and contributions to another user's guest book
  - Links to your friends and groups

- *Private information uploaded by the person*

  - Settings and administrative data such as user name and password, skin, credits and shortcuts

- *History and Logs*

  - Time, date and URL of all Netlog pages visited by you
  - The URL of the referring websites
  - The searches one performs on the website.

A sample data with eight users having 16 features to analyse the social network amongst the users is shown in Table 2.2.

## Methodology and Experimental Setup

We conducted our research on social network analysis to reveal the relationships amongst the terrorist using the terrorist network dataset. We also use Netlog dataset to understand the social networking of a common man. All experiments are conducted in a Pentium-4 Machine with 2.86 GHz CPU, 40 GB HDD, 512 MB RAM. We use UCINET 6.0 tool [46] for our performance evaluations in social network analysis. The Netdraw software produces a visualization of the 2-mode data with all the actors and event nodes. The actor nodes are circles and the event nodes are the squares. The Netdraw visualization works directly from the 2-mode data set in UCINET tool used. More details about the network analysis in 2-mode network can be obtained from Borgatti and Everett [48].

It is evident from Table 2.1 with the concept of relation metric as discussed earlier in section "Step-by-Step Procedure" that Hari Hanjour has some relationship with Majed Moged Nawaf Alhazmi, Salem Alhazmi*, Khalid Al-Mihdhar and Mohamed Atta, where as poses no relationship with Waleed Alshehri, Wail Alshehri and Satam Suqami and so on for all others.

From Table 2.2, we can understand the data as: the person with user_id 1 with a current time value is online now, is a female, aged about 44 years citizen of "Tn" staying in city of Greeneville. He is a member of NETLOG since November 1, 2007

**Table 2.2** A sample of Netlog dataset in 1-mode network

| UI | CT | ON | MS | F | G | O_S | A | City | C | Ph | B | GB | O | SO | SOF |
|----|-----|------|----------------------------------|----|--------|--------|----------|-------------|----------------|----|---|----|---|----|--------|
| 1 | ###### | TRUE | 664 visitors since 1 November 2007 | 23 | Female | Online | 44 years | Greeneville | Tn | 18 | 1 | 17 | 1 | 0 | 42,617 |
| 2 | ###### | TRUE | 232 visitors since 16 May 2007 | 8 | Male | Online | 67 years | Stockton | United States | 6 | 1 | 1 | 1 | 0 | 38,510 |
| 6 | ###### | TRUE | 663 visitors since 6 November 2006 | 23 | Male | Away | 33 years | Catterick | United Kingdom | 5 | 1 | 36 | 1 | 0 | 42,024 |

Where, *UI* user_id, *CT* current time, *ON* online_now, *MS* member since, *F* friends, *G* gender, *A* age, *C* country, *Ph* photos, *O_S* online_now_state, *O* objects, *SO* swfobject, *SOF* size_of_profile, *GB* guestbook, *B* blog with 664 numbers of visitors visited his profile with 23 friends, having 18 photos, 1 blog, 17 guest books with 42,617 as size of her profile.

## Metrics in Social Network Analysis

The following measures (Metrics) are used in social network analysis.

- *Centrality:* This measure gives a rough indication of the social power of a node based on how well they "connect" to the network. "Betweenness", "Closeness", and "Degree" are considered to fall under the measures of centrality.
- *Betweenness:* It is defined as the extent to which a node lies between other nodes in the network. Here, the connectivity of the node's neighbours is taken into account in order to provide a higher value for nodes which bridge clusters. This metrics reflects the number of people who are connecting indirectly through direct links.
- *Closeness:* This refers to the degree with which an individual is nearer to all others in a network either directly or indirectly. Further, it reflects the ability to access information through the "grapevine" of network members. In this way, the closeness is considered to be the inverse of the sum of the shortest distance (sometimes called as geodesic distance) between each individual and all other available in the network.
- *Degree:* It is the count of the number of ties to other actors in the network.
- *Clustering coefficient:* This provides the likelihood that two associates of a node are associates with themselves. A higher clustering coefficient indicates a greater "cliquishness".
- *Centralization:* It is calculated as the ratio between the numbers of links for each node divided by maximum possible sum of differences. While a centralized network will have many of its links dispersed around one or a few nodes, the decentralized network is one in which there is little variation between the number of links each node possesses.
- *Density:* It is the degree that measures the respondent's ties to know one another. The density may be sparse or dense network depends upon the proportion of ties in a network relative to the total number of possibilities.

## Results and Discussion

In order to understand Closeness one must understand geodesic distance; which is the number of relations in the shortest possible "walk" from one actor to another. Therefore, geodesic distance is the most commonly used measure of Closeness. For instance whose inCloseness score of 100 has the lowest total of geodesic distances

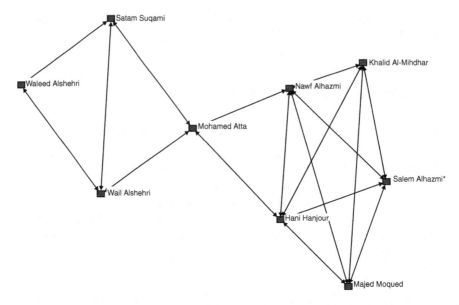

**Fig. 2.3** Social network for Terrorist Network dataset (1-mode network)

from other actors; Nearness can be re-expressed as farness. In other words, actors because of their inFarness score of 210 from Netlog Data have the largest total of geodesic distances from other actors. High closeness centrality indicates the greater autonomy of an individual person, since he or she is able to reach the other members easily (and vice versa). Low closeness centrality indicates higher individual member dependency on the other members, i.e. the willingness of other members to give access to the network's resources.

In the same way, betweenness refers to the number of groups that a node has indirect ties to through the direct links that it possesses. In other words, it represents the number of times that a node lies along the shortest path between two others. UCINET will calculate the betweenness for each node in a dataset automatically using the formula above. Interpreting the results is relatively easy; the larger the number the higher the betweenness the node possesses. UCINET will automatically place them in order of highest to lowest. All these results are presented in sections "1-Mode and 2-Mode Network" and "SNA with Netlog Data" with Netlog Data and Terrorist Network data respectively.

Further, the social network structure for the proposed analysis using Terrorist Network dataset are shown in Figs. 2.3 and 2.4 with 1-mode and 2-mode respectively. The brief description about the 1-mode and 2-mode network is provided below. The similar type of social network structure using Netlog dataset is shown in Fig. 2.5.

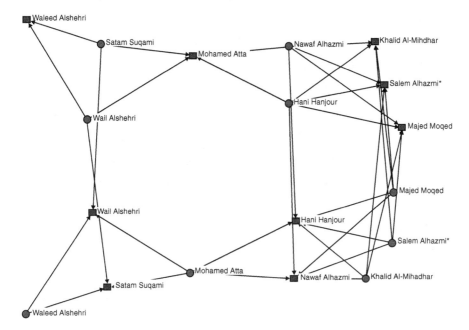

**Fig. 2.4** Same for 2-mode network for Terrorist Network dataset

## 1-Mode and 2-Mode Network

A (2-dimensional) matrix is said to be 2-mode if the rows and columns index different sets of entities (e.g., the rows might correspond to persons while the columns correspond to organizations). In contrast, a matrix is 1-mode if the rows and columns refer to the same set of entities, such as a city-by-city matrix if distances. In social network analysis, 2-mode data refers to data recording ties between two sets of entities. In this context, the term "mode" refers to a class of entities – typically called actors, nodes or vertices – whose members have social ties with other members (in the 1-mode case) or with members of another class (in the 2-mode case). Most social network analysis is concerned with the 1-mode case, as in the analysis of friendship ties among a set of school children or advice-giving relations within an organization. The 2-mode case arises when researchers collect relations between classes of actors, such as persons and organizations, or persons and events. For example, a researcher might collect data on which students in a university belong to which campus organizations, or which employees in an organization participate in which electronic discussion forums. These kinds of data are often referred to as affiliations. Co-memberships in organizations or participation in events are typically thought of as providing opportunities for social relationships among individuals (and also as the consequences of pre-existing relationships). At the same time, ties between organizations through their members are thought to be conduits through which organizations influence each other.

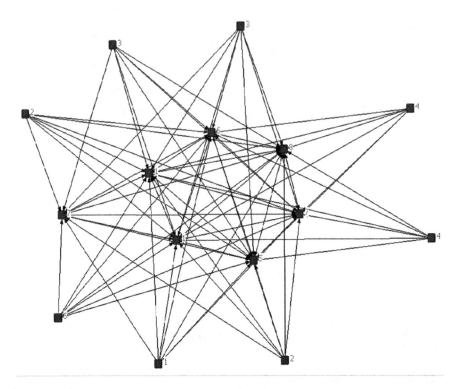

**Fig. 2.5** Social network structure using Netlog1 data_16inst_8users

**Table 2.3** Closeness centrality

|    |   | 1 | 2 | 3 | 4 |
|----|---|-----------|------------|-------------|--------------|
|    |   | inFarness | outFarness | inCloseness | outCloseness |
| 1  | 1 | 14.000    | 126.000    | 100.000     | 11.111       |
| 12 | 5 | 14.000    | 126.000    | 100.000     | 11.111       |
| 10 | 7 | 14.000    | 127.000    | 100.000     | 11.024       |
| 4  | 1 | 14.000    | 126.000    | 100.000     | 11.111       |
| 7  | 1 | 210.000   | 112.000    | 6.667       | 12.500       |
| 9  | 4 | 210.000   | 113.000    | 6.667       | 12.389       |
| 3  | 2 | 210.000   | 112.000    | 6.667       | 12.500       |

## SNA with Netlog Data

### Closeness Centrality with Netlog Data

Closeness Centrality Measures can be understood from Table 2.3:

Closeness centrality approaches emphasize the distance of an actor to all others in the network by focusing on the geodesic distance from each actor to all others.

**Table 2.4** Statistics of the closeness centrality measures

|   |                    | 1<br>inFarness | 2<br>outFarness | 3<br>inCloseness | 4<br>outCloseness |
|---|--------------------|----------------|-----------------|------------------|-------------------|
| 1 | Mean               | 118.733        | 118.733         | 49.046           | 11.831            |
| 2 | Standard deviation | 97.571         | 6.942           | 45.501           | 0.687             |
| 3 | Variance           | 9520.063       | 48.196          | 2070.352         | 0.471             |

One should use either directed or undirected geodesic distances among actors. The sum of these geodesic distances for each actor is the "farness" of the actor from all others. We can convert this into a measure of nearness or closeness centrality by taking the reciprocal of the farness and norming it relative to the most central actor.

From the above sample of the whole result obtained, Let us examine the in-farness, in-closeness, out-farness and out-closeness of the points as a measure of who is "central" or "influential" in this network. In undirected data, actors differ from one another only in how many connections they have. With directed data, however, it can be important to distinguish centrality based on in-degree from centrality based on out-degree. If an actor receives many ties or relationships with others in the network, they are often said to be prominent, or to have high prestige. That is, many other actors seek to have direct ties with them, which may indicate their importance. Actors who have unusually high out-degree are actors who are able to exchange with many others, or make many others aware of their views. Actors who display high out-degree centrality are often said to be influential actors.

From Table 2.3, we can observe that actors 7 & 1, 9 & 4 and 3 & 2 donot have much prominent relationship between each other with low inCloseness value of 6.667 and high inFarness value of 210.000. At the same time, higher outCloseness and lower outFarness between actors 7 & 1 and 3 & 2 are more influential among all relationships present. Relationship between 1 & 1, 12 & 5, 10 & 4 and 4 & 1 are closest or most central with inCloseness of 100.

From Table 2.4, the mean for inCloseness is 49.046 which says that the mean strength of ties across all possible ties (ignoring self-ties). Since the data are binary, this means that 49% of all possible ties are present (i.e. the density of the matrix). The standard deviation is a measure of how much variation there is among the elements. If all elements were one, or all were zero, the standard deviation would be zero, i.e. no variation. Here, the average variability from one element to the next is 45.501, almost same as the mean. So, we would say that there is, relatively, a great deal of variation in ties. With binary data, the maximum variability in ties – or the maximum uncertainty about whether any given tie is likely to be present or absent is realized at a density of .50. As density approaches either zero or unity, the standard deviation and variance in ties will decline accordingly.

**Freeman Betweenness Centrality with Netlog Data**

Supposing that somebody wants to influence you by sending you information, or make a deal to exchange some resources. But, in order to talk to you, he must go

**Table 2.5** Betweenness
centrality measures

|   |   | 1 | 2 |
|---|---|---|---|
|   |   | Betweenness | nBetweenness |
| 1 | 1 | 0.600 | 0.330 |
| 12 | 5 | 0.600 | 0.330 |
| 13 | 8 | 0.600 | 0.330 |
| 4 | 1 | 0.600 | 0.330 |
| 15 | 6 | 0.600 | 0.330 |
| 3 | 2 | 0.000 | 0.000 |

**Table 2.6** Descriptive
statistics for each measure of
betweenness centrality

|   |   | 1 | 2 |
|---|---|---|---|
|   |   | Betweenness | nBetweenness |
| 1 | Mean | 0.200 | 0.110 |
| 2 | Standard Deviation | 0.283 | 0.155 |
| 3 | Variance | 0.080 | 0.024 |

through a mediator. For example, let's suppose that I wanted to try to convince the Director of my institute to provide a laptop. According to the rules of the institution, I must forward my request through department head and then administrative officer. Each one of these people could delay the request, or even prevent my request from getting through. This gives the people who lie "between" me and the Director power with respect to me. Having more than one channel makes me less dependent, and, in a sense, more powerful. Betweenness centrality views an actor as being in a favoured position to the extent that the actor falls on the geodesic paths between other pairs of actors in the network. That is, the more people depend on me to make connections with other people, the more power I have. If, however, two actors are connected by more than one geodesic path, and I am not on all of them, I lose some power. Using the computer, it is quite easy to locate the geodesic paths between all pairs of actors, and to count up how frequently each actor falls in each of these pathways. If we add up, for each actor, the proportion of times that they are "between" other actors for the sending of information in the dataset used by us in this chapter, we get the a measure of actor centrality. We can norm this measure by expressing it as a percentage of the maximum possible betweenness that an actor could have had. The results for this are shown in Tables 2.5 and 2.6.

Here, we get Network Centralization Index = 0.24%, a very low one with Unnormalized centralization of 6.000.

We can see from Table 2.5 that there is a variation in actor betweenness (from zero to 0.6), and that there is a variation (std. dev. = 0.283 relative to a mean betweenness of 0.2) and the overall network centralization is very low. This is important in the sense that, because we know that most of the connections can be made in this network with the aid of any intermediary – hence there can be a lot of "betweenness" with same value of 0.600. In the sense of structural constraint, the network contains lots of power that could be important for group formation and stratification.

**Table 2.7** Degree centrality measure

|    |   | 1<br>Degree | 2<br>NrmDegree | 3<br>Share |
|----|---|-------------|----------------|------------|
| 15 | 6 | 581320.000  | 90.316         | 0.264      |
| 1  | 1 | 561374.938  | 87.217         | 0.255      |
| 12 | 5 | 86341.547   | 13.414         | 0.039      |
| 6  | 3 | 85508.977   | 13.285         | 0.039      |
| 5  | 3 | 85508.977   | 13.285         | 0.039      |

**Table 2.8** Descriptive statistics for degree centrality

|   |                    | 1<br>Degree      | 2<br>NrmDegree | 3<br>Share |
|---|--------------------|------------------|----------------|------------|
| 1 | Mean               | 146766.125       | 22.802         | 0.067      |
| 2 | Standard deviation | 166598.547       | 25.883         | 0.076      |
| 3 | Variance           | 27755075584.000  | 669.951        | 0.006      |

**Freemans Degree Centrality Measures**

Actors who have more ties to other actors are considered to be in advantageous positions for having many ties, many alternative ways to satisfy needs, and hence are less dependent on other individuals. Since they have many ties, they may have access to, and be able to call on more of the resources of the network as a whole. Also, they can act as third parties and deal makers in exchanges among others, and finally able to get benefit from this brokerage. So, degree centrality measure provides a very simple, but often very effective measure of an actor's centrality and power potential in a social network analysis. The results obtain for this is provided in Tables 2.7 and 2.8. Table 2.6 shows that actor 12 & 5 has highest degree with a value of 86341.547 and mean of 146766.125 and deviation of 166598.547. In this, Network Centralization = 77.90%, Heterogeneity = 15.26%, Normalized = 9.20%.

The degree of points is important because it tells us how many connections an actor has. Actors that receive information from many sources may be prestigious with high value (other actors want to be known by the actor, so they send information), and actors that receive information from many sources may also be more powerful. But, actors that receive a lot of information could also suffer from "information overload" or "noise and interference" due to contradictory messages from different sources. Hence, choosing a degree is of paramount importance in order to build a good social network model.

**K-Clusters Using Tabu Search**

As discussed earlier in section "Data Mining", Tabu search is a numerical method for finding the best division of actors into a given number of partitions on the basis of approximate automorphic equivalence. With this, it is important to explore a range

**Table 2.9** Density table

|   | 1 | 2 | 3 | 4 | 5 |
|---|---|---|---|---|---|
| 1 | 19410.510 | 19.778 | 4.750 | −0.500 | 0.000 |
| 2 | 13561.036 | 15332.223 | 0.333 | −0.500 | 0.000 |
| 3 | 13058.829 | 2.500 | 22987.500 | −0.500 | 0.000 |
| 4 | 13066.239 | 4.667 | 0.500 | 22987.250 | 0.000 |
| 5 | 13310.836 | 6.000 | −0.500 | −0.500 | 22987.500 |

of possible numbers of partitions, one has to determine intelligently on how many partitions are useful. Having selected a number of partitions, it is useful to re-run the algorithm a number of times to insure that a global, rather than local minimum has been obtained. The detail parameter settings used in our experiments using Tabu Search algorithm is provided below.

Number of clusters:          5
Type of data:                Similarities/Strengths/Cohesion
Method:                      correlation
Starting fit: 1.174; Starting fit: 0.609; Fit: 0.608; Fit: 0.605; Fit: 0.607; Fit: 0.605 (smaller values indicate better fit). r-square = 0.156

Clusters:
   1: 1 3 3 5 8 6
   2: 1 1 7
   3: 4 7
   4: 2 2
   5: 4 6

Table 2.9 provides the density table for analysing the relationships amongst the actors present in the network, where Density is defined as the total number of ties divided by the total number of possible ties. It is especially relevant for knowledge community building within and between organizations, for a thorough understanding about the overall linkage between network members. The more the value of the density, the better will be the knowledge flow and denser will be the network. However, a negative value indicates less dense network.

## SNA with Terrorist Network Data

Followed by the usefulness and description of all performance measures in Netlog dataset, we here use the terrorist dataset obtained from UCINET tool for our social network analysis. The closeness centrality is shown in Table 2.10.

**Table 2.10** Closeness centrality measures using a sample of terrorist dataset

|  |  | 1 | 2 |
| --- | --- | --- | --- |
|  |  | Farness | nCloseness |
| 6 | Mohamed Atta | 107.000 | 57.944 |
| 11 | Marwan Al-Shehhi | 134.000 | 46.269 |
| 1 | Hani Hanjour | 141.000 | 43.972 |
| 3 | Nawaf Alhazmi | 141.000 | 43.972 |
| 21 | Zacarias Moussaoui | 144.000 | 43.056 |
| 51 | Jean-Marc Grandvisir | 250.000 | 24.800 |
| 52 | Abu Zubeida | 250.000 | 24.800 |
| 35 | Nabil Almarabh | 257.000 | 24.125 |

**Table 2.11** Closeness centrality statistics

|  |  | 1 | 2 |
| --- | --- | --- | --- |
|  |  | Farness | nCloseness |
| 1 | Mean | 183.460 | 34.773 |
| 2 | Standard deviation | 30.430 | 6.081 |
| 3 | Variance | 925.963 | 36.978 |

**Closeness Centrality**

As discussed in section "SNA with Netlog Data" with Netlog dataset, more the closeness and less the farness value, better is the relationship between the terrorists in the network. From Table 2.10, it is evident that Nabil Almarabh is having more distant relationship in the network. The various statistics with mean farness of terrorist in the network is 183.460 with a deviation of 30.430, which is shown in Table 2.11 with a Network Centralization of 47.48%

**Freeman Betweenness Centrality**

In this, the Un-normalized centralization for the network using terrorist dataset is 65911.478. From Table 2.12, it can be observed that Essid Sami Ben Khamais has a high value of betweenness measure with 470.473, which indicates that among all others, he can work as a most vital mediator of knowledge flows with a high potential of control on the indirect relations of the other members in the network. The corresponding descriptive statistics are shown in Table 2.13. In the whole process of measuring betweenness centrality, our simulation gives a Network Centralization Index of 56.22%.

**K-Clusters Using Tabu Search**

Finally, we use Tabu search algorithm with 5-cluster to analyse our proposed social network analysis with following parameters, same as to that of taken for analysing Netlog dataset.

**Table 2.12** Betweenness centrality measures for terrorist dataset

|   |                         | 1 Betweenness | 2 nBetweenness |
|---|-------------------------|------------|-------------|
| 6  | Mohamed Atta           | 1106.944   | 58.538      |
| 37 | Essid Sami Ben Khemais | 470.473    | 24.880      |
| 21 | Zacarias Moussaoui     | 434.533    | 22.979      |
| 3  | Nawaf Alhazmi          | 287.580    | 15.208      |
| 1  | Hani Hanjour           | 233.759    | 12.362      |
| 46 | Djamal Beghal          | 195.683    | 10.348      |

**Table 2.13** Descriptive statistics for each measure of betweenness centrality

|   |                    | 1 Betweenness | 2 nBetweenness |
|---|--------------------|------------|-------------|
| 1 | Mean               | 60.730     | 3.212       |
| 2 | Standard deviation | 162.565    | 8.597       |
| 3 | Variance           | 26427.225  | 73.904      |

**Table 2.14** Density table analysis

|   | 1     | 2     | 3     | 4     | 5     |
|---|-------|-------|-------|-------|-------|
| 1 | 0.433 | 0.029 | 0.024 | 0.005 | 0.059 |
| 2 | 0.029 | 0.260 | 0.050 | 0.009 | 0.020 |
| 3 | 0.024 | 0.050 | 0.260 | 0.018 | 0.013 |
| 4 | 0.005 | 0.009 | 0.018 | 0.355 | 0.000 |
| 5 | 0.059 | 0.020 | 0.013 | 0.000 | 0.333 |

Number of clusters: 5

Type of data: Similarities/Strengths/Cohesion

Method: correlation

Starting fit: 1.050; Starting fit: 0.539; Fit: 0.543; Fit: 0.550; Fit: 0.543; Fit: 0.539 (smaller values indicate better fit). r-square = 0.212

Cluster 1: Mohamed Atta Waleed Alshehri Wail Alshehri Satam Suqami Abdul Aziz Al-Omari* Marwan

Cluster 2: Zacarias Moussaoui Kamel Daoudi Mamduh Mahmud Salim Faisal Al Salmi Bandar Alhazmi

Cluster 3: Raed Hijazi Nabil Almarabh Nizar Trabelsi Djamal Beghal Abu Qatada Ahmed Khalil

Cluster 4: Essid Sami Ben Khemais Haydar Abu Doha Mohamed Bensakhria Tarek Maaroufi Lased Ben

Cluster 5: Hani Hanjour Majed Moqed Nawaf Alhazmi Salem Alhazmi* Khalid Al-Mihdhar Ahmed

The density table after Tabu search algorithm applied in the dataset is provided below in Table 2.14. The information flow will be better for high value of density.

# Conclusions

We presented the cluster based data mining method to extract relationships in social network analysis using Netlog data and Terrorist network data. We used different performance measures in order to build a useful social relationship amongst the users. The social network analysis using cluster analysis made it very much useful for organizations to analyse the social network to understand the internal and external association of an organization, which further will be of immense use for collaborative work for innovation and dissemination of knowledge.

# References

1. Wasserman, S., Faust, K.: Social Network Analysis: Methods and Applications (Structural Analysis in the Social Sciences). Cambridge University Press, Cambridge (1994)
2. Schtt, J.: Social Network Analysis: A Handbook. Sage Publications, Newbury Park (1991)
3. Hanneman Robert, A., Mark, R.: Introduction to Social Network Methods. University of California, Riverside, Riverside (2005)
4. Finin, T., Joshi, A., Kolari, P., Java, A., Kale, A., Karandikar, A.: The information ecology of social media and online communities. Artif. Intell. Mag. 28, 1–12 (2008)
5. Eagle, N., Portland, A.: Reality mining: sensing complex social systems. Pers. Ubiquit. Comput. 10, 255–268 (2005)
6. Boyd, D.M., Ellison, N.B.: Social network sites: definition, history and scholarships. J. Comput. Mediat. Commun. 13(1), 210–230 (2008). Wiley
7. Tufekci, Z.: Grooming, gossip, Facebook and MySpace: what can we learn about these sites from those who won't assimilate? Inf. Commun. Soc. 11(4), 544–564 (2008)
8. Sheldon, P.: The relationship between unwillingness to communicate and students Facebook use. J. Media Psychol: Theor. Method. Appl. 20(2), 67–75 (2008)
9. Thelwall, M., Wilkinson, D., Uppal, S.: Data mining emotions in social network communications: gender differences in MySpace. J. Am. Soc. Sci. Technol 61, 1–14 (2009). Wiley
10. Zhou, L., Ding, J., Wang, Y., Cheng, B., Cao, F.: The social network mining of BBS. J. Netw. 4(4), 298–305 (2009)
11. Lewis, K., Kaufman, J., Gonzalez, M., Wimmer, A., Christakis, N.: Tastes, ties and time: a new social network dataset using FaceBook.com. Soc. Netw. 30, 330–342 (2008). Elsevier
12. Vaidyanathan, A., Shore, M., Billinghurst, M.: Data in social network analysis. In: Computer-Mediated Social Networking. Lecture Notes in Computer Science, vol. 5322, pp. 134–149. Springer, Berlin/New York (2009)
13. Lusseau, D., Schneider, K., et al.: Behavioural ecology and sociology, vol. 54. Addison-Wesley, US (2003)
14. Academic, L.A., Glance, N.: The political blogosphase and the 2004 US election. In: Proceedings of the 2005 Workshop on the Weblogging Ecosystem, Chiba, Japan, 10–14 May 2005
15. Snasel, V., Horak, Z., Abraham, A.: Understanding social networks using formal concept analysis. In: IEEE/WIC/ACM International Conference on Web Intelligence and Intelligent Agent Technology, WI-IAT '08, Vol. 3, pp. 390–393, 2008
16. Choa, A., Hernandez, A., Gonzalez, S., Castro, A., Gelbukh, A., Hernandez, A., Iztebegovic, H.: Social data mining to improved bio-inspired intelligent systems. In: Giannopoulou, E.G. (ed.) Data Mining in Medical and Biological Research, pp. 291–320. I-Tech, Vienna (2008)
17. Bhattacharya, I., Getoor, L.: Iterative record linkage for clearing and integration. In: Proceedings of the SIGMOD 2004 Workshop on Research Issues on Data Mining and Knowledge Discovery, Paris, France, pp. 1–18, 13 June 2004

18. Kubica, J., Moore, A., Schneider, J.: Tractable group detection on large link datasets. In: Proceedings of the 3rd IEEE International Conference on Data Mining, Melbourne, FL, pp. 573–576, 19–22 Dec 2003
19. Lu, Q., Geetoor, G.: Link based classification. In: Proceedings of the 2003 International Conference on Machine Learning, Washington, DC, pp. 496–503, 21–24 Aug 2003
20. Liben-Nowell, D., Kleinberg, J.: The link prediction problem for social networks. In: Proceedings of the 2003 International Conference on Information and Knowledge Management, New Orleans, LA, pp. 556–559, 2–8 Nov 2003
21. Krebs, V.: Mapp. Netw. Terror. Cell Connect. **24**, 43–52 (2002)
22. Page, L., Brin, S., Motwani, R., Winograd, T.: The PageRank Citations Ranking: Bringing Order to the Web, Technical Report. Stanford University, Stanford (1998)
23. Kleinberg, J.: Autoritive success in a hyper linked environment. J. ACM **5**, 604–632 (1999)
24. Wasserman, S., Faust, K.: Social Network Analysis. Cambridge University Press, Cambridge (1994)
25. Milgram, S.: The small world problem. Psychol. Today **2**, 60–67 (1967)
26. Travers, J., Milgram, S.: An experimental study of the small world problem. Sociometry **32**, 425–443 (1969)
27. Guare, J.: Six Degrees of Separation: A Play. Vintage, New York (1990)
28. Marsden, P.V.: Network data and measurement. Ann. Rev. Sociol. **16**, 435–463 (1990)
29. Katzir, L., Liberty, E., Somekh, O.: Estimating sizes of social networks via biased clustering. In: Proceedings of the International Conference on World Wide Web (WWW-2011), Hyderabad, India, 28 Mar–1 Apr 2011, pp. 597–605. ACM Press, New York (2011)
30. Amaral, L.A.N., Scala, A., Barthélémy, M., Stan-ley, H.E.: Classes of small-world networks. Proc. Natl. Acad. Sci. USA **97**, 11149–11152 (2000)
31. Newman, M.E.J., Strogatz, S.H., Watts, D.J.: Random graphs with arbitrary degree distributions and their applications. Phys. Rev. E **64**, 026118 (2001)
32. Newman, M.E.J.: The structure of scientific collaboration networks. Proc. Natl. Acad. Sci. USA **98**, 404–409 (2001)
33. Barabási, A.-L., Jeong, H., Ravasz, E., Néda, Z., Schu-berts, A., Vicsek, T.: Evolution of the social net-work of scientific collaborations. Physica A **311**, 590–614 (2002)
34. Davis, G.F., Greve, H.R.: Corporate elite networks and governance changes in the 1980s. Am. J. Sociol. **103**, 1–37 (1997)
35. Mariolis, P.: Interlocking directorates and control of cor-porations: the theory of bank control. Soc. Sci. Quart. **56**, 425–439 (1975)
36. Aiello, W., Chung, F., Lu, L.: A random graphmodel for massive graphs. In: Proceedings of the 32nd Annual ACM Symposium on Theory of Computing, Portland, 21–23 Mar 2000, pp. 171–180. Association of Computing Machinery, New York (2000)
37. Aiello, W., Chung, F., Lu, L.: Random evolution of massive graphs. In: Abello, J., Pardalos, P.M., Resende, M.G.C. (eds.) Handbook of Massive DataSets, pp. 97–122. Kluwer, Dordrecht (2002)
38. Ebel, H., Mielsch, L.-I., Bornholdt, S.: Scale-freetopology of e-mail networks. Phys. Rev. E **66**, 035103 (2002)
39. Abraham, A., et al.: Reducing social network dimensions using matrix factorization methods. In: Proceedings of the 2009 Advances in Social Network Analysis and Mining, 19 Jan 2009, pp. 348–351. IEEE press, Piscataway (2009)
40. Freeman, L.C.: Graphical techniques for exploring social network data. In: Carrington, P.J., Scott, J., Wasserman, S. (eds.) Models and Methods in Social Network Analysis. Cambridge University Press, Cambridge (2005)
41. Bulkley, N., Alstyne, V., Marshall, W.: An Empirical Analysis of Strategies and Efficiencies in Social Networks, 1 Feb 2006. Boston University School of Management Research Paper No. 2010–29, MIT Sloan Research Paper No. 4682–08. Available at SSRN: http://ssrn.com/abstract=887406

42. Abraham, A., et al.: Social aspects of web page contents. In: Abraham, A., Snásel, V., Wegrzyn-Wolska, K. (eds.) Proceedings of the International Conference on Computational Aspects of Social Networks, CASoN 2009, Fontainebleau, France, 24–27 June 2009, pp. 80–87. IEEE Computer Society, Washington, DC (2009)
43. Divjak, B., Peharda, P.: Social network analysis of study environment. JIOS **34**(1), 67–80 (2010)
44. Han, J., Kamber, M.: Data Mining: Concepts and Techniques, 2nd edn. Morgan Kauffman, San Francisco (2006)
45. Glover, F.: Heuristics for integer programming using surrogate constraints. Decis. Sci. **8**(1), 156–166 (1977)
46. Halgin, D.: An introduction to UCINET and NetDraw. In: 2008 NIPS UCINET and NetDraw Workshop, Harvard University, Cambridge, 13–14 June 2008, pp. 1–47
47. Gyarmati, L., Tuan, A.T.: Measuring user behaviour in online social networks. IEEE Netw. **24**(5), 26–31 (2010)
48. Borgatti, S.P., Everett, M.G., Freeman, L.C.: Network analysis of 2-mode data. Soc. Netw. **19**, 243–269 (2002). Elsevier

# Chapter 3
# Bio-inspired Clustering and Data Diffusion in Machine Social Networks

Iva Bojic, Tomislav Lipic, and Vedran Podobnik

**Abstract** At the end of 2010, we are at the effective end of the second phase of research in the field of Social Networks (SNs) and aspects such as Human-to-Human (H2H) interactions have pretty much had their day due to advances in Machine-to-Machine (M2M) interactions. This chapter will provide a useful insight into the differences between those two types of SNs: the human SNs (hSNs) based on H2H interactions and the machine SNs (mSNs) based on M2M interactions. During the last two decades rapid improvements in computing and communication technologies have enabled a proliferation of hSNs and we believe they will induce the formation of mSNs in the next decades. To this end, we will show how to carry out successful SN analyses (e.g. clustering and data diffusion) by connecting ethological approaches to social behaviour in animals (e.g. the study of firefly synchronization) and M2M interactions.

## Introduction

"For connecting more than half a billion people and mapping the social relations among them, for creating a new system of exchanging information and for changing how we live our lives," Mark Zuckerberg was named TIME's 2010 Person of the Year [28]. And just 7 years ago, Zuckerberg's online Social Network (SN) Facebook did not even exist.

I. Bojic (✉) • V. Podobnik
Faculty of Electrical Engineering and Computing, University of Zagreb, Unska 3,
HR-10000, Zagreb, Croatia
e-mail: iva.bojic@fer.hr; vedran.podobnik@fer.hr

T. Lipic
Centre for Informatics and Computing, Rudjer Boskovic Institute, Bijenicka 54,
HR-10000, Zagreb, Croatia
e-mail: tlipic@irb.hr

A. Abraham (ed.), *Computational Social Networks: Mining and Visualization*,
DOI 10.1007/978-1-4471-4054-2_3, © Springer-Verlag London 2012

There is no single definition of a SN, which is probably due to the fact that the study of SNs is one of the most interdisciplinary areas of science – for a comprehensive understanding of SNs one requires knowledge of sociology, mathematics (specifically graph theory), economics, computer science, statistical physics and others [33]. However, almost all SN definitions have one idea in common: a notion of *common interest*, which connects the entities (e.g. people) involved in SNs [1, 15, 17, 53, 66].

SNs are a well-developed area of study in social sciences, with a history longer than 50 years. Everything begun in the 1960s with Brown's identification of "a need for understanding complexities of collective human behaviour at a level that is more objective and more scientific than the approach of psychology and sociology to the same problem" [13] and Milgram's "small world experiment" which demonstrated the idea of "six degrees of separation" [42, 59]. A solid theoretical foundation in the field of SN research was developed in the 1970s [20, 22, 27, 67], while the next two decades were mainly dedicated to practical studies that applied theoretical knowledge from the field to real-world situations, such as an investigation about the interconnections of supervisory boards of various companies [44], an analysis of human social structure [61], or a discussion about the spreading of new ideas within a community [55]. Furthermore, the research by social scientists confirmed the importance of SNs in provisioning of social support among community members [69], in structuring unrest and other political conflicts [58], in analysis of immigration processes [56], as well as in studying internal processes within companies [48]. In this chapter, we refer to this phase in SN evolution as *Phase 1: The age of human Social Networks as the field of study in social sciences.*

However, at the beginning of the 2000s SNs experienced a proliferation grounded on the advent of ICT-enabled (*Information and Communication Technology*) Social Networking Services (SNSs). This was a huge shift for both scientists, who now had access to an unprecedented source of data on human behaviour [31], and people in general, who now became able to interconnect at a global scale in just a few seconds and with just a few mouse-clicks. Implementation of SNs based on ICT infrastructure not only allows people to map their social relationships from the real world to a virtual one, but also to build virtual communities with other people that share the same interests/activities. This is achieved through creating (semi-)public user profiles and defining a list of other user profiles (i.e. people) with whom they are associated. Although the SNSs [11, 71] less than a decade ago represented only a drop in the sea of web pages with different themes and purposes, today they are not only the most popular services based on ICT infrastructure, but also a truly global phenomenon which greatly affects the modern way of life. Between 2002 and 2006 many SNSs appeared on the scene – the first to begin was *Friendster,*[1] then

---

[1] The SN was established in 2002. It is active today (http://www.friendster.com) and has over 115 million registered users, of which over 90% come from Asian countries (in Western countries it is no longer popular).

*MySpace*[2] and *LinkedIn*,[3] and then came *Facebook*[4] [62], *Bebo*[5] and *Twitter*[6] [76]. Some of the aforementioned SNSs have grown into the most popular SNs supported by ICT infrastructure. Today, the list of major SNSs has around 200 names (more than 50 million registered users, apart from those already mentioned, have *Flixster, Habbo, hi5, MyLife, Netlog, Orkut, Qzone, Tagged, vkontakte* and *Windows Live Spaces*). In this chapter, we refer to this phase in SN evolution as *Phase 2: The age of ICT-enabled human Social Networks.*

At the end of 2010, although the real effects of Facebook's advent are yet to be seen in the years to come, we are at the effective end of the second phase in the evolution of SNs. We believe Human-to-Human (H2H) interactions have pretty much had their day due to advances in Machine-to-Machine (M2M) interactions. This chapter will provide a useful insight into the differences between two types of SNs: human SNs (hSNs) based on H2H interactions and machine SNs (mSNs) based on M2M interactions. The continuation of rapid improvements in computing and communication technologies, which enabled the proliferation of hSNs during the last decade, will induce the formation of mSNs in the next decade. In this chapter, we refer to this phase in SN evolution as *Phase 3: The age of machine Social Networks.*

---

[2] The SN was established in 2003. This SN (http://www.myspace.com) gained the first million users in 2004, while in early 2007 the number of its users reached the 100 million mark. The period between 2005 and 2007 was a time when MySpace was the most popular SNS in the world, after which Facebook assumed primacy. Today, the number of MySpace users is around the 130 million mark (70% of users are Americans). Since 2005 MySpace has been owned by News Corporation (the second largest media company in the world), which bought it for 580 million US dollars.

[3] The SN was established in 2003. It is active today (http://www.linkedin.com) and has over 100 million users from over 200 countries representing today's most important professional SN in which more than 150 different industries are represented, and whose members are leading people of all Fortune 500 global companies.

[4] The SN was established in 2004 and today is the most popular SNS (http://www.facebook.com/) with over 700 million users worldwide (more than 10% of the entire world population) and is constantly growing. The value of the Facebook brand was estimated at a staggering 50 billion US dollars. General statistics about Facebook are available at http://www.facebook.com/press/info. php?statistics and http://www.socialbakers.com

[5] The SN was established in 2005. The name Bebo is an acronym for "Blog early, blog often." The target users of this SN (http://www.bebo.com/) are primarily residents of Ireland, UK, Australia, New Zealand and US, and their total number is about 40 million. Since 2008 Bebo has been owned by AOL (one of the world's major Internet and media companies), who bought it for 850 million US dollars.

[6] The SN was established in 2006. It is based on the microblogging principle – users can post and read short messages (text messages to a maximum of 140 characters long) called tweets. The similarities with the concept of the SMS (*Short Message Service*) in mobile telecommunications is responsible for Twitter being called the "SMS of the Internet." This SN (http://www.twitter.com) recorded staggering user growth rates (greater than 1,000% per year), but the problem with Twitter is the fact that it has a large number of inactive users (compared to other leading SNSs – it is estimated that only 40% of Twitter users are actually active, while this number for Facebook and MySpace is around 70%). The current total number of Twitter users has exceeded 200 million, while the dizzying growth rate has began to calm down. There is, on average, 150 million tweets sent per day.

**Table 3.1** Phases in Social Network evolution

| Phase | Time period | Description |
|-------|-------------|-------------|
| 1st phase | 1960s–2000s | Human Social Networks as the field of study in social sciences |
| 2nd phase | 2000s–2010s | ICT-enabled human Social Networks |
| 3rd phase | 2010s–2020s | Machine Social Networks |

To conclude this introduction, Table 3.1 lists described phases in the evolution of SNs. Please note that the next phase in evolution does not exclude properties of the current phase, but rather presents a major technological/conceptual add-on.

This chapter is organized as follows. In section "Machine Social Networks," we define the mSN and compare it with the hSN. Section "Synchronization in Machine Social Networks" gives formal definitions and theorems of Pulsed Coupled Oscillators (PCO) used for machines representation in mSNs. Section "Analysis of Social Networks" verifies our model of PCO in mSNs mapping currently used techniques for SNs analyses in hSNs into mSNs where machines are presented as fireflies. Section "Real World Examples of Machine Social Networks" brings forth some real word examples where machines form their SNs within interacting in M2M manner. Finally, section "Conclusion" concludes the chapter.

## Machine Social Networks

Is the name *machine Social Network* pretentious or at least contrived? We argue it is not and explain why.

Firstly, we will start with the numbers. There are almost seven billion people in the world, two billion of whom are on the Internet. Intel estimated that by 2015 the world will have 15 billion connected devices [23] and Ericsson predicted that by the end of 2020 there will be 50 billion devices (i.e. machines) connected to the Web [72]. Whether these predictions will come true or not, one thing is certain – the number of interconnected machines will greatly exceed the number of interconnected people.

Secondly, these machines are not "dummy" devices that use energy to perform some activity, such as a steam engine or chronometer. On the contrary, we refer to "smart" machines, equipped with hardware (such as processors and memory storages) and software (such as Artificial Intelligence algorithms) providing them with a certain level of intelligence and autonomy. Already today there exist *autonomous vacuum cleaners* which are in charge of cleaning *smart homes*. And this is only the beginning. Although many years will pass until machines eventually reach or even surpass human intelligence, it is not science fiction to imagine two machines talking to each other. Moreover, later in this chapter we will explain one mechanism that exists today and makes this possible.

**Fig. 3.1** Mappings between:
(1) people in the real world
and human Social Networks,
(2) machines in the real world
and machine Social Networks

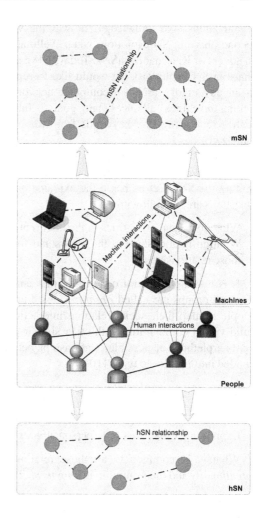

These are the reasons why we think it is of vital importance to be able to understand machines' interactions within the SN context. Figure 3.1 presents mappings between: (1) people in the real world and human Social Networks, (2) machines in the real world and machine Social Networks. It can be noted that machines are owned by people who give them tasks. We will continue explaining our vision of an mSN through a comparison with a hSN.

## Human Verses Machine Social Networks

In his viewpoint entitled "Computer networks as Social Networks" Wellman [68] wrote "computer networks are inherently Social Networks, linking people, organizations, and knowledge." It was the year 2001 (i.e. the beginning of the second phase in SN evolution) when Wellman presented this thought, referring to an advent of ICT-enabled hSNs. Today, 10 years later (i.e. the beginning of the third phase in SN evolution), we would like to rephrase Wellman's sentence, referring to an advent of mSNs – "computer networks are inherently Social Networks, linking machines, alliances, and goals." Table 3.2 explains our motivation for such a rephrasing (the keywords from the original and rephrased sentences are italicized).

The two basic notions in SNs are *entities* (nodes/vertices in a graph representing SN) and *relationships* between these entities (edges/connections in a graph representing the SN). Let us begin the explanation of Table 3.2 by focusing on hSNs. Questions are the following:

- What do (group of) entities in the hSN represent?
- What do relationships in the hSN stand for and what are the characteristics of those relationships?

It is a straightforward conclusion that entities in hSNs are *people*, while the (formal) groups are called *organizations*. Furthermore, the fact that hSNs enable people to map their social relations/interactions/flows from the real world, or to build virtual communities with other similar people, bring us to answer that there exists a plethora of possible relationships between people in hSNs, which can be divided into four basic types [10]:

- Expressing a *social relation* (e.g. person *A* *is a friend* of person *B*);
- Expressing an *interaction* (e.g. person *A* *had sex* with person *B*);
- Expressing a *flow* (e.g. person *A* *gave money to* person *B*); and
- Expressing a *similarity* (e.g. person *A* *goes out in the same clubs* as person *B*).

What is in common to all those relationships is that they are being made *intentionally* and their duration is *long term*. These relationships have a goal of:

- *Renewing old/broken, maintaining current and boosting future social relations/interactions/flows*;
- *Building virtual communities with other people that share the same interests/activities.*

Entities (i.e. people) in the hSN are represented by profiles, which can be:

- *Public* (accessible to everybody), or;
- *Semi-public* (accessible only to "friends," i.e. other people with whom the ego-person is in a relationship).

These profiles can include one or more of the following information types:

- *Basic information* describing the person (such as age, sex, gender, etc.);
- The person's *interests* (such as favourite books/music/movies, etc.);
- The person's *activities* (such as hobbies, sports, memberships, etc.);

**Table 3.2**  A comparison between human Social Networks and machine Social Networks

| Property | hSNs | mSNs |
|---|---|---|
| Entities | *People* | *Machines* |
| Group of entities | *Organization* | *Alliance* |
| Relationships | • Social relations<br>• Interactions<br>• Flows, and<br>• Similarities | Cooperative relations |
| How are relationships formed? | Intentionally, based on *knowledge* about<br>• Existing social relations<br>• Historic interactions<br>• Established flows, and<br>• Discovery of people who share similar interests/activities | Serendipitously, based on a common *goal* |
| Why are relationships being made? | • To renew old/broken, maintain current and boost future social relations/interactions/flows, and<br>• To build virtual communities with other people that share the same interests/activities | To meet a goal more efficiently (in terms of time, cost, energy consumption, etc.) through collaboration |
| How long do relationships last? | Long term | Short term |
| What does a profile look like? | • Basic information<br>• Interests<br>• Activities<br>• Photo, and<br>• Links to "friends" | Description of capabilities |
| Level of profile availability | (Semi-)public | Public |

- The person's *photo*, and;
- The person's *"friends."*

Let us now shift our focus to mSNs. Here, the questions are the following:

- What do (group of) entities in mSNs represent?
- What do relationships in the mSN stand for and what are the characteristics of those relationships?

Again, it is a straightforward fact that entities in mSNs are *machines*. However, here we refer to (formal) groups of entities as *alliances* and we identify only one type of relationship – *cooperative relations* (e.g. machine *A collaboratively downloads data with* machine *B*). The reason for that is the fact that machines connect *serendipitously* and their relationships are *short term*. The only goal for machines to connect is meeting a common goal more efficiently (in terms of time, cost, energy consumption, etc.) by collaborating. Machine profiles consist only of the description of their capabilities (such as list of tasks which the machine can execute, the location and time where and when these tasks can be executed, etc.) because this is the only information required by other machines interested in collaboration. Furthermore, machine profiles are usually publicly available so they can be accessed from a broad set of other machines, which augments the possibility of collaboration.

## Challenges for Machine Social Networks

Interactions in hSNs are achieved using a common human communication interface, i.e. human languages. Although, there is more than one human language, the mapping between them can be easily done. However, in order to enable interactions in mSNs, one common machine communication interface must be set. That interface must be independent of communication technologies (e.g. Bluetooth, WiFi) allowing different machines to communicate.

Today there exist mechanisms which enable machines to understand each other while communicating (such as the semantic web [6]). However, they do not fully support SN interactions. In this chapter, we explain how entities (i.e. machines) in mSNs can be represented as Pulsed Coupled Oscillators (PCO) fulfilling the vision of one common machine language.

Modelling machine interactions within their SNs with PCOs preserves all the good characteristics of hSNs (e.g. amenability for social analysis) and enables some new ones (e.g. data visualization techniques). In the next section we will firstly provide proofs that mobile and partially connected machines in a dense network, with interferences and collisions within it, can communicate at different points of time (i.e. different time frames). Afterwards, we will provide some examples of how social analysis (e.g. clustering and data diffusion) is currently performed in hSNs. Finally, we verify our model by showing that when machines are represented by PCOs the same social analysis can be performed in mSNs.

## Synchronization in Machine Social Networks

The PCO model is inspired by the synchronization of fireflies in Nature. In certain parts of south-east Asia alongside riverbanks, male fireflies gather on trees at dawn and start emitting flashes regularly. Over time, synchronization emerges from randomness, which makes it seem as though the whole tree is flashing in perfect synchrony [4]. Furthermore, for various species of fireflies, an emission of light represents communication which helps female fireflies distinguish males of its own species. This allows a female to recognize a specific male. She responds to him with a flash after a species-specific time delay [14].

In mSNs, the term synchronization is connected with machine interactions (i.e. communication). Only when synchronized, can machines interact. Modelling mSNs with PCOs does not enable interactions between machines to be smooth (i.e. continuous), but to occur in intervals (i.e. pulses). Pulse-like communication has several advantages compared to continuous communication – it generates less traffic, allows the same machines to communicate in different time frames, consumes less energy, etc.

Additionally, the PCO model does not presume that machines have to be fixed (i.e. they can move). Finally, the PCO model enables some machines to have good/bad influence on others (i.e. they can be excitatory or inhibitory coupled). In the rest of this section we will present a formal PCO model, together with proofs for achieving synchronization in partially connected networks, in which:

- Realistic radio effects (e.g. delays) are not neglected;
- Nodes are mobile, and;
- Nodes can be excitatory or inhibitory coupled.

## Types of Interconnections in Machine Social Networks

The mSN can be modelled as a network of $\mathcal{N}$ oscillators, where each machine is one oscillator, characterized by a voltage-like *state variable* $x_i$:

$$x_i' = f_i(x_i) + \varepsilon \sum_{j=1}^{\mathcal{N}} g_{ij}(x_i) \delta\left(t - t_j^*\right),\qquad(3.1)$$

where $x_i'$ denotes the first derivation of $x_i$ over a time of duration $\Delta t$, $f_i(x_i)$ describes the dynamics of the $i$-th oscillator, $\varepsilon$ is the small coupling constant, $g_{ij}(x_i)$ is the coupling function between oscillators $i$ and $j$, $\delta$ is the Dirac delta function and $t_j^*$ is the firing time of the $j$-th oscillator. When $x_i$ reaches the upper boundary (e.g. the value is equal to 1), the $i$-th oscillator "fires" (i.e. is able to communicate), and $x_i$ then jumps back to the lower boundary (e.g. the value is equal to 0). State variable $x_i$ not only depends on its previous state, but also on its neighbour's state variable $x_j$. Namely, $x_j$ increments $x_i$ by an amount given by $\varepsilon g_{ij}(x_i)$:

$$x_j = 1 \Rightarrow \begin{cases} x_i \to x_i + \varepsilon g_{ij}(x_i) & if\ x_i + \varepsilon g_{ij}(x_i) < 1 \\ x_i \to 0 & \text{otherwise} \end{cases}.\qquad(3.2)$$

If the oscillators evolve according to identical uncoupled dynamics we can write

$$f_i(x) = f(x) > 0,\ \forall x \in [0, 1].\qquad(3.3)$$

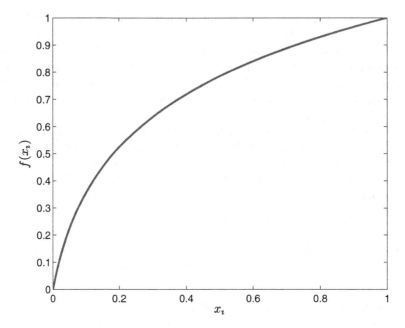

**Fig. 3.2** Graph of the function $f$

Moreover, (3.1) can then be written as

$$x'_i = f(x_i) + \varepsilon \sum_{j=1}^{\mathcal{N}} g(x_i)\delta(t - t_j^*), \quad x_i \in [0, 1]. \tag{3.4}$$

**Theorem 1.** *If the state function $f$ is smooth, monotonically increasing and concave down, then the set of $\mathcal{N}$ oscillators will always converge to synchronicity for any $\mathcal{N}$ and any initial conditions $x_i(0)$ $\forall i$ [43].*

In Theorem 1, Mirollo and Strogatz (M&S) have proven that synchronization can be achieved for the *state function* $f : [0, 1] \to [0, 1]$ that satisfies $f' > 0$ and $f'' < 0$ (see Fig. 3.2), under the assumption of all-to-all communication in a network. All-to-all communication in the mSNs would mean that each machine affects all others. Considering Ericsson's prediction of 50 billion connected machines [72], this sort of interaction would generate huge network traffic.

Furthermore, if the pulse-coupled oscillators are weakly connected (i.e. $\varepsilon \ll 1$) and each oscillator exhibits autonomous oscillatory behaviour, then (3.4) can be transformed into a simpler *phase model* formation

$$\phi'_i = \omega_i + \varepsilon \sum_{j=1}^{\mathcal{N}} \gamma_{ij}(\phi_j - \phi_i), \tag{3.5}$$

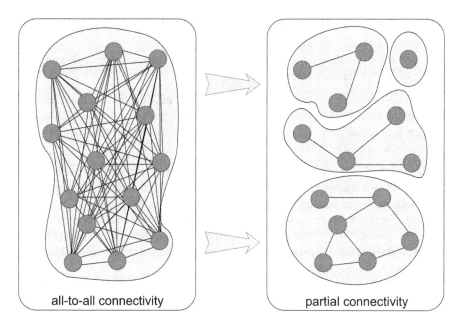

**Fig. 3.3** Transition from all-to-all communication to partial communication

where $\phi_i$ is *phase variable*, $\omega_i$ is the *natural frequency* of uncoupled oscillator $i$ and $\gamma_{ij}$ is a connection function between oscillators $i$ and $j$

$$\gamma_{ij}(\psi) = \frac{\omega^2}{2\pi} \frac{g_{ij}\left(\xi(\frac{\psi}{\omega})\right)}{f\left(\xi\left(\frac{\psi}{\omega}\right)\right)}. \tag{3.6}$$

For different formulations of function $\gamma_{ij}$ see [32]. Fourteen years after the M&S model, Lucarelli and Wang (L&W) relaxed the assumption about all-to-all communication, allowing nearest neighbour communication (see Theorem 2).

**Theorem 2.** *Let $\mathcal{G}^c$ be a connected graph describing the coupling topology of the system of oscillators presented with (3.4). If $\gamma \propto g/f$ is an uneven function such that $\gamma(0) = 0$ and $\psi \cdot \gamma(\psi) > 0, \forall \psi \neq 0$, then in the limit $\varepsilon \to 0$, the system asymptotically synchronizes for any initial condition $x_0 \in \mathcal{D}$, where $\mathcal{D}$ is a compact subset of $[0, 1]^N$ [39].*

Theorem 2 allows the usage of the PCO model in partially connected networks, which is a realistic assumption for mSNs. Figure 3.3 illustrates how the assumption of all-to-all communication in Theorem 1 was relaxed in Theorem 2 (i.e. by allowing communication between only close neighbours).

## Message Loss and Message Delays in Machine Social Networks

M&S and L&W models have assumed idealized nodes and have neglected the realistic effects of network communication:

- Machines observe all events emanating from their neighbours (i.e. there are no message losses), and;
- When a machine fires, its neighbours instantaneously observe that event (i.e. there are no message delays).

However, both assumptions are very unrealistic for any communication technology, since when a machine $\iota$ sends out a firing event message at time $t$, its neighbour $\jmath$ will not receive the message until time $t + \tau$ (where the delay $\tau$ is not known in advance). Therefore, in the case of delays between the sender and receiver those two models are no longer capable of providing synchronization. Namely, in [18, 19] Ernst et al. showed that the presence of delays causes the synchronization to become out of phase by a finite time lag.

Nevertheless, Lundelius and Lynch showed in [40] that the presence of an uncertainty $\zeta$ in the message delivery time, affects synchronization precision. The parameter $\zeta$ is defined as $\zeta = \nu - \mu$, where $\mu$ denotes the smallest message delay in the network, and $\nu$ is the largest message delay.

**Theorem 3.** *No clock synchronization algorithm can synchronize a system of $\mathcal{N}$ processes to within time $\beta$, for any*

$$\beta < \zeta \left( 1 - \frac{1}{\mathcal{N}} \right). \tag{3.7}$$

Although, message loss and message delays negatively affect synchronization time and precision in the PCO model, modification of certain model properties can lead to synchronization. Thus, Kuramoto introduced an absolute *refractory period*, during which the individual oscillators are assumed to be completely insensitive to effects from the outside world [36]. He modified (3.5) in the following way:

$$\phi_\iota' = \omega_\iota + \mathcal{H}(\phi_\iota) \left[ \varepsilon \sum_{\jmath=1}^{\mathcal{N}} \gamma_{\iota\jmath} (\phi_\jmath - \phi_\iota) \right], \tag{3.8}$$

where the inserted function $\mathcal{H}$ is defined by

$$\mathcal{H}(\phi_\iota) = \begin{cases} 0 & \phi_\iota \in \mathcal{R} \\ 1 & \text{otherwise} \end{cases}. \tag{3.9}$$

The interval $\mathcal{R}$ is chosen as

$$\mathcal{R}[h_1, h_2] \ 0 < h_1, h_2 < 2\pi. \tag{3.10}$$

Furthermore, in [32] Izhikevich showed that the activity of a weakly pulse-coupled network with transmission delays described with

$$x_i' = 1 + \varepsilon \sum_{j=1}^{\mathcal{N}} g_{ij}(x_i) \delta \left( t - t_j^* - \tau_{ij} \right),$$  (3.11)

where $\tau_{ij} \geq 0$ denotes some delay, converges to an $\varepsilon$-neighbourhood of a limit cycle. He also proved that every non-constant function $f$ can be transformed into a constant one by a continuous change of variables. Therefore, without losing any generality, in (3.11) for function $f$ can be taken $f = 1$, so that each oscillator has period $\mathcal{T} = 1$ and frequency $\Omega = 2\pi$.

**Theorem 4.** *Consider the weakly pulse-coupled network* (3.11) *and the corresponding phase model* (3.5). *Let $g(x)$ be an arbitrary odd function having period 1 and let $g_{ij}^0$, $g_{ji}^0$, $w_{ij}$ and $w_{ji}$ be arbitrary constants. If the connection functions have the form*

$$g_{ij}(x_i) = g_{ij}^0 + g(w_{ij} + x_i),$$  (3.12)

$$g_{ji}(x_j) = g_{ji}^0 + g(w_{ji} + x_j),$$  (3.13)

$$\eta_{ij} + w_{ij} + \eta_{ji} + w_{ji} = 0 \ (mod \ 1)$$  (3.14)

*where (mod 1) means modulo 1. Then the activity of the pulse-coupled network* (3.11) *converges to an $\varepsilon$-neighbourhood of a limit cycle. On the limit cycle all neurons fire with equal frequencies and constant phase differences, which corresponds to synchronization of the network activity [32].*

More recently, Werner-Allen et al. proposed the *Reachback Firefly Algorithm* that takes into account realistic radio effects and provides synchronization [70].

**Theorem 5.** *Two oscillators $i$ and $j$, governed by Reachback Firefly Algorithm dynamics, will be driven to synchrony irrespective of their initial phases.*

In the *Reachback Firefly Algorithm*, unlike the M&S model, $j$ will not jump immediately upon hearing $i$'s fire; instead, $j$ will record the time and then execute the appropriate jump after its next firing. The jump is defined as

$$\Delta(\phi) = g(f(\phi) + \varepsilon) - \phi,$$  (3.15)

where $g = f^{-1}$ and $\varepsilon \ll 1$.

Figure 3.4 (where a cross denotes message loss and a star message delay) illustrates communication without and with delays and message loss. In this subsection we have shown that even in networks with realistic radio effects synchronization can be achieved.

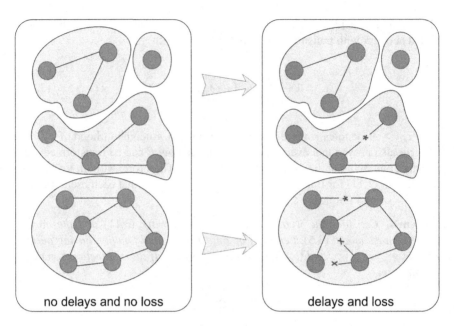

**Fig. 3.4** Transition from communication without delays and loss into communication with delays and loss

## *Inhibitory Coupling in Machine Social Networks*

So far we have assumed that all neighbours from a certain machine have a positive effect on it, and we have neglected the possible negative effect. However, in the PCO model, oscillators can be either *excitatory coupled* or *inhibitory coupled*. In the excitatory coupled model when one oscillator fires, phases of all its other neighbours are raised by an amount $\varepsilon$:

$$\phi_j = 1 \Rightarrow \begin{cases} \phi_i \to \phi_i + \varepsilon\, g_{ij}(\phi_i) & if \ \ \phi_i + \varepsilon\, g_{ij}(\phi_i) < 1 \\ \phi_i \to 0 & \text{otherwise} \end{cases}. \qquad (3.16)$$

Analogously, inhibitory coupled oscillators affect their neighbours by lowering their phases (i.e. $\varepsilon < 0$):

$$\phi_j = 0 \Rightarrow \begin{cases} \phi_i \to \phi_i - \varepsilon\, g_{ij}(\phi_i) & if \ \ \phi_i - \varepsilon\, g_{ij}(\phi_i) > 0 \\ \phi_i \to 1 & \text{otherwise} \end{cases}. \qquad (3.17)$$

Note that phase variable $\phi_i$ in (3.16) and (3.17) is normalized, meaning its value can be between 0 and 1.

The M&S model showed that biological oscillators always synchronize their firing in homogeneous networks with *excitatory* all-to-all coupling if the rise function has a concave shape. L&W relaxed the assumption about all-to-all communication, but still kept the assumption of *excitatory* coupling. Furthermore, Ernst et al. have proved that in cases of delays, *excitatory* coupled oscillators may receive echoes of their own pulses that drive their phases further apart and prohibits the overall system to reach synchrony. However, when certain adjustments are made (e.g. as in the Reachback Firefly Algorithm or Kuramoto model) *excitatory* coupled oscillators can reach the synchronization phase. In this subsection we will present the results of mSN modelling based on *inhibitory* coupled oscillators.

Ernst et al. investigated the effects of non-zero delays in *inhibitory* coupled networks [18, 19]. They concluded that synchronization depends on the inhibition strength $\varepsilon$. Therefore, they presented three scenarios:

- For $\varepsilon \in \langle 0, 1 - f(2\tau)\rangle$ oscillators synchronize either in phase $\phi^\infty = 0$ or in antiphase $\phi^\infty = \mathcal{T}/2$ depending on initial conditions $\phi^0$, where $\mathcal{T} = \mathcal{T}(\varepsilon)$ denotes the average period between two firing events of one oscillator;
- For $\varepsilon \in \langle 1 - f(2\tau), f(\tau)\rangle$ oscillators always synchronize with zero phase, and;
- For $\varepsilon \in \langle f(\tau), \infty\rangle$ the system can achieve marginally stable synchronization similar to that for excitatory couplings.

In 2009 Klingmayr et al. presented their inhibitory coupling approach that leads to synchronization of all oscillators, where synchrony is always granted, independent of initial conditions and delays [35]. More precisely, in their model an oscillator after firing does not reset its phase to zero, but adjusts it according to a simple linear transfer function $\mathcal{L}$

$$\mathcal{L}(\phi(t)) = (1 + \alpha) \cdot \phi(t), \qquad (3.18)$$

that mediates the phase adjustment due to interaction. Parameter $\alpha$ is within the $\langle -1, 0\rangle$ interval which guarantees that $\phi(t) \in [0, 1]$ for any $t$. Moreover, for systems with delays they adopted the *refractory period* from Kuramoto's model. During that period, an oscillator does not react to firing pulses, and hence the receiving oscillator just considers the first received pulse, ignoring the others.

In Fig. 3.5 the dot-filled nodes denote inhibitory coupled oscillators. In this subsection we proved that an inhibitory coupled network with realistic radio effects can synchronize even faster than the excitatory coupled one.

## Mobility in Machine Social Networks

In 2010 Tyrrell et al. proposed the *Meshed Emergent Firefly Synchronization* (MEMFIS) concept [60] that supports partly connected dense networks where network topology can change over time. So far, we have assumed that machines in mSNs are static (i.e. they could not move), but MEMFIS guarantees network

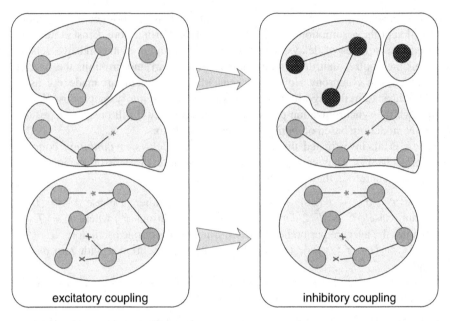

excitatory coupling

inhibitory coupling

**Fig. 3.5** Transition from communication with excitatory coupling into communication with mixed coupling (i.e. excitatory and inhibitory coupling)

synchrony even when nodes change their positions. Moreover, this algorithm is shown to be robust against interferences and collisions in the network as well.

All previously mentioned models made a clear distinction between an *acquisition phase* (where nodes in a network synchronize) and a *communication phase* (where nodes transmit and receive data). The acquisition phase always comes before the communication phase and these two phases never mix. Therefore, those models do not support the dynamics of the network (i.e. that previously synchronized parts of networks can be merged forcing the rest of the network to resynchronize). Conversely, MEMFIS integrates the acquisition phase into the communication phase, since the synchronization word, common to all nodes, is embedded into each packet along with payload data.

Figure 3.6 illustrates one node (black) that has changed its position. The MEMFIS algorithm provides synchronization within a network that supports node moving and position changing, as well as relationships.

## Analysis of Social Networks

This section first defines SNs as graphs where nodes represent individuals (i.e. humans, machines) in SNs and links their connections. Secondly, we show how two common SN analysis methods (*social clustering* and *data diffusion*) can be

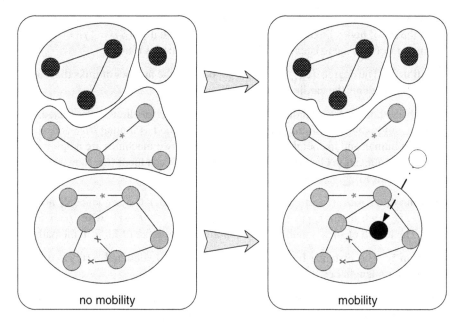

**Fig. 3.6** Transition from communication without mobility into communication with mobility

successfully applied when representing machines in mSNs using a PCO model. This verifies that the PCO model in mSNs can provide the same functionality as currently used mechanisms in hSNs. Finally, we will show how machines in mSNs can be used for data visualization of data generated by outside sources. The key idea is to use the flashes of fireflies to visualize the data.

## *Representation of Social Networks As Graphs*

Graph theory has been commonly used to describe different SNs including friendship, affiliation and collaboration networks. From an abstract perspective, the term network is used as a synonym for a mathematical *graph*.

**Definition 1.** A pair $\mathcal{G} = (\mathcal{V}, E)$ with $E \subseteq E(\mathcal{V})$ is called a graph. The elements of $\mathcal{V}$ are the vertices of $\mathcal{G}$, and those of $E$ the edges of $\mathcal{G}$. The vertex set of a graph $\mathcal{G}$ is denoted by $\mathcal{V}_{\mathcal{G}}$ and its edge set by $E_{\mathcal{G}}$. Therefore, $\mathcal{G} = (\mathcal{V}_{\mathcal{G}}, E_{\mathcal{G}})$.

In SNs, the term *node* is used instead of *vertex* to represent individuals in SNs. All individuals in the network can be presented with a set of nodes $\mathcal{N} = \{1, 2, \ldots, n\}$. Furthermore, social relationships in SNs can be presented with a set of *links* in graphs.

**Definition 2.** For any graph $\mathcal{G}$ and node $\imath$, let $\mathcal{N}_\imath(\mathcal{G})$ be the neighbourhood of $\imath$ in $\mathcal{G}$, that is, the set of nodes linked to $\imath$ in the network $\mathcal{G}$, so that $\mathcal{N}_\imath(\mathcal{G}) = \{\jmath \mid \imath\jmath \in \mathcal{G}\}$. The link $\imath\jmath$ denotes the existence of the path between nodes $\imath$ and $\jmath$.

**Definition 3.** The degree $deg_\mathcal{G}(\imath) = |\mathcal{N}_\imath(\mathcal{G})|$ denotes the number of links that each node has, and equals the cardinality of $\mathcal{N}_\imath(\mathcal{G})$.

Neighbourhood in SNs denotes a set of individuals that are directly connected. In hSNs the neighbourhood of one person can be understood as mutual *friendship* between that human and his neighbours, while in mSNs two machines are neighbours when a communication channel of any kind exists between them (i.e. they are able to communicate).

**Definition 4.** A path in a graph $\mathcal{G}$ between nodes $\imath$ and $\jmath$ is a sequence of nodes $\imath_1\imath_2, \ldots, \imath_\mathcal{K}$ such that $\imath_k\imath_{k+1} \in \mathcal{G}$ for each $k \in \{1, \ldots, \mathcal{K}-1\}$, with $\imath_1=\imath$ and $\imath_\mathcal{K}=\jmath$. The length of such a path is $\mathcal{K}-1$ denoting the number of links in the path.

**Definition 5.** The distance between two nodes $\imath$ and $\jmath$, denoted $d(\imath, \jmath)$, is the minimum path length between $\imath$ and $\jmath$.

**Definition 6.** The diameter of a graph $\mathcal{G}$, defined as $\overline{d}(\mathcal{G}) = max_{\imath,\jmath} d(\imath, \jmath)$, is the maximum distance between any two nodes in a graph.

Diameter denotes connectivity in a graph. As many SNs are not connected (i.e. there are at least two nodes that have no path between them), the diameter is often reported for the largest component (i.e. a maximally connected subgraph). Subgraphs in SNs can be understood as clusters.

**Definition 7.** A graph $\mathcal{G}'$ is a subgraph of a graph $\mathcal{G}$, denoted by $\mathcal{G}' \subseteq \mathcal{G}$, if $\mathcal{N}_{\mathcal{G}'} \subseteq \mathcal{N}_\mathcal{G}$ and $E_{\mathcal{G}'} \subseteq E_\mathcal{G}$.

In terms of defining clusters in graphs, a *clustering coefficient* can be defined. Watts and Strogatz defined the clustering coefficient of a node $c(\imath)$ as a measure that represents the likeliness that two adjacent nodes of $\mathcal{N}$ are connected [65], while Brinkmeier and Schank defined it in terms of triangles and triples [12].

**Definition 8.** A triangle $\Delta = \{\mathcal{N}_\Delta, E_\Delta\}$ is a complete subgraph of $\mathcal{G}$ with exactly three nodes. $\lambda(\mathcal{G})$ is the number of triangles in $\mathcal{G}$, $\lambda(\imath) = |\{\Delta \mid \imath \in \mathcal{N}_\Delta\}|$ is the number of triangles of a node. A triple is a subgraph with three nodes and two links and the number of triples $\tau(\imath)$ at a node $\imath$ depends on its $deg(\imath)$:

$$\tau(\imath) = \frac{deg(\imath)^2 - deg(\imath)}{2}. \tag{3.19}$$

The number of triples for the whole graph is

$$\tau(\mathcal{G}) = \sum_{i \in \mathcal{N}} \tau(i). \tag{3.20}$$

The clustering coefficient of a node $\iota$ is defined as:

$$c\left(\iota\right) = \frac{\lambda\left(v\right)}{\tau\left(v\right)}.\tag{3.21}$$

In SNs a low clustering coefficient indicates that individual's friends are rather loosely connected, whereas a highly clustered network has a high clustering coefficient. Furthermore, the link *betweenness* measure assesses the centrality of a link in a graph. It is calculated by summing up the number of shortest paths that pass the observed link.

**Definition 9.** The link betweenness of a link $e$ in a graph $\mathcal{G}$ is defined as the number of shortest paths along it. The proportion of shortest paths between $s$ and $t$ that pass link $e$ is defined as

$$\delta_{st}\left(e\right) = \frac{\sigma_{st}\left(e\right)}{\sigma_{st}}.\tag{3.22}$$

The betweenness centrality $c_B\left(e\right)$ of a link $e$ is

$$c_B\left(e\right) = \sum_{s\in\mathcal{N}}\sum_{t\in\mathcal{N}}\delta_{st}\left(e\right).\tag{3.23}$$

The bridges between clusters, so-called weak ties, are responsible for the efficient diffusion of information. If all communication is conducted along shortest paths, the link betweenness centrality can be interpreted as the probability that a link $e$ is involved in a communication between $s$ and $t$, while $\delta_{st}\left(e\right)$ can be interpreted as the amount of communication that passes if one message is sent from $s$ to $t$.

## Clustering in Social Networks

Participants in SNs have a high tendency to cluster into structures called *communities* [65]. A community consists of a group of participants that are relatively densely connected to each other but sparsely connected to other dense groups in SNs.

Identifying communities provides understanding of properties of nodes just from the network topology as all nodes in a cluster may be somewhat related or one node that appears in more than one cluster may have a special role. Additionally such cluster-grained structure of large networks may provide a more insightful overview of hardly visible network properties. Accordingly, Murata [45] enumerated reasons for detecting communities from a given SN:

- Firstly, since members of the communities often have similar tastes and preferences, communities can be used for *information recommendation* (e.g. within recommendation systems);

- Secondly, through communities the *structure* of given SN can be easily understood, and;
- Finally, communities play an important role in the *visualization* of large-scale SNs.

Since members of the same community share common properties, they can be represented as one group, and not as individuals. Membership of detected communities is the basis of member collaboration, allowing the introduction of group-oriented services [9, 51]. Moreover, the notion of community clarifies the processes of information sharing and information diffusion.

Community detection in SNs should not be confused with the technique of data clustering, which is a way of detecting groupings of data points in high-dimensional data spaces. However, as these two procedures have some common features, SN community detection can be implemented by adjusting algorithms originally designed for finding clusters of similar objects in statistics and data mining. Those "classic" clustering techniques include *partitional* clustering techniques (e.g. k-means clustering algorithm), *neural network* clustering techniques (e.g. self-organizing maps) and *multi-dimensional scaling* techniques (e.g. singular value decomposition or principal component analysis). This section will present community detection methods that can be used for SNs and will discuss synchronization-based methods that can be used for mSNs.

**Community Detection Methods**

In the past the concept of community detection methods was mainly related to graph partitioning. The goal was to divide a graph into an arbitrarily given number of partitions minimizing the number of edges between those partitions. A downside of this approach is a demand to initially know the number, as well as sizes of partitions. The foundations for defining community detection were laid with the Girvan and Newman (GN) algorithm [46]. This algorithm started a new era in the field of community detection [21]. The GN algorithm is an iterative divisive method based on recursively finding and removing the edges with the largest *betweenness*, until the network breaks up into partitions. In [47] Newman and Girvan gave the most popular definition of the quality function for a partition:

$$Q = \frac{1}{2m} \sum_{ij} \left( A_{ij} - \frac{k_i k_j}{2m} \right) \delta \left( C_i, C_j \right),$$

(3.24)

where $A_{ij}$ denotes the weight of the link between $i$ and $j$, $k_i = \sum_j A_{ij}$ the sum of the weights of the links attached to node $i$, $C_i$ is the community to which node $i$ is assigned, the $\delta$-function $\delta(u, v)$ is 1 if $u = v$ and 0 otherwise, and finally, $m = \frac{1}{2} \sum_{ij} \left( A_{ij} \right)$.

Fortunato presented a comprehensive survey about community detection and comparison analysis of algorithms for community detection [21, 37]. Fortunato also stated that the first problem in community detection was to look for a quantitative definition of community and that no definition was universally accepted. The definition of community often depends on the context of the analysis. The basis of the definition of community for SNs is higher density of interactions between individuals in particular social groups than between individuals in other groups. Wasserman and Faust defined general properties of such social groups [63].

Several types of community detection algorithms can distinguish among *divisive*, *agglomerative* and *optimization* approaches. Divisive algorithms detect inter-community links and remove them from the network [24, 47], agglomerative algorithms merge similar nodes/communities recursively [52], while optimization methods maximize an objective function [74]. These algorithms detect communities based on a particular snapshot of the network at the given time. The next section will present a dynamic algorithm used to analyze network characteristics through a synchronization process.

**Clustering in Machine Social Networks Through Synchronization**

Synchronization can be applied to find communities in a network where nodes are represented as oscillators. Community detection employing synchronization is founded on the fact that, before reaching the full network synchronization state, oscillators in the same community (i.e. cluster) synchronize locally first. This is because the more densely connected groups of oscillators synchronize more easily than those with sparse connections [3, 30, 41]. In [30] the authors even gave a theoretical analytical formula describing how inter-cluster connections are related to global synchronization in clustered networks. MacGraw and Menzinger [41] studied the effects of the clustering coefficient on the synchronization of networks of Kuramoto-like phase oscillators. It is found that a high clustering coefficient promotes synchronization at low coupling, while it suppresses it at higher coupling. Another interesting observation is that at higher clustering levels synchronization dynamics introduce an additional subset of oscillators, each synchronized at a different frequency.

Fortunato [21] in his review of community detection algorithms also mentions works about dynamic algorithms for community detection based on synchronization [3, 7, 38]. In [3] the authors studied the effects of local synchronization in a network with nodes represented as in the Kuramotos oscillator model. In [7] the authors designed a community detection algorithm based on the de-synchronization properties of the dynamic system mapped to the network using a variation of the Kuramotos model, called the Opinion Changing Rate (OCR) that was previously introduced for the modelling of opinion consensus in social networks [49]. In [38] a synchronization-based method for detection of overlapping communities is presented. All these results indicate that highly connected clusters within networks can be found through studying the path to global synchronization.

Another way, instead of identifying communities through analysis of the synchronization path, is to detect communities in the final synchronization state through *phase-locked phenomenon*. Here we focus on models of PCOs where the type and number of oscillators that synchronize in clusters can be controlled. Rhouma and Frigui proposed a model of PCO interactions in which a system of $\mathcal{N}$ oscillators is divided into $k$ disjoint subgroups $\mathcal{G}_l$, each containing $n_l$ oscillators, where $l \in \langle 1, k \rangle$ [54]. We can further assume that whenever oscillator $i$ fires, then for every other oscillator $j$ with phase $\phi_j$, we have

$$
\begin{cases}
\dfrac{f'(\phi_j)+\varepsilon_i'(\phi_j)}{f'(f^{-1}(f(\phi_j)+\varepsilon_i(\phi_j)))} > 1 & \text{if oscillators } i \text{ and } j \\[2ex]
& \text{belong to the same group .} \\[2ex]
0 < \dfrac{f'(\phi_j)+\varepsilon_i'(\phi_j)}{f'(f^{-1}(f(\phi_j)+\varepsilon_i(\phi_j)))} < 1 & \text{otherwise}
\end{cases}
\tag{3.25}
$$

Under the above assumptions, any two oscillators will synchronize if and only if they belong to the same subgroup $\mathcal{G}_l$.

Clusters in mSNs can be understood as groups of machines that are able to synchronize themselves. Similarly, the authors in [70], in terms of sensor networks, defined the concept of synchronicity as the ability of nodes to agree on a firing period and phase of collective action across a sensor network and distinguish it from the concept of time synchronization.

## *Data Diffusion in Social Networks*

One individual in a SN can greatly affect how other individuals behave and interact. Individual actions are influenced by their friends, acquaintances and neighbours, while relationships between them form the basis of SNs. In a SN we can represent individuals with *nodes*, and relations or information flows between them can be represented as *links* in graphs. These links can represent different types of relations between individuals, including exchange of information, transfer of knowledge and collaboration.

Innovation, topics, and even malicious rumours propagate through SNs in the form of so-called "world-of-mouth" communication. Through this propagation process we can conclude useful information about the SN such as the best group of people to spread the desired information, types of topics that propagate faster, a mechanism of forming public opinions or acceptance of the same information in different communities.

Studies, investigating the effects of social interactions, can be classified as *cross-sectional* or *longitudinal*. Cross-sectional studies concentrate on analyzing social interactions for one snapshot in time (static perspective), while longitudinal studies take into account the dynamic nature of diffusion (an over time perspective). These empirical studies can be mapped to various diffusion models that help us to predict how behaviour should evolve and how it interacts with the social structure. In this section we will describe diffusion models used for hSNs, and present how to propagate information in mSNs.

## Data Diffusion Models

A great number of research on diffusion modelling is based on the Bass model [5] which formalizes the aggregate level of penetration of a new product, emphasizing two processes: *external* and *internal*. The external process influences consumers via advertising and mass media, while the internal process influences consumers via word-of-mouth. Although this form of study can be used in hSNs for modelling data diffusion, the Bass model does not specify the consumer decision-making process or how they communicate with each other and influence one another at the micro level. It also assumes the population of consumers to be homogeneous (such models are referred to as *aggregate* models). However, consumers in the real world are different, they can realize different aspects of the benefits and costs of a particular innovation, hear about the innovation at different times, or delay in acting on the information they receive. Furthermore, in [75] Young analyzed the effect of incorporating heterogeneity and identified three broad classes of models: *contagion*, *social influence* and *social learning*.

Another approach is to model the diffusion of information, rumours, or gossip through SNs after the spread of infectious diseases. The basic diffusion model in this group is the Susceptible-Infected-Recovered (SIR) model, in which nodes are initially susceptible to the disease and can become infected from infected neighbours. The SIR model assumes that a node, once infected, can never be reinfected again once it has been cured. The other class of model for the spread of a disease is the so-called Susceptible-Infective-Susceptible (SIS) model, where a node once infected moves to a susceptible state and can be reactivated multiple times.

Finally, fundamental information diffusion models are the Independent Cascade (IC) models [25, 29, 34] and the Linear Threshold (LT) models [34, 64]. In these models, the diffusion processes unfold in discrete time-steps $t \geq 0$, and it is assumed that nodes can switch from being inactive to being active, but cannot switch from being active to being inactive. IC is a fundamental probabilistic model of information diffusion, which can be regarded as the SIR model for the spread of disease. In threshold models all propagation is not the simple activation of nodes after exposure to multiple active neighbours. In this model each node has a threshold that determines the proportion of neighbours required to activate it.

## Data Diffusion in Machine Social Networks Through Synchronization

One aspect of data diffusions in mSNs can be seen through usage of gossip protocols [26]. Generally, gossip protocols provide a robust technique for message propagation from one node of a group to another until all the nodes in that group receive the same message. In [73] the authors present an adaptive firefly gossip protocol that provides a robust technique for distributing data in machine networks, guaranteeing the receiving of the message even if some nodes become disconnected.

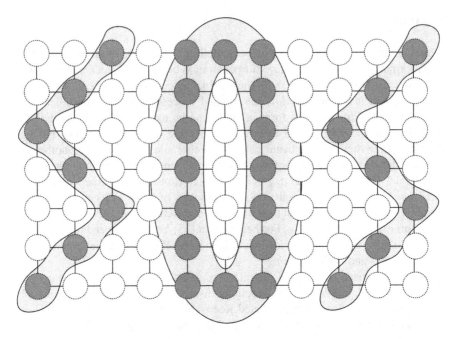

**Fig. 3.7** Visualization of the word "SOS" with machines in mSNs

Another approach for data diffusion was proposed by Taniguchi et al. in [57] where the PCO model was adopted in order to accomplish the periodic data gathering without centralized controls. Information propagation through a machine network can be observed as travelling waves. The authors showed how to control the frequency, the form, and the direction of these waves by adjusting parameters and functions in the model.

## Data Visualization with Machine Social Networks Through Synchronization

In Nature, when fireflies achieve synchrony, they flash together giving out a green-like illumination. If we present machines with two colours (e.g. white and green), with them we can visualize different information. Data that machines in mSNs visualize can either be some information about themselves, but can also come from external sources (e.g. some words). For instance, Fig. 3.7 shows how machines can be used to visualize the word "SOS." For that purpose, three groups of machines are formed in $7 \times 11$ grid of partially connected machines.

# Real-world Examples of Machine Social Networks

Today, M2M communication is not only a commonly used buzzword, but a paradigm present in many spheres of human life. In this section we will present three scenarios with M2M interactions: collaborative downloading between mobile devices, smart home environments and smart cities.

## *Collaborative Downloading*

In our previous work we presented a collaborative downloading model for mobile devices [8, 50]. Collaborative downloading is a distributed model of a service provisioning process for machines (i.e. mobile devices) that share a common interest in a content offered by the service provider.

Our model is based on an idea that such machines could individually acquire disjunctive parts of content from a remote server (via a wide area mobile network), and then subsequently exchange them among themselves using M2M interactions in a Peer-to-Peer fashion, thus allowing each machine to reassemble the entire content for its own use.

The benefits of this approach include lowering the load on the "expensive" link to the telco's network and saving the energy initially used for wide-area communication among mobile devices.

## *Smart Home*

The term Smart Home is commonly used to define a residence that uses a *smart controller* to integrate the residence's various machines subsystems [2, 16]. Today smart vacuum cleaners,[7] smart washing machines,[8] smart fridges,[9] smart heating and cooling subsystems[10] can already be found on the market.

When an owner leaves the Smart Home, all lights are turned off, as well as heating and cooling systems. And then, when the owner gets back, everything is just the way it was before he left. To provide the described functionality, Smart Homes are filled with various network-aware machines. The only thing all machines have in common is their ability for communication through wireless or wireline channels.

---

[7]Smart vacuum cleaners – http://bestvacuumcleanerreviews.co.uk/

[8] Smart washing machines – http://weblogs.asp.net/ssivakumar/archive/2004/09/21/232359.aspx

[9] Smart fridges – http://www.guardian.co.uk/environment/2008/dec/02/energy-efficient-dynamic-demand-fridges

[10] Smart heating and cooling subsystems – http://smartheat.com.au/

## *Smart City*

Even more fascinating than Smart Homes are Smart Cities. Smart Cities can be identified along six main axes or dimensions[11]:

- A smart economy;
- Smart mobility;
- A smart environment;
- Smart people;
- Smart living, and;
- Finally, smart governance.

For instance, a *smart economy* can be connected with a *smart environment* through a scenario including Smart Electric Cars. In the not so distant future, Smart Electric Cars will be able to communicate with Smart Grids in Smart Cities to determine where and when to charge batteries. Namely, some cars will charge their batteries in places with a lot of energy (where energy is cheap), and later sell at a higher price any remaining power to other machines in places with no energy. Obviously, all of those interactions in Smart Cities will take place in a M2M domain.

## **Conclusion**

This chapter provided a useful insight into the development of Social Networks (SN) and predicted the next phase in SN evolution – the 3rd phase of social networking called *Machine Social Networks* (mSNs). Although the age of Machine-to-Machine interactions has already begun (e.g. in Smart Homes and Smart Cities), mSNs will surely experience a global proliferation if Ericsson's predictions of 50 billion machines connected to the Web by the end of 2020 comes true.

However, before a deployment of large-scale mSNs occurs, both academia and industry will have to find solutions for a number of challenges – one of them will be to design and implement inter-machine communication within an mSN. To propose a solution for this challenge, in this chapter we introduced the concept of Pulse Coupled Oscillators (PCOs) into mSNs. Namely, machines represented as PCOs can interact in partially connected networks, and they can also even change their position in the network as time passes. Moreover, the PCO-based model enables us to model inter-machine communication without neglecting packet loss, making our mSN model a realistic abstraction of real-world inter-machine communication. Finally, in PCO-based mSNs social analysis (e.g. clustering and data diffusion) can be conducted, which will eventually lead towards designing innovative and value added services for machines forming an mSN, as well as machines' owners.

---

[11] Smart cities – http://www.smart-cities.eu/

**Acknowledgements**  The authors acknowledge the support of the research project "Content Delivery and Mobility of Users and Services in New Generation Networks" (036-0362027-1639), funded by the Ministry of Science, Education and Sports of the Republic of Croatia.

# References

1. Adamic, L.A., Adar, E.: Friends and neighbors on the web. Soc. Netw. **25**(3), 211–230 (2003)
2. Arcelus, A., Goubran, R., Sveistrup, H., Bilodeau, M., Knoefel, F.: Context-aware smart home monitoring through pressure measurement sequences. In: IEEE International Workshop on Medical Measurements and Applications, Ottawa, pp. 32–37 (2010)
3. Arenas, A., Díaz-Guilera, A., Pérez-Vicente, C.J.: Synchronization reveals topological scales in complex networks. Phys. Rev. Lett. **96**(11), 114102–114106 (2006)
4. Attenborough, D.: Talking to strangers. In: The Trials of Life: A Natural History of Behaviour, vol. 10. Collins/BBC Books, London (1990)
5. Bass, F.: A new product growth model for consumer durables. Manag. Sci. **13**(5), 215–227 (1969)
6. Berners-Lee, T., Hendler, J., Lassila, O.: The Semantic Web: Scientific American. Munn, New York. http://www.scientificamerican.com/article.cfm?id=thesemantic-web (2001)
7. Boccaletti, S., Ivanchenko, M., Latora, V., Pluchino, A., Rapisarda, A.: Detecting complex network modularity by dynamical clustering. Phys. Rev. E **75**(4), 045102–045106 (2007)
8. Bojic, I., Podobnik, V., Kusek, M., Jezic, G.: Collaborative Urban Computing: Serendipitous Cooperation between Users in an Urban Environment. Cybernetics and Systems **42**(5), 287–307 (2011)
9. Bojic, I., Podobnik, V., Petric, A.: Swarm-oriented mobile services: Step towards green communication. Expert systems with applications. **39**(9), 7874–7886 (2012)
10. Borgatti, S., Mehra, A., Brass, D., Labianca, G.: Network analysis in the social sciences. Science **323**(5916), 892–895 (2009)
11. Boyd, D., Ellison, N.: Social network sites: definition, history, and scholarship. J Comput. Med. Commun. **13**(1), 210–230 (2008)
12. Brinkmeier, M., Schank, T.: Network statistics. In: Network Analysis: Methodological Foundations, vol. 3418, pp. 293–317. Springer, Berlin/New York (2005)
13. Brown, R.: Social Psychology. Free Press, New York (1965)
14. Camazine, S., Deneubourg, J.L., Franks, N.R., Sneyd, J., Theraulaz, G., Bonabeau, E.: Self-Organization in Biological Systems. Princeton University Press, Princeton (2001)
15. Chi, E.: The social Web: research and opportunities. IEEE Comput. **41**(9), 88–91 (2008)
16. Cook, D.J., Youngblood, M., Edwin O., Heierman, I., Gopalratnam, K., Rao, S., Litvin, A., Khawaja, F.: Mavhome: An agent-based smart home. In: IEEE International Conference on Pervasive Computing and Communications, Fort Worth, pp. 521–524 (2003)
17. Donath, J., Boyd, D.: Public displays of connection. BT Technol. J. **22**(4), 71–82 (2004)
18. Ernst, U., Pawelzik, K., Geisel, T.: Synchronization induced by temporal delays in pulse-coupled oscillators. Phys. Rev. Lett. **74**(9), 1570–1573 (1995)
19. Ernst, U., Pawelzik, K., Geisel, T.: Delay-induced multistable synchronization of biological oscillators. Phys. Rev. E **57**, 2150–2162 (1998)
20. Fischer, C.: To Dwell Among Friends: Personal Networks in Town and City. University of Chicago Press, Chicago (1982)
21. Fortunato, S.: Community detection in graphs. Phys. Rep. **486**(3–5), 75–174 (2010)
22. Freeman, L.: Centrality in social networks conceptual clarification. Soc. Netw. **1**(3), 215–239 (1979)
23. Gantz, J.: The Embedded Internet: Methodology and Findings. Intel Development Center. http://download.intel.com/embedded/15billion/applications/pdf/322202.pdf (1965)

24. Girvan, M., Newman, M.E.J.: Community structure in social and biological networks. Proc. Natl. Acad. Sci. USA **99**(12), 7821–7826 (2002)
25. Goldenberg, J., Libai, B., Muller, E.: Talk of the network: a complex systems look at the underlying process of word-of-mouth. Mark. Lett. **3**(12), 211–223 (2001)
26. Golding, R.A., Long, D.D.E.: Modeling replica divergence in a weak-consistency protocol for global-scale distributed data bases. Technical report, University of California, Santa Cruz (1993)
27. Granovetter, M.: The strength of weak ties. Am. J. Sociol. **78**(6), 1360–1380 (1973)
28. Grossman, L.: Person of the Year 2010. In Time (15 December 2010): http://www.time.com/time/specials/packages/article/0,28804,2036683_2037183_2037185,00.html
29. Gruhl, D., Guha, R., Nowell, D.L., Tomkins, A.: Information diffusion through blogspace. In: 13th International Conference on World Wide Web, New York, pp. 491–501 (2004)
30. Guan, S., Wang, X., Lai, Y.C., Lai, C.H.: Transition to global synchronization in clustered networks. Phys. Rev. E **77**(4), 046211–046216 (2008)
31. Hogan, B., Fielding, N., Lee, R., Blank, G.: Analyzing social networks via the Internet. In: The SAGE Handbook of Online Research Methods, pp. 141–160. SAGE, Los Angeles/London (2008)
32. Izhikevich, E.M.: Weakly pulse-coupled oscillators, FM interactions, synchronization, and oscillatory associative memory. IEEE Trans. Neural Netw. **10**(3), 508–526 (1998)
33. Jackson, M.O.: Social and Economic Networks. Princeton University Press, Princeton (2008)
34. Kempe, D., Kleinberg, J., Tardos, E.: Maximizing the spread of influence through a social network. In: 9th ACM SIGKDD International Conference on Knowledge Discovery and Data Mining, Washington, DC, pp. 137–146 (2003)
35. Klinglmayr, J., Bettstetter, C., Timme, M.: Globally stable synchronization by inhibitory pulse coupling. In: 2nd International Symposium on Applied Sciences in Biomedical and Communication Technologies, Bratislava, pp. 1–4 (2009)
36. Kuramoto, Y.: Collective synchronization of pulse-coupled oscillators and excitable units. Phys. D Nonlinear Phenom. **50**(1), 15–30 (1991)
37. Lancichinetti, A., Fortunato, S.: Community detection algorithms: a comparative analysis. Phys. Rev. E **80**(5), 056117 (2009)
38. Li, D., Leyva, I., Almendral, J.A., Sendiña Nadal, I., Buldú, J.M., Havlin, S., Boccaletti, S.: Synchronization interfaces and overlapping communities in complex networks. Phys. Rev. Lett. **101**(16), 168701–168705 (2008)
39. Lucarelli, D., Wang, I.J.: Decentralized synchronization protocols with nearest neighbor communication. In: Proceedings of the 2nd International Conference on Embedded Networked Sensor Systems, Baltimore, pp. 62–68 (2004)
40. Lundelius, J., Lynch, N.A.: An upper and lower bound for clock synchronization. Inf. Control **62**(2/3), 190–204 (1984)
41. McGraw, P.N., Menzinger, M.: Clustering and the synchronization of oscillator networks. Phys. Rev. E **72**(1), 015101–015105 (2005)
42. Milgram, S.: The small world problem. Psychol. today **1**(1), 61–67 (1967)
43. Mirollo, R.E., Strogatz, S.H.: Synchronization of pulse-coupled biological oscillators. SIAM J. Appl. Math. **50**(6), 1645–1662 (1990)
44. Mizruchi, M.S.: The Corporate Board Network. Sage, Thousand Oaks (1982)
45. Murata, T.: Detecting communities in social networks. In: Handbook of Social Network Technologies and Applications, pp. 269–280. Springer, New York (2010)
46. Newman, M.E.J.: The structure and function of complex networks. SIAM Rev. **45**(2), 167–256 (2003)
47. Newman, M.E.J., Girvan, M.: Finding and evaluating community structure in networks. Phys. Rev. E **69**(2), 026113–026128 (2004)
48. Nohria, N.: Networks and Organizations: Structure, Form and Action. Harvard Business School Press, Boston (1994)
49. Pluchino, A., Latora, V., Rapisarda A.: Compromise and synchronization in opinion dynamics. Eur. Phys. J. B **50**(1), 169–176 (2006)

50. Podobnik, V., Bojic, I., Vrdoljak, L., Kusek, M.: Achieving collaborative service provisioning for mobile network users: the colldown example. Infocommun. J. **65**(3), 46–52 (2010)
51. Podobnik, V., Galetic, V., Trzec, K., Jezic, G.: Group-oriented service provisioning in next-generation network. In: Srinivasan, D., Jain, L. (eds.) Innovations in Multi-Agent Systems and Applications - 1. Studies in Computational Intelligence, vol. 310, pp. 277–298. Springer, Berlin/ Heidelberg (2010)
52. Pons, P., Latapy, M.: Computing communities in large networks using random walks. J. Gr. Algorithm Appl. **10**(2), 284–293 (2004)
53. Reid, M., Gray, C.: Online social networks, virtual communities, enterprises, and information professionals part 1. Past and present. Searcher **15**(7), 32–51 (2007)
54. Rhouma, M.B.H., Frigui, H.: Self-organization of pulse-coupled oscillators with application to clustering. IEEE Trans. Pattern Anal. Mach. Intel. **23**(2), 180–195 (2001)
55. Rogers, E.: Diffusion of Innovations. Free Press, New York (1995)
56. Salaff, J., Fong, E., Wong, S.: Using social networks to exit Hong Kong. In: Networks in the Global Village: Life in Contemporary Communities, pp. 299–329. Westview, Boulder (1999)
57. Taniguchi, Y., Wakamiya, N., Murata, M.: A Distributed and self-organizing data gathering scheme in wireless sensor networks. In: 6th Asia-Pacific Symposium on Information and Telecommunication Technologies, pp. 299–304. Yangon (2005)
58. Tilly, C.: Big structures, large processes, huge comparisons. Sage, New York (1984)
59. Travers, J., Milgram, S.: An experimental study of the small world problem. Sociometry **32**(4), 425–443 (1969)
60. Tyrrell, A., Auer, G., Bettstetter, C.: Emergent slot synchronization in wireless networks. IEEE Trans. Mobile Comput. **9**(5), 719–732 (2010)
61. Wallerstein, I.: The Modern World System: Capitalist Agriculture and the Origins of the European World Economy in the Sixteenth Century. Academic Press, New York (1997)
62. Wan, Y., Kumar, V., Bukhari, A.: Will the overseas expansion of facebook succeed? Internet Comput. IEEE **12**(3), 69–73 (2008)
63. Wasserman, S., Faust, K.: Social Network Analysis: Methods and Applications (Structural Analysis in the Social Sciences). Cambridge University Press, New York (1994)
64. Watts, D.J.: A simple model of global cascades on random networks. Proc. Natl. Acad. Sci. U. S. A. **99**(9), 5766–5771 (2002)
65. Watts, D.J., Strogatz, S.H.: Collective dynamics of 'small-world' networks. Nature **393**(6684), 440–442 (1998)
66. Weaver, A., Morrison, B.: Social networking. Computer **41**(2), 97–100 (2008)
67. Wellman, B.: The community question: the intimate networks of East Yorkers. Am. J Sociol. **84**(5), 1201–1231 (1979)
68. Wellman, B.: Computer networks as social networks. Science **293**(5537), 2031–2034 (2001)
69. Wellman, B., Wellman, B.: Domestic affairs and network relations. J Soc. Personal Relatsh. **9**(3), 385–239 (1992)
70. Werner-Allen, G., Tewari, G., Patel, A., Welsh, M., Nagpal, R.: Firefly-inspired sensor network synchronicity with realistic radio effects. In: Proceedings of the 3rd international conference on Embedded networked sensor systems, San Diego, pp. 142–153 (2005)
71. Westland, J.: Critical mass and willingness to pay for social networks. Electron. Commerce Res. Appl. **9**(1), 6–19 (2010)
72. Wibergh, J.: (Ericsson News: Johan Wibergh on 50 billion connected devices. In: Ericsson Business Innovation Forum. Shanghai: http://www.ericsson.com/news/100603_wibergh_50b_244218601_c (2010)
73. Wokoma, I., Liabotis, I., Prnjat, O., Sacks, L., Marshall, I.: A weakly coupled adaptive gossip protocol for application level active networks. In: Third IEEE International Workshop on Policies for Distributed Systems and Networks, Monterey. pp. 244–247 (2002)
74. Wu, F., Huberman, B.A.: Finding communities in linear time: a physics approach. Eur. Phys. J. B – Condens. Matt. Complex Syst. **38**(2), 331–338 (2004)
75. Young, H.P.: Innovation diffusion in heterogeneous populations: contagion, social influence, and social learning. Am. Econ. Rev. **99**(5), 1899–1924 (2009)
76. Zeichick, A.: A-twitter over twitter. NetWorker **13**, 5–7 (2009)

# Chapter 4
# Mining Geo-Referenced
# Community-Contributed Multimedia Data

Milan Mirkovic, Dubravko Culibrk, and Vladimir Crnojevic

**Abstract**  Besides connecting users and allowing interactions between them, social networks are becoming an increasingly popular medium for sharing multimedia content, such as images and videos. Due to technological advances it has become extremely simple to create and share such content in (near) real-time, and even associate it with a location where it was made (i.e. geo-reference it). All of this has caused tremendous amounts of geo-referenced multimedia content to become publicly available, which made it suitable for analysis by employing different visualization and data-mining techniques. This chapter presents some of the techniques and methods for mining geo-referenced multimedia content in order to discover patterns and trends in it, which can lead to better understanding of the phenomena driving the data generation in the first place.

Nowadays, many web platforms exist that provide users with easy, fast, and convenient means of sharing information with the online community. Social networks (Facebook, MySpace and LinkedIn), image and video-sharing services (Flickr, YouTube, Picasa), and blogs are just some of them. What all of those applications and services have in common is that they store a large amount of user-generated data that is just a query away from anyone interested in taking a look at it. By default, much of that data is time-stamped, allowing for various temporal analysis to be performed, that can uncover interesting patterns and models of behavior – which in turn can be used to achieve different goals by interested parties. Ability to perform such analysis comes with a certain amount of responsibility, since many privacy issues might arise in the process [1, 6]. In addition, explosion of the mobile-devices market and a constant decrease of their price coupled with the increase of their capabilities introduced another dimension to the equation; for instance, GPS

Milan Mirkovic (✉) • Dubravko Culibrk • Vladimir Crnojevic
Faculty of Technical Sciences, University of Novi Sad, Trg Dositeja Obradovica 6,
21000 Novi Sad, Serbia
e-mail: mirkovic.milan@gmail.com; dubravko.culibrk@gmail.com; crnojevic@uns.ac.rs

A. Abraham (ed.), *Computational Social Networks: Mining and Visualization*,
DOI 10.1007/978-1-4471-4054-2_4, © Springer-Verlag London 2012

receivers can now be found in most devices ranging from phones over cameras to laptops, effectively enabling them to tag content created through their usage with geographic information, adding the spatial dimension to the data. That, combined with already existing data, enables researchers to answer many questions regarding human behavior, since they are able to discover new trends in who (user), what (content), when (time), and where (place).

## Social Networks

Social networks – in terms of web services – are relatively new, but increasingly popular and heavily used tools for communication, information-sharing, and collaboration. While functionalities that a web service needs to provide in order for it to qualify as a social network somewhat vary, loosely speaking, it has to allow individuals to: (1) create a profile (or equivalent) that contains their personal information, (2) make connections to other users within the system/service – either directly through a dedicated list or indirectly through posting comments/interacting with other users' activities, and (3) browse other users' profiles/posted content [5]. In other words, when someone signs up for a profile with some service provider, browses other users' profiles and/or comments on their activities/uploaded content, that person is effectively a part of a social network. It is clear that these loose criteria allow for existence of plethora of social networks, and that such abundance inevitably leads to competition and specialization in order to attract and keep users. While a solid line between types of services that respective social networks offer to their users is hard to be drawn (caused by constant improvement of services and implementation of new functionalities either as a part of innovative process or as imitation), some distinction can be made if primary focus of respective network is considered. Hence exist social networks that promote inter-user communication and on-line community building (e.g., Facebook, MySpace, LinkedIn), those that focus on sharing user-generated multimedia content (YouTube, Flickr, Panoramio), those that favor information dissemination and propagation (various types of blogs, Twitter), and others. Many other categorizations might certainly be made depending on the criteria one defined (e.g., one might take the number of users as a primary criterion, or usage in local community, etc.), but for purposes of demonstrating methods and techniques presented in this chapter, only those networks dealing with multimedia content will be explored.

As can be seen from Table 4.1, there are over 925 million users on listed social networks alone, and those are only world-wide known networks; many others exist that are popular only in certain countries or on one continent, but have several (hundred) millions of users (e.g., Google owned Orkut which is popular in India and Brazil has more than 100,000,000 users [21], Qzone which is very popular in China [22] has circa 200,000,000 users).

The number of discrete users of social networks is very hard to obtain or even estimate, due to some users having several accounts within the same service, some

**Table 4.1** Some popular social networks

| Name | Estimated number of users | Established in | Focus |
|---|---|---|---|
| delicious | 8,900,000 | 2003 | Community/content-sharing |
| deviantART | 9,100,000 | 2000 | Community/artwork-sharing |
| Facebook | 500,000,000 | 2004 | Community/communication |
| Flickr | 32,000,000 | 2004 | Photo sharing |
| Friendster | 90,000,000 | 2002 | Community/communication |
| Last.fm | 30,000,000 | 2002 | Music |
| LinkedIN | 80,000,000 | 2003 | Community/communication |
| MySpace | 130,000,000 | 2003 | Community/communication |
| YouTube | 48,000,000 | 2005 | Video sharing |

users having accounts with several services, and some users being inactive but not closing their account/profile. Nevertheless, the number of users – if observed for social networks as a phenomenon without making a distinction between particular services – is increasing by the day, and that trend is likely to continue in the future as new services emerge and existing services develop and offer new features.

## Community-Contributed Multimedia Data

As mentioned in section "Social Networks", social networks are becoming an increasingly popular way of sharing various content among users. Depending on the primary focus of a particular social network, that content can be in form of text, audio, or video recordings, images, or any combination of those. Wide acceptance and exploitation of those focusing on multimedia sharing began when two technological criteria were met: (1) devices able to make digital multimedia content became common and affordable and (2) development and advancements in networking products/technologies made sharing of that content possible. In addition, most of that content – regardless of form – usually has some additional data attached to it, known as meta-data. Meta-data (or data about data) is used to describe the content it is attached to in more detail, so advanced search and indexing can be performed efficiently. It is usually created in either automated or semi-automated fashion; even though purely manual creation of meta-data is certainly possible, for modern applications this approach would be just too time-consuming, and is hence avoided. In the former case, meta-data is attached to content at creation time, effectively embedding itself in the data, if the format allows it. In the latter case, the user adds missing (or potentially useful) data manually at publish time. Good example for automatic meta-data creation would be taking of a photo; when the user presses the shoot button, not only the content in terms of pixels that make up the photo is stored but some additional data that describes that photo (Fig. 4.1a) is stored as well, such as time and date of creation, make and model of the device used to make it, image resolution and color depth, and possibly even

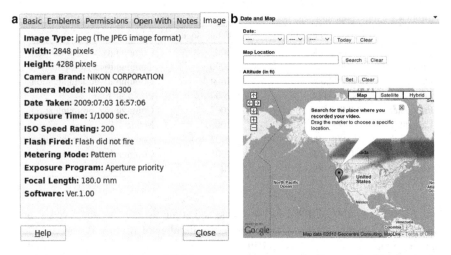

**Fig. 4.1** Meta-data examples. (**a**) JPEG image meta-data (automatically created when the picture was taken). (**b**) YouTube meta-data (user added, after the video was uploaded)

the geographical location (latitude and longitude coordinates). Sometimes devices do not automatically store additional description of the content they produce, or that description is scarce for specific purposes and requires some expansion. That is when users have to – either manually or by using appropriate tools for auto-creation – enter missing information themselves. Uploading a video clip to YouTube is a nice example of this. Once the video has been uploaded, users are required to enter a name for it, pick one of the categories that describes the content the best, and they can enter a short description of it or even pick a place where the video was taken from the accompanying map (or enter precise geographic coordinates in appropriate fields (Fig. 4.1b)).

Whatever the method of meta-data creation, once it is there, it can be treated just like regular data: it can be indexed, searched, and analyzed. While benefits of searching for content using meta-data are obvious (faster and more meaningful results obtained, extended search capabilities depending on the amount of meta-data available), some issues exist – mainly due to human factor and ambiguity – that might cancel all the upsides of this approach. Incomplete, missing, ambiguous, or false meta-data can lead to unexpected or unwanted results. For example, someone might record a game and tag it only as "football"; while having best intentions and acting to the best of their knowledge, if that person was from say Europe, it is more likely than not that the content will be soccer-related. So when someone from USA searches for "football" and ends up with the previous video clip, they will not be getting what they expected (since "football" in the USA refers to American Football, or NFL; European football is called soccer). This particular problem might be overcome to some degree by search engine taking into account geographical location of the device that the query was initiated from (by looking at its IP address or some similar mechanism) and then applying a filter of some

**Fig. 4.2** Automatic meta-data creation and its import to Google Earth. (**a**) HTC Footprints. (**b**) Data imported to Google Earth

sort (e.g., recommending videos that were uploaded from USA rather than from the rest of the world if the query is originating from the USA), or by taking into consideration previous searches (if applicable) and then favoring results that are most likely to be relevant considering the historical data.

Or consider another example: someone might upload a video of Statue of Liberty, and tag it as recorded in Miami. While even now recognition technology exists that would be able to automatically correct some of such errors, its implementation would be extremely computationally intensive and time expensive, and therefore hardly feasible for large-scale application. That is why it is easier and makes more sense to try and automate meta-data creation (preferably at content-creation time) as much as possible in order to avoid missing, false or incomplete data.

A lot of tools exist that perform automatic meta-data creation rather well; and not only that – they usually provide means for sharing the created content (sometimes even in real time). In addition, they make possible exporting it to other formats for convenient exchange and display in different software suites. For instance, HTC Footprints (Fig. 4.2a) automatically assigns latitude, longitude, date, and time of creation to each photo taken through its interface (provided that the GPS signal is available). Once users have made several photos, they can browse them, assign them to some predefined categories, and export them for viewing in other software (in particular, HTC Footprints exports its content to .KMZ files that can easily be read by Google Earth). In fact, once the data has been successfully imported to Google Earth, placemarks for each photo are placed on the map (with a thumbnail of the actual photo available upon clicking the placemark, as can be seen from Fig. 4.2b), which can be dynamically shown and hidden by using a slider that represents the time span during which the respective photos were taken. Slider can also be put to "play" mode that shows placemarks for photos sequentially (in respect to time of creation), effectively simulating the route the user had followed. This makes visual exploration of aforementioned data particularly easy and interesting.

# Data Mining and Geographic Information Systems

Data is everywhere. In modern world, little can be done that leaves no trace in one form or another. Whether it is withdrawing cash from an ATM, browsing the web, making a phone call, taking a picture or driving through a pay toll, almost any activity generates new data. Even trivial activities such as riding an elevator, walking down the street, or making a photocopy of a document can be sources of new data. This is especially true in the era of smart and integrated devices that not only store that data but use it to try to guess what the user will do next, so – among other things – they can make themselves available and ready for action when called upon. And if such analysis are complex enough for the devices not to be able to perform them "on-the-fly", advancements in storage technologies are making prices per unit of storage plummet, effectively enabling users to warehouse the gathered data for later inspection. Taking into consideration the number of devices able to store it, low prices of storage media and the constantly increasing amount of places and ways to gather various forms of data, it is easy to see that not all of it can be processed. What is more, never in history of mankind has data been multiplied at such a rate – it is estimated that the amount of it stored in the world's databases doubles every 20 months [23] – making conventional methods of (statistical) analysis effectively obsolete. All of this called for new methods and techniques for making sense out of, discovering patterns in, and creating rules from the abundance of available data. Hence data mining emerged as a process of automated (or more commonly semi-automated), computer augmented, useful structure pattern discovery in data. In short, it aims to find new structure patterns that can be used to enhance knowledge and understanding of processes underpinning generated data, and to be able to act on that new knowledge (i.e., predict new instances/occurrences).

While a lot of algorithms exist that are suitable for aforementioned pattern discovery, most of them can be broadly divided into following categories: (1) classification, (2) association learning, (3) clustering, and (4) numerical prediction. Classification is a data mining technique used to predict group membership for data instances. For example, one might want to predict if the day will be sunny, rainy, or foggy based on other available attributes (such as humidity, visibility, temperature). Popular techniques for classification are decision trees and neural networks. Association learning is a set of methods used for discovery of relations between variables (usually in large datasets). For instance, if a supermarket stores POS (Point Of Sale) data, by analyzing it they might discover that certain relations among bought products exist: if someone bought bagels, onions, and potatoes, they probably also bought some burgers, or if someone bought a lot of snacks they were likely to buy some beer or soda as well. Clustering methods are used for discovering groups of records in data that are similar to one another within the group in some way. Numerical prediction encompasses various methods and techniques applied in order to predict numerical data (as opposed to nominal data that cannot be subjected to all arithmetic operations, but can be processed using some of the previously described techniques).

Alongside these "traditional" data mining techniques, a special subset of methods exists that can be applied to extracting interesting and regular knowledge from large spatial databases. In particular, they can be used for better understanding of spatial data, capturing characteristics of it, discovering relationships between spatial and non spatial data, etc. They have a wide application in geographic information systems, remote sensing, robot navigation and similar fields. For example, thematic maps can be used to present the spatial distribution of one or several attributes, as opposed to traditional maps which aim to show position of objects in relation to other objects. Spatial rules extraction are another example of those special methods, since they are customized for application with spatial data (as opposed to traditional association learning that works with nominal or numerical data) – for instance, a rule that states that real estate prices are extremely high in a certain city area, or that income is below average in another, might be extracted from a database containing geographically referenced data (spatial data) [15].

Geographic information systems (GIS) are systems that integrate hardware, software, and data for capturing, managing, analyzing, and displaying all forms of geographically referenced information. GIS allow users to view, understand, question, interpret, and visualize data in many ways that reveal relationships, patterns, and trends in the form of maps, globes, reports, and charts; they also help users answer questions and solve problems by looking at data in a way that is quickly understood and easily shared [12]. In effect, GIS enable users to discover knowledge using avilable data. This process is usually a complex one, and requires a skilled person with a good set of tools and techniques at their disposal to be performed successfully. Selection, preprocessing, mining and reporting techniques have to be applied in a thoughtful manner, based on intermediate results and background knowledge; hence, human intelligence is usually at the centre of the whole process [17]. GIS excel at visualization, which is a powerful way of integrating human intelligence in knowledge discovering process, since human visual system and pattern recognition capabilities outperform any artificial system yet deployed in terms of usefulness of results.

Many studies have been conducted combining data mining and GIS, yielding some very interesting results. For example, a few studies try to identify attractive places using only publicly available images (Flickr and Panoramio) and their meta-data as input for various visualization techniques, and even aim to map characteristic tourist flows and movement patterns within regions in focus of research [3,9–11,13]. Another study analyzes the usage of online maps (provided by Google, Yahoo!, and Microsoft), in a way that it tries to identify what are the most commonly looked-at regions in the world using the access logs of service providers [7]; yet another one [24] introduces new ways of representing and visually encoding existing data, thus creating "tag clouds" and "tag maps". Several studies extend research done using publicly available images, and use data retrieved from publicly available videos – arguing that patterns discovered among movie-making population differ from those discovered within image-taking population, since videos, in contrast to still images, are able to capture events (and sounds) [16,18]. Several of these studies are presented in next sections, and methods and techniques used for data analysis and visualization, as well as knowledge discovery are explored and explained in detail.

## More than the Sum of Parts: Mining and Visualizing the Data

### *Flickr Example*

Flickr is an image hosting and sharing website, initially created by Ludicorp (in 2004), and later acquired by Yahoo! (in 2005). It enables its users to upload images and organize them by using tags (a form of meta-data) or by assigning them to one or more groups (called sets and collections). On September 19th, 2010, flickr had its five-billionth image uploaded [8], making it one of the largest online image storages in the world. What is more, upload rate at the time the milestone image had been uploaded, was 3,000 images per minute, with that number steadily increasing (Flickr homepage can be seen on Fig. 4.3).

So much content requires an efficient way for performing searches and browsing through images that might be interesting to visitors (or related to respective image), and that is where meta-data comes in handy. By using tags, searchers can find images that are related to particular topics – such as landmarks, certain events, people – or simply see what words are most commonly used to describe shared images; the latter technique is also known as "weighted list" or "tag cloud". It provides users with a visual representation of the most frequent terms, such that

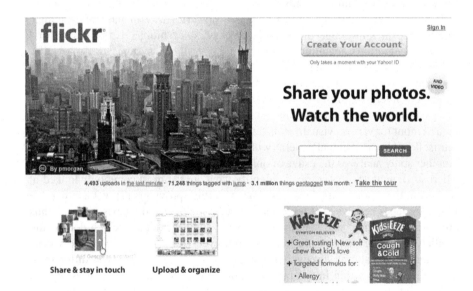

**Fig. 4.3** Flickr homepage

those with the highest frequency are written using largest fonts (or brightest colors, or some similar method of distinction) and those with the least frequent are written in smaller letters. This list is usually dynamically updated to reflect changes in data.

Besides adding tags that are used to describe content of the photos, users can – as mentioned earlier – assign geographical information to images by either using an automated system (devices with embedded GPS receiver that add latitude and longitude coordinates to images at creation time) or doing it manually when the images are uploaded. Flickr uses a scale to represent precision of geographical information related to images: 1 being the least accurate (world level), 6–8 being accurate at the region/city level and 16 being the most accurate, precise to the street level.

Studies dealing with retrieval and analysis of this publicly available data have already yielded some interesting results. While the exact scope and volume of obtained data depend on the specific aims of the research in question, most of it – after a bit of preprocessing perhaps – can be used for some basic statistical analysis and is usually suited for a number of data mining algorithms, if nothing else then for its sheer abundance. Visualization techniques can turn out particularly useful in geo-referenced data analysis, since they can provide additional insight into human behavior patterns and dynamics.

### Attractive Locations

In order to perform analysis of any kind, data that is going to be subjected to it has to be obtained first. Conveniently, Flickr has an API (Application Programming Interface) publicly available, that can be used to access almost all of the content and data stored in its repositories, as well as functionality offered to its users through the website. What is more, there are a dozen of API kits readily available (though none of them are supported by Flickr officially) that were developed in different environments (ranging from Actionscript, over Python, Ruby, and C to .Net and PHP) and can be used by all interested parties to interact with Flickr.

One of the first things that comes to mind of researchers when looking at a large dataset of geo-tagged content is to see the spatial distribution of it. Once plotted on a map, geo-referenced data can tell many interesting stories. For example, one research [11] analyzed roughly 81,000 photos taken over the period of 2 years, in a particular region. Based on the time and disclosed location (i.e., geo-tagged content), records of the people presence and movement were extracted. In particular, tourists were in focus of the research. To separate tourists from residents, authors decided to use the presence in the area over time as a discriminating factor – if a particular photographer took all of his/her pictures during a 30 day period in the area examined, he/she is considered a visitor; otherwise (if photos were made over the 30 day threshold in the area by the same photographer) they're considered a resident (since it is rather unlikely that many tourists would stay for more than a month in the same region). Once the tourists were identified, their nationalities were looked up, using a Flickr social function that enables users to provide more information about themselves. Even though some of the information was missing, incorrect or incomplete, authors managed to gather city/country of residence for around 65% of the population in question. That is a large percentage for a purely optional information to be disclosed.

With all of that data, authors sought to identify what was the spatio-temporal behavior of the tourists in the region in the focus of the research? Several conclusions were made with the help of various visualization and analysis techniques (some of which are explained in more detail in following sections) – that there are "hot-spots" when it comes to tourist concentration in the region, that tourist concentration in respective attractive places (and in region in general) oscillates depending on the time of the day, time of the week, time of the month and time of the year, as well as that there are some characteristic trajectories to and from the region, as well as patterns of flow that are common to all tourists or some nationalities in particular.

To identify a location as attractive, authors of the study required for it to be photographed many times, by different photographers (and during a different time period). The more photos there were – geo-referenced as taken at the same location by different authors – the more attractive the place was. In fact, a heat map was created for the region in question, where different colors represented different concentration of photos in a particular area. As expected, some well-known tourist attractions in the region turned out to be the most frequently photographed objects – cathedrals, bridges, monuments, etc. However, tourists' movement patterns were somewhat surprising, when nationality of visitors was taken into account – domestic visitors (visiting from within the country) seemed to take different paths and indeed to have different interests than foreign visitors (visiting from abroad). While the latter concentrated mostly on well-known attractions and did not deviate much from going straight from one to another – thus producing a somewhat predictable movement path – the former were roaming the area more freely, their movement resembling a web when plotted on a map.

## YouTube: An In-Depth Case Study

YouTube is a video-sharing web service, that enables anyone to upload their video content for the whole world to see. Or, as the company itself states: "YouTube provides a forum for people to connect, inform, and inspire others across the globe and acts as a distribution platform for original content creators and advertisers large and small." YouTube [25] It was founded in early 2005 by three ex-PayPal employees: Chad Hurley, Steve Chen, and Jawed Karim. Nowadays, YouTube has hundreds of millions of users from around the world, 24 h of content uploaded each minute and as of May 2010 – more than two billions of views per day. It all makes it the largest and the most heavily used service of its kind in the world. Such a variety of users and publicly available content provide a fertile ground for researchers to conduct various analysis. Just like Flickr, YouTube also provides a public API that enables anyone interested to interact with the service, and query it for data they are interested in. A study that explores geo-tagged content publicly available on YouTube and aims to discover attractive places in a region (those with high concentration of videos in their vicinity), as well as to improve understanding of some behavioral aspects of its users, is presented in following sections.

## The Data

For users to be able to upload their video content to YouTube, first thing they need to do is open an account – also known as a profile. Aside mandatory information one needs to provide in order to create an account – a unique e-mail address and user name, location, date of birth and gender – there are several other categories that enable users to enter additional information about themselves. Those are:

- About Me (users can provide a picture, write something about themselves and leave a homepage address)
- Personal Details (first and last name, relationship status and an option to show/hide age to other users)
- Hometown/Location (provide a hometown and current place/country of residence as well as a current ZIP/postal code)
- Jobs/Career (list occupations and companies one has been working for)
- Education
- Interests (favorite books, movies and shows, music and other interests)

Once they have created an account, users can log in and start uploading video content. The process is pretty straightforward: upon clicking the Upload link, a window is brought up offering users to upload a file already existing on their device (PDA, mobile phone, computer) or to capture a video stream from their web cam. By far more commonly used option is the former one. YouTube supports a wide variety of formats it can accept and convert to be displayed via Adobe Flash-enabled devices – MPEG-4, MPEG, WMV and even 3GP – as well as container formats, such as .avi, .mkv., .mov, .mp4, .flv Only a few restrictions apply when it comes to content users can upload (purely technically speaking, copyright issues aside), such as that file size cannot exceed 2 GB and that its duration cannot be more than 15 min; but even these restrictions are prone to changes, due to technological advancements (most notably those affecting storage and bandwidth costs).

Once the content has been uploaded, users have to choose a category that best describes it (there are a total of 15 categories currently, ranging from Autos and Vehicles, Comedy, Education and Entertainment, over Gaming, Music and Travel, to Sports and Science), provide a title for the video, assign at least one tag to it (there are some automatically generated that users may or may not accept) and choose a privacy setting – Public for everyone to be able to search and see it, Unlisted for only people with direct link to be able to view the video, or Private for only certain YouTube users to be able to access the content (Fig. 4.4).

Additional information can, but does not have to be provided. Among that additional information, users can choose to enter date when and location where the

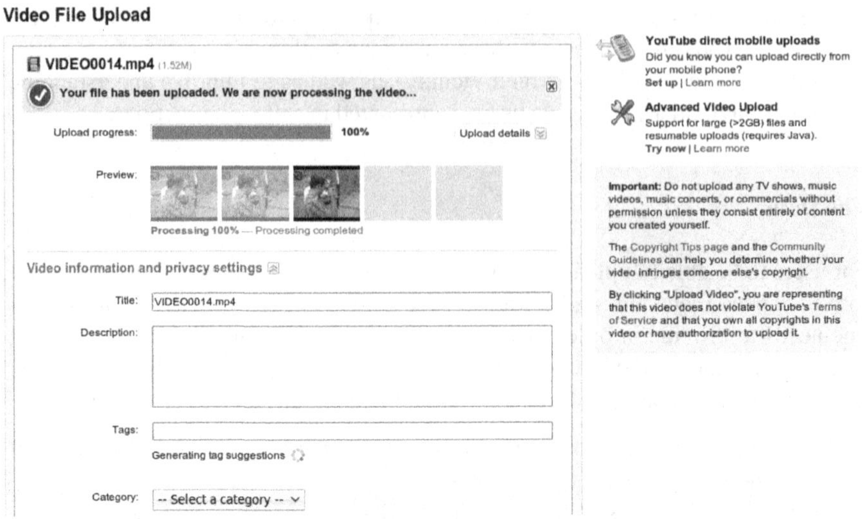

**Video File Upload**

**Fig. 4.4** Web form for uploading a video and adding information to it

video was recorded (Fig. 4.1b), they can add annotations, captions and subtitles to the video, swap soundtrack (or add one if none exists) and enable or disable various options that affect privacy settings and community interaction (such as ability to comment on the video, rate it, respond to it by another video, etc.). Once everything has been set up, depending on the privacy settings and the level of details provided, the video will be returned as a search result when a query is initiated.

### Crawling for Publicly Available Geo-Referenced Videos

In order to identify attractive locations, one needs a specific set of data. First of all, that data has to be geo-referenced, for if it is not, one would have a very hard time determining where the video was taken and manually assigning it with a location (most of the time this wouldn't even be possible). Secondly, while not strictly necessary, it is very useful to have a time stamp attached to the content – since, as will be discussed later, high concentration of videos in the same area during the same time period might mean that there was some event going on instead of some monument existing there. Lastly, user description of the video (its title, as well as tags added) is usually very helpful for performing searches, since terms used there will certainly rate it better when called upon through a query.

To obtain the data that conforms to the previously mentioned requirements, a few things had to be considered and a few issues addressed. Most of them were of technical nature, and were a result of search limitations imposed by YouTube (apparently in order to avoid clogging the servers and wasting resources). YouTube API enables programmers to perform automated searches that can be highly customized. For instance, one can search for videos that contain the word "handball" in the title, and were categorized as "Sport". Or one can search for videos that were recorded during last year, uploaded by a specific user and have captions in a specific language. But the API has also some restrictions, most notably that it does not allow for pure spatial queries (i.e., to return all of the videos tagged as recorded in a particular region) and that maximum number of results returned by a query is 1,000 (one thousand). Also, it is possible to restrict search to only a particular region, defined by a specific set of coordinates (latitude/longitude) and a radius that may not exceed 1,000 km. This restriction makes sense only for geo-referenced videos, of course. While these limitations might not seem too harsh for the average user, they quickly become a major obstacle for a researcher trying to retrieve as much data as possible in order to subject it to data-mining algorithms and visualization techniques.

Hence, a custom tool was needed that performs specific searches and stores obtained results in a format that is suitable for further processing and analysis; what started as a small modification of already existing open-source software [20] quickly led to heavy customization and development of a whole new set of features specifically needed for this kind of research to be conducted. Furthermore, since different countries (i.e., regions of interest) use quite different languages, a search mechanism that would return meaningful and useful results was needed too (e.g., while searching Scandinavian area for videos using Thai language might not return exactly empty, using Finnish, Swedish, or Norwegian words as search terms is bound to yield better results). These issues were addressed as follows:

1. To begin looking for attractive places, it was necessary to have geo-referenced data – hence, only videos that were geo-tagged were included in the search. While this might eliminate a good deal of available content, it was the only way to link (more or less precisely as is discussed later) video to a particular location.
2. Since English is one of the most commonly understood and used language nowadays, an English frequentation list (i.e., list of the most commonly used words in a language) was used to perform initial search for videos. While a full dictionary search would probably yield more results, that approach is too time consuming to be efficiently applied. Also, many videos contain at least one of the most common words from the list in their name or tags, so probability of their inclusion is rather high.
3. Second pass (i.e., search) was performed using a frequentation list of the language dominant in the region in focus (e.g., Italian for Italy, French for France, Greek for Greece, etc.) – but not all of the languages of interest had those lists readily available. Since constructing such a list is a rather long and complex process requiring knowledge and resources specific to the given region (i.e., books and literature), a more crude – yet probably not much less effective – solution was applied. A list of electronic media that operated in the region was made, and their RSS channels were scanned for all articles (often without much understanding of what they were exactly about, since the language, let alone the alphabet was sometimes utterly incomprehensible to the researchers), which

were then broken down to individual words. These, in turn, have been counted and then words that appeared most commonly (first 3,000 of them) were favored and included as search terms. While this method might be biased a bit toward events that got more media coverage, it was also sure to include current events and places that were definitely attractive for one reason or another and received public attention.

4. Region of interest was broken down to a series of overlapping circles (their radii depending on the size of the region – from 1,000 km for large areas to only a few kilometers when observing city-sized areas) that were each queried for terms from frequentation lists.

Once the search was performed for each predefined location using every word from the frequentation lists, results were unified and filtered for duplicates. It should be noted that results in this case were web addresses of videos, which could be pasted in a browser to visually inspect desired video, or passed on to a downloader to save the video locally for further analysis. The process is graphically presented in Fig. 4.5.

## Data visualization

Usually one glimpse at the properly plotted data can tell the viewer more than a couple of minutes' worth reading of numbers used to make that plot. This could not be more true when it comes to geo-referenced data. In fact, the only way this kind of data makes much sense is when it is plotted and overlay over another map – and it is up to the user to interpret the results. In the case study presented here – that shows analysis and visualization techniques applied to data obtained as recorded in Japan – CommonGIS (Visual Analytics ToolKit) [2] and Open Heatmap [19] software were used to visually represent retrieved data.

Obtained data was stored in .CSV files (Comma Separated Values), since that format could be used by both tools, with little modification. Data fed to the CommonGIS software was formatted so that each row presented one record, containing:

1. ID – string uniquely identifying the video, assigned by YouTube
2. Category – one of the 15 categories, selected by the user
3. Viewed – number of times the video was viewed, at the time the data were obtained
4. Published – time and date when the video was put online
5. Duration – duration of the video in seconds
6. Latitude – latitude of the location where the video was made
7. Longitude – longitude of the location where the video was made
8. User – user name of the user who uploaded the video

Once the data was imported, various analysis were performed and layers made that represented transformations of it, and their close inspection revealed some

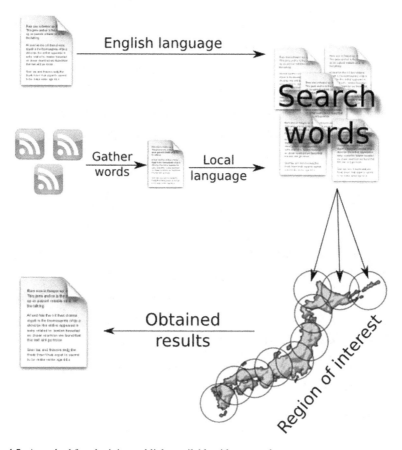

**Fig. 4.5**   A method for obtaining publicly available video meta-data

interesting patterns. Firstly, raw data was plotted on a map, in such a way that each circle marked the location of a video from the dataset. The application enables (among other things) fast switching between different types of maps (i.e., backgrounds) – the three default being Open Street Maps, Google Maps Terrain map, and Google Maps Hybrid map – and panning and zooming functionality very similar to the browser version of Google Maps. Fig. 4.6a shows some 95,000 records presented in this simple fashion (one dot – one video) [18]. Even so, some conclusions could be drawn by applying this crude visualization technique: that either the area under scrutiny is densely populated and people living there have the habit of sharing their videos or it has a lot of places people travel to and make recordings about. By merely zooming-in on the map (Fig. 4.6b), more details about the geographical distribution of the data emerge; populated areas – such as cities – can be more easily distinguished since they usually contain high amount of videos concentrated in a relatively small area. Also, some other areas might prove to be

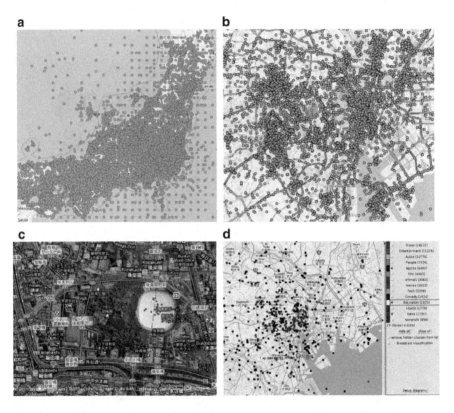

**Fig. 4.6** Sample plots of Japan data set. (**a**) Country-wide view of the data. (**b**) City-wide view of the data. (**c**) Landmark with the hybrid map background. (**d**) Data after classification, with three categories displayed

catching the fancy of video makers, easily visually identified by distinct clusters of dots. Once such regions are spotted, further zooming-in and switching from street to hybrid view can give more insight into what they exactly are (since hybrid view merges labels with aerial imagery of an area). Figure 4.6c shows the Tokyo Dome – the largest concert hall in Japan, zoomed in at the block level with the background changed to a hybrid map.

Classification of the data was performed next in order to further inspect it. The most obvious criterion for classification (among attributes in the dataset) was the category assigned to the video, which produced another layer with 15 switchable options for showing/hiding each class. Alongside the number of items, their percentage was calculated and displayed. It turned out, for the Japan data subset, that almost a quarter of videos were categorized as "Music" (23.8%), followed by "Travel" (16.9%), "Entertainment" (11.8%), and "Autos" (11.3%) categories. Figure 4.6d shows the distribution of videos classified as "Sports" (represented by blue color), "Education" (yellow), and "News" (red), referenced as recorded in

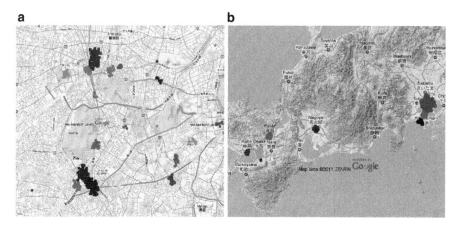

**Fig. 4.7** OPTICS density clustering example. (**a**) Radius: 100 m/minimum number of points: 50 (Tokyo city center). (**b**) Radius: 1,000 m/minimum number of points: 10 (Central Japan)

Tokyo, Japan. It would appear that sports and education recordings are more widely dispersed over the city area than news (which tend to be concentrated in business blocks of Tokyo).

Data exploration was continued by density-based cluster analysis, using the OPTICS (Ordering Points To Identify the Clustering Structure) algorithm [4]. This algorithm creates an ordering of a database, additionally storing the core distance and a suitable reachability distance for each object. In contrast to another popular clustering algorithm DBSCAN (Density-Based Spatial Clustering of Applications with Noise) [14], OPTICS responds well to datasets with varying densities. Density clusters are then built using only two parameters: the neighborhood radius and a minimum number of points in the neighborhood. Resulting clusters can have different shapes and there is no need to predefine their number (which is of essence when working with large datasets and area-dependent parameters). Depending on the results desired, those parameters can be widely varied; if one wished to take a broad look at the clusters country wide, they could set the distance parameter to a few kilometers and minimum number of points to a dozen or so (this would ensure that large areas were covered). In contrast, to see the real "hot spots" of activity, one could set the distance parameter to, say, a 100 m or less, and number of points to several dozens. Of course, there is no general rule on the size of parameters to use – they are heavily dependent on the data at hand, and need to be considered carefully prior to starting the calculations, since odd values might lead to linear, quadratic or even worse complexities and respective calculation costs in appropriate time units. Figure 4.7 shows data visualized using the OPTICS clustering algorithm with small area and a large number of points defined (Fig. 4.7a) when fewer, smaller clusters were obtained for this dataset, and with large area and a small number of points defined (Fig. 4.7b) when more large clusters were obtained.

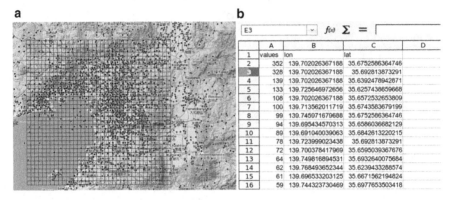

**Fig. 4.8** OpenHeatmap data preparation. (**a**) Coarse-detail matrix, cell edge set to 1,500 m. (**b**) Data sorted and ready for export to CSV format

Even though plotting every video location on the map gave researchers some idea of the density of their spatial distribution, it was hard to tell just by looking at that image (e.g., Fig. 4.6b) exactly how dense was each cluster, number wise (since a lot of circles might be overlapping and covering each other). To get a better idea of what the real "hot spots" were (areas densely packed with videos), following method was applied:

1. Firstly, it was necessary to construct a matrix with arbitrary number of rows and columns over the area that was observed; the number of cells depended on level of details needed and size of the area in question. For example, if the country as a whole was observed, matrix would be comprised of square cells whose edge length would be a few kilometers. If a district was observed, the edge length would be a few hundred meters perhaps. If only a city center was under scrutiny, edges of cells would be no more than 50 m long.
2. Number of videos that each cell encompassed was counted, latitude and longitude coordinates of the center of the cell were extracted and stored in a table. Each row in this table contained data about one cell (i.e., latitude/longitude coordinates and number of videos inside its boundaries).
3. This table was then sorted on the number of videos (in descending order), and trimmed to contain only rows that had more than one video count, and exported to a simple CSV file.
4. The CSV file was then imported in the OpenHeatmap on-line software, for further tweaking and visualization.

The method is illustrated on Fig. 4.8, where data for a low-detail heat map of the Osaka prefecture was being prepared. OpenHeatmap is an on-line tool for heat map creation; a heat map is very similar to a choropleth map, except that it usually displays continuous data in such a fashion that lower values are presented in one pattern/color and higher values are presented using a different pattern/hue/lightness/color [7] (a choropleth map is a thematic map in which areas

**Table 4.2** Japan dataset
basic statistics

| Number of videos | 95,516 |
|---|---|
| Time frame | 2005–2010 |
| Mean number of views | 6,036 |
| Median number of views | 286 |
| Mean duration | 215 s |
| Median duration | 178 s |
| Unique uploaders | 35,920 |

are shadowed or patterned in proportion to the measurement of the statistical variable being displayed on the map, usually aggregated to designated enumeration units – countries, cities, city blocks, etc.). OpenHeatmap allows users to (once the data has been imported) set desired colors for representing high, intermediate, and low data values, set zoom level of the area in focus, and to set opacity of the generated heat map. It also enables users to save their maps on-line once they are done customizing them, and share them via URLs. When opened in a browser, maps can be zoomed and panned; they also display a legend explaining values for the colors used, and when users hover the cursor over the map, a small text box is shown displaying the exact data value under the cursor.

Figure 4.9a shows a heat map for the better part of Japan. Red (dark) color represents high concentration of videos in the area, while yellow (light) color represents low concentration (orange is intermediate concentration). It can be seen that most of the videos are concentrated in or near urban areas (i.e., major cities), but in order to get more insight into where exactly are the videos the most densely clustered (remember spatial resolution is determined by the cell size, which is rather large at country level), several more maps had to be constructed. Figure 4.9b demonstrates a heat map for the wider area of city of Tokyo, while Fig. 4.9c shows the same kind of map for the city center. As new maps containing more details are constructed, they, understandably, deviate somewhat from their coarser counterparts due to different number of videos counted for different cell sizes, but provide more information about the exact location of the videos.

Besides visualization techniques applied to gain more insight into patterns existing in the geo-referenced data described here, a few more statistical methods were applied in order to further describe and understand the data. Simple time-series analysis revealed that most of the videos were uploaded during late summer and early autumn (August, September, and October), that the most inactive months as far as uploads go are December through February and that uploads occur most frequently during the weekend (Friday through Sunday). Hourly distribution of video uploads was as expected, with peaks during the late afternoon and early evening (6–9 p.m.) and least activity during late night and early morning (2–8 a.m.). Basic statistics describing the data retrieved for Japan area are given in Table 4.2; majority of the videos (just over 75%) analyzed were up to 300 s (5 min) long, and most of the videos (91%) had been viewed less than 15,000 times.

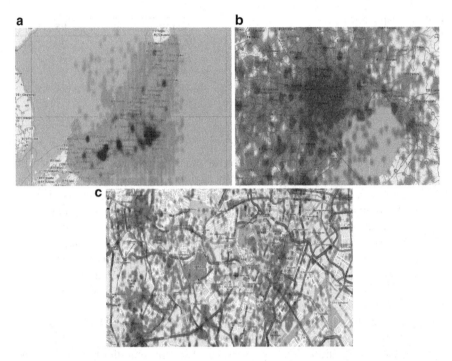

**Fig. 4.9** Some heat map examples, for different zoom levels. (**a**) Better part of Japan area. (**b**) Wider Tokyo area. (**c**) Tokyo city center

## Conclusion

Web platforms for sharing multimedia content (e.g., images and videos) are becoming increasingly popular, mostly due to advancements in technologies enabling lower storage and bandwidth (communication) costs. Miniturization and integration of various components (GPS receivers, wireless modules, cameras, etc.) into mobile devices has also helped this trend a lot, while at the same time tremendously increasing the amount of meta-data attached to the content being created by these mobile devices. This, in turn, has enabled researchers to come up with novel ways of using that meta-data, and to perform various analysis that yielded interesting results.

This chapter presented several methods proposed in past and ongoing research for pattern discovery using publicly available meta-data (attached to images and videos). Specific problems that arise during data retrieval and ways to circumvent them were discussed, and since geo-referenced data was in focus – suitable visualization techniques that make pattern discovery easier were demonstrated. Putting this new knowledge to practical use does not require too much imagination; urban planners and local authorities might include results like these in their decision and policy-making processes, marketing practitioners and tourist organizations might target specific end groups with customized offers once they have learned their movement patterns when visiting particular area, cultural heritage organizations might gain new insight into which monuments get the most publicity tourist wise, social analysts could link certain service usage habits to some already known or new behavioral patterns, etc. In brief – many different disciplines might benefit from application of these methods and techniques to data that is already there, just waiting to be analyzed. Of course, some ethical issues might arise in the process, and good care should be taken in order to avoid misuse of personal data that users inadvertently disclosed publicly – for as it is doubtlessly true, knowledge and responsibility go hand in hand.

# References

1. Acquisti, A., Gross, R.: Imagined communities: awareness, information sharing, and privacy on the facebook. In: Privacy Enhancing Technologies, pp. 36–58. Springer, Berlin (2006)
2. Andrienko, N., Andrienko, G.: Exploratory Analysis of Spatial and Temporal Data: A Systematic Approach. Springer, Berlin/New York (2006)
3. Andrienko, G., Andrienko, N., Bak, P., Kisilevich, S., Keim, D.: Analysis of community-contributed space-and time-referenced data (example of Panoramio photos). In: Proceedings of the 17th ACM SIGSPATIAL International Conference on Advances in Geographic Information Systems, Seattle, pp. 540–541. ACM (2009)
4. Ankerst, M., Breunig, M.M., Kriegel, H.P., Sander, J.: OPTICS: ordering points to identify the clustering structure. ACM SIGMOD Rec. **28**(2), 49–60 (1999)
5. Boyd, D.M., Ellison, N.B.: Social network sites: definition, history, and scholarship. J. Comput. Mediat. Commun. **13**(1), 210–230 (2008)
6. Dwyer, C., Hiltz, S.R., Passerini, K.: Trust and privacy concern within social networking sites: a comparison of Facebook and MySpace. In: Proceedings of AMCIS, Keystone. Citeseer (2007)
7. Fisher, D.: Hotmap: looking at geographic attention. IEEE Trans. Vis. comput. graph. **13**(6), 1184–1191 (2007)
8. flickr blog. 5,000,000,000. http://blog.flickr.net/en/2010/09/19/5000000000/, 09 (2010)
9. Girardin, F., Fiore, F.D., Blat, J., Ratti, C.: Understanding of tourist dynamics from explicitly disclosed location information. In: 4th International Symposium on LBS and Telecartography, Hong-Kong (2007)
10. Girardin, F., Calabrese, F., Fiore, F.D., Ratti, C., Blat, J.: Digital footprinting: uncovering tourists with user-generated content. IEEE Pervasive Comput. **7**(4), 36–43 (2008)
11. Girardin, F., Fioreb, F.D., Rattib, C., Blata, J.: Leveraging explicitly disclosed location information to understand tourist dynamics: a case study. J. Locat. Based Serv. **2**(1), 41–56 (2008)
12. GIS.com. What is gis? http://www.gis.com/content/what-gis, 12 (2010)
13. Kisilevich, S., Mansmann, F., Bak, P., Keim, D., Tchaikin, A.: Where would you go on your next vacation? A framework for visual exploration of attractive places. In: 2010 Second International Conference on Advanced Geographic Information Systems, Applications, and Services, St. Maarten, pp. 21–26. IEEE (2010)
14. Kisilevich, S., Mansmann, F., Keim, D.: P-DBSCAN: a density based clustering algorithm for exploration and analysis of attractive areas using collections of geo-tagged photos. In: Proceedings of the 1st International Conference and Exhibition on Computing for Geospatial Research & Application, Washington, pp. 1–4. ACM (2010)

15. Koperski, K., Adhikary, J., Han, J.: Spatial data mining: progress and challenges survey paper. In: Proceedings of ACM SIGMOD Workshop on Research Issues on Data Mining and Knowledge Discovery, Montreal (1996)
16. Milisavljevic, S., Mirkovic, M., Culibrk, D., Crnojevic, V.: Detecting attractive locations using publicly available user-generated video content central Serbia case study. In: Proceedings of 18th TELFOR, Belgrade. TELFOR (2010)
17. Miller, H.J.: Geographic data mining and knowledge discovery. In: Wilson, J.P., Fotheringham, A.S. (eds.) The Handbook of Geographic Information Science. Blackwell Publishing Ltd., Oxford, UK (2008)
18. Mirkovic, M., Culibrk, D., Crnojevic, V.: Detecting behavior patterns using publicly available user-generated video content – comparative study of Serbia and Japan. In: Proceedings of 8th DOGS. Dogs 2010, Novi Sad, Serbia (2010)
19. OpenHeatMap.com. Openheatmap. http://www.openheatmap.com/, 12 (2010)
20. Shah, C.: Tubekit – a query-based YouTube crawling toolkit. Proceedings of the 8th ACM/IEEE-CS joint conference on Digital libraries, pp. 433–433. Pittsburgh, PA, USA (2008)
21. The economic Times. Google unveils new look for orkut. http://economictimes.indiatimes.com/Google-unveils-new-look-for-Orkut/articleshow/5181314.cms 12 (2009)
22. Wauters, R.: China's social network qzone is big, but is it really the biggest? http://techcrunch.com/2009/02/24/chinas-social-network-qzone-is-big-but-is-it-really-the-biggest/, 2 (2009)
23. Witten, I.H., Frank, E.: Data Mining: Practical Machine Learning Tools and Techniques. Morgan Kaufmann Publishers, Amsterdam/Boston (2005)
24. Wood, J., Dykes, J., Slingsby, A., Clarke, K.: Interactive visual exploration of a large spatio-temporal dataset: reflections on a geovisualization mashup. IEEE Trans. Vis. Comput. Graph. **13**(6), 1176–1183 (2007)
25. YouTube. About YouTube. http://www.youtube.com/t/about_youtube, 12 (2010)

# Chapter 5
# Correlation Mining for Web News Information Retrieval

Jing Liu, Zechao Li, and Hanqing Lu

**Abstract** In this chapter, we focus on the problem of correlation mining in news retrieval. To this end, we present a framework of multimodal multi-correlation news retrieval, which integrates news event correlation, news entity correlation, and event-entity correlation simultaneously by exploring both text and image information. The proposed framework enables a more vivid and informative news browsing by providing two views of result presentation, namely, a query-oriented multi-correlation map and a ranking list of news items with necessary descriptions including news image, title, central entities and relevant events. First, we preprocess news articles using common natural language techniques, and initialize the three correlations by statistical analysis about events and entities in news articles and face images. Second, considering the sparsity of the known event-entity correlation, an algorithm of Multi-correlation Probabilistic Matrix Factorization (MPMF) is proposed to reconstruct it with joint consideration of the three correlations. Third, the result ranking and visualization are conducted to present search results. Experimental results on a news dataset collected from multiple news websites demonstrate the attractive performance of the proposed solution.

## Introduction

Along with information technology development and Internet globalization, online news articles have enjoyed explosive growth and received high popularity from over half of web users. Such spurting growth urges the necessity for efficiently organizing the large amount of news articles from multiple new sources.

A news article is defined as a specific event arose by specific people or an organization which happens at a certain time and place. That is, a news article

J. Liu (✉) • Z. Li • H. Lu
Institute of Automation, Chinese Academy of Sciences, Beijing, China
e-mail: jliu@nlpr.ia.ac.cn; zcli@nlpr.ia.ac.cn; luhq@nlpr.ia.ac.cn

A. Abraham (ed.), *Computational Social Networks: Mining and Visualization*,
DOI 10.1007/978-1-4471-4054-2_5, © Springer-Verlag London 2012

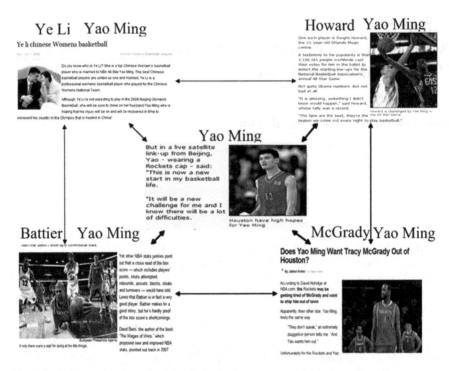

**Fig. 5.1** An illustrative example of correlations among news entities and news events

corresponding to a specific news event can be identified according to the following
"4W" elements: Who (person or organization), When (time), Where (location),
and What (event). In particular, "Who" as a news entity should be paid special
attention because the social network among different persons can be viewed as a
kind of indirect connection among news events as well as their textual relevance.
Accordingly, news event and news person should be considered as the two basic
items in news retrieval, special for person-centric news retrieval in this chapter.
both the items are correlated to each other. Specifically, different news articles may
be relevant when the news events happen on the same or related persons, and the
persons appearing in the same news event should also be related by certain social
interaction. As shown in Fig. 5.1, the five news articles are related to some extent
due to a shared person (*Yao Ming*), and different persons appearing in these articles
are connected with specific social relationships, such as *Yao Ming* is the teammate
of *McGrady* and *Battier*, the husband of *Ye Li*, and the rival of *Howard*. It is an
important and challenging problem to effectively explore these two items and their
intra- and inter-correlations to organize and search possible relevant news events on
Internet, so as to enable an informative overview about a target news topic.

Some researchers have fixed their attentions on exploring correlations within
news events or news entities in various news-related applications. However, most
of them depend on the textual analysis to estimate such intra-correlations, and
furthermore neglect the inter-correlation mining between event and entity. Usually,

news web pages contain news images to vividly describe a specific news event, in which central news actors (persons or an organization) and locations may appear. Thus, the importation of news images as well as textual details is valuable to deeply understand news articles, and to describe them more precisely. Currently, few work attempt to employ the multimodal analysis in news description, and jointly explore available correlations among events and entities to discover or correct some implicit ones during news retrieval.

In this chapter, we propose a framework of Multi-modal Multi-correlation Person-centric News Retrieval (MMPNR), in which both text information and image information are explored, and news event correlations, news entity correlations, and event-entity correlations are incorporated simultaneously and seamlessly. First, we initialize the three correlations using common natural language techniques and face recognition technologies. Second, a complete and refined event-entity correlation is estimated by a Multi-correlation Probabilistic Matrix Factorization (MPMF) model, which is an extended version of traditional Probabilistic Matrix Factorization (PMF) [1] with additional consideration of the within-item correlations, i.e., the event correlation and the entity correlation. Third, the result ranking and visualization are conducted to present news search results. Different from a typical news browser, which only presents a ranking list of relevant news items, we will additionally provide user a query-oriented multi-correlation map as an intuitive and concise resulting presentation. Experimental results on a news dataset collected from multiple sources demonstrate the effectiveness of the proposed MMPNR framework.

The rest of this chapter is organized as follows. Section "Related Work" presents a brief review of related work. Section "Overview of Our System" gives an overview of our news retrieval system. Section "Correlation Initialization" presents the correlation initialization using multimodal analysis. We introduce the proposed MPMF model to complete and refine the three correlations in section "Correlation Reconstruction". Section "Ranking and Visualization" gives the result ranking and visualization in MMPNR. Section "Experiments" shows our experimental evaluations on a large news article set. Section "Conclusion" concludes this chapter.

# Related Work

## *Correlation Mining*

Correlation mining is recognized as one of the most important data mining tasks for its ability to capture underlying dependencies between objects, which can be reduced to the problem link prediction. In this section, we give a review on methods for link prediction. These methods can mainly fall into three categories in accordance with the intuitions of their solutions: similarity-based algorithms, maximum likelihood methods, and probabilistic models [2].

The simplest framework of link prediction methods is the similarity-based algorithm, where each pair of nodes is assigned a score, defined as the similarity (or proximity) between them. And the link prediction is achieved by putting an edge between nodes that are similar enough. Many similarity measures have been proposed, such as information content relevance [3], mutual information [4], dice coefficient [5], cosine coefficient, and so on. Lin [6] defined similarity in information-theoretic terms. Bennett et al. [7] and Li et al. [8] also developed a mathematical theory of similarity distances and showed that there is a universal similarity distance. Pan et al. [9] tried to train a binary classifier to determine the similarity. There also exist some approaches, which are based on Markov chains [10, 11] and statistical relational learning [12–14].

Maximum likelihood methods usually suppose some organizing principles of network structure with some detailed rules and specific parameters obtained by maximizing the likelihood of the observed structure. The likelihood of any non-observed link can be calculated according to those rules and parameters. There are two recently proposed algorithms: hierarchical structure model and stochastic block model. Empirical evidence indicates that many real networks are hierarchically organized, where nodes can be divided into groups, further subdivided into groups of groups, and so forth over multiple scales [15] (e.g., metabolic networks [16] and brain networks [17]). As described in [18], focusing on the hierarchical structure inherent in social and biological networks might provide a smart way to find missing links. A general technique [19] was proposed to infer the hierarchical from network data and further applied it to predict the missing links. Stochastic block model [20–24] can capture the factors for the establishing of connections, especially when the group membership plays the considerable roles in determining how nodes interact with each other, which usually could not be well described by the simple assortativity coefficient [21, 22] or the degree–degree correlations [23, 24].

Probabilistic models aim at abstracting the underlying structure from the observed network, and then predicting the missing links by using the learned model. There are three popular methods, respectively, called Probabilistic Relational Model (PRM) [25], Probabilistic Entity Relational Model (PERM) [26], and Stochastic Relational Model (SRM) [27]. PRM attempts to build a joint probability distribution over the attributes of a relational dataset. There are three types of PRM-like algorithms: Relational Bayesian Networks (RBNs) [25,28], Relational Markov Networks (RMNs) [29] and Relational Dependency Networks (RDNs) [30]. A specific type of PERM is the directed acyclic PERM, which uses directed arcs to describe the relationship between attributes [26]. The key idea of SRM is to model the stochastic structure of entity relationships (i.e., links) via a tensor interaction of multiple Gaussian Processes (GPs), each defined on one type of entities [31].

## *Matrix Factorization*

Factor analysis [32] has been widely utilized in many fields [1, 33–39]. Zhu et al. [33] proposed a joint matrix factorization combining both linkage and document-term matrices to improve the hypertext classification. The content information and link structures were seamlessly combined through a single set of latent factors.

The discovered latent factors (bases) explained both content information and link structures, and were used to classify the web pages. A variety of probabilistic factor-based models have been proposed [34–36], which can be viewed as graphical models in which latent factor variables have directed connections to variables that represent user ratings. The major drawback is that potentially slow or inaccurate approximations are required for the estimation of the posterior distribution over latent factors. Probabilistic Matrix Factorization (PMF) [1] was proposed to find only point-wise estimation of model parameters and hypermeters, instead of inferring the full posterior distribution over them. It models the user-item matrix as a product of two low-rank user and item matrices. The computation cost of PDF is linear with the number of observations. A social recommendation has been proposed based on the probabilistic matrix factorization model, named as SoRec [37]. It fused the user-item matrix with the users' social trust networks by sharing a common latent low-dimensional user feature matrix. A probabilistic polyadic factor model [38] was proposed to analyze multiple-dimensional data such as networked data in social networks and directly model all the dimensions simultaneously in a unified framework. In order to discover community structure from various social contexts and interactions, MetaFac (MetaGraph Factorization) [39] proposed an efficient factorization approach through analyzing time-varying and multirelational data.

To make full use of the intra- and inter-correlations among events and entities, in this chapter, we propose an MPMF model to learn the person latent space and the event latent space by exploring the three correlation matrices simultaneously and seamlessly. Based on the reconstructed correlations over the latent spaces, we provide users a concise and informative result browsing with a query-oriented correlation map and a ranking list of news items. As far as we know, the proposed MPMF-based news retrieval is the first one attempting to mine the intra- and inter-correlations among events and entities in a simultaneous and seamless form.

## Overview of Our System

In this section, we will briefly overview the framework of the proposed MMPNR (shown in Fig. 5.2), which includes four components, namely, data preprocessing, correlation initialization, correlation reconstruction, and result ranking and visualization.

First, we collect and preprocess news data. A large scale of news articles are crawled from some distinguished news sites including ABCNews.com,[1] BBC.co.uk[2], and CNN.com.[3] We first parse these news articles into news titles, summaries, texts, URLs and images of news pages. Necessary text preprocessing

---

[1]http://abcnews.go.com/

[2]http://www.bbc.co.uk/

[3]http://edition.cnn.com/

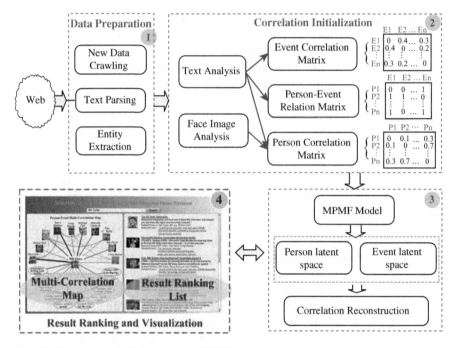

**Fig. 5.2** The framework of the proposed MMPNR

including word separation and stop-words filtering are conducted. Then we extract news entities (Time, Person or Organization, and Location) according to [40]. In this chapter, we view Person (or Organization) as entities, while the Time and Location are used to identify news events.

The second component introduced in section "Correlation Initialization" aims to initialize three kinds of correlations: the event correlation, the person correlation, and the person-event correlation. In particular, the event correlation is estimated via the TF-IDF model on text information (news title, summary, and details) from news web pages. For the person correlation, a linear combination of the two co-occurrences of entities within text information and faces on news images, respectively. We utilize the occurrence of a specific person in an event to obtain a binary relationship between the person and the event.

The third component is the basic one in MMPNR, which is demonstrated in section "Correlation Reconstruction". We apply the MPMF model to mine the hidden correlations. We connect these three different correlations simultaneously and seamlessly through the shared latent person space and the shared latent event space. That is, the latent person space in the news person relational matrix is same to the one in the person-event correlation matrix, and a similar case is available for the latent event space. Through the factor analysis via MPMF, the low-dimension latent person features and latent event features are learned, which can be used to reconstruct the news person-event correlations.

The fourth component described in section "Ranking and Visualization" is the result ranking and visualization in MMPNR, which obtains and displays query-related search results to the end users. To give users a vivid and informative organization of news results, we divide the user interface into two parts. The left part gives users a query-oriented relation graph, in which the relations between the query and events (or persons) are illustrated. In the right part, we present a ranking list of related news events with their titles, and the most relevant persons and events, respectively.

## Correlation Initialization

In this section, we will explain how to estimate the three correlations based on multi modal information from news web pages. The estimated correlations are viewed as the initialized input of the MPMF model, which will be introduced in section "Correlation Reconstruction". The details about the correlation initialization are presented as follows.

### *Person-Event Correlation Matrix*

We employ the binary relationship to measure the person-event correlation matrix **R**, which is defined as follows.

$$R_{ij} = \begin{cases} 1, & \text{if person } i \text{ appears in news event } j, \\ 0, & \text{otherwise.} \end{cases} \tag{5.1}$$

Since the amount of online news articles is too large and the number of persons appearing in one news article is small, the person-event relation matrix **R** is very sparse, which is one of the reasons we select the probabilistic matrix factorization model.

### *Event Correlation Matrix*

To discover the intra-correlation among news articles (corresponding to one event in this chapter), we adopt the widely utilized TF-IDF model and cosine similarity to estimate the news event similarity matrix **S**. Considering the different importance of news title, news summary, and its detailed textual report to a news event, we process them separately and combine them in a linear form. Specifically, we assume that the title information is the most important and the news summary is more important than the detailed textual report to the news event. In our implementation, we combine these three kinds of similarities as

$$\mathbf{S} = \alpha \times \mathbf{S}^{\text{title}} + \beta \times \mathbf{S}^{\text{summary}} + (1 - \alpha - \beta) \times \mathbf{S}^{\text{text}}, \qquad (5.2)$$

where $\mathbf{S}$, $\mathbf{S}^{\text{title}}$, $\mathbf{S}^{\text{summary}}$, and $\mathbf{S}^{\text{text}}$ represent the similarity of event, title, summary and text, respectively. In our experiments, we set $\alpha = 0.5$ and $\beta = 0.3$.

## *Person Correlation Matrix*

In view of current news web pages containing images and persons always appearing in images of news articles, we propose to utilize not only the text information but also the news images to calculate the person correlation in news events. First, we use the formula $C_{iq}^{\text{Text}} = 2f(i,q)/(f(i) + f(q))$ to calculate the co-occurrence of person names in news articles, where $f(i,q)$, $f(i)$ and $f(q)$ denote the count of news articles including person $i$ and person $q$ simultaneously, the count of news articles containing person $i$, and the count of news articles containing person $q$, respectively. We apply the face detection and matching methods to recognize the person in each news images, then we employ the similar formula as above to calculate the co-occurrence of person faces in news images.

In the following, we will introduce the details for the person recognition in news images. We first submit names of persons to Wikipedia,[4] crawl and parse the corresponding returned web pages, and download images in the resume tables. Then we adopt the face detection approach to detect the face part in the images. To determine whether a specific person appears in the news images or not, the SIFT flow approach [41] is used to match the face part of the specific person's image from Wikipedia with any face part detected from news images. An illustrate example is given in Fig. 5.3. The face parts (b) of images derived by submitting persons' names in (a) are used to be matched with the face parts in images (c) from news web pages. According to the matching results, we derive the person co-occurrence matrix based on news images in (d).

The SIFT flow approach assumes SIFT descriptor extracted at each pixel location is constant with respect to the pixel displacement field and allows a pixel in one image to match any other pixel in the other image. We still want to encourage smoothness of the pixel displacement field by encouraging close-by pixels to have similar displacements. It formulates the correspondence search as a discrete optimization problem on the image lattice with the following cost function:

---

[4]http://en.wikipedia.org/wiki/Main_Page

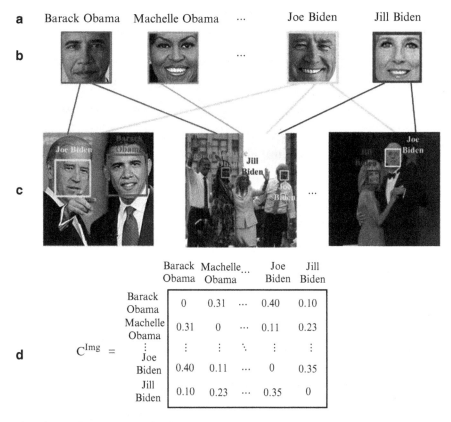

Fig. 5.3 An illustrative example of face detection and matching. (a) The names of news persons; (b) the faces detected in images crawled from Wikipedia by submitting names in (a); (c) the face matching results; (d) the co-occurrence matrix based on (c). The *red, green, blue,* and *yellow* boxes represent "Barack Obama", "Michelle Obama", "Joy Biden" and "Jill Biden", respectively

$$l(\mathbf{w}) = \sum_{\mathbf{p}} \|s_1(\mathbf{p}) - s_2(\mathbf{p} + \mathbf{w})\|_1 + \frac{1}{\sigma^2} \sum_{\mathbf{p}} (u_{\mathbf{p}}^2 + v_{\mathbf{p}}^2)$$

$$+ \alpha \sum_{(\mathbf{p},\mathbf{q}) \in \varepsilon} \min\left(|u(\mathbf{p}) - u(\mathbf{q})|, \frac{d}{\alpha}\right) + \min\left(|v(\mathbf{p}) - v(\mathbf{q})|, \frac{d}{\alpha}\right), \quad (5.3)$$

where $\mathbf{w}(\mathbf{p}) = (u(\mathbf{p}), v(\mathbf{p}))$ is the displacement vector at pixel location $\mathbf{p} = (x, y)$, $s_i(\mathbf{p})$ is the SIFT descriptor extracted at location $\mathbf{p}$, in image $i$, and $q$ is the spatial neighborhood of a pixel. Parameters $\sigma = 300$, $\alpha = 0.5$ and $d = 2$ are fixed in our experiments. Based on the matching results, we can decide whether a person exists in a news image. Finally, we obtain an indicator matrix with each column representing whether a news person appears in news images or not. The person faces' co-occurrence is calculated as above for text processing, denoted as $C_{iq}^{\text{Img}}$, and then we linearly integrate these two co-occurrences as follows:

$$C_{iq} = (1 - \gamma) \times C_{iq}^{\text{Text}} + \gamma \times C_{iq}^{\text{Img}}. \tag{5.4}$$

In our experiments, we set $\gamma = 0.4$.

## Correlation Reconstruction

After the correlation initialization, we will preform the correlation reconstruction via MPMF, to further complete and refine those initialized correlations. For clarity, we first introduce the standard PMF model. Then, we present our proposed MPMF model with additional consideration of the intra-correlations about events and entities.

## *PMF Model*

Probabilistic Matrix Factorization (PMF) model [1] was proposed to handle very large, sparse, and imbalanced dataset in collaborative filtering, based on the assumption that users who have rated similar sets of movies are likely to have similar preferences. In the following, we take such collaborative filtering for example, to illustrate the probabilistic matrix factorization model, whose graphical model is shown in Fig. 5.4.

In order to learn any user's preference to any movie, matrix factorization is employed to factorize the user-item matrix. Suppose we have $m$ users, $n$ movies, and a rating matrix of $\mathbf{R} \in \mathcal{R}^{m \times n}$. Let $R_{ij}$ denote the rating of user $i$ for movie $j$. The basic idea of probabilistic matrix factorization is to derive two high-quality $d$-dimensional ($d$ is lower than $\min(m, n)$) latent feature spaces $\mathbf{P} \in \mathcal{R}^{d \times m}$ and $\mathbf{E} \in \mathcal{R}^{d \times n}$, which denote the latent user and movie feature spaces, respectively. The column vectors $\mathbf{p}_i$ and $\mathbf{e}_j$ represent user-specific and movie-specific latent feature vectors, which are not unique. A probabilistic model with Gaussian observation noise is employed as shown in Fig. 5.4, and the conditional distribution over the observed rating is defined as:

$$p(\mathbf{R}|\mathbf{P}, \mathbf{E}, \sigma_R^2) = \prod_{i=1}^{m} \prod_{j=1}^{n} [\mathcal{N}(R_{ij}|g(\mathbf{p}_i^T \mathbf{e}_j), \sigma_R^2)]^{I_{ij}}, \tag{5.5}$$

where $\mathcal{N}(x|\mu, \sigma^2)$ denotes the probabilistic density function, in which the conditional distribution is defined as the Gaussian distribution with mean $\mu$ and variance

**Fig. 5.4** Graphical model for probabilistic matrix factorization (PMF)

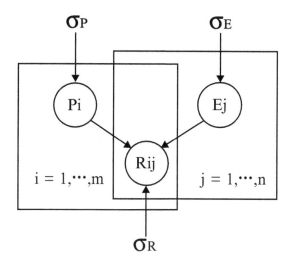

$\sigma^2$, and $I_{ij}$ is the indicator function that is equal to 1 if user $i$ rated movie $j$ and equal to 0 otherwise. The function $g(x)$ is a logistic function defined as $g(x) = 1/(1 + \exp(-x))$, which makes it possible to bound the range of $\mathbf{p}_i^T \mathbf{e}_j$ within the interval $[0, 1]$. As described in [42, 43], zero-mean spherical Gaussian priors are placed on the latent user and movie feature vectors as:

$$p(\mathbf{P}|\sigma_P^2) = \prod_{i=1}^{m} \mathcal{N}(\mathbf{p}_i|0, \sigma_P^2 \mathbf{I}), \tag{5.6}$$

$$p(\mathbf{E}|\sigma_E^2) = \prod_{j=1}^{n} \mathcal{N}(\mathbf{e}_j|0, \sigma_E^2 \mathbf{I}), \tag{5.7}$$

where $\mathbf{I}$ is an identity matrix.

Through a simple Bayesian inference, the jointly posterior distribution over user and movie is given by:

$$p(\mathbf{P}, \mathbf{E}|\mathbf{R}, \sigma_R^2, \sigma_P^2, \sigma_E^2) \propto p(\mathbf{R}|\mathbf{P}, \mathbf{E}, \sigma_R^2) p(\mathbf{P}|\sigma_P^2) p(\mathbf{E}|\sigma_E^2)$$

$$= \prod_{i=1}^{m} \prod_{j=1}^{n} [\mathcal{N}(R_{ij}|g(\mathbf{p}_i^T \mathbf{e}_j), \sigma_R^2)]^{I_{ij}}$$

$$\times \prod_{i=1}^{m} \mathcal{N}(\mathbf{p}_i|0, \sigma_P^2 \mathbf{I}) \times \prod_{j=1}^{n} \mathcal{N}(\mathbf{e}_j|0, \sigma_E^2 \mathbf{I}). \tag{5.8}$$

Thus, we can derive the log of the posterior distribution in Eq. 5.8 as:

$$\ln p(\mathbf{P}, \mathbf{E} | \mathbf{R}, \sigma_R^2, \sigma_P^2, \sigma_E^2)$$

$$= -\frac{1}{2\sigma_R^2} \sum_{i=1}^{m} \sum_{j=1}^{n} I_{ij}^R (R_{ij} - g(\mathbf{p}_i^T \mathbf{e}_j))^2$$

$$- \frac{1}{2\sigma_P^2} \sum_{i=1}^{m} \mathbf{p}_i^T \mathbf{p}_i - \frac{1}{2\sigma_E^2} \sum_{j=1}^{n} \mathbf{e}_j^T \mathbf{e}_j$$

$$- \frac{1}{2} (\sum_{i=1}^{m} \sum_{j=1}^{n} I_{ij}^R \ln \sigma_R^2 + md \ln \sigma_P^2 + nd \ln \sigma_E^2) + \mathcal{C}, \qquad (5.9)$$

where $\mathcal{C}$ is a constant. Maximizing the log-posterior distribution given by Eq. 5.9 with hyperparameters (i.e., the observation noise variance and prior variances) kept fixed is equivalent to minimizing the following sum-of-squared-errors objective functions with quadratic regularization terms:

$$L(\mathbf{P}, \mathbf{E}) = \frac{1}{2} \sum_{i=1}^{m} \sum_{j=1}^{n} I_{ij}^R (R_{ij} - g(\mathbf{p}_i^T \mathbf{e}_j))^2 + \frac{\lambda_P}{2} \|\mathbf{P}\|_F^2 + \frac{\lambda_E}{2} \|\mathbf{E}\|_F^2, \qquad (5.10)$$

where $\lambda_p = \sigma_R^2 / \sigma_P^2$, $\lambda_E = \sigma_R^2 / \sigma_E^2$, and $\| \cdot \|_F^2$ denotes the Frobenius norm. Eq. 5.10 can be solved using gradient methods, such as the conjugate gradient, quasi-Newton methods, and steepest descent method. Through performing gradient descent over $P$ and $E$ as described in Eqs. 5.11 and 5.12, we can find a local minimum of the objective function given by Eq. 5.10.

$$\frac{\partial L}{\partial \mathbf{p}_i} = \sum_{j=1}^{n} I_{ij}^R g'(\mathbf{p}_i^T \mathbf{e}_j)(g(\mathbf{p}_i^T \mathbf{e}_j) - R_{ij})\mathbf{e}_j + \lambda_P \mathbf{p}_i \qquad (5.11)$$

$$\frac{\partial L}{\partial \mathbf{e}_j} = \sum_{i=1}^{m} I_{ij}^R g'(\mathbf{p}_i^T \mathbf{e}_j)(g(\mathbf{p}_i^T \mathbf{e}_j) - R_{ij})\mathbf{p}_i + \lambda_E \mathbf{e}_j \qquad (5.12)$$

where $g'(x)$ is the derivative of logistic function $g'(x) = \exp(x)/(1 + \exp(x))^2$.

The experimental results in [1] demonstrate that PMF model performs very well on a very large, sparse, and imbalanced dataset and takes time linear in the number of observations using steepest descent. However, traditional PMF-based recommender systems assume that all the users and the items are independent and identically distributed. This assumption ignores the social connection among users and the similarity among items. Considering that connected users should have preference on similar item, we will propose an improved PMF algorithm to integrate the user-item correlation, users, social network and items similarity simultaneously and seamlessly.

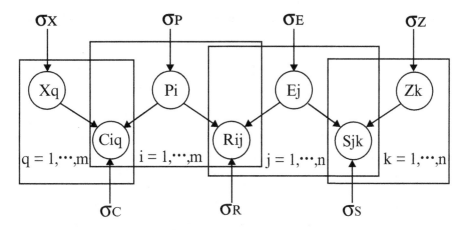

**Fig. 5.5** Graphical model for multi-correlation probabilistic matrix factorization (MPMF)

## MPMF Model

During the person-centric news retrieval, we aim to provide the news search result when submitting a person name as a query. Thus the inter-correlation estimation between news person and news event is the key problem in the task. The person-event correlation in news retrieval is analogous to user-item relation in recommender system. Furthermore, due to the fast explosion of online news articles, the inter-correlation between news persons and news events are usually very sparse. The PMF-like algorithm is employed as a natural and feasible option to conduct our work. However, the standard PMF model can only employ one relation. Then we extend the model to integrate the news person correlation and news event correlation, named as Multi-correlation Probabilistic Matrix Factorization (MPMF). We employ the probabilistic factor analysis to factorize person-event correlation matrix, person correlation matrix, and event correlation matrix, and connect these three different data resources with the shared latent person space and the shared latent event space, as introduced in section "Overview of Our System".

To learn the latent person and event spaces, we model our problem using the graphical model shown in Fig. 5.5. Suppose we have $m$ persons and $n$ events. Let $\mathbf{R} \in \mathcal{R}^{m \times n}$, $\mathbf{C} \in \mathcal{R}^{m \times m}$ and $\mathbf{S} \in \mathcal{R}^{n \times n}$ denote the person-event relation matrix, person correlation matrix and event similarity matrix, respectively. Let $R_{ij}$ represent the correlation between person $i$ and event $j$ within the range $[0, 1]$, $C_{iq} \in [0, 1]$ denote the relation between person $i$ and person $q$, and $S_{jk} \in [0, 1]$ denote the similarity between event $j$ and event $k$. Let $\mathbf{P} \in \mathcal{R}^{d \times m}$, $\mathbf{E} \in \mathcal{R}^{d \times n}$, $\mathbf{X} \in \mathcal{R}^{d \times m}$ and $\mathbf{Z} \in \mathcal{R}^{d \times n}$ be person, event, person factor and event factor latent feature matrices, with column vectors $\mathbf{p}_i$, $\mathbf{e}_j$, $\mathbf{x}_q$, and $\mathbf{z}_k$ representing person-specific, event-specific, person factor-specific, and event factor-specific latent feature vectors, respectively.

The probabilistic model with Gaussian observation noise is adopted and the conditional distributions are defined as:

$$p(\mathbf{R}|\mathbf{P}, \mathbf{E}, \sigma_R^2) = \prod_{i=1}^{m} \prod_{j=1}^{n} [\mathcal{N}(R_{ij}|g(\mathbf{p}_i^T \mathbf{e}_j), \sigma_R^2)]^{I_{ij}^R}, \tag{5.13}$$

$$p(\mathbf{C}|\mathbf{P}, \mathbf{X}, \sigma_C^2) = \prod_{i=1}^{m} \prod_{q=1}^{m} [\mathcal{N}(C_{iq}|g(\mathbf{p}_i^T \mathbf{x}_q), \sigma_C^2)]^{I_{iq}^C}, \tag{5.14}$$

$$p(\mathbf{S}|\mathbf{E}, \mathbf{Z}, \sigma_S^2) = \prod_{j=1}^{n} \prod_{k=1}^{n} [\mathcal{N}(S_{jk}|g(\mathbf{e}_j^T \mathbf{z}_k), \sigma_S^2)]^{I_{jk}^S}, \tag{5.15}$$

where $I_{ij}^R$ is the indicator function that is equal to 1 if the relation between news person $i$ and news event $j$ is more than 0 and equal to 0 otherwise. $I_{iq}^C$ and $I_{jk}^S$ are defined similarly.

We also place zero-mean spherical Gaussian priors on the latent person, event, person factor and event factor feature vectors.

$$p(\mathbf{P}|\sigma_P^2) = \prod_{i=1}^{m} \mathcal{N}(\mathbf{p}_i|0, \sigma_P^2 \mathbf{I}), \tag{5.16}$$

$$p(\mathbf{E}|\sigma_E^2) = \prod_{j=1}^{n} \mathcal{N}(\mathbf{e}_j|0, \sigma_E^2 \mathbf{I}), \tag{5.17}$$

$$p(\mathbf{X}|\sigma_X^2) = \prod_{q=1}^{m} \mathcal{N}(\mathbf{x}_q|0, \sigma_X^2 \mathbf{I}), \tag{5.18}$$

$$p(\mathbf{Z}|\sigma_Z^2) = \prod_{k=1}^{n} \mathcal{N}(\mathbf{z}_k|0, \sigma_Z^2 \mathbf{I}). \tag{5.19}$$

Hence, similar to Eq. 5.9, through a simple Bayesian inference, we can obtain the log-posterior distribution:

$$\ln p(\mathbf{P}, \mathbf{E}, \mathbf{X}, \mathbf{Z}|\mathbf{R}, \mathbf{C}, \mathbf{S}, \sigma_R^2, \sigma_C^2, \sigma_S^2, \sigma_P^2, \sigma_E^2, \sigma_X^2, \sigma_Z^2)$$

$$= -\frac{1}{2\sigma_R^2} \sum_{i=1}^{m} \sum_{j=1}^{n} I_{ij}^R (R_{ij} - g(\mathbf{p}_i^T \mathbf{e}_j))^2$$

$$- \frac{1}{2\sigma_C^2} \sum_{i=1}^{m} \sum_{q=1}^{m} I_{iq}^C (C_{iq} - g(\mathbf{p}_i^T \mathbf{x}_q))^2$$

$$- \frac{1}{2\sigma_S^2} \sum_{j=1}^{n} \sum_{k=1}^{n} I_{jk}^S (S_{jk} - g(\mathbf{e}_j^T \mathbf{z}_k))^2$$

$$- \frac{1}{2\sigma_P^2} \sum_{i=1}^{m} \mathbf{p}_i^T \mathbf{p}_i - \frac{1}{2\sigma_E^2} \sum_{j=1}^{n} \mathbf{e}_j^T \mathbf{e}_j$$

$$- \frac{1}{2\sigma_X^2} \sum_{q=1}^{m} \mathbf{x}_q^T \mathbf{x}_q - \frac{1}{2\sigma_Z^2} \sum_{k=1}^{n} \mathbf{z}_k^T \mathbf{z}_k$$

$$- \frac{1}{2} \left( \left( \sum_{i=1}^{m} \sum_{j=1}^{n} I_{ij}^R \right) \ln \sigma_R^2 + \left( \sum_{i=1}^{m} \sum_{q=1}^{m} I_{iq}^C \right) \ln \sigma_C^2 \right)$$

$$- \frac{1}{2} \sum_{j=1}^{n} \sum_{k=1}^{n} \mathbf{I}_{jk}^S \ln \sigma_S^2 - \frac{1}{2} md \ln \sigma_P^2$$

$$- \frac{1}{2} (nd \ln \sigma_E^2 + md \ln \sigma_X^2 + nd \ln \sigma_Z^2) + \mathcal{C}. \tag{5.20}$$

As described above, the equivalent optimization problem is to minimize the following objective function:

$$L(\mathbf{P}, \mathbf{E}, \mathbf{X}, \mathbf{Z}) = \frac{1}{2} \sum_{i=1}^{m} \sum_{j=1}^{n} I_{ij}^R (R_{ij} - g(\mathbf{p}_i^T \mathbf{e}_j))^2$$

$$+ \frac{\lambda_C}{2} \sum_{i=1}^{m} \sum_{q=1}^{m} I_{iq}^C (C_{iq} - g(\mathbf{p}_i^T \mathbf{x}_q))^2$$

$$+ \frac{\lambda_S}{2} \sum_{j=1}^{n} \sum_{k=1}^{n} I_{jk}^S (S_{jk} - g(\mathbf{e}_j^T \mathbf{z}_k))^2 + \frac{\lambda_P}{2} \|\mathbf{P}\|_F^2$$

$$+ \frac{\lambda_E}{2} \|\mathbf{E}\|_F^2 + \frac{\lambda_X}{2} \|\mathbf{X}\|_F^2 + \frac{\lambda_Z}{2} \|\mathbf{Z}\|_F^2, \tag{5.21}$$

where $\lambda_C = \sigma_R^2/\sigma_C^2$, $\lambda_S = \sigma_R^2/\sigma_S^2$, $\lambda_P = \sigma_R^2/\sigma_P^2$, $\lambda_X = \sigma_R^2/\sigma_X^2$, $\lambda_E = \sigma_R^2/\sigma_E^2$, and $\lambda_Z = \sigma_R^2/\sigma_Z^2$. A local minimum of the objective function given by Eq. 5.21 can be found by performing gradient descent in $\mathbf{p}_i$, $\mathbf{e}_j$, $\mathbf{x}_q$ and $\mathbf{z}_k$, respectively.

$$\frac{\partial L}{\partial \mathbf{p}_i} = \sum_{j=1}^{n} I_{ij}^R g'(\mathbf{p}_i^T \mathbf{e}_j)(g(\mathbf{p}_i^T \mathbf{e}_j) - R_{ij}) \mathbf{e}_j$$

$$+ \lambda_C \sum_{q=1}^{m} I_{iq}^C g'(\mathbf{p}_i^T \mathbf{x}_q)(g(\mathbf{p}_i^T \mathbf{x}_q) - C_{iq}) \mathbf{x}_q + \lambda_P \mathbf{p}_i \tag{5.22}$$

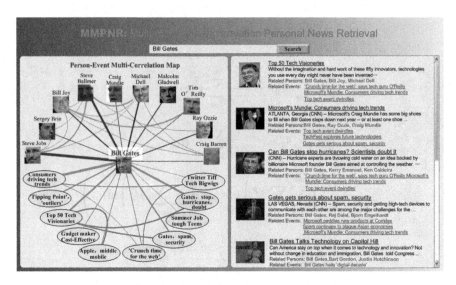

**Fig. 5.6** Interface of MMPNR

$$\frac{\partial L}{\partial \mathbf{e}_j} = \sum_{i=1}^{m} I_{ij}^{R} g^{'}(\mathbf{p}_i^T \mathbf{e}_j)(g(\mathbf{p}_i^T \mathbf{e}_j) - R_{ij})\mathbf{p}_i$$

$$+ \lambda_S \sum_{k=1}^{n} I_{ik}^{S} g^{'}(\mathbf{e}_j^T \mathbf{z}_k)(g(\mathbf{e}_j^T \mathbf{z}_k) - S_{jk})\mathbf{z}_k + \lambda_E \mathbf{e}_j \qquad (5.23)$$

$$\frac{\partial L}{\partial \mathbf{x}_q} = \lambda_C \sum_{i=1}^{m} I_{iq}^{C} g^{'}(\mathbf{p}_i^T \mathbf{x}_q)(g(\mathbf{p}_i^T \mathbf{x}_q) - C_{iq})\mathbf{p}_i + \lambda_X \mathbf{x}_q \qquad (5.24)$$

$$\frac{\partial L}{\partial \mathbf{z}_k} = \lambda_S \sum_{j=1}^{n} I_{jk}^{S} g^{'}(\mathbf{e}_j^T \mathbf{z}_k)(g(\mathbf{e}_j^T \mathbf{z}_k) - S_{jk})\mathbf{e}_j + \lambda_Z \mathbf{z}_k. \qquad (5.25)$$

To reduce the model complexity, in our implementation, we set $\lambda_P = \lambda_E = \lambda_X = \lambda_Z$.

## Ranking and Visualization

Provided with the latent feature spaces by MPMF, we can present users more information than the traditional news search engines, which can only present the list of related news articles. Figure 5.6 gives the interface of our MMPNR system. It presents the reconstructed correlations and the relative news results to users.

Basically, it comprises two types of views: a query-oriented multi-correlation map on the left view and a ranking list of related news items on the right view.

In the query-oriented multi-correlation map, we give users three query-dependent correlations to answer their queries, namely, person correlation, event correlation and person-event correlation. In the person correlation part, we present a social network about the most relevant persons, which enables users to discover interesting relationships about persons associated with their queries. We also show users a news event relation map about the most related events in the event relation part. Through MPMF, we have got the latent spaces $\mathbf{P}$, $\mathbf{E}$, $\mathbf{X}$, and $\mathbf{Z}$, which can be utilized to reconstruct the three correlation matrices by the following formulas:

$$\hat{\mathbf{R}} = g(\mathbf{P}^T \mathbf{E}) \tag{5.26}$$

$$\hat{\mathbf{C}} = g(\mathbf{P}^T \mathbf{X}) \tag{5.27}$$

$$\hat{\mathbf{S}} = g(\mathbf{E}^T \mathbf{Z}). \tag{5.28}$$

If a user submits a query corresponding to the person $i$ in our dataset, we can rank persons and events by sorting the $i$-th column of $\hat{\mathbf{C}}$ and $\hat{\mathbf{R}}$ with a descending order. We can also derive the relevant events to the query from the matrix $\hat{\mathbf{S}}$. We only present the top ten relevant persons in the social network and the top ten relevant events in the news event relation map. As shown in the left part of Fig. 5.6, we give names and face images of persons and keywords of events. The weighted edges between persons or events denote the relations between them. The thicker the line between persons or events, the stronger the relation they have. The person-event items shows the correlation between the relative news events and the query person using weighted edges. Users can also see the detailed information about a specific event or person through putting the mouse pointer on the suitable position.

On the right view, as done in a traditional news searcher, we also present a ranking list of relative news events with general introduction. We present news event not only with the title and a shot part of summary similar to the traditional news searcher, but also with the top three relevant persons and the top three relevant news events, which can be obtained by sorting the reconstructed event correlation matrix $\hat{\mathbf{S}}$. Users can browse more details through clicking the title of the corresponding events.

## Experiments

The objective of our experiments is to examine the effectiveness of our proposed model in news retrieval. We first explain the collected dataset for our evaluation, the evaluation measure, and the parameter setting in our experiments. Then we present the experimental results using our algorithm as well as its comparison with other methods.

**Table 5.1** Details of our web news dataset

| Web site           | ABC    | BBC    | CNN    | Total  |
|--------------------|--------|--------|--------|--------|
| Number of articles | 47,163 | 11,073 | 41,649 | 99,885 |

**Table 5.2** The graded relevance

| Relevance level | Weight |
|-----------------|--------|
| Very relative   | 3      |
| Relative        | 2      |
| Irrelative      | 1      |

## Experimental Design

Our experiments are performed on a web news dataset, in which news articles were crawled from ABCNews.com, BBC.co.uk and CNN.com. Two news articles are considered to be duplicate when they correspond to the same news event according to the "4W" criterion. With the crawled news articles, we first remove the duplicate ones and conduct the evaluation on the deduplicated dataset. That is, one news article stands for a news event in our experiments. We got 99,885 articles in total, whose distribution over the three websites is shown in Table 5.1. In addition, we extracted 9,345 person names as the entities from the news dataset after deleting the ones which appear less than ten times.

Similar to previous work on information retrieval, we adopt normalized Discounted Cumulative Gain (nDCG) [44] as a measure to evaluate the effectiveness of the web search algorithm, which is defined as

$$nDCG@k = \frac{DCG[k]}{IDCG[k]}. \tag{5.29}$$

DCG (Discounted Cumulative Gain) is to measure the cumulative gain of the resulting documents on its position and IDCG is the ideal discounted cumulative gain vector. The DCG is defined as

$$DCG[k] = \sum_{j=1}^{k} \frac{G[j]}{\log_2(1+j)}$$

where $G[j]$ is the graded relevance of the result at position $j$. At last, nDCG values for all queries can be averaged to obtain a measure of the average performance of a ranking algorithm.

No well-defined ground-truth dataset can be used to evaluate the performance of news retrieval. Thus, we invite a group of ten people to judge the relevance of search results. As defined in Table 5.2, the participators can present three types of graded relevance, which is used in the calculation of nDCG. The specific task of

**Table 5.3** The query list used in experiments

| Allen Craig | Andre Owens | Ayrton Senna |
|---|---|---|
| Barack Obama | Blake Griffin | Bobby Simmons |
| Caster Semenya | Charlie Villanueva | Chase Utley |
| Chelsea Clinton | Chris Samuels | Christopher Dodd |
| Christopher Plummer | Clarence Thomas | Claudio Pizarro |
| Cole Aldrich | Darren Fletcher | David Brinkley |
| Eddie Griffin | Edgar Davids | Edison Miranda |
| Elie Wiesel | Emily Blunt | Eric Schmidt |
| Frank Lloyd | Gene Hackman | George Washington |
| Greg Kinnear | Harry Hopkins | Howard Baker |
| Hugh Grant | Imam Khomeini | Indiana Jones |
| Jack Coleman | Jackie Chan | James Baker |
| James Steinberg | Jarno Trulli | Jason Kendall |
| Jerry Siegel | Jesse Ventura | John Conyers |
| John Huston | John McGraw | John Paul Jones |
| Julie Christie | Justin Timberlake | Katie Hoff |
| Kelly Clarkson | Landon Donovan | Larry McReynolds |
| Lionel Messi | Lord Mandelson | Mark Hatfield |
| Martin Demichelis | Meredith Whitney | Mike Schmidt |
| Neil Armstrong | Ottoman Sultan | Patrick Cowan |
| Penelope Cruz | Peter Bergen | Prince William |
| Randi Weingarten | Robert Kubica | Samantha Ronson |
| Sarah Ferguson | South Vietnam | Stephen Hendry |
| Steve Cohen | Steve Jobs | Terry Nichols |
| Troy Murphy | Wayne Rooney | William Wallace |

each participator is to randomly select ten queries from the query list as shown in Table 5.3 to search news information and evaluate the performance according to our predefined evaluating criterions.

There are some parameters to be set in advance. We set $\alpha = 0.5$, $\beta = 0.3$, $\gamma = 0.4$, $\lambda_P = \lambda_E = \lambda_X = \lambda_Z = 0.001$, $\lambda_C = 10$, $\lambda_S = 25$, and $d = 100$. The initial values for **P** are set by Random Acol [45] through averaging 1,000 columns randomly chosen from **R**. The matrices **E**, **X**, and **Z** are initialized similarly.

## *Comparison on Retrieval Performance*

We perform the experimental comparisons among six news search systems. They are MMPNR considering both person correlation and event correlation (our proposed system), MMPNR-Text only employing text information in correlation initialization, EPMF only considering event correlation, PPMF only considering person

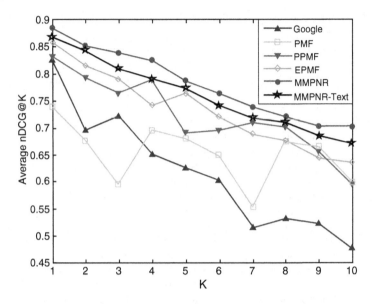

**Fig. 5.7** Comparison on nDCG@k

correlation, and PMF with no consideration of both correlations. Additionally, Google News search engine[5] is employed as a baseline in the comparison.

In the first experiment, the participators were asked to search on the six systems to give scores about the relevance to queries as shown in Table 5.3. The ranking quality is measured using the average nDCG@$k$ for $k$ from 1 to 10. Figure 5.7 presents the average scores on the top ten events returned for each query. Figure 5.8 presents the corresponding gains of ranking quality over baseline. From Figs. 5.7 and 5.8, we can draw the following observations. First, all the factor analysis-based methods achieve the superior effectiveness over Google News, which only considers the text relevance to a given query. Among these, the proposed MMPNR achieves the best performance by simultaneously employing the three correlations and multimodal information analysis. Second, the worse performance is achieved by MMPNR-Text compared with MMPNR. This demonstrates that the process of face detection and matching is useful in the entity correlation initialization. Third, with additional consideration of entity (or event) correlation, PPMF (or EPMF) obtains more attractive performance than PMF. Fourth, PMF is better than Google news when $k$ is no less than 4, because PMF is able to find more relevant results by mining hidden correlations between entities and events. However, when $k$ is less than 4, i.e., the top 1–3 returned results are considered, a little worse performance is obtain by PMF compared with Google News. It is understandable

---

[5]http://news.google.com/

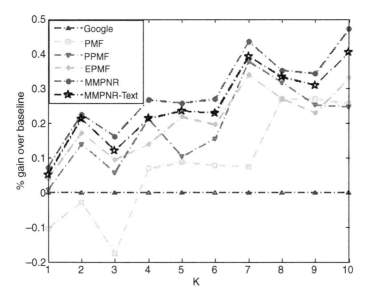

**Fig. 5.8** Gains over Google news

because Google News adopt a more comprehensive ranking strategy (e.g., PageRank and log analysis in search) to measure the query-oriented relevance.

Second, we evaluate our system from a subjective view. While browsing results of the ten queries, each participator was asked to give a score within the interval [1, 5] (the bigger the score is, the better the result is) based on the following aspects:

- *Relevancy*: How about the whole relevancy between the results and queries? Are the results useful?
- *Person Relevancy*: How about the social network? Are the presented persons relative to the query person?
- *Event Relevancy*: How about the event relation map? How about the relevance among the presented events?
- *Efficiency*: How long does the system cost to return the search results to users for each query?
- *Friendliness*: Do the users enjoy the interface? Does the interface seem comfortable?
- *Convenience*: Is it convenient to search and browse the news?
- *Multiplicity*: Does the system show users many kinds of information? Can it present users multi-view effectively?

We average the scores given by participators for each aspect and present the average scores in Fig. 5.9. It is obvious that users prefer the interface of our system and our system can give relevant and various results conveniently and efficiently. Additionally, the users are satisfied with the presented social network and the

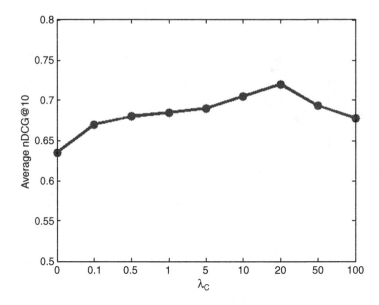

**Fig. 5.9** The average scores of the subjective evaluation

relevant event map, which demonstrates that the MPMF model is effective to mine the hidden relationships. Additionally, our system is useful and convenient for user to understand news events.

In summary, the above experiments demonstrate that our system is able to mine more relations and give users multi-view relations. They can more easily understand the news events and obtain more information about their queries.

## *Discussion on Parameters of $\lambda_C$ and $\lambda_S$*

The main advantage of our person-centric news retrieval is that it incorporates the social network information and event correlation information. In our model, parameters $\lambda_C$ and $\lambda_S$ balance the information from the person-event relation matrix, person social network, and event correlation matrix. If $\lambda_C = 0$ (or $\lambda_S = 0$), it is equivalent to EPMF (or PPMF), respectively. Figures 5.10 and 5.11 show the impacts of $\lambda_C$ (while holding $\lambda_S = 25$ fixed) and $\lambda_S$ (while holding $\lambda_C = 10$ fixed) on nDCG@10, respectively, which demonstrate that the values of $\lambda_C$ and $\lambda_S$ impact the results. As $\lambda_C$ increases, the average nDCG@10 increases at first, but when $\lambda_C$ surpasses a certain threshold, the average nDCG@10 decreases with further increase of the value of $\lambda_C$. The impact of parameter $\lambda_S$ is similar to $\lambda_C$. This phenomenon coincides with the intuition that purely using the person-event relation matrix, the person social network or the event correlation matrix cannot generate better performance that fusing these three sources.

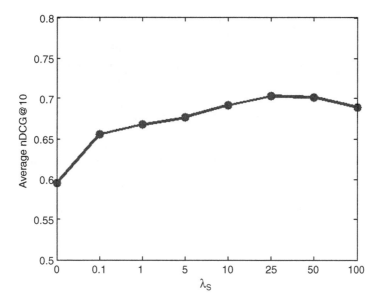

**Fig. 5.10**  Impact of parameter $\lambda_C$ on MMPNR

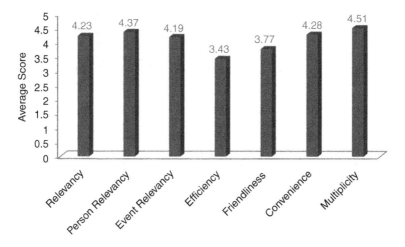

**Fig. 5.11**  Impact of parameter $\lambda_S$ on MMPNR

## Conclusion

In this chapter, we propose a news retrieval approach based on multimodal analysis and multi-correlation exploration. We explore the information of both text and corresponding images for the initialization of entity correlation. In particular, we adopt statistical co-occurrences in the two modalities to derive the news entity correlations. To fully employ the multi-correlation information, namely, news entity correlation, news event correlation, and entity-event correlation, we proposed the MPMF model to complete and refine the three correlation and further to vividly present the ranking news events and news persons relevant to a given query. Finally, the reasonable and comprehensive evaluations are performed to demonstrate the effectiveness of our system.

The MPMF model opens a broad way for future improvement and extension. As part of future work, we will investigate the following directions: (1) kernel-based representation for the two low-dimensional vectors; (2) considering the information diffusion between persons (events). We believe the issues would lead us to more promising results.

**Acknowledgements** This work was supported by 973 Program (Project No. 2010CB327905) and National Natural Science Foundation of China (Grant No. 60903146 and 90920303).

# References

1. Salakhutdinov, R., Mnih, A.: Probabilistic matrix factorization. Adv. Neural Inf. Process. Syst. **20**, 1257–1264 (2008)
2. Lü, L., Zhou, T.: Link prediction in complex networks: a survey. CoRR 1010.0725 (2010)
3. Resnik, P.: Using information content to evaluate semantic similarity in a taxonomy. In: International Joint Conferences on Artificial Intelligence, Montréal, pp. 448–453 (1995)
4. Hindle, D.: Noun classification from predicate-argument structures. In: Annual Meeting of the Association for Computational Linguistics, Pittsburgh, pp. 268–275 (1990)
5. Frakes, W.B., Baeza-Yates, R.: Information Retrieval: Data Structures and Algorithms. Prentice Hall PTR, Englewood (1992)
6. Lin, D.: An information-theoretic definition of similarity. In: Proceedings of the Fifteenth International Conference on Machine Learning, pp. 296–304. San Francisco, CA, USA (1998)
7. Bennett, C.H., Gács, P., Li, M., Vitáyi, P.M.B., Zurek, W.H.: Information distance. IEEE Trans. Inf. Theory **44**(4), 1407–1423 (1998)
8. Li, M., Chen, X., Li, X., Ma, B., Vitányi, P.M.B.: The similarity metrix. IEEE Trans. Inf. Theory **50**(12), 3250–3264 (2004)
9. Pan, R., Zhou, Y., Chao, B., Liu, N.N., Lukose, R., Scholz, M., Yang, Q.: One-class collaborative filtering. In: Proceedings of IEEE International Conference on Data Mining, pp. 502–511. Washington, DC, USA (2006)
10. Sarukkai, R.R.: Link prediction and path analysis using markov chains. Comput. Netw. **33**, 377–386 (2000)
11. Zhu, J., Hong, J., Hughes, J.G.: Using markov chains for link prediction in adaptive web sites. In: Proceedings of the 13th ACM conference on Hypertext and Hypermedia, College Park (2002)
12. Popescul, A., Ungar, L.H.: Statistical relational learning for link prediction. In: Workshop on Learning Statistical Models from Relational Data. ACM Press, New York (2003)
13. Yu, K., Chu, W., Yu, S., Tresp, V., Xu Z.: Stochastic relational models for discriminative link prediction. In: Advance in Neural Information Processing Systems, vol. 19. MIT Press, Cambridge (2007)
14. Bilgic, M., Namata, G., Getoor, L.: Combining collective classification and link prediction. In: Workshop of IEEE International Conference on Data Mining, Omaha, pp. 381–386 (2007)
15. Carmi, S., Havlin, S., Kirkpatrick, S., Shavitt, Y., Shir, E.: A model of Internet topology using k-shell decomposition. Proc. Natl. Acad. Sci. U.S.A. **104**(27), 11150–11154 (2007)

16. Ravasz, E., Somera, A.L., Mongru, D.A., Olyvai, Z.N., Barabási, A.-L.: Hierarchical organization of modularity in metabolic networks. Science **297**(5586), 1551–1555 (2007)
17. Zhou, C., Zemanovaá, L., Zamora, G., Hilgetag, C.C., Kurths, J.: Hierarchical organization unveiled by functional connectivity in complex brain networks. Phys. Rev. Lett. **97**(23), 238103 (2006)
18. Redner, S.: Networks: teasing out the missing links. Nature **453**(7191), 47–48 (2008)
19. Clauset, A., Moore, C., Newman, M.E.J.: Hierarchical structure and the prediction of missing links in networks. Nature **453**, 98–101 (2008)
20. Guimerà, R., Sales-Pardo, M.: Missing and spurious interactions and the reconstruction of complex networks. Proc. Natl. Acad. Sci. U.S.A. **106**(52), 22073–22078 (2009)
21. Newman, M.E.J.: Assortative mixing in networks. Proc. Natl. Acad. Sci. U.S.A. **89**(20), 208701–208704 (2002)
22. Newman, M.E.J.: Mixing patterns in networks. Proc. Natl. Acad. Sci. U.S.A. **67**(2), 026126–026138 (2003)
23. Pastor-Satorras, R., Vázquez, A., Vesspignani, A.: Dynamical and correlation properties of the Internet. Proc. Natl. Acad. Sci. U.S.A. **87**(25), 258701–258704 (2001)
24. Vázquez, A., Pastor-Satorras, R., Vespignani, A.: Large-scale topological and dynamical properties of the Internet. Proc. Natl. Acad. Sci. U.S.A. **65**(6), 066130–066131 (2002)
25. Friedman, N., Getoor, L., Koller, D., Pfeffer, A.: Learning probabilistic relational models. In: Proceedings of the 16th International Joint Conference on Artificial Intelligence, Stockholm (1999)
26. Heckerman, D., Meek, C., Koller, D.: Probabilistic entity-relationship models, PRMs, and plate models. In: Proceedings of the 21st International Conference on Machine Learning, Banff (2004)
27. Yu, K., Chu, W., Yu, S., Tresp, V., Xu, Z.: Stochastic relational models for discriminative link prediction. In: Proceedings of Neural Information Precessing Systems. MIT Press, Cambridge (2006)
28. Heckerman, D., Geiger, D., Chickering, D.: Learning Bayeaian networks: the combination of knowledge and statistical data. Mach. Learn. **20**(3), 197–243 (1995)
29. Taskar, B., Wong, M.-F., Abbeel, P., Koller, D.: Link prediction in relational data. In: Proceedings of Neural Information Precessing Systems. MIT Press, Cambridge (2004)
30. Heckerman, D., Chickering, D.M., Meek, C., Rounthwaite, R., Kadie, C.: Dependency networks for inference, collaborative filtering, and data visualization. J. Mach. Learn. Res. **1**, 49–75 (2000)
31. Yu, K., Chu, W., Yu, S., Tresp, V., Xu, Z.: Stochastic relational models for discriminative link prediction. In: Proceedings of Neural Information Precessing Systems. MIT Press, Cambridge (2006)
32. Spearman, C.: "General Intelligence", objectively determined and measured. Am. J. Psychol. **15**(2), 201–292 (1904)
33. Zhu, S., Yu, K., Chi, Y., Gong, Y.: Combining content and link for classification using matrix factorization. In: Proceedings of the 30th Conference on Research and Development in Information Retrieval, Amsterdam (2007)
34. Hofmann, T.: Probabilistic latent semantic analysis. In: Proceedings of the 22nd Annual International ACM SIGIR Conference on Research and Development in Information Retrieval, pp. 50–57. New York, NY, USA (1999)
35. Marlin, B.: Modeling user rating profiles for collaborative filtering. In: Processing of the Neural Information Processing Systems, Vancouver (2003)
36. Marlin, B., Zemel, R.S.: The multiple multiplicative factor model for collaborative filtering. In: Proceedings of the 21st International Conference on Machine Learning, Banff (2004)
37. Ma, H., Yang, H., Lyu, M.R., King, I.: Sorec: social recommendation using probabilistic matrix factorization. In: Proceeding of the 17th ACM Conference on Information and Knowledge Management, Napa Valley (2008)
38. Chi, Y., Zhu, S., Gong, Y.: Probabilistic polyadic factorization and its application to personalized recommendation. In: Proceeding of the 17th ACM Conference on Information and Knowledge Management, Napa Valley (2008)

39. Lin, Y.-R., Sun, J., Castro, P., Konuru, R., Sundaram, H., Kelliher, A.: MetaFac: community discovery via relational hypergraph factorization. In: Proceedings of the 15th ACM SIGKDD International Conference on Knowledge Discovery and Data mining, Paris (2009)
40. Sekine, S., Sudo, K., Nobata, C.: Extended named entity hierarchy. In: Proceedings of the 3rd International Conference on Language Resources and Evaluation, Canary Islands, Spain (2002)
41. Liu, C., Yuen, J., Torralba, A., Sivic, J., Freeman, W.T.: SIFT flow: dense correspondence across different scenes. In: Proceedings of the 10th European Conference on Computer Vision, Marseille (2008)
42. Dueck, D., Frey, B.: Probabilistic sparse matrix factorization. Technical Report PSI TR 2004-023 (2004)
43. Tipping, M.E., Bishop, C.M.: Probabilistic principal component analysis. J. R. Stat. Soc. Ser. B, **61**, 611–622 (1997)
44. Järvelin, K., Kekäl"ainen, J.: Cumulated gain-based evaluation of IR techniques. ACM Trans. Inf. Syst. **20**(4), 422–446 (2002)
45. Langville, A.N.: Algorithms for the nonnegative matrix factorization in text mining. In: SSIAM Southeastern Section Annual Meeting. Charleston, SC, USA (2005)

# Chapter 6
# Mining Micro-blogs: Opportunities and Challenges

**Yang Liao, Masud Moshtaghi, Bo Han, Shanika Karunasekera,
Ramamohanarao Kotagiri, Timothy Baldwin, Aaron Harwood,
and Philippa Pattison**

**Abstract** This chapter investigates whether and how micro-messaging technologies such as Twitter messages can be harnessed to obtain valuable information. The interesting characteristics of micro-blogging services, such as being user oriented, provide opportunities for different applications to use the content of these sites to their advantage. However, the same characteristics become the weakness of these sites when it comes to data modelling and analysis of the messages. These sites contains very large amount of unstructured, noisy with false or missing data which make the task of data mining difficult. This chapter first reviews some of the potential applications of the micro-messaging services and then provides some insight into different challenges faced by data mining applications. Later in this chapter, characteristics of a real data collected from the Twitter are analysed. At the end of chapter, application of micro-blogging services is shown by three different case studies.

## Introduction

With the wide uptake of the Internet, micro-blogging services such as Tumblr and Twitter have become popular means of communication. Most of today's popular social networking sites such as Facebook and MySpace also support micro-

Y. Liao (✉) • M. Moshtaghi • B. Han • S. Karunasekera • R. Kotagiri • T. Baldwin • A. Harwood
Department of Computer Science and Software Engineering, The University of Melbourne, Melbourne, VIC, Australia
e-mail: liaoy@student.unimelb.edu.au; m.moshtaghi@student.unimelb.edu.au; hanb@student.unimelb.edu.au; karus@unimelb.edu.au; kotagiri@unimelb.edu.au; tbaldwin@unimelb.edu.au; aharwood@unimelb.edu.au

P. Pattison
Faculty of Medicine, Dentistry and Health Sciences Psychological Sciences, The University of Melbourne, Melbourne, VIC, Australia
e-mail: pepatt@unimelb.edu.au

A. Abraham (ed.), *Computational Social Networks: Mining and Visualization*,
DOI 10.1007/978-1-4471-4054-2_6, © Springer-Verlag London 2012

blogging features. Superficially, the main factor differentiating micro-blogging from traditional blogging is the limited message size, with a hard limit on messages in micro-blogging services typically of around 150 characters. Micro-blogs have evolved to include rich social networking features, however, most notably via the ability to "follow" another user and thereby receive the feed of all messages posted by them. Via this social networking feature, information propagation in micro-blogs resembles epidemic propagation in social communities. The highly connected nature of these dynamic networks and the explosive nature of message passing lead to rapid and efficient data dissemination and very targeted information fluxes.

Although micro-blogging technologies were originally created as a means of personal communication, they have many unique characteristics that offer opportunities beyond simple communication and make them a ripe target for data mining. Some applications that have recently been explored over micro-blog data are disaster detection [22], trend identification [4], and online marketing [6]. However, effective mining of micro-blogging sites have associated challenges.

In this chapter, we discuss and demonstrate the opportunities and the challenges associated with data mining in micro-blogs, with specific focus on Twitter. We classify the information generated in micro-blogs into three categories and identify important characteristics of information in each of them. A high-level data mining architecture for micro-blogs is then presented. We identify a number of applications which fall into three application areas: event detection, trend identification, and social behaviour analysis. We analyse characteristics of Twitter data based on a data set which we collected over a 4 week period. This chapter also presents three case studies based on Twitter data. Based on the observation that the number of messages related to an event increases due to elevated user interest in the event, the first case study demonstrates how epidemic models combined with frequency-domain deconvolution techniques can be used for event identification. The second case study demonstrates how a Markov chain model and a distance computation algorithm can be used for identifying social clusters. The third case study demonstrates how the frequency of keywords within clusters can be used for trend identification.

Section "Characteristics" describes some of the characteristics of micro-blogs. Section "Opportunities" discusses how these characteristics provide opportunities for data mining to support different classes of applications. The challenges faced in text mining micro-blogs are discussed in section "Text Mining Challenges." Section "Analysis: Twitter Data" shows the analysis of Twitter data we collected over a 4-week period, and section "Case Studies" shows three different case studies of using Twitter data for different applications.

## Characteristics

Micro-blogs provide a means for users to generate content and connections. In this section, we briefly review the general characteristics of micro-blogs and classify these characteristics into three categories: *Users, Social Connections, and Messages.*

## User Properties

Users are the content generators of micro-blogs. Due to privacy issues and the fear of identity theft, users usually limit the public information they share about themselves to fields such as name, location, and spoken language(s). Privacy also affects the reliability of the shared information. For example, a user providing a bogus location could result in erroneous interpretation of information in the content they post. In addition, micro-blogs commonly contain *virtual users* with a very short active life as a means of identity obfuscation. For example, a business owner might want to start a rumour about the quality of the products of a rival company using multiple virtual users. This property further reduces the reliability of the data on micro-blogs. It also underscores the importance of selecting data analysis approaches which can deal with uncertainty in the information.

Similar to other types of social networks, behavioural properties of users in micro-blogs change with time. Level of activity, location, and even the language used by the user to share information may change. Also, users come and go with time.

## Social Connections

Social connections create the connectivity in micro-blogs. Social connections in a micro-blog can be classified into two categories: *social links* and *social interactions*. Social connections are highly dynamic and are created and deleted between users over time.

*Social Links:* These links are created between two users and last till one or both users decide to end the relation. These links are either *bidirectional* or *unidirectional*. Bidirectional links, also known as friendship links, are mutual connections where both users are interested in the content generated by each other. On the other hand, with unidirectional links—also known as follower links—one user is interested in the content generated by the other, but not vice versa. Social links can also be classified into *direct* and *indirect* links. While direct links directly connect users, it is also possible for users to be connected indirectly through their selection of followed threads.

Micro-blogs usually contain large numbers of social links. The number of social links in a network directly affects the propagation of content, and as such, social structure is an important aspect of micro-blogs.

*Social Interactions:* Social interactions are one-off links between two users, regardless of social links. Interactions in micro-blogs are made via messages. One form of such interaction is a user posting a message in reply to another post or user in a network. Other forms of interaction are relaying another user message and mentioning the name of other users in the body of a message. Social links are potentially more socially meaningful than one-off interactions.

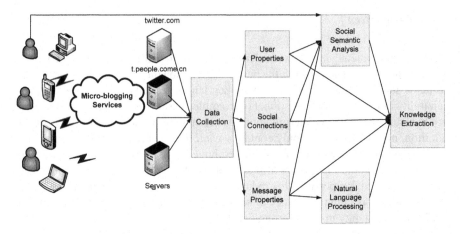

**Fig. 6.1** Schematic representation of the activities related to data mining in micro-blogs

## Message Properties

In micro-blogs, messages—also known as *status updates* or *posts*—are short and usually limited to around 150 characters. These short messages allow users to share personal and professional information, as well as links to other sites. The length limit forces users to be succinct in expressing the information they want to share, which in turn leads to various linguistic devices for abbreviating the message length, and creates challenges for language processing techniques, as we survey in section "Text Mining Challenges."

Based on the above classification of the data in micro-blogs, we propose the high-level data mining architecture shown in Fig. 6.1 for identification of events and trends from mining micro-blogs. As shown, the main activities involved are data collection, natural language processing (NLP), social semantic analysis, and knowledge extraction. The first step in data mining process is data collection. The data from micro-blogs can be collected using web crawlers and official APIs. Though a complete dump is very useful for knowledge extraction, privacy constraints and the sheer volume of data mean there are access restrictions on the data, influencing the design of data mining techniques. Our basic approach is to use NLP techniques and social semantic analysis to extract features from raw data of users and their connections as well as message information in micro-blogs, for further processing for knowledge discovery.

## Opportunities

Several characteristics of the data available in micro-blogs make them appealing for applications. In this section, we outline a number of possible applications, which fall into three broad categories: event detection, trend identification, and social group identification. Events correspond to real-world happenings which usually have a short-term interest period among micro-bloggers; *event detection* techniques try to predict or identify an event based on user messages. *Trend identification* relates to analysis of the effects of real-life developments on user opinions and behaviour. Finally, *social behaviour analysis* deals with relations between users and tries to group users based on their social links, social interactions, and interests. Note that these three categories might be used in tandem in a single application. For example, an event detection technique might be used to identify an event, then the extent of the event can be predicted by trend inference or identification techniques, while social group analysis could aid in the preparation of a response.

## *Event Detection*

Micro-messages tend to be constrained to essential facts due to the enforced brevity, which makes automated analysis more efficient. These characteristics can be exploited to help identify and provide rapid response in emergency situations, including natural disasters such as bush fires and accidental or deliberate chemical, biological, and radiological releases. Our first case study in section "Case Studies" (quantitative analysis of information propagation in Twitter) is used for identifying the new events.

*Disaster Detection:* Micro-blogs can play an important role as an emergency alert system. For example, during the recent Haiti earthquake, Mumbai terror attacks, and political unrest in Iran, many people found Twitter to be a useful means of getting real-time updates on the situation. In some recent natural disasters, these networks are reported to have been able to even beat commercial news networks such as CNN and BBC with situation updates. Because of the effectiveness of these social networks, some organizations (Red Cross and some government agencies in the USA) have made use of these networks to promptly provide updates on evacuation routes and other information.

During times of major disasters, telecommunication networks have been known to fail due to traffic overload. Internet micro-messaging communication technologies are able to alleviate traffic overloads due to queued transmission and the limited message size. The failure to provide adequate warnings to affected communities on Black Saturday in Australia was one of the key contributors to the large number of casualties in the bush fire. Therefore, investigating the suitability of these emerging micro-messaging technologies to complement the existing communication techniques is of vital importance.

In recent work, Twitter has been leveraged to detect earthquakes and send alerts to relevant communities ahead of impending shockwaves [22]. In this work, an event detection algorithm was developed on the basis of Twitter users being social sensors for a disaster. First, the posting time and volume of earthquake-related tweets was modelled as an exponential distribution, and a Kalman filter and Particle filters were applied for location estimation.

*Anomalous Change Detection:* Internet-based syndromic surveillance using predefined keywords such as disease symptoms has been used in the area of epidemiology, as a possible means of early detection of infectious disease outbreaks [4]. Similarly, rapid increases in message traffic related to specific keywords occurring in micro-messaging systems may be used to detect anomalous events.

Research has shown the potential use of micro-blogs in providing early warning for events like swine flu outbreak [18, 21]. In addition, first story detection within the Twitter stream has been addressed in recent work [17]. By finding the relaxed nearest neighbour of a tweet, an optimized locality sensitive hashing (LSH) algorithm is used to meet the need of high-volume data in speed and memory usage.

## Trend Identification

In many applications, we are interested in finding the effects of a phenomenon, such as its extent or user opinions on it. The effects of a phenomenon can be analysed through trend identification in micro-blogs. In trend identification, unlike event detection, the trigger is known a priori and the focus is on its consequence.

*Opinion Polls:* Micro-blogs are a great way for users to express their opinion. Analysis of the sentiments of users and extraction of meaningful information from user messages by means of NLP techniques enables the determination of user opinions. This information can be used as a supplement to traditional polling [3]. Separately, conventional positive/negative sentiment detection over micro-blog messages has been investigated [2].

*Marketing:* Market analysis provides feedback to companies. Mining micro-blogs may facilitate market analysis by providing cheaper, faster, and more comprehensive information about their products and market campaigns. In section "Case Studies," we demonstrate how to identify short-term events using an epidemic model; the same methodology is useful in collecting feedback for short-term marketing campaigns, such as immediate reactions to a new advertisement. On the other hand, the long-term trend of the market may be observed using the approach that we introduce in the third case study, where Twitter messages are used to predict attendance trends at the World Expo 2010 in Shanghai, China.

## Social Group Identification

It is interesting to study reciprocated and repeated unidirectional relations between users of a micro-blog through analysis of social connections between users, for example to find out who is the most influential user in the network or what makes one user follow another. User profile and network analysis can offer hints in this regard.

TwitterRank [27] has been proposed to determine the most influential users on different topics in Twitter. The topologies of Twitter users can also be analysed for relationship distribution [13]. Alternatively, it is possible to develop recommender systems for users to recommend a set of users that a given user is likely to benefit from following [8].

In our second case study, we introduce an experiment for grouping users into clusters by measuring the velocity of information flows between them; the results show that users in the same cluster have same or similar backgrounds, such as geological location, interests, and age groups.

## Text Mining Challenges

Micro-blog messages differ from conventional text. They feature many unique symbols like mentions, hashtags, and urls and the popular use of colloquial words and Internet slang. Message quality varies greatly, from newswire-like utterances (e.g. *The United Nations Security Council will hold an emergency meeting Sunday on tensions in the Korean Peninsula*) to babble (e.g. *O_o haha wow*). In terms of text processing, there are significant research challenges, as outlined below.

First, popular micro-blogs such as Twitter attract users from a variety of language backgrounds and are thus highly multilingual in content. This language diversity poses obstacles in text processing, as most text processing tools such as word tokenizers and syntactic parsers are language dependent. Thus, it is important to perform language identification before further text processing.

Second, typos, ad hoc abbreviations, phonetic substitutions, and ungrammatical structures in micro-blog messages hamper text processing tools [7, 20, 24]. For example, given the Twitter message *I was talkin bout u lol* (or in standard English: *I was talking about you (lol).*), the Stanford parser [5, 12] analyses *talkin bout u* as a noun phrase rather than a verb phrase. Noise of this type restricts the performance of text mining without proper normalization or inbuilt robustness in the text processing.

Third, micro-blog data is user generated and as such subjective and, at times, unreliable in content. Anyone who can access the micro-blog service can post a message, possibly containing false or offensive information. The unreliability of micro-blog data can cause grief for applications such as information extraction and analysis of the authority and trustworthiness of different users/messages is a significant challenge.

In addition, algorithm efficiency is critical for data mining over popular micro-blogs due to the high rate of data generation: around 65 millions tweets were posted on Twitter per day in June 2010, for example [25]. In order to keep pace with the real-time stream of data, processing time must be kept to a minimum, particularly for real-time applications like event alert services where the response time is critical [17].

In summary, although micro-blogs are a highly attractive target for knowledge extraction due to the large amount of real-time data generated by their users, there are many challenges associated with text mining these sites.

## Analysis: Twitter Data

In this section, we present an analysis of a data set gathered from Twitter, with focus on the analysis of the characteristics of the messages introduced in section "Characteristics." We start by introducing the data collection process.

### Data Collection

Data from Twitter can be gathered by crawling the Twitter website, or via a set of official APIs. Full public information about the messages and users can only be obtained through APIs. Twitter APIs consist of a REST API and a Streaming API. The REST API supports keyword or user ID-based querying but is subject to rate limiting, currently set to 350 requests per hour for authenticated users. The Streaming API provides access to a random sample of 5% of public status updates from its users. The results reported in this chapter are based on two different data sets we gathered from Twitter.

*Data Set 1:* This data set was collected in a 1-moth period starting from the 26th of October 2010 using the Twitter Streaming API. We collected about 200 million messages generated by around 15 million users during this period. The results reported in the remainder of this section and, expect where explicitly mentioned, the case studies are based on this data set.

*Data Set 2:* This data set consists of messages in the Chinese language, collected over a period of 5 months from April to September 2010, using an in-house crawler. By searching for particular Chinese keywords relating to the World Expo 2010, we were able to constrain messages to the Chinese language and specifically posts relating to the Expo.

### User Information

Twitter has a very large number of users spread across different countries. In 2010, 100 million new Twitter accounts were created. These users are from different age groups, despite Twitter being targeted at a young demographic. Ten million visitors to the Twitter website in February 2009 were over 35 years old. In the US, 10%

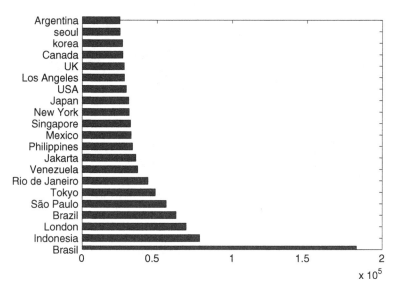

**Fig. 6.2** Top locations specified by Twitter users

of users are aged between 55 and 64, almost equalling the number of users aged between 18 and 24 [19]. This shows the diversity of the population contributing content to Twitter.

The location information provided by users shows their geographical diversity. However, this information is specified by the user and can be both unreliable and inconsistent in format/granularity. For example, a user in San Francisco may list their location as *USA, CA, CA USA, San Francisco, San Francisco CA, San Francisco CA US(A)*, etc. The top 20 locations declared by users in the collected data set are shown in Fig. 6.2.

Figure 6.3 (left) depicts the distribution of spoken language(s) using user-declared information. Our own analysis of Twitter messages based on automatic language identification [1] over a random subset of 600,000 messages points to a higher diversity of languages used on Twitter (see Fig. 6.3 (right)). This language diversity shows the global reach of Twitter and emphasizes the need for language-specific methods for processing Twitter data.

## Connection Information

An important characteristic of Twitter users is their interconnectivity or *social links*. In Twitter, a user can create a social link by *following* another user or adding a user as a *friend*. Figure 6.4 shows the distribution of the number of followers and friends in our data set. The data contains over two billion social links.

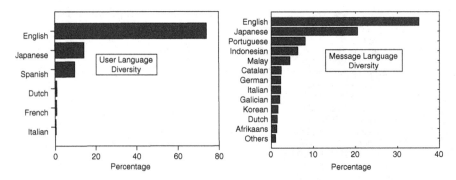

**Fig. 6.3** The language diversity among Twitter users specified by the users (*left*) and obtained by a language identification tool (*right*)

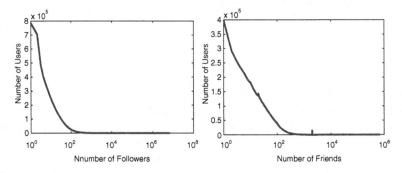

**Fig. 6.4** Distribution of the number of followers (*left*) and friends (*right*) in the Twitter data set

Social interactions are more complicated to infer from messages, and it requires analysis of the message content. Twitter provides some additional information that helps identification of social interactions. These additional fields indicate whether a message is in response to another message or user. Thirty-four percent of the messages in our data set are responses. Twitter users themselves first introduced this feature informally by prefixing user names with @, but this is now officially supported by Twitter.

## Message Information

Messages in Twitter, known as *tweets*, are limited to 140 characters. A tweet can be *re-tweeted* by other users, to share the content with followers. Re-tweeting is a simple mechanism of message dissemination. Beside the content of the message, Twitter APIs provide additional information about the message. In this section, we briefly review these complementary fields that can aid data analysis and knowledge extraction.

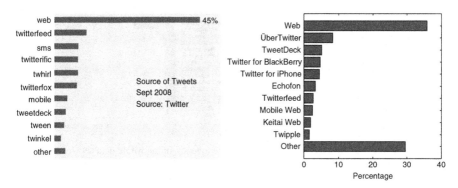

**Fig. 6.5** Client applications used to access Twitter reported by Twitter 2008 (*left*) and obtained from our data set (*right*)

## Complementary Information

The date and time of each message is an attribute that is included with each tweet. This data can be used along with the message content to find popular trends among users and how they evolve over time. Another piece of information optionally provided with each tweet is the geolocation of the user when posting the message. This data is important for many applications, notably event detection and emergency response. Many modern smartphones have built-in GPS, which facilitates geotagging. Therefore, the number of tweets with geolocation information is expected to rise with the increasing number of users accessing Twitter via a smartphone. Figure 6.5 shows a 10% decrease in the number of users accessing Twitter via the web interface and an increase in the usage of smartphones and custom-made applications to access Twitter from 2008.

## Message Content

To conclude this section, we analyse the contents of English messages. Messages contain a lot of information and are usually the focus of data mining applications. Natural language processing and text mining techniques are widely used to extract useful information from the messages. Challenges faced by these techniques are discussed in section "Text Mining Challenges." In Twitter, user-generated features such as specifying the topic of a tweet with hashtags (#) help to categorize the message content. According to [16], around only 2% of tweets in 2008 contained hashtags, while in our collection 12% of tweets contain hashtags. Hashtags can be used to identify long- and short-term trends. Short-term trends quickly reach a peak number of messages and then drop off. Long-term trends, on the other hand, take longer to reach their peak and then to dissipate. When a subject becomes popular among users, hashtags related to that subject become frequent in the data. Figure 6.6 (left) shows top 15 popular hashtags in the data set. If we want to see short-term

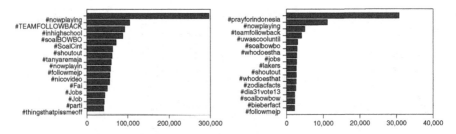

**Fig. 6.6** Popular hashtags and their corresponding frequency in the whole data set (*left*) and in a 1 day period (*right*)

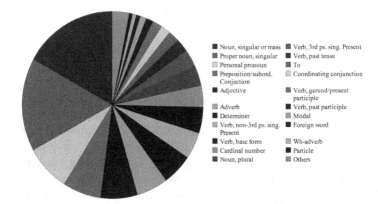

**Fig. 6.7** Part-of-speech distribution in our sample of English tweets

trends, we need to look at frequent hashtags in a smaller time window. Figure 6.6 (right) shows popular hashtags on the 27th of October 2010. In comparison to the most popular hashtags overall, we can see hashtags related to more short-term events such as those corresponding to a natural disaster in Indonesia and election in Brazil. Therefore, in order to capture short-term trends, smaller time windows should be considered for data analysis.

Though hashtags are an important feature in data mining applications, they are not usually sufficient for trend analysis. NLP techniques and keyword analysis are required to complement this analysis. In terms of language-specific information, the part-of-speech distribution of 3.6 million words[1] is listed in Fig. 6.7. The Penn part-of-speech tagset [23] used by the Stanford parser treats different morphological variations of the same word class as different types, e.g. verbs are separated by inflectional type.

---

[1]The data is based on the output of the Stanford parser over a 0.3-million sample of English tweets, as identified using automatic language identification over our primary data set.

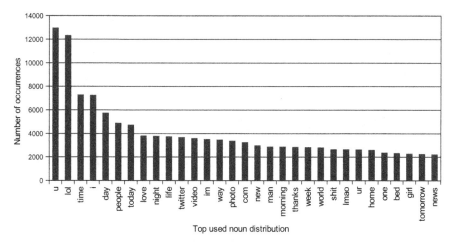

**Fig. 6.8** Top 30 nouns in our sample of English tweets

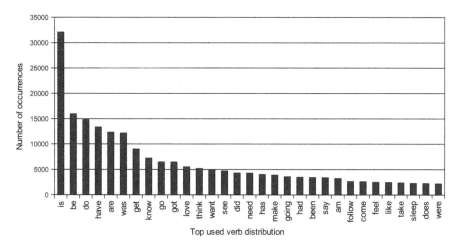

**Fig. 6.9** Top 30 verbs in our sample of English tweets

Unsurprisingly, nouns and proper nouns occupy the top 2 positions in our data, followed by personal pronouns, prepositions, and adjectives.

In addition, the top 30 most frequent nouns, verbs, and adjectives are listed in Figs. 6.8, 6.9, and 6.10, respectively. These figures indicate the language preference of Twitter users and reflect the trends of public attention at the time of data collection. Especially in Fig. 6.10, sentiment-bearing adjectives like *good, happy, great, bad, nice, funny, amazing*, and *awesome* are commonplace.

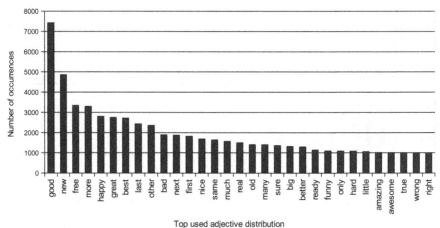

Top used adjective distribution

**Fig. 6.10** Top 30 adjectives in our sample of English tweets

# Case Studies

In this section, we describe three case studies, each from one of the opportunity areas identified in section "Text Mining Challenges." Although the data sets used in these case studies were from Twitter, the same techniques can be used in data from other micro-blogs that have a structure similar to Twitter.

## *Case Study 1: Event Identification*

### Background

In this case study, we use an epidemic model to characterize the intensity of information flow between micro-blog users and reveal the sequence of events behind the information flows using frequency-domain deconvolution techniques. The methods shown in this case study are useful in identifying new events by mining micro-blogs.

### The Epidemic Model

Epidemic models [11] characterize the way epidemics propagate in communities, which may resemble information flow in cyberspace. Different epidemic models have been proposed, including the susceptible-infected-recovered (*SIR*) model, susceptible-infected-recovered-susceptible (*SIRS*) model, and the susceptible-infected-susceptible (*SIS*) model. We used the SIR model to analyse patterns of interest in events. In the SIR model, the population is considered to be in one of three states:

- Susceptible—when an individual is yet to be infected but is exposed to the risk of being infected.
- Infected—when an individual has been infected and is a source of infection.
- Recovered—when an individual has been infected and recovered. A recovered individual is considered to be immune to reinfection.

Based on [11], equations for predicting the number of the people in the population in the different states at a given time point are

$$\frac{dS(t)}{dt} = -\beta S(t) I(t), \tag{1}$$

$$\frac{dI(t)}{dt} = \beta S(t) I(t) - \lambda I(t), \tag{2}$$

$$\frac{dR(t)}{dt} = \lambda I(t), \tag{3}$$

where the coefficient $\beta$ denotes the expected number of people an infected individual is in contact with and $\lambda$ denotes the rate of infected individuals recovering in a given period; $S(t)$, $I(t)$, and $R(t)$, respectively, denote the number of people that are susceptible, infected, and recovered at time point $t$. Assuming a constant size for the population $S_0$, and that a given individual must be in only one of the three states at a given point in time, $S_0 \equiv S(t) + I(t) + R(t)$. The basis of $S(t)$, $I(t)$, and $R(t)$ come from [9]; different equations may be used in real-world applications to approximate the number of individuals at different states at discrete time points.

If the epidemic is seen as an impulse to the social system, $I(t)$ can be seen as a reaction function to the impulse. Figure 6.11 shows an example of the variation of $I(t)$ over time for the case of $S_0 = 10,000$, $\beta = 0.01$, $\lambda = 0.13$.

Information propagation in micro-blogs resembles the course of an epidemic. A new event is perceived (experienced directly or learned about from external sources) by a user, who is the first infected individual. The messages reporting the event are contagious to all users who were not aware of that event. After a period of cooling, a user may lose interest in the event, i.e. recover from the contagion. After losing interest, subsequent exposure to the same event will not raise the interest level of the user again, i.e. reinfection does not occur. Based on these observations, we can apply epidemic models to study the flow of information.

We assume that each user who is interested in an event posts messages about the event at a constant frequency, so that the number of messages that mention an event in a period is proportional to the number of the interested users (i.e. the "infected" individuals in the epidemic model). We name the time-dependent function of message numbers $m(t) = c \times I(t)$, where $c$ denotes the frequency of messages. Figure 6.12 illustrates the relationship between the weekly numbers of messages

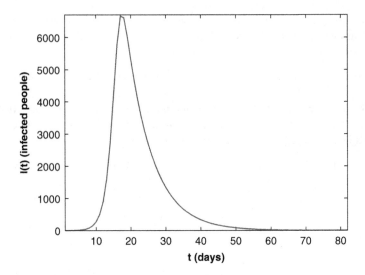

**Fig. 6.11** $I(t)$ for an ideal epidemic

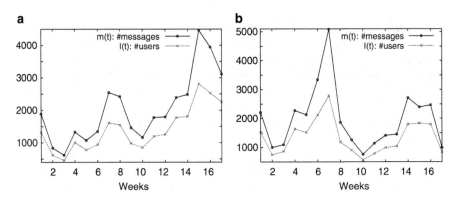

**Fig. 6.12** The relationships between numbers of messages about an event and the number of individual users who posted these messages. (**a**) Earthquake. (**b**) Expo

containing the two keywords *earthquake* (left) and *expo* (right) in our primary data set, and the corresponding numbers of individual users who posted these messages per week, namely, $m(t)$ and $I(t)$, respectively. The very high correlation coefficients between $m(t)$ and $I(t)$ give support to our assumption—$c$ in both cases is equal to 1.46.

We show in Fig. 6.13 two examples of significant events which generate reactions on a micro-blog. Since each message is published at a time point, we need to define a time granularity for grouping and counting the messages, so that the discrete messages are converted into a time-dependent density function. In our case, the granularity is set to a day. The two curves in the figure show the density of messages

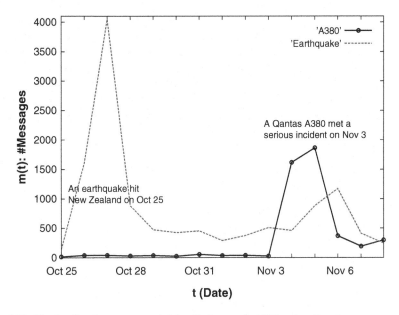

**Fig. 6.13** The density of messages containing the keywords A380 and earthquake

mentioning the keywords *A380* and *earthquake*, respectively, in the primary data set. As shown, the frequency of messages about *A380* was clearly raised by the occurrence of a mid-air incident involving a Qantas A380 on the 3rd of November. There are two peaks, differing in significance, on the curve for *earthquake*: the first peak, the more significant one, can be attributed to an earthquake, with a magnitude of 7.2, in New Zealand on the 25th of October, while the second peak can be attributed to a minor earthquake, with a magnitude of 6.1, in Indonesia on the 3rd of November. One may notice that the three peaks and the ideal epidemic model in Fig. 6.11 have similar shapes. The two earthquakes differ in magnitude, and the different demographic backgrounds of the two countries further result in differences in the number of people who are potentially concerned. As a result, we have two peaks with different $S_0$ and $\beta$ for the two earthquakes.

**Deconvolution**

The epidemic model characters the process of a single event arousing reactions from users. However, there is usually a very large number of events happening in the real world in any short period, each of which can be seen as an impulse to the system; the output of the system in that period (e.g. the number of messages mentioning these events at each time point) is thereby the accumulation of influence from all these events. Hence, each peak of message numbers may not be exclusively mapped to an event, and the outcome from minor events may be overshadowed by major events.

To recover the original events from the mixture of these footprints, we used the method of deconvolution to convert the time-series data into the frequency domain, wherein we recovered the strengths and the time points of the potential events.

The reader will recall that $m(t)$ is a time-dependent function of message numbers. This function can be seen as the convolution of pulses (the event) and reaction functions (the epidemic model). The significance of each event is the energy of the pulse, and the impressiveness/attentiveness of the event determines the parameters of the epidemic model. Therefore

$$m(t) = w(t) * e(t) + \text{noise}(t), \tag{4}$$

where $w(t)$ is the event function to be recovered and $e(t)$ is the reaction function to each impulse; it equals to $I$ when there is only one impulse to the system. Hereafter, we will use $*$ to denote the operation of convolution.

Considering the noise-free case, we used the Fourier transform to restore the original $w(t)$ from $s(t)$ by calculating

$$W(\omega) = \frac{M(\omega)}{E(\omega)}, \tag{5}$$

where $W(\omega)$, $M(\omega)$ and $E(\omega)$ are the frequency-domain functions corresponding to the three time-domain functions. From $W(\omega)$, we calculate the approximation of $w(t)$ by the inverse Fourier transform

$$\hat{w}(t) = FT^{-1}\{W(\omega)\}. \tag{6}$$

Note that there are three parameters of $e(t)$: $S_0$, $\beta$, and $\lambda$, which are unknown. However, a large number of optimistic algorithms, e.g. the Expectation-Maximization (EM) algorithm, can be used to determine $e(t)$ and $w(t)$, as demonstrated in [14] and [15] if additional information about the events is available. We used a simple approach, by trying a number of parameters and selecting the set of parameters that trims $w(t)$ most effectively.

**Natural Language Processing**

As mentioned above, micro-blogs provide no or very limited meta-data about each message. The only available information is the date of publication and, for some newer applications, the location of the publisher and a handful of tags. Therefore, NLP is necessary to extract more useful information from each message, including the topic of any events, the names of people who are involved in the event, the location where the event took place (which may differ from the location of the message author), and the date/time of the event (which may also differ from the time when the message is published).

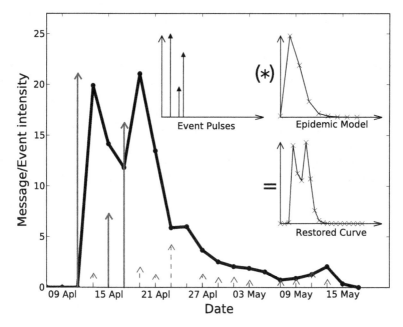

**Fig. 6.14** Using deconvolution to rationalize the events behind the messages that mentioned *Yushu* in the given period. The symbol ∗ denotes convolution. Note that the small chart of the restored curve is the result of convolution of the identified events and the ideal epidemic model, which is very similar to the trend of the observed messages

NLP is particularly critical for processing micro-blog messages in languages such as Chinese and Japanese, which are non-segmenting languages which do not represent word breaks in their orthography. In our case, we use NLP to split sentences into words to identify the names of locations that are mentioned in the messages. In this case study, we used the location name as a keyword filter to efficiently removing irrelevant messages.

**Data Analysis**

The events were identified by a two-step routine. First, we calculated the mean message frequency for each location as a baseline, so that the locations that temporarily received markedly high attention could be spotted. Second, those locations spotted in the first step were analysed using the epidemic model to evaluate whether events happened in these locations.

There was a number of locations mentioned in our primary data set that emerged as being unusual, amongst which the most significant location which attracted a great deal of momentary attention was Yushu. We then analysed the messages about that location using deconvolution and show our result in Fig. 6.14. The main chart in the figure illustrates the relationship between the number of messages mentioning

*Yushu* each day and the potential background events, based on deconvolution. The three smaller charts show how the outcome function, $m(t)$, is accumulated by the reactions to the three events, each expressed as a peak based on the epidemic model. Note that the "restored curve" is the result of re-calculating the convolution of $w(t)$ with $e(t)$ but not the observation results. The restored curve has a very similar shape to the observed curve, lending support to the validity of our methodology.

We mapped the resulting events to real-world incidents by manually reviewing the messages. The significant event behind these messages is an earthquake in Yushu on the 14th of April, resulting in thousands of fatalities. There are three potential events identified. The first event was the earthquake itself which generated an initial flood of messages from concerned people, the second event was reporting of the high death toll, and the third event was the official nationwide mourning which was announced on the 20th of April and conducted on the 21st.[2] Note that the date labels are based on Coordinated Universal Time.

## Challenges

Reliably identifying events based on messages from micro-blogs has several associated challenges, which are identified below:

- Some users simply re-post news stories via Twitter instead of reporting their own experience. These messages may reflect the social reaction raised by the media, but they have little, if any, effect on the identification of new events before they are reported in traditional ways.
- Some users do not care about authenticity of information; they just re-post messages that they found interesting. Thereby, rumours are propagated along with true information; rumours may be propagated even faster because of the characteristic implications of scandal.
- Information propagation of some events does not perfectly match the curve derived from the epidemic model: sometime there are multiple peaks for a single event, sometime there is a long tail after the event happened, and sometimes the curve rapidly dissipates. Also, noise may come from outside sources, such as biassed media coverage, variable user interest levels, weekdays and weekends, and even the different time zones users live in.
- Some of the assumptions in our SIR model are too simplistic, which could affect the reliability of our technique. For example, a recovered user may be reinfected by the bombardment of media reports, and users may have very different cooling down periods. By using a more sophisticated model, we may discover more latent factors behind the messages.

---

[2]There is a minor impulse on the 25th of April. This impulse cannot be explained by any single event but by the accumulation of a large number of minor events in the aftermath of the earthquake.

## Case Study 2: Social Cluster Identification

### Background

This second case study presents our approach for identifying social clusters in micro-blog users. A cluster is defined in graph theory as a set of vertexes in a graph between which there is a complete sub-graph. Our definition of user clusters resembles the definition in graph theory, by characterizing a user cluster to be a set of users who interact with each other intensively, such that information can rapidly propagate between the users. However, we do not expect the complete sub-graph between all members of a cluster because information can still quickly propagate between a given pairing of users which is not directly linked but shares a large number of friends; instead, we used the Markov chain model and random walks to measure the distance between each pair of users.

The forms of social connections and social links differ in the ability of reflecting the relationships between users. In [10], the authors analyse the forms of interactions between the groups of users and reveal that links made by mentioning (i.e. re-tweeting and replying), rather than by following, have more significant correlation to the user groups; hence, we followed only the links by mentioning in this case study.

### Markov Chain Model

The Markov chain model is widely used for measuring the distances between vertexes in a graph. The probability of a user being reached in $\tau$ steps of propagation is defined by

$$
U_\tau = \begin{bmatrix} p_\tau(u_1, u_r|x) \\ p_\tau(u_2, u_r|x) \\ \vdots \\ p_\tau(u_m, u_r|x) \end{bmatrix},
\tag{7}
$$

where $p_\tau(u_k, u_r|x)$ is the probability that the $k$-th user is reached by message $x$ generated by user $r$ in $\tau$ steps. This probability vector is derived using an iterative equation

$$
U_\tau = \mathbf{A}U_{\tau-1}.
\tag{8}
$$

In this formula, matrix $\mathbf{A}$ is the adjacency matrix defining the probability of a step taken between any two directly connected users. The initial vector, $U_0$, is a zero vector but with the $i$-th element being 1, where $i$ denotes the starting node in a random walk. Adjacency matrix $\mathbf{A}$ is derived by the normalized weight of out-degrees of each user, which is defined by the number of messages from this user and mentions of each other user.

We note that the damping factor that is defined in the PageRank algorithm may be important to characterize the means of the random walk, namely, a walk terminates at any node with a given probability. However, we did not introduce this factor in our case.

**Distance Measurement**

The Markov chain model provides a measurement of the probability with which a walk stops at each node after a given number of steps. Given enough time, the probability of a walk reaching any node will converge to one if there is a path between the target node and the original node in the graph, and the probability of the walk stopping at a node converges to a value that is independent of where the walk started. On the other hand, we need an approach for distance measurement, which is only determined by the structure of the network and is sensitive to the starting node.

Considering the epidemic model mentioned in the first case study, an individual is infected when the epidemic reaches this individual for the first time. The time cost for propagating the epidemic can be measured by the expected number of steps taken in a walk in the social network, from a given node to reach a target node for the first time. This expectation is only determined by the structure of the network, and is more suitable for measuring the ease of information propagating between two nodes; hence, we used these expectations as the distance measurement for clustering users. An algorithm, proposed in [26, 28], was used to calculate these expectations.

By knowing the distance between each pair of users, one may use an existing clustering algorithm to group the users that are close to each other; we used the $k$-means algorithm in our case study, which requires the manual specification of the value $k$. We tried a number of different values of $k$ and selected the one that results in no predominantly large clusters. Note that, in a practical application, the process of finding $k$ can be done using an optimistic algorithm.

For evaluating the validity of our method, we assume that, being closer to each other on the path of information propagation, users in the same cluster have similar backgrounds. We manually evaluate the clusters identified in our data set and show the similarity between the profiles of their members.

**Revealed Clusters**

We ran our algorithm on the primary data set and identified six major user clusters that have many members. Figure 6.15 shows members of these clusters, as well as inner- and inter-connections between these members. The number of inter-cluster connections in the figure are far fewer than those connecting users in the same cluster, which gives the basic support to the validity of the distance measurement and clustering algorithms.

Each link shown in the figure denotes at least 14 re-tweets or replying messages between the two users. The structure of the connections with each cluster is rather like the conjunction of star structures: some users have significantly more connections to other users, and there are relatively fewer links between inactive users. This confirms to Zipf's law, which is often used to analyse the popularity of objects in social systems, such as people in social networks and websites on the Internet. It is also worth noting that we referenced not only the links shown in the

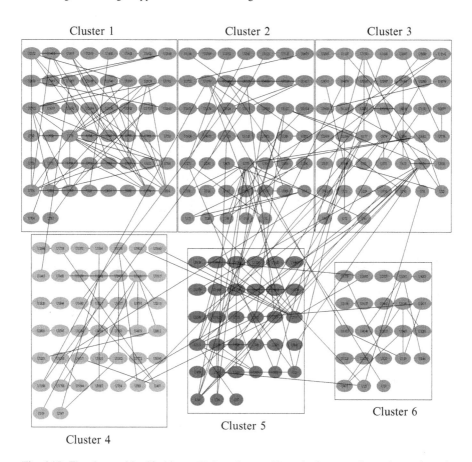

**Fig. 6.15** The clusters identified in our Twitter data set. From the large numbers of users in each cluster, we selected only those who have the largest numbers of connections to others in drawing the graph. Cluster are rendered by bounding rectangles. Clusters that have very few members are not rendered, for readability purposes. The user identities are not shown in the graph

figure in clustering but also the links that have low weights, i.e. instances of less than 14 interactions between a given pairing of two users. These links are omitted from the figure for readability purposes. From Table 6.1, we can see that users in a given cluster may share the same social background, the same occupation, the same political ideology, and even the same geological location. This results in them having similar interests, such that a message from a cluster member has a high probability of being noticed by other users in the same cluster. Please note that the clusters are roughly divided and the description may be not applicable to all members of the cluster.

The exclusiveness of the clusters strongly supports the validity of our algorithm. The figure shows that the second cluster, formed mainly from people living in

**Table 6.1** Descriptions of the clusters that are identified using the random walk model; the descriptions are summarized by manually reviewing the messages and the self-descriptions of the cluster members

| Mark | Members | Description |
|------|---------|-------------|
| Cluster 1 | 366 | Young people living in Taiwan and Hong Kong |
| Cluster 2 | 507 | People living in mainland China who tend to talk about critical politic issues |
| Cluster 3 | 669 | Young people living in mainland China, sharing popular things |
| Cluster 4 | 369 | IT workers in China who tend to talk about technical issues |
| Cluster 5 | 667 | People in their 30s living in mainland China, sharing deeper and more intellectual subjects |
| Cluster 6 | 365 | Similar to the third cluster |
| Sum | 2,493 | |

Taiwan and Hong Kong, is the most exclusive cluster, due to its intense inner links and very few outer links. The imbalanced connections between clusters reflect the extend to which users share same interests. Different economic, cultural, and political backgrounds make the second cluster share few interests with other groups. Another exclusive cluster, the first one, is a turn-off for other users because of the detailed technical subjects.

Even though the unique backgrounds of each cluster tend to exclude irrelevant users, it does not mean that all topics in the cluster are unique. We noted that more than half of the topics in every cluster are irrelevant to the background and circumstance of the cluster members; however, people are more likely to share general topics of interest with users in the same cluster.

## Challenges

The validity of the methodology introduced in this section may be influenced by factors including:

- Clusters may be temporal in nature. A new event may lead to interactions between a particular set of users, who interact solidly over a short time period; however, as their interest in the event fades, the cluster may dissipate.
- The hard cluster membership defined in our model may be over simplistic. A particular combination of circumstances may result in a user belonging to multiple clusters, between which there is very low similarity. Ignoring such overlaps in membership can result in inappropriate merging of two unrelated clusters.

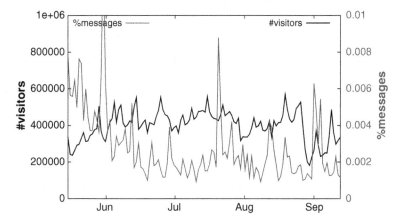

**Fig. 6.16** The number of the visitors to Expo 2010 on each day versus the proportion of messages mentioning the event. The three abnormal peaks on the message number curve correspond to three short-term events: a stampede incident on the 30th of May, a rumour about injuries in the very congested park in late July, and a critical news report which was published in early September and disclosed unpleasant behaviour of visitors and aroused discussion

## Case Study 3: Trend Identification

### Background

In this case study, we present a technique for identifying trends in long-term events by observing trends in micro-blog messages mentioning them. Expo 2010 took place in Shanghai from May to November in 2010. In the 184 days, there were around 70 million visitors to the exhibition park and disclosure of daily and hourly updates on visitor numbers on the official website. This publicly available data served as a good reference for analysing how micro-blog messages reflect the public perception of events. Figure 6.16 shows the number of visitors and the number of Twitter messages referencing the event. In contrast to the figures shown in the first case study, long-term events do not usually raise a single peak of interest but a rather smooth and continuous curve of attention. Nevertheless, the curve still reflects the interests of the users, so that it may reveal event trends.

### Methodology

We used the following three-step process to identify the relationship between the number of messages mentioning Expo 2010 and the daily visitors to the event:

- The interlinks between the users were extracted from the messages for clustering the users into clusters, using the clustering technique presented in Case Study 2.

- From each cluster, we extracted messages that potentially mention experience and/or intention of visiting Expo 2010 and also counted the number of messages from that cluster.
- We calculated the correlation coefficients between the relative proportion on Expo-related messages from each cluster and the official visitor numbers. A higher correlation coefficient denotes the cluster being a better indicator of visitor number prediction.

**Micro-blog Message Refinement**

From the 13.5 million messages in our primary data set, 35,000 explicitly mentioned *Expo 2010*. We divided the number of messages each day mentioning *Expo* by the total message number for the day, in order to remove the variance resulting from accessibility to Twitter in mainland China.

As mentioned in the first case study, some messages posted on micro-blogs may not reflect the experiences and intentions of the users. We further reviewed messages from Twitter mentioning Expo 2010 and found that users have different motivations for writing messages mentioning an event:

- Some users copy stories from outer websites or re-tweet other user's message about the event.
- Some users post comments on news reports or to others' messages about the event.
- Some users report the intention or experience of other people to the event, who may have no access to Twitter.
- Some users report the intention or experience of themselves with regard to the event.

Only the last two message categories, which report the experience and the intention in visiting Expo 2010, are valuable to us. We distinguished these messages using the following heuristics:

- These messages are more authentic and as such are re-tweeted by fewer, if any, users.
- These messages contain more subjective and relative temporal expressions like *I*, *we*, *will*, *go*, *today*, or *tomorrow*.

Only messages which satisfy these two heuristics (i.e. which were not re-tweeted, and contain one of a small set of keywords) were considered for analysis.

**Data Analysis**

Figure 6.17a shows the real visitor numbers and the proportion of messages from each cluster based on our technique. This figure seems very noisy because of the three reasons: (1) high-frequency noise over the weekly period, (2) the great

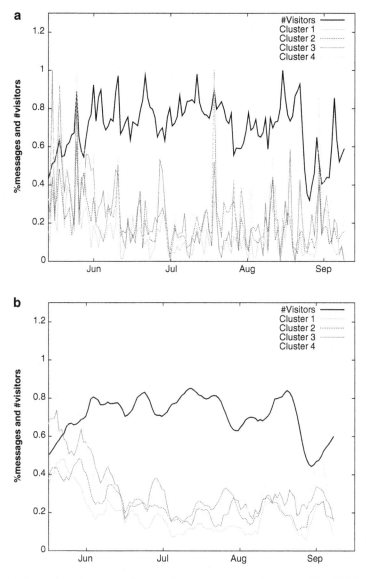

**Fig. 6.17** The number of messages from the four major user clusters versus the official numbers of visitors. Note that the message numbers are normalized; from the four clusters, the maximum average number of messages is approximately five times larger than the minimal number. (**a**) Raw figures; (**b**) 7-day moving average after trimming

**Table 6.2** The correlation coefficients between the official visitor numbers and the the message numbers from the four clusters, as well as the total number of messages mentioning the Expo. The correlation coefficients are calculated over the 7-day moving average values. Note that a negative lag denotes that the message numbers can be used in predicting future visitor numbers, while a positive lag denotes that the message numbers can be used in recovering past visitor numbers

| Lag | Cluster 1 | Cluster 2 | Cluster 3 | Cluster 4 | Total Msgs |
|---|---|---|---|---|---|
| −6 | 0.3656 | 0.3475 | 0.0554 | 0.2775 | 0.0708 |
| −5 | 0.4139 | 0.3719 | 0.0761 | 0.2875 | −0.0086 |
| −4 | 0.4319 | 0.3939 | 0.0944 | 0.2946 | −0.1010 |
| −3 | 0.4210 | 0.4098 | 0.1138 | 0.2879 | −0.1990 |
| −2 | 0.3869 | 0.4216 | 0.1320 | 0.2724 | −0.2717 |
| −1 | 0.3366 | 0.4324 | 0.1459 | 0.2468 | −0.3298 |
| 0 | 0.2847 | 0.4449 | 0.1681 | 0.2191 | −0.3575 |
| 1 | 0.2282 | 0.4521 | 0.2007 | 0.1938 | −0.3391 |
| 2 | 0.1817 | 0.4554 | 0.2394 | 0.1722 | −0.2856 |
| 3 | 0.1527 | 0.4534 | 0.2851 | 0.1451 | −0.1878 |
| 4 | 0.1191 | 0.4413 | 0.3102 | 0.1283 | −0.0974 |
| 5 | 0.0968 | 0.4287 | 0.3342 | 0.1179 | 0.0028 |
| 6 | 0.0688 | 0.4035 | 0.3366 | 0.0995 | 0.1075 |
| 7 | 0.0208 | 0.3604 | 0.2913 | 0.0620 | 0.2090 |

enthusiasm at the very beginning of the exhibition, and (3) the impulses from the three special events described above. We manually removed these abnormal peaks and plot the result as a 7-day moving average in Fig. 6.17b.

The correlation between the numbers of messages from clusters and the official numbers of visitors is perceivable, while each cluster has a different lag, either positive or negative, over the trend of the official visitor numbers. We show in Table 6.2 the correlation coefficient with the official visitor number for the message numbers of each cluster and also the overall Twitter population community. We ignored the first 30 days to remove noise from the great enthusiasm at the beginning of the Expo.

This table shows that the clusters vary in their ability in predicting or recovering the numbers of visitors. The first cluster is useful as an indicator of the users' intention in 4 days later because the maximum correlation coefficient is with a 4-day lag, whereas the second and the third clusters may be used to recover the attendance trend in following days. It is also shown that, without user clustering, the total numbers of messages have very little correlation, if any, with the trend of the event.

We further tested our methodology by comparing trends of messages containing other irrelevant keywords to the trend of Expo 2010. The keywords that we selected are *officer* and *house price*, both of which are popular but intuitively irrelevant to Expo 2010. The results showed that the maximum positive correlation coefficients of these irrelevant message trends to the numbers of attendants are 0.12 and 0.21 respectively, much lower than the correlation coefficients of the message trends that are relevant to Expo 2010; namely, the message trends for irrelevant keywords are largely meaningless for predicting or recovering the trend of attendance to Expo 2010.

### Challenges

This case study provides only a preliminary example of trend identification by mining micro-blogs. We point out some issues to be further improved for making our methodology more practical in real mining applications.

- As we pointed out in Case Study 2, user clusters may change from time to time. This may influence the approach to utilizing the cluster-wise information in two ways: (1) the membership of clusters may change with time and (2) the correlation and the lag between the behaviour of a cluster and the trend of the event may differ for a long-term event.
- The method for clustering users may be further guided by the ability of the resulting clusters to predict event trends. Given that users who have similar reactions to events are more likely to share the same interests, these clusters will be better suited to event trend prediction.
- In this case study, we manually removed noise the data. Nonetheless, as we showed in the first case study, this task can be automatically done using deconvolution and the EM algorithm. Further studies are needed to build the model for analysing the mixture of long-term trends and short-term events.

## Conclusion

This chapter has served as an introduction to data mining of micro-blogs, with a particular focus on Twitter. We first described characteristics of micro-blogs, and different data mining tasks that can be performed over them, including both opportunities and challenges. We then presented an analysis of Twitter data, based on data collected over a 4-week period. Finally, we presented three case studies using Twitter data: event identification using an epidemic model, social cluster identification using a Markov chain model, and trend identification using keyword frequencies within user clusters.

## References

1. Baldwin, T., Lui, M.: Language identification: the long and the short of the matter. In: Proceedings of Human Language Technologies: The 11th Annual Conference of the North American Chapter of the Association for Computational Linguistics (NAACL HLT 2010), Los Angeles, pp. 229–237 (2010)

2. Barbosa, L., Feng, J.: Robust sentiment detection on Twitter from biased and noisy data. In: Proceedings of the 23rd International Conference on Computational Linguistics (COLING 2010), Posters Volume, Beijing, pp. 36–44 (2010)
3. Connor, B., Balasubramanyan, R., Routledge, B.R., Smith, N.A.: From tweets to polls: linking text sentiment to public opinion time series. In: Proceedings of the Second International AAAI Conference on Weblogs and Social Media, Washington, DC, pp. 122–129 (2010)
4. Culotta, A.: Towards detecting influenza epidemics by analyzing Twitter messages. In: Proceedings of the KDD 2010 Workshop on Social Media Analytics, Washington, DC, (2010)
5. de Marneffe, M., MacCartney, B., Manning, C.D.: Generating typed dependency parses from phrase structure parses. In: Proceedings of the 5th International Conference on Language Resources and Evaluation (LREC 2006), Genoa, (2006)
6. Goorha, S., Ungar, L.: Discovery of significant emerging trends. In: Proceedings of the 16th ACM SIGKDD International Conference on Knowledge Discovery and Data Mining, Washington, DC, pp. 57–64. ACM (2010)
7. Han, B., Baldwin, T.: Lexical normalisation of short text messages: Makn sens a #twitter. In: Proceedings of the 49th Annual Meeting of the Association for Computational Linguistics: Human Language Technologies (ACL HLT 2011), pp. 368–378. Stroudsburg, PA, USA (2011)
8. Hannon, J., Bennett, M., Smyth, B.: Recommending Twitter users to follow using content and collaborative filtering approaches. In: Proceedings of the Fourth ACM Conference on Recommender Systems, Barcelona, pp. 199–206 (2010)
9. Hethcote, H., Tudor, D.: Integral equation models for endemic infectious diseases. J. Math. Biol. **9**(1), 37–47 (1980)
10. Huberman, B., Romero, D., Wu, F.: Social networks that matter: Twitter under the microscope. First Monday **14**(1), 8 (2009)
11. Kermack, W.O., McKendrick, A.G.: A contribution to the mathematical theory of epidemics. Proc. R. Soc. A **115**, 700–721 (1927)
12. Klein, D., Manning, C.D.: Fast exact inference with a factored model for natural language parsing. In: Advances in Neural Information Processing Systems 15 (NIPS 2002), Whistler, pp. 3–10 (2003)
13. Kwak, H., Lee, C., Park, H., Moon, S.: What is Twitter, a social network or a news media? In: Proceedings of the 19th International Conference on World Wide Web, Raleigh, pp. 591–600 (2010)
14. Lane, R.: Methods for maximum-likelihood deconvolution. JOSA A **13**(10), 1992–1998 (1996)
15. Likas, A., Galatsanos, N.: A variational approach for Bayesian blind image deconvolution. IEEE Trans. Signal Process. **52**(8), 2222–2233 (2004)
16. Milstein, S., Chowdhury, A., Hochmuth, G., Lorica, B., Magoulas, R.: Twitter and the micro-messaging revolution: communication, connections, and immediacy – 140 characters at a time. O'Reilly Radar Report (2008)
17. Petrović, S., Osborne, M., Lavrenko, V.: Streaming first story detection with application to Twitter. In: Proceedings of Human Language Technologies: The 11th Annual Conference of the North American Chapter of the Association for Computational Linguistics (NAACL HLT 2010), Los Angeles, pp. 181–189 (2010)
18. Quincey, E., Kostkova, P.: Early warning and outbreak detection using social networking websites: the potential of Twitter. In: Electronic Healthcare, vol. 27, pp. 21–24. Springer, Heidelberg (2010)
19. Reuters-Web: Twitter older than it looks. URL http://blogs.reuters.com/mediafile/2009/03/30/twitter-older-than-it-looks/. Reuters MediaFile blog (2009). Accessed 15 Dec 2011
20. Ritter, A., Cherry, C., Dolan, B.: Unsupervised modeling of Twitter conversations. In: Proceedings of Human Language Technologies: The 11th Annual Conference of the North American Chapter of the Association for Computational Linguistics (NAACL HLT 2010), Los Angeles, pp. 172–180 (2010)
21. Ritterman, J., Osborne, M., Klein, E.: Using prediction markets and Twitter to predict a swine flu pandemic. In: Proceedings of the 1st International Workshop on Mining Social Media, Sevilla (2009)

22. Sakaki, T., Okazaki, M., Matsuo, Y.: Earthquake shakes Twitter users: real-time event detection by social sensors. In: Proceedings of the 19th International Conference on World Wide Web, Raleigh, North Carolina, pp. 851–860 (2010)
23. Santorini, B.: Part-of-speech tagging guidelines for the Penn Treebank project. Techinical report, Department of Computer and Information Science, University of Pennsylvania (1990)
24. Sproat, R., Black, A.W., Chen, S., Kumar, S., Ostendorf, M., Richards, C.: Normalization of non-standard words. Comput. Speech Lang. **15**(3), 287–333 (2001)
25. Twitter: Big goals, big game, big records. http://blog.twitter.com/2010/06/big-goals-big-game-big-records.html (2010). Retrieved 4 Aug 2010
26. Wasow, W.: A note on the inversion of matrices by random walks. Math. Table Other Aid Computat. **6**(38), 78–81 (1952)
27. Weng, J., Lim, E.P., Jiang, J., He, Q.: Twitterrank: finding topic-sensitive influential twitterers. In: Proceedings of the Third ACM International Conference on Web Search and Data Mining, WSDM '10, New York, pp. 261–270 (2010)
28. Yen, L., Vanvyve, D., Wouters, F., Fouss, F., Verleysen, M., Saerens, M.: Clustering using a random walk based distance measure. In: Proceedings of the 13th Symposium on Artificial Neural Networks (ESANN 2005), Bruges, pp. 317–324 (2005)

# Chapter 7
# Mining Buyer Behavior Patterns Based on Dynamic Group-Buying Network

Xiao Liu and Jianmei Yang

**Abstract** New challenges arise as analysts started to apply traditional network analysis techniques to social network in the Web 2.0 era. Many business modes in e-commerce emerged based on online or offline social network, such as group-buying, social buying and viral marketing. The target environments are those involving large amounts of relational data that is time-dependent. Such characteristics require time-sensitive network analyses to support decision making. For example, in the dynamic online markets, understanding changes in buyer behavior and the dynamics of social networks can help manager to establish effective promotion campaigns. However, traditional single snapshot approach does not exactly fit in the time-sensitive network representation scenarios. Thus, this chapter first proposed a time-sensitive network by using timestamp to enhance edge representation, and then provided a methodology based on the framework of business intelligence platform to support dynamic network modeling, analysis and data mining. Finally, China's case study described the process of dynamic group-buying network modeling and analysis, as well as the results of the buyer behavior pattern analysis and mining.

## Introduction

Group-buying has been in vogue for many years in various industries [1, 2]. Demand aggregation in group-buying benefits sellers, offered lower marketing costs and coordinated distribution channels, while buyers also enjoy these lower costs for product purchases [3].

X. Liu (✉)
College of Economics, Jinan University, Guangzhou, China
e-mail: lxchdd@jnu.edu.cn

J. Yang
School of Business Administration, South China University of Technology, Guangzhou, China
e-mail: fbayang@scut.edu.cn

A. Abraham (ed.), *Computational Social Networks: Mining and Visualization*,
DOI 10.1007/978-1-4471-4054-2_7, © Springer-Verlag London 2012

The Internet enables low-cost transaction-making via a variety of market mechanisms. It also facilitates the exchange of information between buyers and sellers more quickly and without the limitations of time and space than we have seen in any market mechanism heretofore [4]. The Internet provides a powerful tool for demand aggregation and hence is a natural platform to facilitate group-buying. It is thus not surprising that online group-buying was perceived as one of the most innovative business models of e-commerce, and has been employed by many companies.

Although some early pioneers failed, online group-buying has been reviving in North America, Europe and Asia in recent years, following the success of Groupon's mode (e.g., groupon.com). Groupon (Group + Coupon), which is different from traditional online group-buying auctions, not only offers one deal for something fun to do or buy at a great discount every day, but also takes advantage of the social media(such as Facebook and Twitter) to gather their buyers. Over the past years, some companies have launched websites offering daily deals that are triggered once a minimum number of people express an interest in them.

The emergence of online group-buying model on the Internet has got great interest of leading researchers around the world. There are several group-buying papers based on the empirical study or theoretical work. Some of the early works are predominantly focused on two issues.

One is the pricing mechanism from sellers' perspective in group-buying markets. Seller's pricing is crucial because in group-buying 1.0 price is set according to the numbers of buyers gather in the group. Anand and Aron [5] analyzed the value of group-buying and the optimal price curve. Chen et al. [6–9] analyzed buyers' bidding strategies in a group-buying auction and compared group-buying with fixed pricing mechanisms, examined the effect of uncertain customer values, and analyzed the benefits of buyer collusion.

The other critical issue faced by many group-buying markets is how to improve customer participation [10]. A buyer will not join a group if she expects to pay a price higher than her willingness-to-pay. Kauffman and Wang [10, 11] explored consumer behavior in online group-buying through analysis of transactional data from Mobshop in San Francisco, California, and other real-world online group-buying Web sites. Anand and Aron [5] and Ho et al. [12] used online experiments to study customer participation in group-buying. Anand and Aron [5] focused on the effect of textual comments and existing orders, and Ho et al. [12] investigated in different incentive mechanisms that overcome startup participation inertia.

Most of these researches tended to explore the problem from the perspective of economics, seldom from the perspective of network approach. In fact, "network" has two aspects of definition, ontology and methodology. The former refers to the real network, e.g., transportation network, telephone network, etc. The latter refers to the methodology, such as social network analysis (SNA) or complex network analysis originated in physics and computer science.

A use of networks as models of complex systems and processes brings a number of advantages. First, networks have a convenient graphical representation: network nodes and links can be visualized as graph vertices and edges respectively. Visualization of networks as graphs has value in itself for understanding intricate relationships within complex systems. Second, graph theory is well-developed and can provide a solid theoretical foundation to such new areas as complex social systems, while graph measures and computational tools are readily available. Last and most importantly, network approach provides a powerful abstraction of structure and dynamic graph of all kinds of people or people-to-event interaction.

With the language of network, group-buying is a bipartite network which the buyers are linked to the deals they purchased. Because the deal is good if only a specific numbers of people decide to buy, all interested parties are incentivized to send the deal to their friends, family and coworkers. Thus, social buying is conducive to starting viral marketing in multiple social circles. Therefore, along with an online group-buying network forming, a recommendation relation network or a Word-of-Mouth social network will very likely emerge.

New challenges have arisen because the real environment involves large amounts of relational data that is dynamic. According to the rule of "one day one deal" on social buying websites, group-buying network and Word-of-Mouth network is dynamically changed over time. In other words, the nodes and edges (relations) may appear, disappear, or change in strength over time as new information arrives. These situations require time-sensitive network analyses to support decision-making as real world events alter the networks.

However, a snapshot of a network, in essence, is not suitable for dynamic network modeling and analysis. So the biggest challenge is the networks technique beyond simple snapshots. On the other hand, large-scale data can be gathered from different online transaction database. These large data streams require more powerful tools to digest and manipulate, and extract network topology with minimal computational overhead. New analytical techniques, such as data mining, reveal hidden patterns in complex social networks, should be further explored.

The aim of this chapter is to propose a comprehensive methodology framework which combines dynamic network approach with data mining, supporting empirical study of online group-buying. We are particularly interested in questions as following: network topology changes with time, changes in buyer behavior and the factors that lead to network changes. Answers of these questions will help us to understand the structure and the formation mechanism of online group-buying network or word-of-mouth network.

To achieve this, we first proposes a social buying metanetwork to describe buyer and buyer-to-deal interaction in a group-buying website in section "Concepts and Model," and then shows how to represent a time-sensitive network by enhancing edges definition with timestamp. Section "Modeling and Analysis Methodology" provides a methodology framework based on Business Intelligent platform. This framework build a problem-solving environment to support data storing and integrating, dynamic network modeling and analysis, as well as patterns identifying or rules mining based on network data. Section "A Framework of Modeling and Analysis" describes four modules of the methodology framework combining various analysis techniques. Section "Dynamic Network Databases" describes the details of how to create dynamic network database. Section "Dynamic Network Modeling" provides two ways in modeling dynamic network for different purpose.

Section "Dynamic Network Analysis" introduces concepts of sequence pattern mining. Case study of China is presented in section "Case Study." Section "Data Source" describes the background of case study and data source. Section "Dynamic Network Analysis" illustrates the application of ORA to the dynamic group-buying network. Section "Buyer Behavior Analysis" analyzes and partitions buyers according to four variables describing buyer behavior (e.g., recency, frequency, monetary and activity) during online shopping. Section "Time-Interval Sequence Pattern Mining" shows the results of time-interval sequence pattern mining. A brief conclusion is presented in section "Conclusion," and some unsolved problems are issued for further research.

## Concepts and Model

### *Social Buying Metanetwork*

The idea of group-buying is again gaining popularity in Web 2.0, in part thanks to the increasing connection of people in online forums and social networks [13]. Applications, such as Groupon, SocialBuy and LivingSocial, offer discounts for reviewing a product, and give points for recommending a purchase to friends and family. So people have an economic incentive to promote products in their social network in order to reach those thresholds more rapidly and consistently. Thus, the new term "social buying" emerged, i.e., group-buying 2.0.

From network approach perspective, data from online group-buying or social buying websites has the main features as following:

- Multi-entities: there are a number of different entity sets or objects, such as user, buyer, products, items, deals, etc. Each type of entity has its own attributes.
- Multi-ties: there are various types of relation, such as purchasing, recommending, reviewing, and so on.
- Multi-mode network: one-mode network (different kind of connections can link the entities of one sort, e.g., Mouth-of-Word network among people); two-mode network (so-called bipartite networks contain nodes of two kinds, e.g., customers purchase the deals).

These networks of concern are "meta-networks" that are multi-modal (different types of nodes) and multi-link (different types of relations). The resulting social buying metanetwork is shown in Table 7.1.

There are three types of nodes and three networks in the social buying meta-network shown in Table 7.1. The node types are: individual buyer (SNA class "actor"), groups or deals (SNA class "event," i.e., join in a group or purchase a product), communities (social media community on internet, e.g., Facebook, MSN or QQ in China). The networks included are: Word-of-Mouth network which

**Table 7.1** Meta-network of social buying

|        | Buyers (actor)    | Groups/deals (event) | Communities (organization) |
|--------|-------------------|----------------------|----------------------------|
| Buyers | Word-of-Mouth net | Group-Buying net     | Membership net             |
|        | Who recommend whom | Who has bought what | Who is a member of what    |

The concept of Meta-network was proposed by Carley [14], which is a multicolor, multiplex representation of the entities and the connections among them [15]. In the metanetwork, the nodes could be people, knowledge, resources, locations, etc., and the links that connect them could be of different strength/weight [14].

represents that a buyer has recommended another buyer to buy a special deal, group-buying network which links buyers and their purchasing items or deals, and membership network which shows affiliations of buyers with online community.

The advantages of the metanetwork representation are clearly identifiable. In the metanetwork, "hidden" relationships or multiple social relations between entities can be identified through analyzing their connections to nodes of different kinds. For example, co-purchasing or co-interest for two buyers as they purchase the same deal, and co-membership in an online community (e.g., Facebook), emerges or can be transformed from inter-linked networks. Even more significantly, changes in one network cascade through the entire metanetwork.

## *Dynamic Network Representation with Timestamp*

The majority of well-known Network Representation Languages (e.g., CSV, UCINET-native) are very good at representing static networks. But, the real environments involve large amounts of relational data that is dynamic. In the scenarios, the representation of network should be suitable for temporal analysis and sensitivity analysis. To analyze such data, a simple solution is to divide it into time periods and then assess a sequence of networks. For example, Fig. 7.1 shows two 2-mode data matrices at different time point.

However, from a computational perspective, the solution of multiple data matrices often faced the problem of scalability, due to high IO costs and complexity in modeling and data processing. Furthermore, attribute data representation about the node or the edge of network is crucial in the process of network data mining.

Three key improvements are needed to handle the limit of traditional Network Representation Languages [16]: Enhanced Edge Representation (EER, details including strength, direction, and change in these factors), Enhanced Node Representation (ENR, details including existence, attributes about the state of the node such as age or gender), and Enhance Meta-Data Representation (EMR, details about who generated the data, why, when, how, etc.). In our study, we propose the time-sensitive network, which enhanced edge representation with timestamp, as the foundation of dynamic network modeling and analysis.

| **a** | two-mode network (t=1) | | | | | | |
|---|---|---|---|---|---|---|---|
|  | a | b | c | d | e | f | g |
| c1 | 1 | 0 | 0 | 0 | 0 | 0 | 0 |
| c2 | 1 | 0 | 0 | 0 | 0 | 0 | 0 |
| c3 | 0 | 0 | 0 | 0 | 1 | 1 | 0 |
| c4 | 0 | 0 | 0 | 0 | 1 | 0 | 0 |

| **b** | two-mode network (t=2) | | | | | | |
|---|---|---|---|---|---|---|---|
|  | a | b | c | d | e | f | g |
| c1 | 1 | 0 | 0 | 0 | 0 | 0 | 0 |
| c2 | 1 | 0 | 0 | 1 | 0 | 0 | 0 |
| c3 | 0 | 0 | 0 | 0 | 1 | 1 | 0 |
| c4 | 0 | 0 | 0 | 0 | 1 | 0 | 0 |

| **c** two-mode network with timestamp | | | |
|---|---|---|---|
| actor | event | strength | timestamp |
| c1 | a | 1 | 1 |
| c2 | a | 1 | 1 |
| c2 | d | 1 | 1 |
| c3 | e | 1 | 1 |
| c3 | f | 1 | 1 |
| c4 | e | 1 | 1 |
| c1 | a | 1 | 2 |
| c1 | b | 1 | 2 |
| c1 | c | 1 | 2 |
| c2 | c | 1 | 2 |
| c3 | a | 1 | 2 |
| c3 | b | 1 | 2 |
| c4 | g | 1 | 2 |

**Fig. 7.1** (**a–b**) Two-mode network which usually represents a rectangular matrix of actors (*rows*) by events (*column*); (**c**) two-mode network with timestamp

A two-mode network of EER with timestamp can be defined as DBN = (A, E, AE, T), where A is the set of actors, E is the set of events, AE is the set of links (A × E), and T is the set of timestamps. The edge list format of DBN is ($a_i$, $e_j$, $w_{ij}$, t), where $w_{ij}$ is the weight of link between $a_i$ and $e_j$, representing the i-th actor attend j-th event at time t. The timestamp can be the exact time, time period or the sequence that event occurs.

Figure 7.1c shows a two-mode network of EER with timestamp, which integrates data of two network snapshots in Fig. 7.1a, b. We name a two-mode network of EER with timestamp as the dynamic bipartite network.

Thus, dynamic group-buying network is namely GBN = (G, B, E, T). G is the set of nodes representing deals or products on social buying website. B is the set of nodes representing buyers. All edges in E are links between buyers and deals at time t. Dynamic Word-of-Month social network is namely BSN = (B, E, T). B is the set of nodes representing buyers. The links or arcs in E represent that the i-th buyer recommends the j-th buyer to buy some special deal at time t. Both GBN and BSN are dynamic and time-sensitive networks.

# Modeling and Analysis Methodology

## A Framework of Modeling and Analysis

Business Intelligent (BI) is a set of concepts, methods and processes that aim at not only improving business decisions but also at supporting realization of

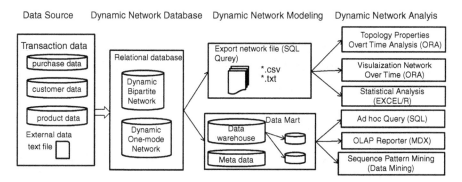

**Fig. 7.2** A framework of modeling and analysis based on Business Intelligent platform

an enterprise's strategy. With appropriate BI a company will be able to develop intelligent decision support systems to gain the competitive advantage of the industry [17]. Business Intelligence's key techniques include data warehouses, OLAP techniques and data mining. These techniques have ability to support data integration, complex network modeling and data mining [18].

In this section, we proposed a dynamic network modeling and analysis framework based on business intelligence platform, which can adequately support the automatic extracting of network relation from online transaction database, dynamic network representation, as well as the continuous ingestion of data into dynamic network package such as ORA or data mining software such as SPSS Clementine.

Figure 7.2 shows the four modules of the framework.

**Data Source**

The data for analysis are derived from the database, which is the transaction database of an online group-buying website. The database includes data on the product, customer, purchasing record, customer comments and customer recommending record. Other data source includes demographic data of customer, communication records on social media websites, etc. These data stream is the foundation of dynamic network modeling and analysis.

**Dynamic Network Database**

The primary goal of the dynamic network database design is to translate the logical description in transaction database into network representation specifications for modeling. Once the dynamic network database design is completed, the data access languages are developed for the final decision analysis requirement.

**Dynamic Network Modeling**

There are two ways to model dynamic network. One way is to use the SQL query to directly export the network data in the database to a data file. Another way is to set up a data warehouse for OLAP analysis and data mining.

**Dynamic Network Analysis**

To meet network analysis and the decision analysis needs, we propose a comprehensive techniques solution as following:

Dynamic network analysis tool allows an analyst to see how a network measures change over multiple time periods, observe who (actor) and what (event) in a network might change, and detect and interpret patterns of social ties change among actors.

Statistical analysis tool offers a wide range of techniques to describe attributes and investigate the association between attributes, but it cannot handle relational data directly. Nevertheless, continuous structural indices, such as node centrality, can be stored as vectors or attributes data which are the bridge between network analysis and statistics.

OLAP is tools for business reporting and ad hoc inquiring. They let analysts access and analyze business problems and share information that stored in data warehouses.

Data mining involves the use of tools, such as machine learning and pattern indentify, to discover previously unknown, valid patterns and relationships in large data set. This study employs the sequence pattern mining technique to discover buyer behavior patterns hidden in a dynamic group-buying network.

## *Dynamic Network Databases*

Use of database technology to store dynamic network (i.e., network with timestamp) data has four advantages: (1) supporting large-scale data storage; (2) using SQL query to directly indentify network relation from transaction database with minimum time cost; (3) using SQL query to extract network snapshot by defining the sliding time windows of different lengths; (4) providing data sources for decision analysis or data mining.

Now we use two-mode network as an example and explain how we set up the database. Three basic tables will be created to store dynamic two-mode network data. Figure 7.3a shows the structure of three tables: bipartite-network, actor-network and event-network.

Because special network techniques for two-mode networks are very complicated and limited, the commonly used solution is to transform a two-mode network

7 Mining Buyer Behavior Patterns Based on Dynamic Group-Buying Network                    169

**a**

The structure of tables

**b**

```
select n1.source actor1,n2.source actor2,n1.target event,n1.time
into actor_network
from "bipartite-network"n1 ,"bipartite-network" n2
where n1.target=n2.target and n1.time=n2.time
and n1.source<n2 source
```

```
select n1.target item1 ,n2.target item2,n1 .source actor,n1.time
into event_network
from "bipartite-network" n1 ,"bipartite-network" n2
where n1.source=n2. source and n1.time=n2.time
and n1.target<n2.target
```

Projection of dynamic bipartite network with SQL query

**c**

| actor1 | actor2 | event | time |
| --- | --- | --- | --- |
| c1 | c2 | a | 1 |
| c3 | c4 | e | 1 |
| c1 | c3 | a | 2 |
| c1 | c3 | b | 2 |
| c1 | c2 | c | 2 |

| item1 | item2 | actor | time |
| --- | --- | --- | --- |
| a | d | c2 | 1 |
| e | f | c3 | 1 |
| a | b | c1 | 2 |
| a | c | c1 | 2 |
| b | c | c1 | 2 |
| a | b | c3 | 2 |

The result tables

**Fig. 7.3** (**a**) The structure of three tables; (**b**) SQL statement of projection operation; (**c**) the result tables after projection

into two one-mode networks, which can be analyzed with standard techniques. However, the traditional projection process may lead to important information (in bipartite structure) loss or other problems [19]. Moreover the time cost of dealing with large networks is very high, leading to failure of Projection. Multi-time point network projection is also very troublesome. Hence, analysts need a simple and efficient method, which is also scalability and information lossless.

Luckily, the process of projection is straightforward in dynamic network database. Figure 7.3b shows two examples of the projection using SQL query. Projection is complete; there is no loss of bipartite structure information. This information is important to explain the evolution of network relation among actors: who, when, how, what happen.

Table actor-network and Table event-network are used to store networks data (projection obtained). Actor-network is the network of Enhanced Edges Representation by using timestamp and "event" information. Event-network is the network of Enhanced Edges Representation by using timestamp and "actor" information. For example, the result tables show (see Fig. 7.3c): the actor "c1" and the actor "c2" have link relationship because both of them attend the same event "*a*" at time 1, and the actor "c1" and the actor "c3" have link relationship because both of them attend the same event "*a*" and "*b*" at time 2.

## Dynamic Network Modeling

There are two ways to model dynamic network. For network structure analysis and visualization, analysts can use SQL query to export network snapshot to a CSV file or a text file (Fig. 7.4), then load into network analysis software package (e.g., ORA or Pajek). Nowadays, some network analysis tools (e.g., ORA) can directly read network data from database through ODBC.

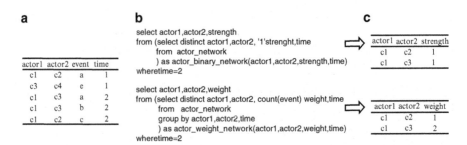

**Fig. 7.4** (**a**) Dynamic actor-network table; (**b**) extract network data with SQL query; (**c**) two network snapshots, one is the binary network, another is the weighted network

For data mining, data warehouse is a proper tool to integrate all kinds of data source, including network relation data and nodes' attribute data. Integrated data is the data source of modeling complex networks. The multi-dimensional model (cube) can meet the needs of various network mode modeling. OLAP technology can help analysts to access data through ad hoc queries. The main data manipulation include: pivoting, drilling down and drilling up, slicing and dicing, rotating and ranking.

## Dynamic Network Analysis

Methods of the over time network data analysis has actually been present in the social sciences literature for quite some time [20]. The dominant methods of longitudinal social network analysis include Markov chain models, multi-agent simulation models, and statistical models. A complete review of these methods is beyond this chapter. Further related reading can be found in [20, 21].

The ORA is a statistical analysis package for analyzing complex systems as dynamic social network. The ORA helps the user to evaluate one or more networks. Using ORA, the following questions can be addressed: what is critical, any groups of interest, any patterns of interest, which is critical, any emerging groups, how the network changes. From the website of CASOS users can download the latest version software [22].

In ORA software package, "The View Measures over Time" is one of ORA tools to assess the network change over time, i.e., the topology change of a network. Consequently, who or what is critical in a network might change over time. Apart from this, it applies statistical process control to graph-level network measures to detect changes in longitudinal network data. So, for the analysis of over time network data, the ORA software is a very good choice.

**a**

| BID | SID | Sequence |
|-----|-----|----------|
| B1 | 1 | `<a(abc)(ac)d(cf)>` |
| B2 | 2 | `<(ad)c(bc)(ae)>` |
| B3 | 3 | `<(ef)(ab)(df)cb>` |
| B4 | 4 | `<eg(af)cbc>` |

Sequences (Horizontal Format)

**b**

| SID | EID | ITEMS |
|-----|-----|-------|
| 1 | 1 | a |
| 1 | 2 | abc |
| 1 | 3 | ac |
| 1 | 5 | d |
| 1 | 3 | cf |
| 2 | 1 | ad |
| ... | ... | .... |

Sequences (Vertical Format)

**c**

| BID/SID | Sequence |
|---------|----------|
| B1/S1 | `<(a,1)(c,3),(a,4)(b,5),(a,6),(c,6),(c,10)>` |
| B2/S2 | `<(d,5),(a,7),(b,7),(c,7),(d,9),(c,9),(c,14)>` |
| B3/S3 | `<(a,8),(b,8),(c,11),(d,13),(b,16),(c,16),(c,20)>` |
| B4/S4 | `<(b,15),(f,17),(c,18),(b,22),(c,23)>` |

Sequences (with timestamp)

**Fig. 7.5** Three formats of purchase sequences data

## *Dynamic Network Data Mining*

Recently, many studies have focused on how to develop new technologies for data mining in social network. Some new models or algorithms have been proposed, but also faces many challenges. This study will apply sequence pattern mining technique to explore the buyer shopping sequence of group-buying.

### Sequence Pattern Mining

Sequential pattern mining is the mining of frequently occurring ordered events or subsequences as patterns. There are many applications involving sequential pattern. Typical examples include customer shopping sequences, Web click streams, sequences of events in science and engineering, and in natural and social development.

In the social buying model, the most interesting question in decision making is "Customers who bought that special deal are likely to buy this special deal within a month," or "Customers who have recommended a deal to their friends are likely to make recommendation this time." In fact, the answers of these questions are the link prediction problem, i.e., we are given a snapshot of a network at time $t$ and wish to predict the edge that will be added to the network during the interval from time $t$ to a given future time, $t'$ [23].

The buyer purchase sequence, which is an ordered list of events, can be extracted from the dynamic network database (i.e., tables) using SQL program. Figure 7.5 shows three types of sequence data: the horizontal format, the vertical format of sequence data, and the format with timestamp.

A sequence describes the process of network node's link growth. Let us look at sequence 1, which is $<a\ (abc)\ (ac)\ d\ (cf)>$, That means the buyer "c1" chose the item "$a$" at time period 1, and chose items "$a$, $b$, $c$" at time period 2, and so on.

Typically, sequence size and sequence length are two commonly used measures. The number of items contained in a sequence corresponds to the sequence size. The number of item sets in the sequence equals its length. For example, sequence 1 has a length of nine and a size of five.

A sequence is a subsequence of another sequence if the first can be derived by deleting itemsets from the second. For example, sequence $<a(bc)df>$ is a subsequence of sequence 1. A sequence that is not a subsequence of another sequence is defined as a maximal sequence.

The support for a sequence equals the proportion of transactions that contain the sequence. For example, for a threshold of 0.50, sequence $<a\ b>$ is a frequent sequence because its support level is 0.75.

The sequential pattern mining problem is "Given a set of sequences, where each sequence consists of a list of events, and given a user-specified minimum support threshold, sequential pattern mining finds all frequent subsequences, that is, the subsequences whose occurrence frequency in the set of sequences is no less than the minimum support." The model of pattern mining is an abstraction of customer-shopping sequence analysis. Some algorithms for sequential pattern mining can be found in [23].

## Time-Interval Sequence Pattern Mining

For decision maker of the social buying websites, a time-interval sequential pattern provides more valuable information than a conventional sequential pattern [18, 24]. For example, with the time-interval sequential pattern, the web manager learns not only the interests and needs of his customers, but also their shopping timing. From the perspective of network dynamics, the time-interval sequential pattern is helpful to explain the evolution of network.

A sequence with timestamp is represented as $S((a_1,t_1),(a_2,t_2),(a_3,t_3),\ldots,(a_n,t_n))$, where $a_j$ is an item and $t_j$ stands for the time at which $a_j$ occurs, $1 \le j \le n$, and $t_{j-1} \le t_j$ for $2 \le j \le n$.

In addition, let $t$ represent the time interval between two successive items, and let $T_k$ be the given constants for $1 \le k \le r-1$. Then, the time interval is divided into $r+1$ ranges, where

- $I_0$ denotes the time interval $t$ satisfying $t = 0$;
- $I_1$ denotes the time interval $t$ satisfying $0 < t \le T_1$;
- $I_j$ denotes the time interval $t$ satisfying $T_{j-1} < t \le T_j$ for $1 < j < r-1$;
- $I_r$ denotes the time interval $t$ satisfying $T_{r-1} < t < \infty$.

Let the set of time intervals be represented as $T_I = \{I_0; I_1; I_2; \ldots; I_r\}$: Then, the time-interval sequential pattern can be defined as follows.

Definition: Let $I = \{i_1; i_2; \ldots; i_m\}$ be the set of all items and $T_I = \{I_0; I_1; I_2; \ldots; I_r\}$ be the set of time intervals. A sequence $\beta = (\beta_1; \&_1; \beta_2; \&_2; \ldots; \beta_{s-1}; \&_{s-1}; \beta_s)$ is a time-interval sequence if bi belong to $I$ for $1 \le i \le s$ and $\&i$ belong to $T_I$ for $1 \le i \le s-1$.

For example, consider the sequence dataset shown in Fig. 7.5c with $T_I = \{I_0; I_1; I_2; I_3\}$; where $I_0: t = 0$; $I_1: 0 < t \le 3$; $I_2: 3 < t \le 6$ and $I_3: 6 < t < \infty$.

The time-interval sequence $(b; I_1; e; I_2; c)$ includes three items, and therefore has a length of 3. It is called a 3-time-interval sequence. The time-interval sequence

$(b; I_1; e; I_2; c)$ is a time-interval subsequence of buyer B4. Besides, $(b; I_1; e; I_2; c)$ is also contained in $S_1$ and $S_3$. Therefore, its support is 75%. If Minsup = 50% is set, then $(b; I_1; e; I_2; c)$ is a time-interval sequential pattern.

## Case Study

### Data Source

Following the success of online Groupon's business mode (i.e. group-buying 2.0) on the Internet, similar interest and activity can be seen in China with a number of dedicated online group-buying sites in recent years. Web-facilitated group-buying is under the name "tuangou" or "team buying" in Chinese [25], for example, Liba.com (at www.liba.com), TeamBuy (at www.teambuy.com.cn) and Meituan (at www. meituan.com). These fast-growing dot companies will provide large data stream to the empirical study of social-buying phenomenon.

UUlike.com (at www.uulike.com) is a new social buying website in Shenzhen, the most modern city in South China. UUlike gathers and recommends daily deal, including great local restaurants, spa, concerts, movies, fitness, events and special foods, etc. The objective customers of UUlike are local residents aged 20–40, fashionable and familiar with web shopping. UUlike's business started their online group-buying service in June 2010. Lack of popularity, they started with "one deal one week," "two deals one week," and then move to "one deal one day" when their site got increasing attention.

We gathered continuous 24 weeks data in the June 15th to November 30th period from transaction database of UULike.com. After data cleaning, all transaction data was loaded into the network database. These data was as the data source of the dynamic network modeling and analysis. The timestamp is the exact time of occurrence of customer purchase.

### Dynamic Network Analysis

Six network snapshots (ordered by month) were exported to the six text files, using SQL query from the dynamic network database, and then all data files were loaded into ORA software to create a dynamic meta-network (see Fig. 7.6).

Let us highlight the "Dynamic Meat-Networks" and select from the main menu "Visualizations > View Measures over Time," which is one of the basic tools for dynamic network analysis. That allows an analyst to observe network measures how to change over time.

Table 7.2 shows the growth of the numbers of nodes and edges, average degree of node and the variation of network density over time.

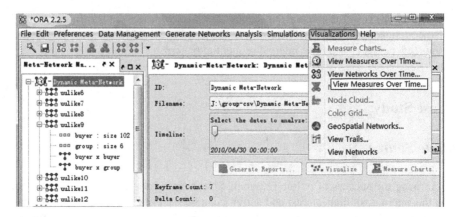

**Fig. 7.6** Dynamic meta-network of social buying in ORA

**Table 7.2** Basic network statistic of dynamic group-buying

| Statistic | June | July | August | September | October | November | Union |
|---|---|---|---|---|---|---|---|
| The number of groups | 5 | 6 | 7 | 6 | 15 | 26 | 65 |
| The number of buyers | 90 | 94 | 400 | 102 | 389 | 455 | 1,341 |
| The number of links | 180 | 121 | 428 | 121 | 488 | 627 | 1,965 |
| The average buyers each group | 36 | 20.2 | 61.14 | 20.17 | 32.5 | 24.12 | 20.6 |
| The average deals each buyer | 2 | 1.29 | 1.07 | 1.186 | 1.25 | 1.378 | 1.46 |
| The density of network | 0.4 | 0.21 | 0.15 | 0.198 | 0.08 | 0.053 | 0.023 |

The "union" network consists of six networks

Counting the number of links maintained by each node is the first way to describe network topology property. This measure is referred to as node in-degree and out-degree. In group-buying network, out-degree for each buyer measures the frequency of attendant group-buying. In-degree for each deal measures the size of group or the number of buyers.

Although the number of nodes, particularly from September, has significantly increased over time, the average degree of node stays in low level. The maximum size of group is close to 350 (see Fig. 7.7a), but the average size of group is about 25 (see Fig. 7.7b). So to say, most of the groups just involved in small collective buying. This implies that business of UUlike is not successful at the beginning. The company should modify business strategies according to market investigation and buyers' behavior research.

The network density of group-buying network (i.e., GBN) reduced from 0.4 to 0.053 (see Fig. 7.8a). This means that the relationship have grown slower than the size of network. The lower average degree of buyer node over time confirms the result for network density.

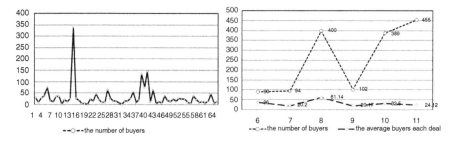

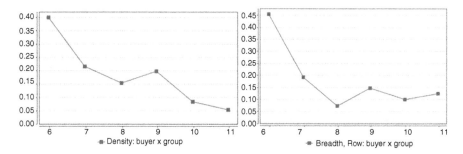

**Fig. 7.7** (**a**) The number of buyers for each group (there are 65 groups during 6 months); (**b**) the variation of two statistics (the number of buyers and the average degree for each group or) from June to November

**Fig. 7.8** (**a**) The variation of network density; (**b**) the variation of row breadth over time

Row Breadth is the fraction of entities with row nodes (i.e., buyer) with degree greater than one. In a given group-buying network, this measure tells us how many people whose purchase frequency is greater than one. Figure 7.8b shows the percentage of purchase frequency greater than one has fluctuated from June to November. The percentage of buyers with purchase frequency greater than one decreased from 45% to about 10%. That means nearly 90% of their customers never return to UUlike.com after participating once in their online group-buying.

Key-Entity analysis tool indentifies the central events and actors. Figure 7.9 shows that the size of each group is different. Some groups attracted large numbers of buyer, although the average size of each group is small. According to the in-degree of column nodes (i.e., group), the most popular deals included G014, G040, G038, G039 and G005. G040 is special food provided by a local restaurant with discount 70%; G005 is another special food with discount 50%, G038 is one time Yoga course for free; G039 is one time Spa service for free; and G014 is a free gift package for the special Chinese festivals. Obviously, lots of customers like free lunch.

Table 7.3 shows Top 10 buyers according to their normalized out-degree. The repeating buyers in different snapshot are underlined. The observation of the tables shows the customers' buying history as followed: c81 has participated in 27 deals,

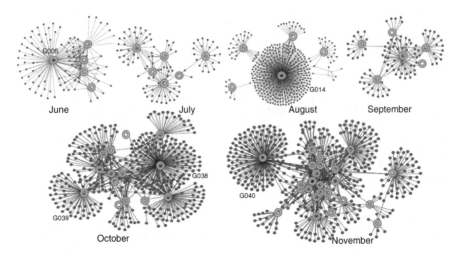

**Fig. 7.9** Dynamic group-buying network from June to November (*circle nodes* and *diamond nodes* represent the buyer and the deal, respectively)

**Table 7.3** Top 10 buyers ranked by out-degree of row nodes in different period

| Rank | 6 | 7 | 8 | 9 | 10 | 11 | Union |
|------|-----|------|-------|------|-------|-------|-------|
| 1 | c14 | c41 | c2133 | c44 | c70 | c1093 | c81 |
| 2 | c30 | c11 | c70 | c70 | c81 | c141 | c48 |
| 3 | c12 | c21 | c81 | c768 | c7 | c1398 | c7 |
| 4 | c21 | c4 | c141 | c769 | c370 | c36 | c70 |
| 5 | c22 | c48 | c268 | c141 | c48 | c81 | c141 |
| 6 | c3 | c67 | c282 | c370 | c82 | c755 | c67 |
| 7 | c34 | c7 | c299 | c50 | c1034 | c912 | c36 |
| 8 | c36 | c8 | c300 | c67 | c1061 | c48 | c370 |
| 9 | c39 | c103 | c307 | c68 | c67 | c1369 | c1093 |
| 10 | c4 | c12 | c310 | c720 | c804 | c7 | c82 |

The smaller the number the customer got, the earlier that customer registered in the web

a little more than once a week; C48, C7 and C70 have all participated in more than 20 deals. They are so-called loyal clients, whose participation rankings were always listed in the top 10 according to the monthly buying records.

So the strategy of "keep them coming back" and "lock-in" to using this site is the key to business success. An in-depth study upon one's likelihood of returning to the same site is significant for UUlike.com's growth. As the world of dot.com businesses began to emerge, it was clear that the race to attract customers is just on. The challenge was not simply bringing the customers in the door but also to retain these customers for future purchases.

An amazing phenomenon is that the size of Word-of-Mouth social network (buyer × buyer) on UUlike website is very small; few buyers have recommended or reviewed special deals. Only three buyers recommended each other during 6 months

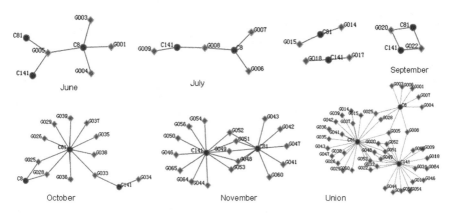

**Fig. 7.10** The subgraph of dynamic group-buying among three buyers (c8, c81 and c141) from June to November (*circle nodes* and *diamond nodes* represent the buyer and the deal, respectively)

(see Fig. 7.10). The reason is that the rapid growth of group-buying in China has led to fierce competition. For the purpose of gathering audience, some social buying websites, e.g., UUlike, cancel restrictions of minimum threshold of the number of buyers, while encouraging recommendation among people with extra bonus.

Although such network is in small scales, but it is clear that multi-recommendation will bring in enough numbers of buying participations. So the marketing based on the social network of customers regularly got greater attention of the decision makers in companies.

## Buyer Behavior Analysis

For customer behavioral analysis, researchers have observed that RFM (such as recency, frequency, and monetary) is a widely used technique that can effectively investigate customer values and segment markets [26].

In this section, we define four buyers' behavior variables based on social buying metanetwork:

- Frequency: How often a customer buys. Use the 20/80 rule for marketing. Twenty percent of customers may contribute 80% of business. Knowing frequency can help manager target these customers and also turn more customers into the 20/80 crowd when leveraged properly. The value is the degree of row node in the binary group-buying network
- Monetary: How much a customer spends. This information helps manager to categorize your customers into monetary groups (like: frugal spender, average spender, and luxury spender) and gain insight into which products and services to target to which individuals. The value is the strength of row node in the weighted (by amount of deal) group-buying network divide degree of row node, measures the average monetary expenditure on purchasing during a specific period.

**Table 7.4** Basic statistic of variables

| Variables | Mean | Standard deviation | Median | Mode | Max |
|---|---|---|---|---|---|
| Frequency of purchase | 1.46 | 0.05 | 1 | 1 | 26 |
| Total expenditure (RMB, Yuan) | 118.5 | 610.3 | 48 | −1 | 14,277 |
| Average expenditure(Monetary) | 61.23 | 131.3 | 48 | −1 | 2,980 |

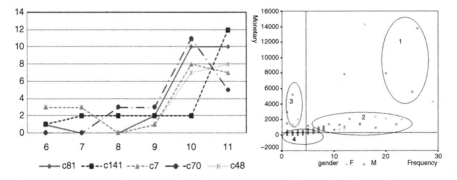

**Fig. 7.11** (a) Purchase frequency from June to November for Top 5 buyers ranked by the total of purchase frequency; (b) Buyer segmentation according to Frequency and Monetary

- Recency: How recently a customer bought. By tracking customers' purchase history, manager will be better able to anticipate their buying habits and market to them more effectively. The value is the interval between the most recent transaction time of individual buyers and the evaluation time.
- Activity: How activity a customer on social media website. The value measures the participation in social buying, by calculating the degree of node in the Word-of-Mouth social network.

UUlike.com has 4,278 registered users between June 15th and November 30th, but only 1,341 attended the group-buying, among them 70% of buyers are female users. In the dynamic network database, four measures can be calculated by using SQL statement. But in our empirical study, the value of activity variable cannot be calculated because Word-of-Mouth social network is small; most buyers have no recommend records. Now the manager has began to pay attention to this problem. Some techniques will be use to monitor users' behavior on the site.

Table 7.4 shows the basic statistic of variables. Most frequent buyer has 26 group-buying experiences. The value of expenditure "−1" means the deal is not only free but also returned 1 dollar (i.e., RMB, Yuan) to the customer, in order to attract customers.

Figure 7.11a shows the top 5 buyers in Frequency, where their purchasing frequencies are more than 20. That means they have bought one deal for each week in 6 months. Customer purchase behavior is very different: sometimes more, sometime less, changing every month.

The RFM values constitute the basis for customer segmentation. Such segmentation well demonstrates significant difference of buyers' behavior. Buyers are divided into four clusters based on purchase frequency and average monetary expenditure (see Fig. 7.11b). The clusters are:

Cluster 1 represents the most valuable customers (higher purchase frequency and higher monetary expenditure, i.e., higher node degree and higher node strength); Clusters 2 represents frequent buyers (higher purchase frequency, i.e., higher connectivity but lower strength of nodes); Cluster 3 represents spenders (higher monetary expenditure, i.e., lower connectivity but higher strength of nodes); Cluster 4 represents uncertain customers (least valuable, i.e., lower node connectivity and lower node strength).

When recency is used for cross analysis of the four customer clusters, customers in Clusters 1and 2 have made regular purchases recently. Cluster 1 also has higher average expenditure and purchase frequency; therefore, Cluster 1 is concluded to be the most valuable for the business. Meanwhile, Cluster 4 is customers who have not made purchases recently.

## *Time-Interval Sequence Pattern Mining*

We generated time-interval sequence based on dynamic bipartite network with SQL program, and then use I-Apriori algorithm for mining time-interval sequential patterns [24].

There are 204 buyers whose purchase frequency is more than one in UUlike dataset, i.e., the length of sequence is more than 1. We define $TI = \{I_0; I_1; I_2; I_3; I_4\}$; where $I_0$: $t = 0$; $I_1$: $0 < t \leq 7$; $I_2$: $7 < t \leq 15$; $I_3$: $15 < t \leq 21$ and $I_4$: $21 < t < \infty$.

If Minsup = 2% is set, that means if more than 26 buyers support then the time-interval sequential pattern is frequent. The empirical results show: (restaurant; $I_1$; KTV; $I_2$; restaurant) and (spa; $I_1$; yoga) are frequent time-interval sequential patterns. There are two typical customers' groups. A group of customers are interested in special food and amusement, another group of customers like the fashionable lifestyle.

## Conclusions

Social buying is an innovative online business model of e-commerce. This chapter first proposed a metanetwork framework to describe people and people-event interaction on the social-buying site. Second we provided modifications to standard Network Representation Languages and enabled this capability by enhancements to the representation of dynamics, along with reduced computational overhead. Third in order to meet the analysis and data mining need, we proposed a methodology framework for supporting large-scale data storing, dynamic network modeling and analysis, based on the Business Intelligent platform.

The Case study was about a new company providing social buying in Shenzhen, China. The empirical results can help managers identify problems and take appropriate strategies or measures.

However, the limitation of this research is that UUlike's data source cannot completely support modeling and analysis of the social-buying metanetwork, because of missing Word-of-Mouth social network data.

In fact, a major problem with traditional SNA is that people in the networks are not treated as active adaptive agents that capable of taking action, learning, and altering their networks [14]. From this point of view, buyers are active adaptive agents that can take action, retrieve information and make decision during the online shopping. These actions result in the emerging of dynamic social network, and the co-evolving of set of networks linking people, items and events.

Therefore, the formation of online or offline social network how to influence customer's web shopping behavior, and how to build collective buying group through social media, are most valuable problems for business decision maker. In the future, we will try to explore these issues.

# References

1. Hannon, D.: Big U.S. companies unite to make group buying work. Purchasing. Magazine Online, 23 Aug 2001
2. Mitchell, P.: Internet-enabled group purchasing: get a buy with a little help from your friends. Technical Report, AMR Research, Feb 2002
3. Dolan, R.: Quantity discounts: managerial issues and research opportunities. Mark. Sci. 6(1), 1–22 (1987)
4. Kauffman, R.J., Lai, H., Lin, H.-C. et al.: Do textual comments and existing orders affect consumer participation in online group-buying? In: Proceedings of the 42nd Hawaii International Conference on System Sciences, Waikoloa, 5–8 Jan 2009
5. Anand, K.S., Aron, R.: Group buying on the web: a comparison of price-discovery mechanisms. Manag. Sci. 49(11), 1546–1562 (2003)
6. Chen, J., Chen, X., Song, X.: Bidder's strategy under group-buying auction on the internet. IEEE Trans. Syst. Man Cybern. A Syst. Human 32(6), 680–690 (2002)
7. Chen, J., Chen, X., Song, X.: Comparison of the group-buying auction and the fixed pricing mechanism. Decis. Support Syst. 43(2), 445–459 (2007)
8. Chen, J., Chen, X., et al.: Should we collude? Analyzing the benefits of bidder cooperation in online group-buying auctions. Electron. Commer. Res. Appl. 8(4), 191–202 (2009)
9. Chen, J., Kauffman, R.J., et al.: Segmenting uncertain demand in group-buying auctions. Electron. Commer. Res. Appl. (2009). doi:10.1016/j.elerap. 03.001
10. Kauffman, R.J., Wang, B.: New buyer's arrival under dynamic pricing market microstructure: the case of group-buying discounts on the internet. J. Manag. Inf. Syst. 18(2), 157–188 (2001)
11. Kauffman, R.J., Wang, B.: Bid together, buy together: on the efficiency of group-buying business models in internet-based selling. In: Lowry, P., Cherrington, J., Watson, R. (eds.) Handbook of Electronic Commerce in Business and Society. CRC Press, New York (2002)
12. Ho, C.-T., Kauffman, R.J., Lai, H.: Incentive mechanisms, fairness and participation in online group-buying auctions. Electron. Commer. Res. Appl. (2009). doi:10.1016/j.elerap. 2008.11.009
13. United We may Stand. Wall Street J., 12 May 2008. http://online.wsj.com/article/SB121018834137874437.html. Accessed on June 2012

14. Carley, K.M.: Dynamic network analysis. In: Breiger, R., Carley, K.M. (eds.) The NRC Workshop on Social Network Modeling and Analysis. National Research Council, National Academies Press, Washington, DC (2003)
15. Irene, P.: Dynamic Network Analysis for Understanding Complex Systems and Processes. DRDC CORA TM (2009). http://www.drdc-rddc.gc.ca.document320
16. Belov, N., Martin, M.K., Patti, J. et al.: Dynamic networks: rapid assessment of changing scenarios. Social Computing and Behavioral Modeling (2009). http://www.springer.com/computer/database+management+%26+information+retrieval/book/978-1-4419-0055-5
17. Davis, M.: Using business intelligence for competitive advantage. CRM Today (2002)
18. Liu, X., Yang, J.: Business intelligence approach to support modeling and analysis of complex economic networks. Int. J. Netw. Virtual Organ. **8**(3/4), 281–291 (2011)
19. Latapy, M., Magnien, C., Del Vecchio, N.: Basic notions for the analysis of large two-mode networks. Soc. Netw. **30**, 31–48 (2008)
20. McCulloh, I.A., Carley, K.M.: Social Network Change Detection. Carnegie Mellon University, School of Computer Science, Institute for Software Research, Technical Report, CMU-ISR-08-116 (2008)
21. McCulloh, I., Carley, K.: Longitudinal Dynamic Network Analysis: Using the Over Time Viewer Feature in ORA. Carnegie Mellon University, School of Computer Science, Institute for Software Research, Technical Report CMU-ISR-09-118 (2009)
22. http://www.casos.ece.cmu.edu/projects/ORA/index.html
23. Han, J., Kamber, M.: Data Mining: Concepts and Techniques, 2nd edn, pp. 555–575. China Machine Press, Beijing (2006)
24. Chen, Y.-L., Chiang, M.-C., Ko, M.-T.: Discovering time-interval sequential patterns in sequence databases. Expert Syst. Appl. **25**, 11 (2003)
25. Kauffman, R.J., Lai, H., Ho, C.-T.: Incentive mechanisms, fairness and participation in online group-buying auctions. Electron. Commer. Res. Appl. **9**, 14 (2010)
26. Hu, Y.-H., Huang, T.C.-K., Yang, H.-R., Chen, Y.-L.: On mining multi-time-interval sequential patterns. Data Knowl. Eng. **68**, 6 (2009)

# Chapter 8
# Reliable Online Social Network Data Collection

**Fehmi Ben Abdesslem, Iain Parris, and Tristan Henderson**

**Abstract** Large quantities of information are shared through online social networks, making them attractive sources of data for social network research. When studying the usage of online social networks, these data may not describe properly users' behaviours. For instance, the data collected often include content shared by the users only, or content accessible to the researchers, hence obfuscating a large amount of data that would help to understand users' behaviours and privacy concerns. Moreover, the data collection methods employed in experiments may also have an effect on data reliability when participants self-report inaccurate information or are observed while using a simulated application. Understanding the effects of these collection methods on data reliability is paramount for the study of social networks; for understanding user behaviour; for designing socially aware applications and services; and for mining data collected from such social networks and applications.

This chapter reviews previous research which has looked at social network data collection and user behaviour in these networks. We highlight shortcomings in the methods used in these studies and introduce our own methodology and user study based on the experience sampling method; we claim that our methodology leads to the collection of more reliable data by capturing both those data which are shared and not shared. We conclude with suggestions for collecting and mining data from online social networks.

## Introduction

An increasing number of online social network (OSN) services have arisen recently to allow Internet users to share their activities, photographs, and other content with one another. This new form of social interaction has been the focus of much recent

F. Ben Abdesslem (✉) • I. Parris • T. Henderson
School of Computer Science, University of St Andrews, St Andrews, UK
e-mail: fehmi@cs.st-andrews.ac.uk; ip@cs.st-andrews.ac.uk; tristan@cs.st-andrews.ac.uk

A. Abraham (ed.), *Computational Social Networks: Mining and Visualization*,
DOI 10.1007/978-1-4471-4054-2_8, © Springer-Verlag London 2012

research aimed at understanding users' behaviours. In order to do so, collecting data on users' behaviour is a necessary first step. These data may be collected as follows: (1) from OSNs, by retrieving data shared on social network websites; (2) from surveys, by asking participants about their behaviour; and (3) through deployed applications, by directly monitoring users as they share content online.

The first source of data, OSNs, contains large quantities of personal information, shared everyday by their users. For instance, Facebook stores more than 30 billion pieces of new content each month (e.g. blog posts, notes, photo albums), shared by over 500 million users.[1] These data not only provide information on the users themselves but also describe their social interactions in terms of how, when and to whom they share information. Nevertheless, while collecting the data available from OSNs can help in studying users' social behaviour, the content made available may often be filtered beforehand by the users according to their particular preferences, resulting in important parts of data being inaccessible to researchers. When studying users' behaviour, ignoring privacy choices by discarding these inaccessible data may lead to a biased analysis and a truncated representation of users' behaviour. Including personal information that the users do not want to share may be vitally important, for instance, if privacy concerns are the focus of one's research.

The second source of data for studying users' behaviour consists of asking users how, when and to whom they would share content using, for instance, question-naires. When using such survey instruments, however, participants might forget the particular context in which they share content in their everyday lives and thus end up unconsciously providing less accurate data on their experiences. Conducting surveys in situ allows researchers to overcome this issue: participants are asked to report their experiences in real time whenever they interact with the observed system; in this case, when they use an OSN. But for ease of implementation or to allow controlled studies, in situ research surveys often involve simulated interactions with the participants' social networks. If a participant knows that their content will never actually be shared, or that their interactions are simulated, then the resulting data may also be biased, as the users' behaviour might have been primed by the simulation.

Finally, deploying a custom application is the third source of data. This method usually consists in collecting data by deploying a custom application used by participants to share content on OSNs. This method provides more flexibility to monitor users' behaviour in situ, and the content that participants do not share to their social network can still be collected by the researchers.

Data collected with these different methods may be biased, suggesting inaccurate interpretations of users' actual behaviours. In this context, we define *data collection reliability* as the property of a method to collect data that can describe users' behaviour with accuracy. In this chapter, we review previous research in the study of online social networks, highlighting the data collection methods employed and evaluating their reliability. We next introduce our methodology that combines

---

[1]http://www.facebook.com/press/info.php?statistics

existing methods to address some of their drawbacks by collecting more reliable data through in situ experiments. The remainder of this chapter is organised as follows. First, commonly used data collection methods are described in section "Existing Data Collection Methods". Section "Experience Sampling in Online Social Networks with Smartphones" details our methodology for collecting more reliable data. Finally, we provide our guidelines to collect more reliable data by discussing methods and their implications in section "Discussion".

## Existing Data Collection Methods

Many researchers have collected data from OSNs and mined these data to better understand behaviour in such networks. There are many different types of data and collection methods that can help in studying OSN users' behaviour. These data often describe different aspects of user behaviour and can be complementary. This section provides an overview of recent research in collecting data about online social networks and their users.

### *Social Network Measurement*

Most OSN providers are commercial entities and as such are loathe to provide researchers with direct access to data, owing to concerns about competitive access to data, and also their users' privacy concerns.[2] Hence, researchers often collect their own data directly from OSNs, either by collecting data directly from the OSN, or by sniffing the network traffic and parsing the data to and from the OSN.

#### Collecting Social Network Content

The most common way to collect content from OSNs is to use the API (application programming interface) provided by the OSN provider. Relevant queries are sent to the OSN with the API to collect data. Where data available on the website are not available through the API, an alternative method is to crawl the OSN website with an automated script that explores the website and collects data using HTTP requests and responses. OSN research usually employs one of these two methods to collect data, but for very different purposes.

---

[2]That said, one of the most popular OSNs, Twitter, has recently made some effort to provide researchers with access to part of their data by donating an archive of public data to the US Library of Congress for preservation and research (http://blog.twitter.com/2010/04/tweet-preservation.html).

Content-Sharing Behaviour

One frequent focus of OSN research is to study users' behaviour regarding their information sharing. Amichai-Hamburger and Vinitzky [1] collect data from the Facebook profiles of 237 students to study the correlation between quantity of profile information and personality. Lewis et al. [28] collect Facebook public profile data from 1,710 undergraduate students from a single university and study their privacy settings. Lindamood et al. [29] collect the Facebook profiles of 167,390 users within the same geographical network by crawling the website. Their goal is to evaluate algorithms to infer private information.

OSN Usage

Data collection is also useful for studying aspects of OSN usage, such as session lengths or applications. Gjoka et al. [15] characterise the popularity and user reach of Facebook applications. They crawl approximately 300,000 users with publicly available profiles. Nazir et al. [32] developed three Facebook applications and study their usage. Gyarmati and Trinh [18] crawl the websites of four OSNs, Bebo, MySpace, Netlog, and Tagged, retrieving publicly available status information, and study the characteristics of user sessions of 80,000 users for more than 6 weeks.

Comparison Between OSN Data and Other Sources

Data shared on OSNs are also collected to be compared to other sources of information. For instance, Qiu et al. [35] use the Twitter API to collect tweets that contain mobile-performance-related text and compare them with support tickets obtained from a mobile service provider. Guy et al. [17] collect social network data from 343 OSN users of a company intranet and compare their public social networks to their email inboxes.

Interaction Between Users

OSNs not only provide information on what users share but also describe their interaction with their social networks. Valafar et al. [42] collect data by crawling Flickr users and study their interactions. Viswanath et al. [43] crawl a geographical Facebook network to study interactions between users. Wilson et al. [45] crawl Facebook using accounts from several geographical network to study user interactions. Jiang et al. [22] examine latent interactions between users of Renren, a popular OSN in China. All friendship links in Renren are public, allowing the authors to exhaustively crawl a connected graph component of 42 million users and 1.66 billion social links in 2009. They also capture detailed histories of profile visits over a period of 90 days for more than 61,000 users in the Peking University Renren network and use statistics of profile visits to study issues of user profile popularity, reciprocity of profile visits and the impact of content updates on user popularity.


OSN Characteristics

Many other researchers study the properties of OSNs, such as the number of active users, users' geographical distribution, node degree, or influence and evolution. This research is not focused on the behaviours of users as individuals but rather on the behaviour of the network as a whole. Cha et al. [7] collect two billion links amongst 54 million users to study people's influence patterns on the OSN Twitter. They use both the API and website crawling to collect this data. Garg et al. [13] examine the evolution of the OSN FriendFeed by collecting data on more than 200,000 users with the FriendFeed API, along with close to four million directed edges amongst them. Rejaie et al. [36] estimate the size of active users on Twitter and MySpace by collecting data on a random sample of users through the API. Ye and Wu [46] crawl Twitter user accounts to validate their method to estimate the number of users an OSN has. Java et al. [21] study the topological and geographical properties of the social network in Twitter and examine users intentions when posting contents. They use the API to collect 1,348,543 posts from 76,177 distinct users over 2 months. Ghosh et al. [14] study the effects of restrictions on node degree on the topological properties of Twitter, by collecting data from one million Twitter users with the API, including their number of friends, number of followers, number of tweets posted, and other information such as the date of creation of the account and their geographical location.


**Measuring Social Network Activity**

OSN users spend most of their time browsing the content of a social network, rather than sharing content themselves [39], and this browsing activity is typically not broadcast on the OSN website. Hence, to better understand how users spend time in OSNs, and what information is of interest to the users, some researchers have focused on collecting network data between the user and the OSNs. Benevenuto et al. [4] analyse traces describing session-level summaries of over four million HTTP requests to and from OSN websites: Orkut, MySpace, Hi5, and Linked. The data are collected through a social network aggregator during 12 days and are used by the authors to study users' activity on these websites. Eagle et al. [10] measure the behaviour of 94 users over 9 months from their mobile phones using call logs, measurements of the Bluetooth devices within a proximity of approximately five metres, cell tower IDs, application usage, and phone status. They compare these data to self-reported friendship and proximity to others. Schneider et al. [39] analyse the HTTP traces of users from a dataset provided by two international ISPs to study usage of four popular OSNs.

## Self-Reported Data

Where data cannot be collected or interpreted from the OSNs, another useful
method is to directly ask the users about their experience, mainly through online
questionnaires, or in situ surveys.

Questionnaires and Focus Groups

There is a plethora of studies on OSN users' behaviour involving online questionnaires and focus groups. Besmer and Lipford [5] collect data from 14 people
through focus groups to examine privacy concerns surrounding tagged images on
Facebook. Brandtzæg and Heim [6] collect data about 5,233 people's motivations
for OSN usage through an online survey in Norway. Ellison et al. [11] measure
psychological well-being and social capital by collecting data through an online
survey from 286 students about their Facebook usage and perception. They were
paid US$5 credit on their on-campus spending accounts. Krasnova et al. [24] collect
data from two focus groups and 210 OSN users through online surveys to study
privacy concerns. Kwon and Wen [25] use an online survey to study the usage of
229 Korean OSN users. Lampe et al. [26] study changes in use and perception of
Facebook by collecting data on 288, 468 and 419 users, respectively, in 2006, 2007,
and 2009 through online surveys. Peterson and Siek [34] collect data on 20 users of
the OSN couchsurfing.com to analyse information disclosure. Roblyer et al. [37]
survey 120 students and 62 faculty members about their use and perception of
Facebook in class. Stutzman and Kramer-Duffield [40] collect data with an online
survey on 494 undergraduate students and examine privacy-enhancing behaviour in
Facebook. Young and Quan-Haase [47] collect data on 77 students with an online
survey about their information revelation on Facebook.

In Situ Data Collection

Participants in questionnaires or focus groups may forget the context of when they
are using OSNs, and thus they may report their experiences inaccurately. To counter
the inaccuracy of users' memories, the experience sampling method (ESM) [27] is
a popular diary method which consists of asking participants to periodically report
their experiences in real time, either on a predetermined (signal-contingent) basis
or when a particular event happens (event-contingent). By allowing participants
to self-report their own ongoing experiences in their everyday lives, ESM allows
researchers to obtain answers within or close to the context being studied, which
may result in more reliable data. Anthony et al. [2] collect in situ data by asking
25 participants to report during their everyday lives to whom they would share their
location. Pempek et al. [33] use a diary to ask 92 students about their daily activity
on Facebook for 7 days. Mancini et al. [30] study how people use Facebook from

their mobile phone by asking six participants to answer questions every time they perform an action on Facebook, such as adding a friend, or updating a status.

ESM has also been used by researchers to study other topics than social networks. Consolvo and Walker [8] ask participants ten times a day during 1 week about their information needs and their available equipment (e.g. televisions, laptops, printers). Questions are asked through a provided PDA, and participants are required to answer through this same device. They receive an incentive of US$50 for their participation and US$1 per question answered. Froehlich et al. [12] propose MyExperience, a system for mobile phones, to ask participants about their in situ experience. They deploy their system for three case studies. These deployments range from 4 to 16 participants and 1–4 weeks, and cover battery life and charging behaviour, text-messaging usage and mobility, and a study on place visit pattern and personal preference.

## Application Deployment

Another method for collecting data is to deploy a custom application based on a social network and monitor its usage. Iachello et al. [20] study the location-sharing behaviour of eight users. Participants use a mobile phone for 5 days and share their location by text message upon request from the other participants. Kofod-Petersen et al. [23] deploy a location-sharing system over 3 weeks in a three-storey building during a cultural festival.

Thousand six hundred and sixty one participants use ultrasound tags to be located, and several terminals are also distributed throughout the building. Sadeh et al. [38] deploy an application that enables cell phone and laptop users to selectively share their locations with others, such as friends, family, and colleagues. They study the privacy settings of over 60 participants.

## Challenges in Data Collection

Various methods have thus been employed for a broad range of studies. Nevertheless, while they all present benefits and provide useful data, these various methods also raise challenges that need to be addressed.

### Private Information

The data accessible on OSNs are rarely complete, as there are several pieces of information that users do not share, e.g. for privacy concerns. The absence of these data, however, may be an important piece of information for understanding user behaviours, and researchers indeed need to take into account the information that the users decline to share.

Most of the time, researchers disregard inaccessible data or even users with private data. For instance, Garg et al. [13] examine the evolution of an online social aggregation network and dismiss 12% of the users because they had private profiles. For these users, authors were not able to obtain the list of users they follow on Twitter and any other information pertaining to their activities. Gjoka et al. [16] study sampling methods by collecting data on more than six million users by crawling the websites, but the authors had to exclude from their dataset users hiding their friend lists. Lewis et al. [28] study OSN users' privacy by only collecting data on public profiles. Nevertheless, while collecting data on private contents is particularly important when studying privacy, 33.2% of the set had private profiles that could not be included in the data.

Researchers have occasionally resorted to tricks to access data about users. For instance, a common way to access users' Facebook profiles was to create accounts within the same regional network[3] than the target profiles [29, 43, 45]. Since membership in regional networks was unauthenticated and open to all users, the majority of Facebook users belonged to at least one regional network [45]. And since most users do not modify their default privacy settings, a large portion of Facebook users' profiles could be accessed by crawling regional networks. But this trick still did not allow access to all the profiles, as some privacy-sensitive users may have restricted access. Another trick is to log in to Facebook with an account belonging to the same university network as the studied sample. Lewis et al. [28] collect data on undergraduate students from Facebook by using an undergraduate Facebook account to access more data. Profiles can also be accessed by asking target users for friendship. Amongst 5,063 random target profiles, Nagle and Singh [31] were able to gain access to 19% of them after they accepted friend requests. They asked 3,549 of this set's friends for friendship, and 55% of them accepted, providing them with access to even more profiles. But when studying privacy concerns, the set of profiles that have been accessed may be biased, as they belong to users who accept unknown friendship requests.

Even when the information is available to the researchers, knowing to whom information is accessible is essential to understand users sharing behaviours. For instance, Amichai-Hamburger and Vinitzky [1] collect data from Facebook profiles and correlate the amount of information shared to users personality, but they do not take into account privacy settings of profile information: they make no difference between information shared to everyone and information shared to a restricted subset of people.

### Inaccuracy of Self-Reported Information

Participants of questionnaires and focus groups may forget their experience on OSNs and report inaccurate information. Researchers have already observed that users' answers to questionnaires do not always match with their actual OSNs

---

[3]Regional networks have been since removed from Facebook in 2009.

behaviour. For instance, Young and Quan-Haase [47] conducted a survey about information revelation on Facebook. They also interviewed a subset of the participants, and asked them to log on Facebook. The profile analysis showed that the participants are often unaware of, or have forgotten, what information they have disclosed and which privacy settings they have activated.

### The Effects of Using Simulated Applications

Researching user behaviour in online social network systems becomes more challenging if studying a system that does not yet exist, as it is not possible to mine data which have not yet been created. For instance, one might want to study behaviour in location- and sensor-aware social networks, which are only just becoming popular. One approach would be to build the real system and then study how people use it. When such a system is difficult to build, an alternative is to simulate the system. This consists in creating a simulated prototype with limited (or no) true functionality and then examining user behaviour of this prototype.

One potential pitfall is realism of the simulated system. For example, Consolvo et al. [9] investigate privacy concerns in a simulated social location-tracking application, employing the experience sampling method to query participants in situ [8]. They note this very problem with simulation, revealed through post-experiment interviews. Unrealistic, "out-of-character" simulated location requests were rejected by at least one participant.

A second possible pitfall, of particular relevance to studying social networks, is that the lack of real social consequences may affect behaviour. Tsai et al. [41] examine the effect of feedback in a real (i.e. non-simulated) location-sharing application tied to Facebook. Feedback, in the form of a list of viewers of each published location, was found to influence disclosure choices. Although they do not investigate a simulated application, the fact that real feedback has an effect may mean that simulated feedback (e.g. using a randomly generated list of viewers) could also affect behaviour in a different way.

To summarise, existing methods are all useful to capture particular aspects of users' experience, but may also lead to biased data collection. We believe that more reliable data can be obtained by using a new methodology based on the combination of existing methods: this way, the data collected come from different sources and better describe users' behaviours.

## Experience Sampling in Online Social Networks with Smartphones

Section "Existing Data Collection Methods" outlined popular research methods for collecting data in OSNs and discussed some of the drawbacks of each method. We now describe our methodology for collecting more reliable data on users' behaviours and demonstrate how we collected more reliable data by implementing this methodology through a set of real-world experiments.

## *Methodology*

Our methodology consists of observing how users share their location with an OSN using smartphones carried by users. In doing so, we are able to combine in situ data collection with OSN monitoring, thus collecting more reliable data on the sharing behaviour of OSN users.

### Design

We combine existing methods as described in section "Existing Data Collection Methods" to gather more complete and reliable data about users' behaviour. More precisely, our methodology comprises the following features:

- *Passive data collection.* We collect data from a custom application and do not rely only on self-reported information from the users (through questionnaires and interviews). The main reason is not only that collecting data in a passive way avoids disturbing the users but also that data gathered from real applications often describe objective and accurate information on users' behaviours. Hence, our methodology includes passive data collection from a social network application.
- *Private content collection.* While many previous methodologies only gather data about publicly shared content on OSNs, we advocate collecting data about both shared and unshared content. To collect data on this private information, we first automatically collect some content (or suggest the user to share content) and then ask the user whether this content should be shared or not. The users' responses are collected and provide information on what content are shared and what content is not.
- *In situ self-reported data collection.* Data collected passively may be difficult to interpret. Asking questions directly to the users can provide more information and context about the data and helps to understand why and to whom the content has been shared (or not). Hence, our methodology also includes self-reported data collection. For these data to be more reliable, questions are asked of the users and replied in situ using the ESM.
- *Real social interaction.* Some methodologies rely on simulated social interactions to collect data in situ about online sharing behaviours. We have found, however, that users may not behave the same when they are aware that sharing does not have any social consequences. With our methodology, when content is shared through the application, this content is actually uploaded onto an online social network and can be seen by members of the users' social network.

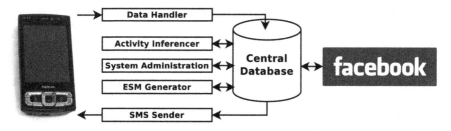

**Fig. 8.1** The testbed architecture and server modules

By implementing these features, our methodology avoids the shortcomings of previous methodologies as described in the last section, allowing more reliable online social network data collection.

We have applied this methodology for studying people's privacy concerns when sharing their location on the Facebook OSN. Participants were given a mobile phone and asked to carry it, using an application that enabled them to share their locations with their Facebook social network of friends. At the same time as they were doing so, they received ESM questions about their experiences, feelings, and location-disclosure choices. Implementing this methodology required the construction of an appropriate testbed and the design of an ESM study. We describe these in turn.

### Infrastructure

The infrastructure is composed of three main elements: the mobile phones, a server, and a Facebook application.

- *Mobile phone.* Every participant is given a smartphone. Each phone is running an application to detect and share locations and to allow participants to answer ESM questions.
- *Server.* Located in our laboratory, the server is composed of different modules (as described in Fig. 8.1) in charge of collecting data from the mobile phones, sending questions to the participants, and inferring their location or activity.
- *Facebook application.* The Facebook application uses the Facebook API (application programming interface) to interact with the phones and the Facebook OSN. This application is also hosted on our server, which allows us to control the dissemination and storage of data, but uses Facebook to share locations with a participant's social network of friends.

Mobile Phone

We use the Nokia N95 8 GB, a smartphone featuring GPS, 802.11, UMTS, a camera, and an accelerometer. This phone runs the Symbian operating system, for which we developed a location-sharing application, *LocShare*, in Python. This is installed on the phones prior to distribution to participants and designed to automatically run on start-up and then remain running in the background. *LocShare* performs the following tasks:

- *Location detection.* Where available, GPS is used to determine a participant's location every 10 s. When GPS is not available (e.g. when a device is indoors), a scan for 802.11 access points is performed every minute.
- *ESM questions.* Questions are sent to the phone using the Short Message Service (SMS) and displayed and answered using the phone.
- *Data upload.* Every five minutes, all collected data, such as locations and ESM answers, are uploaded to a server using the 3G network.

To extend battery life, thus allowing longer use of the mobile phone, the location is only retrieved (using GPS or 802.11) when the phone's accelerometer indicates that the device is in motion, as described in [3].

Server

As shown in Fig. 8.1, the server's role is to process data sent between the mobile phones and Facebook. This is performed using a number of separate software modules.

The collected data (i.e. GPS coordinates, scanned 802.11 access points, ESM responses, and accelerometer data) are regularly sent by the phone through the cellular network and received by the Data Handler module, which is listening for incoming connections and pushing the received data directly into a central SQL database (hereafter referred to as the Central Database).

The Activity Inferencer module runs regularly on the location data in the database and detects when the user stops in a new location. The module then attempts to transform this new location into a place name or activity. This is done by sending requests to publicly available online databases such as OpenStreetMap[4] to convert GPS coordinates and recorded 802.11 beacons into places (e.g. "library", "high street", "the central pub"). We pre-populate the activity database with some well-known activities and locations related to the cities where the experiments take place (e.g. supermarkets, lecture theatres, sports facilities), but by using public databases, we avoid having to manually map all possible location coordinates into places. The places or activity names can then be exploited by the Facebook application.

Since *LocShare* runs on GSM mobile phones, we leverage GSM's built-in SMS to control and send data to the application. SMS messages are handled by the SMS Sender module. The System Administration module allows remote management of the devices by sending special SMS messages handled by *LocShare*, for instance, to reboot the mobile phone if error conditions are observed. More important, the

---

[4]http://www.openstreetmap.org/

**Fig. 8.2**  The Facebook application used to share locations, collected via the mobile phones carried by participants, with a participant's social network of Facebook friends (a test account is displayed to respect participant anonymity). Locations and photos are visible to the participant and any other Facebook users (s)he has chosen

ESM module is in charge of generating questions, according to the current location or activity of a participant, and these questions are also sent using SMS.

Facebook Application

The Facebook application is also hosted on our server but is used through Facebook to display locations and activities of participants to their friends, through their profile or notifications, depending on their disclosure choices (Fig. 8.2).

**Experience Sampling**

To measure participants' privacy concerns when using a location-sharing application, we use the phones to ask participants to share their locations and ask questions about their privacy behaviours.

Before the start of an experiment, participants are asked to categorise their Facebook friends into groups (or "lists" in Facebook terminology), to which they would like to share similar amounts of information. Example groups might include "family", "classmates", "friends in Edinburgh". In addition to these custom lists, we add two generic lists: "everyone" and "all friends", the former including all Facebook users and the latter including only the participant's friends. They were also asked to specify the periods of time in the week when they did not want to be disturbed by questions (e.g. at night, during lectures).

Participants carry the phone with them at all times. Six types of signal- or event-contingent ESM questions are then sent to the participants' phones:

- *Signal-contingent.* Signal-contingent questions are sent on a predetermined regular basis: ten such questions are sent each day, at random times of the day.

   1. *"We might publish your current location to Facebook just now. How do you feel about this?"*
      We ask the participant about his/her actual feeling by reminding that his/her location can be published without any consent. The participant can answer this question on a Likert scale from 1 to 5: 1 meaning "Happy", 3 meaning "Indifferent," and 5 meaning "Unhappy".
   2. *"Take a picture of your current location or activity!"*
      The participant can accept or decline to answer this question. If the participant answers positively, the phone's camera is activated and the participant is asked to take a photograph. The photograph is then saved and uploaded later with the rest of the data. Note that the reasons for declining are difficult to determine and may not be related to privacy concerns (e.g. busy, missed notification, inappropriate location).

- *Event-contingent.* These questions are sent when particular events occur. Up to ten questions per day are sent whenever the system detects that the participant has stopped at particular locations.

   1. *"Would you disclose your current location to:* [friends list]*?"*
      We ask the participant for the friend lists to whom he/she wants to share his/her location. We first ask if the location could be shared with "everyone". If the participant answers "Yes", then the question is over and the participant's location is shared to everyone on Facebook. Otherwise, if the participant answers "No", the phone asks if the participant's location can be shared with "all friends". If so, then the question is over and the location is shared with all of the participant's Facebook friends. Otherwise, we iterate through all of the friend lists that have been setup by the participant. Finally, sharing with "nobody" implies answering "No" to all the questions.
   2. *"You are around* [location]. *Would you disclose this to:* [friends list]*?"*
      This question mentions the detected place. This is to determine whether feedback from the system makes a participant share more.
   3. *"Are you around* [location]*? Would you disclose this to:* [friends list]*?"*
      This is the same question as above, but we ask the participant to confirm the location. If the participant confirms the location, then we ask the second part of the question. Otherwise, we ask the participant to define his/her location by

**Fig. 8.3** The *LocShare* application running on a Nokia N95 smartphone as used in our experimental testbed. The participant is asked whether he/she would share a photograph with his/her social network friends

typing a short description before asking the second part of the question. This is to determine the accuracy of our location/place detection.

4. *"You are around* [location]. *We might publish this to Facebook just now. How do you feel about this?"*

   This question is intended to examine preferences towards automated location-sharing services, e.g. Google Latitude.[5] Locations are explicitly mentioned to determine whether the participants feel happier when the location being disclosed is mentioned. Note that this question does not ask to whom the participant wants the location to be shared: default settings given in the pre-briefing are used instead.

Hence, each participant is expected to answer 10–20 questions each day, depending on the quantity of event-contingent questions. In addition, the application allows participants to share photos and short sentences to describe and share their location whenever they like (Fig. 8.3). We have designed *LocShare* to be fast and

---

[5]http://www.google.com/latitude/

easy to use, so that questions can be answered by pressing only one key and avoid as much as possible disturbing the participant. Moreover, periods of time where each participant do not want to be disturbed by questions have also been taken into account (e.g. at night, during lectures).

## Experiment

We ran a set of experiments in May and November 2010 using our methodology. Our focus was to better understand students' behaviour and privacy concerns when sharing their location on Facebook.

### Participant Recruitment

We recruited participants in the United Kingdom studying in London and St Andrews to participate in an experiment. We advertised through posters, student mailing lists, and also through advertisements on the Facebook OSN itself. In addition, we set up a Facebook "group", to which interested respondents were invited to join. This enabled some snowball recruitment, as the joining of a group was posted on a Facebook user's "News Feed", thus advising that user's friends of the existence of the group. Such recruitment was appropriate since we were aiming to recruit heavy users of Facebook.

Potential participants were invited to information sessions where they filled out a preselection form, and the aims and methodology of the study were explained to them. To avoid priming participants, we did not present the privacy concerns as the main focus of the experiment, both in advertisements and information sessions. More generally, we presented the main goal of the study as being to "study location-sharing behaviour" and "improve online networking systems".

From 866 candidates, we selected participants using the following criteria:

- *Undergraduate students.* We only selected undergraduate students. The main reason for this choice is that undergraduate students are likely to go to more different locations during week days since they are expected to attend generally more courses than postgraduate students. Some postgraduate students only have a project or a thesis and study in the same place (e.g. laboratory, library) most of the time. Maximising the number of different locations to be potentially shared by the participants during the study provides more opportunities to observe privacy concerns.
- *Facebook usage frequency.* We only selected candidates claiming to use Facebook everyday. Since shared locations are disclosed on Facebook, participants must actively use Facebook to see the locations shared by their friends and possibly experience privacy concerns about sharing their own locations.

- *Authors' acquaintances.* We only selected candidates who are not known by us, or studying in the Computer Science department. The main reason is to avoid recruiting participants who have heard about the purpose of the experiment and its privacy focus, as multiple talks have been given about the project in the Computer Science department, revealing the precise focus of the experiment.
- *Availability.* We only selected candidates with the most flexible availabilities to participate in the experiment.

From the remaining candidates, we selected randomly 81 participants, giving priority to those with the most friends. These criteria were not disclosed to any of the candidates to avoid false answers. A reward of £50 was offered as compensation to the selected participants. We used this methodology to collect data about participants' behaviour when sharing their location on Facebook with a mobile phone over seven days. Forty participants from the University of St Andrews used the system in May 2010, and 41 participants from University College London (UCL) used the system in November 2010. One of the participants in UCL did not carry the mobile phone every day, and we therefore discarded the data collected from this participant. Results presented were collected from the 80 remaining participants.

Overall, 7,706 ESM questions were sent to the phones. Not all of these questions were answered, for various reasons. Participants were asked to answer as many questions as they can, but were not obliged to do so in order to avoid false answers. They were also asked to not switch the phone to silent mode or to switch it off. This instruction was not universally followed, however, and five phones were returned at the end of the study in silent mode. Also, if a question has been sent more than 30 min ago without being replied (e.g. when the phone is out of network coverage), it is not displayed on the phone. Of the 7,706 questions, 4,232 were answered (54.8%). The participation rate depended on the participant and ranged from 15.7% to 91.4%, with an average of 55.7% (standard deviation 16.2%).

## Results

We present the results by showing how our methodology can provide more reliable data to study users' behaviour when sharing their location on online social networks. Our methodology provides useful private data that may not be accessible on OSNs, accurate data on application usage that cannot be captured through questionnaires or interviews and real data on sharing behaviours that cannot be measured through simulated applications.

### Private Information

We categorise location sharing into three types:

*Private:*   location is shared with no one.
*Shared:*   location is shared with a restricted set of people.
*Public:*   location is shared with all friends, or everyone.

Determining the category of a given piece of content cannot be done by merely collecting data directly on OSNs, as done by previous works. If a piece of content is accessible to the researchers, it may be either Shared or Public. On the other hand, if the content is not accessible, it may be Private or Shared (to a set of people excluding the researchers). Concretely, when collecting data from OSNs, content shared with a restricted set of people are often misclassified as Private because they are not accessible to the researchers. With our methodology, the category of each content can be determined. This leads to more reliable data collection, especially when studying privacy behaviours.

We define the *private rate* as the proportion of sharing activities that were private, and conversely, the *public rate* is the proportion of sharing activities that were public. If data were to be collected from OSNs, only the public content could be collected, hence misclassifying the other contents as Private. Figure 8.4a shows the distribution of private rates amongst the 80 participants that we observe by collecting data from the participants' Facebook pages. Most of the participants (31) have high private rates (above 90%), while only eight participants have low private rates (under 10%). Data collected with this method would suggest that most of the participants have high private rates and are not happy to share their location. On the other hand, with our methodology, we are able to better classify the contents shared by the participants. What would have been classified as private by collecting data from only OSNs is often actually shared by the participants to a restricted set of friends. Figure 8.4b shows data collected with our methodology. Most of the participants (38) have low private rates and are actually happy to share their location, contradicting the data collected from the OSN. This demonstrates that our methodology allows a better understanding of participants' actual sharing behaviours.

## Additional Data Over Questionnaires

Our methodology includes the collection of data from interviews and questionnaires to better understand participants' privacy concerns. But using only questionnaires and interviews may be insufficient for a reliable picture of participants' behaviours. Before providing the mobile phones to the participants, they were asked to complete a questionnaire discussing whether they have ever shared their location at least once (e.g. through their Facebook status, or with their mobile phone).

Table 8.1 shows that 12 participants reported to have never shared their location, which suggests that they are more likely to keep their location private. Nevertheless, the data collected with our methodology reveal that they actually shared approximately the same proportion of locations than participants who reported to share their location on Facebook.

For the experiments in UCL, we also asked participants more general questions about their privacy through the commonly used Westin-Harris methodology. Specifically, we used the same questions as [44], where Westin and Harris asked a series of four closed-ended questions of the US public:

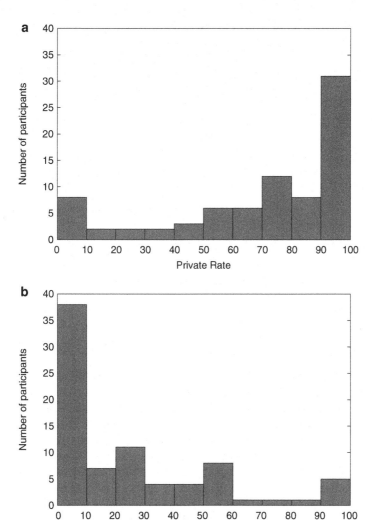

**Fig. 8.4** Comparison between private rates observed with data collected from Facebook and private rates observed with data collected with our methodology. (**a**) Distribution of private rates amongst participants as obtained with data collected from Facebook participants' pages only. (**b**) Distribution of private rates amongst participants as obtained with our methodology

**Table 8.1** Location-sharing choices of participants

| Group | Number of participants | Responses to location-sharing requests | Locations that were shared (%) |
|---|---|---|---|
| Never share location on Facebook | 12 | 127 | 73.2 |
| Share location on Facebook | 68 | 952 | 72.4 |

**Table 8.2** Location-sharing choices of users, grouped by Westin-Harris privacy level

| Group | Number of participants | Responses to location-sharing requests | Locations that were shared (%) |
|---|---|---|---|
| Fundementalist | 9 | 109 | 76.1 |
| Pragmatic | 11 | 168 | 66.7 |
| Unconcerned | 20 | 276 | 64.5 |

- *"Are you very concerned about threats to your personal privacy today?"*
- *"Do you agree strongly that business organisations seek excessively personal information from consumers?"*
- *"Do you agree strongly that the [Federal] government [since Watergate] is [still] invading the citizens privacy?"*[6]
- *"Do you agree that consumers have lost all control over circulation of their information?"*

Using these questions, participants can be divided into three groups, representing their levels of privacy concern:

- *Fundamentalist*: Three or four positive answers
- *Pragmatic*: Two positive answers
- *Unconcerned*: One or no positive answers

Using only questionnaires, one might expect participants falling in the unconcerned category to have fewer privacy concerns and thus share more locations than the participants in the pragmatic category, who should in turn share more locations than the participants in the fundamentalist category. Table 8.2, however, shows that the nine participants in the fundamentalist category actually shared 76.1% of their locations, while participants in the pragmatic category shared only 66.7%. Moreover, the participants in the pragmatic category unexpectedly shared even more locations than the participants in the other categories, with a lower private rate of 64.5%. Once again, data collected with our methodology provide an insight of participants' behaviours that cannot be predicted from questionnaires.

Real Versus Simulated Applications

Participants in each experiment run were randomly divided at the start into two groups. The *real group* experienced real publishing of their location information on Facebook to their chosen friend lists. In contrast, the *simulation group* experienced simulated publishing, where information was never disclosed to any friends,

---

[6]We did not mention the Federal government and Watergate as it was not appropriate to the participants in UK.

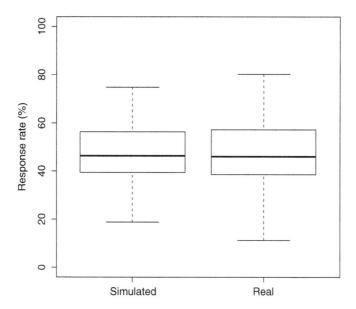

**Fig. 8.5** Question response rate. The response rates are similar for the simulated and the real groups (median 46% for each group.)

regardless of user preferences.[7] Participants were informed to which group they belonged at the start of the experiment. Participants in the simulation group were instructed to answer the questions exactly as if their information were really going to be published to Facebook. To control for differences between experiment runs,[8] half of the participants in each run were assigned to the simulation group and half to the real group. When reporting results, we combine responses from all runs.

We investigate whether publishing the information "for real" (the real group) results in a difference of behaviour compared to simulated publishing (the simulation group). Our results are shown in Figs. 8.5–8.6. Figure 8.5 shows that the response rates for each of the two groups present a median of 46%. We thus observe no significant difference in response rate between the groups and believe participation level in each experiment seems to be neither diminished nor encouraged by simulation.

While response rates are similar, Fig. 8.6 suggests that there is a difference in disclosure choices between the real and simulated applications: the simulation group shares location information on Facebook more openly than the real group. The simulation group less frequently makes their data completely private (available to no

---

[7]To realistically simulate publishing for the simulation group, the information was published using Facebook's "only visible to me" privacy option. Therefore, each user was able to see exactly the information which would have been shared.

[8]We conducted the experiment in four runs because of resource constraints: we had 20 mobile phones available, but 80 participants over the experiment.

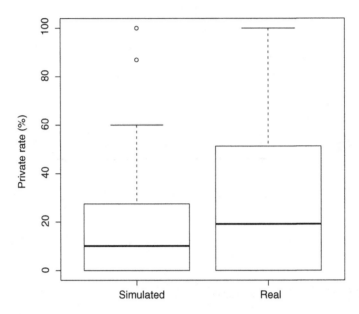

**Fig. 8.6** The simulation group shares locations more openly than the real group: the simulation group has a lower private rate than the real group (medians 10% vs. 19%)

one) than the real group, i.e. the simulation group has a lower private rate (median 10%) than the real group (median 19%). If this difference between behaviour in real and simulated systems holds in the general case, then there are implications for user studies and system design. For example, had our simulation group results been used to inform privacy defaults for a location-sharing system, then these defaults might have been overly permissive.

The reason behind the difference in behaviour cannot be determined solely from data analysis. While the participants in the simulation group were asked to answer questions as if they were in the real group, the participant interviews after the experiment offer some explanation. Members of the simulation group indicated that they were semiconsciously aware that no potential harm could come from their disclosure answers (since, after all, nobody would see the information in any case) and therefore tended to err on the side of more permissive information sharing. We highlight this as a potential problem with studies involving simulated social networks and recommend that results from such studies be interpreted with caution.

## Discussion

Various methods have been used to collect data on online social networks, depending on the focus of the study. In this section, we share our experience by suggesting guidelines to follow when collecting more reliable data with these methods and present some outstanding challenges that still need to be addressed.

## *Guidelines for More Reliable Data Collection and Analysis*

From the experimental results we obtained with our methodology, we propose some guidelines for both data collection and data analysis.

### Data Collection

Data collection can be performed through different methods, as described in section "Existing Data Collection Methods". Nevertheless, the amount and kinds of data generated by social network usage are too rich to be captured by only one of these methods. Hence, we believe that a single data collection method is insufficient to capture all aspects of users' experience. Our experiments show that collecting data from different sources enhances data analysis and provides results that could not be obtained through only one method.

*Data collected from OSNs should be completed by data from deployed applications.* Collecting data directly from OSNs is a passive way of observing users' sharing behaviours that is useful for examining social interactions without being too intrusive to the users. But the data should also be collected from the users themselves through deployed applications. Indeed, data collected from OSNs include neither the content that is not shared by the users nor the content inaccessible to the researchers. In our experiments, from the 1,079 locations detected by the system, only 273 (25.3%) were shared to everyone and 297 (27.5%) were not shared to anyone by the participants. Thus, while our methodology captures all of these data, collecting only from the OSN would only provide the locations shared to everyone (25.3%), as they are the only content available to researchers. Even if the researchers gain access to the participants' accounts, 27.5% of the locations would still be unavailable, as they were not uploaded to the OSN at all.

*Self-reported data should be complemented by measured data.* Self-reported data may also be useful for interpreting and understanding users' behaviour, but they do not always help in predicting users' actual behaviour. In our experiments, we asked participants whether they had ever shared their location on Facebook before using the system, but the answers did not help to predict their actual sharing behaviours. The participants who had never before shared their locations nevertheless shared roughly the same proportion of locations during the study as the other participants. We also asked participants Westin-Harris questions to determine their personality regarding privacy, but, again, their answers did not help predicting their sharing behaviours. Hence, self-reported data must be coupled with measured data from a deployed application.

*Interviews should rely on data collected in situ.* Self-reported information may be inaccurate when the users forget their experience. After our study, participants were interviewed to talk about their experience. We had to rely on the data collected for them to comment on their sharing choices, as they did not remember when and where they shared locations. Hence, data collected in situ help to capture more data from interviews.

*Applications should imply a real social interaction.* Finally, to avoid participants' behaviour being biased by the experiment, their behaviour should be studied under real social interactions by actually sharing content on OSNs. Our experiment suggests that participants experiencing a simulated system may behave differently to those experiencing real social interactions—in this case, by sharing locations more openly in the simulation.

### Data Analysis

Collecting reliable data is an important first step for accurately describing users' behaviours. But analysing these data correctly is also important.

*Give priority to measured data over self-reported data.* In our methodology, we gave priority to measured data over self-reported data. We believe that the observed behaviour better describes the users' behaviour than their self-reported information. Questionnaires and interviews usually do not describe the context with accuracy, and the participants may not consider this context correctly. This leads to an inaccurate answer that differs from the participants' actual behaviour.

*Check the data collected with participants to avoid misinterpretations.* Nevertheless, measured data may also be misleading, and self-reported data remains very useful to interpret them. Interviews helped us to understand participants sharing choices. For instance, some reported that they were unhappy to share their location when at home because they did not want their friends to see they stay home without any social activity for too long (e.g. over the course of a weekend, or on a Saturday night). Another reason was that some did not want people to know where they lived. One participant did not share his home location because the system erroneously reported this location as within a church next to his house, and he did not want his friends to think that he was going to the church everyday. These are examples of self-reported information that do not appear in measured data and that help to understand and analyse them.

## *Outstanding Challenges*

Our methodology was applied to an experiment involving 80 participants. OSNs, however, are used by millions of people (Facebook counts more than 500 million active users). Applying our methodology to a larger number of participants is an outstanding challenge. Our software application could be downloaded and installed to the participants' own smartphones to avoid the purchase and distribution of smartphones to a large number of participants. Nevertheless, interviewing the participants cannot be done at a large scale and thus would be removed from the methodology. Interpretation and analysis of the measured data would then only rely on online questionnaires to be filled in by the participants before and after the study.

Studying social networks usage also raises ethical issues, as the data may contain sensitive information about the users. As the data collected become more reliable, they better describe users' behaviours. Nevertheless, collected data may be deliberately made unreliable by the users, in order to obfuscate information they want to share neither with the social network nor with the researchers. Using collected data from different methods may reveal unexpected information about users' behaviours that they did not intend to provide to the researchers, as it becomes more difficult for them to control the collected data and understand the implications of merging them. Using data from users without their consent is also controversial. Hoser and Nitschke [19] discuss the ethics of mining social networks and suggest that researchers should not access personal data that users did not share for research purpose, even when they are publicly available.

In conclusion, we have shown through experiments that data can be more reliably collected from online social networks using an appropriate methodology. This involves mixing measured data from OSNs and deployed applications and self-reported data from questionnaires, interviews, and in situ experience sampling. Nevertheless, applying this methodology to a larger scale and in an ethical fashion is still an outstanding challenge that needs to be addressed.

# References

1. Amichai-Hamburger, Y., Vinitzky, G.: Social network use and personality. Comput. Hum. Behav. **26**(6), 1289–1295 (2010). doi:10.1016/j.chb.2010.03.018
2. Anthony, D., Henderson, T., Kotz, D.: Privacy in location-aware computing environments. IEEE Pervasive Comput. **6**(4), 64–72 (2007). doi:10.1109/MPRV.2007.83
3. Ben Abdesslem, F., Phillips, A., Henderson, T.: Less is more: energy-efficient mobile sensing with SenseLess. In: ACM MobiHeld'09, Barcelona, pp. 61–62 (2009). doi:10.1145/1592606.1592621
4. Benevenuto, F., Rodrigues, T., Cha, M., Almeida, V.: Characterizing user behavior in online social networks. In: IMC '09: Proceedings of the 9th ACM Internet Measurement Conference, Chicago, pp. 49–62 (2009). doi:10.1145/1644893.1644900
5. Besmer, A., Lipford, H.R.: Moving beyond untagging: photo privacy in a tagged world. In: CHI '10: Proceedings of the 28th International Conference on Human Factors in Computing Systems, Atlanta, pp. 1563–1572 (2010). doi:10.1145/1753326.1753560
6. Brandtzæg, P.B., Heim, J.: Why people use social networking sites. In Hutchison, D., Kanade, T., Kittler, J., Kleinberg, J.M., Mattern, F., Mitchell, J.C., Naor, M., Nierstrasz, O., Rangan, C.P., Steffen, B., Sudan, M., Terzopoulos, D., Tygar, D., Vardi, M.Y., Weikum, G., Ozok, A.A., Zaphiris, P. (eds.) Online Communities and Social Computing, vol. 5621, chapter 16, pp. 143–152. Springer, Berlin/Heidelberg (2009). doi:10.1007/978-3-642-02774-1_16
7. Cha, M., Haddadi, H., Benevenuto, F., Gummadi, K.P.: Measuring user influence in Twitter: the million follower fallacy. In: Proceedings of the 4th International AAAI Conference on Weblogs and Social Media (ICWSM), Washington (2010). Online at http://aaai.org/ocs/index.php/ICWSM/ICWSM10/paper/view/1538/0

8. Consolvo, S., Walker, M.: Using the experience sampling method to evaluate ubicomp applications. IEEE Pervasive Comput. **2**(2), 24–31 (2003). doi:10.1109/MPRV.2003.1203750

9. Consolvo, S., Smith, I.E., Matthews, T., Lamarca, A., Tabert, J., Powledge, P.: Location disclosure to social relations: why, when, and what people want to share. In: CHI '05: Proceedings of the SIGCHI conference on Human factors in computing systems, Portland, pp. 81–90 (2005). doi:10.1145/1054972.1054985

10. Eagle, N., Pentland, A.S., Lazer, D.: Inferring friendship network structure by using mobile phone data. Proc. Natl. Acad. Sci. **106**(36), 15274–15278 (2009). doi:10.1073/pnas. 0900282106

11. Ellison, N.B., Steinfield, C., Lampe, C.: The benefits of Facebook "friends:" social capital and college students use of online social network sites. J. Comput. Mediat. Commun. **12**(4), 1143–1168 (2007). doi:10.1111/j.1083-6101.2007.00367.x

12. Froehlich, J., Chen, M.Y., Consolvo, S., Harrison, B., Landay, J.A.: MyExperience: a system for in situ tracing and capturing of user feedback on mobile phones. In: MobiSys '07: Proceedings of the 5th International Conference on Mobile Systems, Applications and Services, San Juan, pp. 57–70 (2007). doi:10.1145/1247660.1247670

13. Garg, S., Gupta, T., Carlsson, N., Mahanti, A.: Evolution of an online social aggregation network: an empirical study. In: IMC '09: Proceedings of the 9th ACM Internet Measurement Conference, Chicago, pp. 315–321 (2009). doi:10.1145/1644893.1644931

14. Ghosh, S., Korlam, G., Ganguly, N.: The effects of restrictions on number of connections in OSNs: a case-study on Twitter. In: Proceedings of the 3rd Workshop on Online Social Networks (WOSN 2010), Boston (2010). Online at http://www.usenix.org/events/wosn10/tech/full_papers/Ghosh.pdf

15. Gjoka, M., Sirivianos, M., Markopoulou, A., Yang, X.: Poking Facebook: characterization of OSN applications. In: WOSN '08: Proceedings of the First Workshop on Online Social Networks, Seattle, pp. 31–36 (2008). doi:10.1145/1397735.1397743

16. Gjoka, M., Kurant, M., Butts, C.T., Markopoulou, A.: Walking in Facebook: a case study of unbiased sampling of OSNs. In: Proceedings of IEEE INFOCOM 2010, San Diego, pp. 1–9 (2010). doi:10.1109/INFCOM.2010.5462078

17. Guy, I., Jacovi, M., Meshulam, N., Ronen, I., Shahar, E.: Public vs. private: comparing public social network information with email. In: CSCW '08: Proceedings of the ACM 2008 Conference on Computer Supported Cooperative Work, San Diego, pp. 393–402 (2008). doi:10.1145/1460563.1460627

18. Gyarmati, L., Trinh, T.: Measuring user behavior in online social networks. IEEE Netw. **24**(5), 26–31 (2010). doi:10.1109/MNET.2010.5578915

19. Hoser, B., Nitschke, T.: Questions on ethics for research in the virtually connected world. Soc. Netw. **32**(3), 180–186 (2010). doi:10.1016/j.socnet.2009.11.003

20. Iachello, G., Smith, I., Consolvo, S., Chen, M., Abowd, G.D.: Developing privacy guidelines for social location disclosure applications and services. In: SOUPS '05: Proceedings of the 2005 Symposium on Usable Privacy and Security, Philadelphia, pp. 65–76 (2005). doi:10.1145/1073001.1073008

21. Java, A., Song, X., Finin, T., Tseng, B.: Why we Twitter: an analysis of a microblogging community. In: Zhang, H., Spiliopoulou, M., Mobasher, B., Giles, C.L., McCallum, A., Nasraoui, O., Srivastava, J., Yen, J. (eds.) Advances in Web Mining and Web Usage Analysis. Lecture Notes in Computer Science, vol. 5439, chapter 7, pp. 118–138. Springer, Berlin/Heidelberg (2007). doi:10.1007/978-3-642-00528-2_7

22. Jiang, J., Wilson, C., Wang, X., Huang, P., Sha, W., Dai, Y., Zhao, B.Y.: Understanding latent interactions in online social networks. In: IMC '10: Proceedings of the 10th Annual Conference on Internet Measurement, Melbourne, pp. 369–382 (2010). doi:10.1145/1879141.1879190

23. Kofod-Petersen, A., Gransaether, P.A., Krogstie, J.: An empirical investigation of attitude towards location-aware social network service. Int. J. Mobile Commun. **8**(1), 53–70 (2010). doi:10.1504/IJMC.2010.030520

24. Krasnova, H., Günther, O., Spiekermann, S., Koroleva, K.: Privacy concerns and identity in online social networks. Identit. Inf. Soc. **2**(1), 39–63 (2009). doi:10.1007/s12394-009-0019-1

25. Kwon, O., Wen, Y.: An empirical study of the factors affecting social network service use. Comput. Hum. Behav. **26**(2), 254–263 (2010). doi:10.1016/j.chb.2009.04.011
26. Lampe, C., Ellison, N.B., Steinfield, C.: Changes in use and perception of Facebook. In: CSCW '08: Proceedings of the ACM 2008 Conference on Computer Supported Cooperative Work, San Diego,, pp. 721–730 (2008). doi:10.1145/1460563.1460675
27. Larson, R., Csikszentmihalyi, M.: The experience sampling method. New Dir. Methodol. Soc. Behav. Sci. **15**, 41–56 (1983)
28. Lewis, K., Kaufman, J., Christakis, N.: The Taste for privacy: an analysis of college student privacy settings in an online social network. J. Comput. Mediat. Commun. **14**(1), 79–100 (2008). doi:10.1111/j.1083-6101.2008.01432.x
29. Lindamood, J., Heatherly, R., Kantarcioglu, M., Thuraisingham, B.: Inferring private information using social network data. In: WWW '09: Proceedings of the 18th International World Wide Web Conference, Madrid, pp. 1145–1146 (2009). doi:10.1145/1526709.1526899
30. Mancini, C., Thomas, K., Rogers, Y., Price, B.A., Jedrzejczyk, L., Bandara, A.K., Joinson, A.N., Nuseibeh, B.: From spaces to places: emerging contexts in mobile privacy. In: Ubicomp '09: Proceedings of the 11th International Conference on Ubiquitous Computing, Orlando, pp. 1–10 (2009) doi:10.1145/1620545.1620547
31. Nagle, F., Singh, L.: Can friends be trusted? Exploring privacy in online social networks. In: 2009 International Conference on Advances in Social Network Analysis and Mining (ASONAM), Athens, pp. 312–315 (2009). doi:10.1109/ASONAM.2009.61
32. Nazir, A., Raza, S., Chuah, C.N.: Unveiling Facebook: a measurement study of social network based applications. In: IMC '08: Proceedings of the 8th ACM SIGCOMM Conference on Internet Measurement, Vouliagmeni, pp. 43–56 (2008). doi:10.1145/1452520.1452527
33. Pempek, T.A., Yermolayeva, Y.A., Calvert, S.L.: College students' social networking experiences on Facebook. J. Appl. Dev. Psychol. **30**(3), 227–238 (2009). doi:10.1016/j.appdev.2008.12.010
34. Peterson, K., Siek, K.A.: Analysis of information disclosure on a social networking site. In Hutchison, D., Kanade, T., Kittler, J., Kleinberg, J.M., Mattern, F., Mitchell, J.C., Naor, M., Nierstrasz, O., Rangan, C.P., Steffen, B., Sudan, M., Terzopoulos, D., Tygar, D., Vardi, M.Y., Weikum, G., Ozok, A.A., Zaphiris, P. (eds.) Online Communities and Social Computing, vol. 5621, chapter 28, pp. 256–264. Springer, Berlin/Heidelberg (2009). doi:10.1007/978-3-642-02774-1_28
35. Qiu, T., Feng, J., Ge, Z., Wang, J., Xu, J., Yates, J.: Listen to me if you can: tracking user experience of mobile network on social media. In: IMC '10: Proceedings of the 10th Annual Conference on Internet Measurement, Melbourne, pp. 288–293 (2010). doi:10.1145/1879141.1879178
36. Rejaie, R., Torkjazi, M., Valafar, M., Willinger, W.: Sizing up online social networks. IEEE Netw. **24**(5), 32–37 (2010). doi:10.1109/MNET.2010.5578916
37. Roblyer, M., McDaniel, M., Webb, M., Herman, J., Witty, J.V.: Findings on Facebook in higher education: a comparison of college faculty and student uses and perceptions of social networking sites. Int. High. Educ. **13**(3), 134–140 (2010). doi:10.1016/j.iheduc.2010.03.002
38. Sadeh, N., Hong, J., Cranor, L., Fette, I., Kelley, P., Prabaker, M., Rao, J.: Understanding and capturing people's privacy policies in a mobile social networking application. Pers. Ubiquitous Comput. **13**, 401–412 (2009). doi:10.1007/s00779-008-0214-3
39. Schneider, F., Feldmann, A., Krishnamurthy, B., Willinger, W.: Understanding online social network usage from a network perspective. In: IMC '09: Proceedings of the 9th ACM Internet Measurement Conference, Chicago, pp. 35–48 (2009). doi:10.1145/1644893.1644899
40. Stutzman, F., Duffield, J.K.: Friends only: examining a privacy-enhancing behavior in facebook. In: CHI '10: Proceedings of the 28th International Conference on Human Factors in Computing Systems, Atlanta, pp. 1553–1562 (2010). doi:10.1145/1753326.1753559
41. Tsai, J.Y., Kelley, P., Drielsma, P., Cranor, L.F., Hong, J., Sadeh, N.: Who's viewed you?: the impact of feedback in a mobile location-sharing application. In: CHI '09: Proceedings of the 27th International Conference on Human Factors in Computing Systems, Boston, pp. 2003–2012 (2009). doi:10.1145/1518701.1519005

42. Valafar, M., Rejaie, R., Willinger. W.: Beyond friendship graphs: a study of user interactions in Flickr. In: WOSN '09: Proceedings of the 2nd ACM Workshop on Online Social Networks, Barcelona, pp. 25–30 (2009). doi:10.1145/1592665.1592672
43. Viswanath, B., Mislove, A., Cha, M., Gummadi, K.P.: On the evolution of user interaction in Facebook. In: WOSN '09: Proceedings of the 2nd ACM Workshop on Online Social Networks, Barcelona, pp. 37–42 (2009). doi:10.1145/1592665.1592675
44. Westin, A., Harris, L. & Associates: Equifax-Harris Consumer Privacy Survey. Conducted for Equifax Inc. (1991)
45. Wilson, C., Boe, B., Sala, A., Puttaswamy, K.P., Zhao, B.Y.: User interactions in social networks and their implications. In: Proceedings of the Fourth ACM European Conference on Computer Systems (EuroSys), Nuremberg, pp. 205–218 (2009). doi:10.1145/1519065.1519089
46. Ye, S., Wu, F.: Estimating the size of online social networks. In: Proceedings of the IEEE Second International Conference on Social Computing (SocialCom), Minneapolis, pp. 169–176 (2010). doi:10.1109/SocialCom.2010.32
47. Young, A.L., Quan-Haase, A.: Information revelation and internet privacy concerns on social network sites: a case study of Facebook. In: C&T '09: Proceedings of the Fourth International Conference on Communities and Technologies, University Park, pp. 265–274 (2009). doi:10.1145/1556460.1556499

# Chapter 9
# Knowledge Mining from the Twitter Social Network: The Case of Barack Obama

**Marco Guidi, Igor Ruiz-Agundez, and Izaskun Canga-Sanchez**

**Abstract** Social networks build up a representation of the social structure on the Internet by enabling new ways of communication and understanding of human relations. These networks generate big amounts of information on which we can apply mining techniques in order to extract knowledge. Different works have studied many aspects of social networks, but just a few of them focused on text mining in social networks. In this work, we focus on the Twitter social network features and specifically on the use of this network by a representative, and well-known, user's behaviour. We extracted all the contents that previously Senator and then President Barack Obama has shared in this service in the course of the last 3 years and applied a text-analysis knowledge discovery methodology to it. This methodology allowed us to build a meaning-making process on our dataset. In this process, we successfully conducted a cluster analysis that helped collecting Barack Obama's Twitter contents in groups. Studying the results, we perceived that these clusters could be interpreted as a mirror of his political strategy. Finally, we discuss the application of this method for other social networks.

M. Guidi (✉)
Department of Pedagogical, Psychological and Teaching Sciences, Università del Salento, Lecce, Italy
e-mail: marcoguidi73@gmail.com

I. Ruiz-Agundez
DeustoTech, Deusto Institute of Technology, University of Deusto, Basque Country, Spain
e-mail: igor.ira@deusto.es

I. Canga-Sanchez
Sapienza Università di Roma, Roma, Italy
e-mail: izaskun1982@yahoo.com

A. Abraham (ed.), *Computational Social Networks: Mining and Visualization*, 211
DOI 10.1007/978-1-4471-4054-2_9, © Springer-Verlag London 2012

# Introduction

The aim of this work is twofold: to present a research methodology applied to the field of study that transcends the boundaries of several disciplines, such as communication research (in the field of political communication studies and cultural and media research), psycholinguistic research, data mining techniques, new social networks analysis, etc., and to highlight the main findings of this research in order to evaluate the effectiveness and utility of such a methodology for new studies to be made in the future.

More particularly, our interest is linked to two main issues. On the one hand, the analysis of the meaning-making process unfolded (within a specific communication system, that of Twitter) in the course of a complex political communication process (the American election campaign and first 2 years of Barack Obama's presidency). On this plan, we will highlight how new social network systems (as Twitter) have jumped into the world of political communication being taken, as they are, for powerful media to be used and to refer to. The study of the relationship between political communication and social networks provides one of the pillars on which this study grounds. On the other hand, it grounds on the need for improving the analysis of the political communication process through the use of knowledge mining techniques. Specifically, we used a textual-statistical tool for carrying a content analysis and text mining of Twitter social networks messages.

Political information cannot be merely considered a linear presentation of contents and/or information between a sender and a receiver. Each political communication system can be understood in terms of the complex interconnections between political systems, media (and journalistic organisations in general) and citizens [5]. As political communication is itself a historically situated and strategically determined meaning-making process (socially instituted by a (small) group of people to affect, influence or inspire a (larger) group of people), we might regard it as a way of organising and shaping a certain "version of the world" [4]. Because of that, studying the communication processes that a political source enables does not only mean to identify the content roots of the messages given but also to connect this content to the goals that the political source aims to give to its messages [5].

Hereon, we are going to introduce a study about the Tweets (messages posted on the Twitter social network) sent by US president Barack Obama since his presentation to the primaries up to his current presidency.

Twitter offers a social networking and microblogging service, enabling the users to read and post messages, or Tweets, to others. Tweets have certain fixed characteristic. They are text-based and formed by up to 140 characters. They are public on the service web page by default, and users can subscribe to a certain user's messages by becoming a *"follower"* and may follow his/her tweets. The ever increasing impact of Twitter on the Internet, with more than 175 million users [13] since its creation in July 2006, is worth mentioning.

We consider the text-analytical methodology useful for the extraction of the main *"knowledge forms"* provided through the Tweets (messages) available on the Twitter platform selected and furthermore hypothesise that it is helpful for understanding the meaning-making process deployed in the underlying political communication.

Against this background, the contribution of this chapter is fourfold. Firstly, we present a methodology that allows the analysis of the posts of a user on the Twitter social network. Secondly, we conduct an experiment by applying our methodology over a representative user of this social network. Thirdly, we interpret the results of the experiment applying the meaning-making process. Finally, we discuss the proposed methodology and consider its application to other social networks.

The remainder of this chapter is organised as follows. Section "Related Work" presents the related work in knowledge mining in social networks. section "Methodology" gives an overview of the proposed methodology to extract knowledge from the Twitter social network. Section "Experiment and Results" introduces the performed experiment and its results. Section "Conclusion" concludes the study and proposes avenues for future work.

# Related Work

This section introduces the different theories related to meaning-making processes and gives an outlook on text analysis in literature, which are both highly relevant for our study.

## *Theories of Meaning-Making Process*

In the traditional conception, *"meaning"* is statically referred as the way a certain content (significance) associates to a peculiar word (signifier) that carries it and that accounts for it. In this conception, each discrete meaning can be considered as a piece of social knowledge that is usually taken for granted in a certain community. According to this, if one says *"dog"*, it is fairly sure that each bystander will understand that he/she is referring to a domestic, hairy animal, usually considered a man's best friend, which keeps company to its masters.

To have an emblematic example of this vision, let us think of a *"dictionary"*. In a dictionary, any sign (the words) corresponds to a certain meaning (or to few meanings), conceived as the content(s) conveyed by a given definition.

This traditional meaning conception has been strongly criticised. Current meaning conceptions are more and more inclined to shape meaning models by claiming for an intrinsic dynamicity and systemicity concern. These theories, despite their reciprocal differences, converge by underlining three main points:

1. Each way of communicating (e.g. be it a message, a discourse or a piece of information) is not to be intended in a unique, universal and objective manner. Namely, it is not to be conceived as conveying univocal meanings that are to be

interpreted as neutrally taken for granted. These theories rather claim that the meanings that a way of communicating enables should always be interpreted as the by-products of a contingent and socially constructed process that is distributed over time [16]. In this sense, the meaning of a message does not only rely on (and not only depend on) the words that are used to pass on that message (the *what*, i.e. the content, of a way of communicating), but has to be interpreted in the light of the context and of the intentions for which it has been produced (i.e. for its goal, the *why* of the message), according to the ways in which the message was construed (the *how*) and in relation to the type of sender and addressee of that message (the *who* and the *to whom*).

2. A meaning always emerges as a construction procedure occurring in the course of time. It becomes a meaning-making process. In this sense, people understand a meaning in terms of their competence to give sense, within a context, to the associations among present signs and subsequent signs [16].

3. Finally, and as a consequence of the first two points, meaning is not conveyed in terms of a discrete sign, but displays a complex matrix of interacting signs that altogether help build the general meaning of communication. Complex signs (a number of discourses combined together and that people might experience in terms of a theme, a subject, an argument, a thesis and others) structure themselves dynamically (sometimes assuming a transient form, some other crystallising within social representations) in ways that people, on one hand, experience and use to interpret the messages (communication, discourses, information, etc.) they receive in their living context and, on the other hand, are produced and reproduced by people themselves over time, according to how much they are used. Meanings are thus constantly produced and reproduced, over time: some of them are short-living; others structure themselves in long-lasting representations [17, 18].

This basic conception of meaning-making can be applied either to everyday communication or to understand a complex communication process, such as that of political communication and of new social media (or of their combined use), as in the case of this work.

## Text Analysis in Literature

Text mining, also known as text data mining or text analytics, is the research area that seeks to achieve representative information from text. To wit, knowledge mining forms text. The classic text mining procedure is composed by the text structuring, derivation of patterns in the data, evaluation of the results and interpretation of the results.

Some of the most popular techniques in text mining are text categorization, text clustering, concept/entity extraction, production of granular taxonomies, sentiment analysis, document summarising and modelling of relations between instances.

Furthermore, text analysis has been used in many research areas such as security applications, biomedical text mining, software and applications, online media applications, marketing applications, sentiment analysis or academic applications.

In our experiment, we are using T-LAB, a software solution that includes a set of linguistic and statistical tools for content analysis and text mining, which makes it perfect for the purpose of our study. T-LAB features may be classified in three main areas:

- Co-occurrence Analysis (including Word Association, Comparison between Word pairs, Co-Word Analysis, Concept Mapping, Sequence Analysis and Concordances).
- Thematic Analysis (including Modelling of Emerging Themes, Thematic Analysis of Elementary Contexts, Sequences of Themes, Key Contexts of Thematic Words and Thematic Document Classification).
- Comparative Analysis (including Specificity Analysis, Correspondence Analysis, Multiple Correspondence Analysis, Cluster Analysis and Contingency Tables).

These features can be applied over any type of text (speech transcripts, newspaper articles, responses to open-ended questions, transcriptions of interviews and focus groups, legislative texts, company documents, books, etc.). Nevertheless, to our knowledge, this is the very first time that social network texts are studied in this way.

T-LAB has been used broadly in many previous works. We may recall the following in order to refer to the scientific use and references about it [1–3, 10–12, 15, 16, 19].

## Methodology

This section introduces the methodology we used for carrying out this experiment: the model of analysis, the meaning-related methodology and the procedure.

## *Model of Analysis*

According to our standpoint, the Tweets collected can be analysed according to the representational contents they convey. Barack Obama (and his staff) have actually managed to build a certain kind of relationship with the Twitter users through these contents.

Representational contents are to be interpreted as the contingent expressions of the meanings made explicit in the production of tweets. We have to remark that tweets convey their meanings not only by themselves, but according to the contingent conditions in which they have been posted (their chronological disposition, their sequentiality, the kind of message given, etc.).

This means that each representational content is not a ready-made fact but always the fruit of a construction enabled by the production of the messages [20]. Therefore, each tweet works as a signifier by conveying a broad spectrum of meanings, some of which made explicit by the situation and, because of that, probably reproduced over time.

## Proposed Analysis

The method of analysis we use is addressed to the identification of the similarities in the messages' ways of using signifiers (words) in order to connote the meanings they are conveying.

This method is grounded on the general assumption that meanings are shaped in terms of lexical variability. This means that words like *"native"*, *"origin"* and *"residence"* might convey the meaning of *"protective motherland"* (even if this word is not used in the discourse) if, and only if, it is used together with words like *"home"* and *"care"*.

In other cases, on the contrary, if associated with words like *"insecure"*, *"violence"* and *"abuse"*, the same words might contribute to the construction of the meaning of a *"fearful nation"*.

In our view, any word should be seen as a polysemic sign. Words could potentially convey infinite significations, reduced to a finite number thanks to the co-occurrence with other words. Thus, we do not have to look at the meaning of a single word (since, from a theoretical standpoint, its meanings could be infinite) but to the meanings emerging throughout the aggregation to other words.

As a result, the meaning of a message can be intended as the probability distribution value associated to a pattern of associated signs. Thus, after the analysis, a meaning emerges together with the probability of certain signs to be used together, while other signs are absent.

## Procedure

The corpus containing all the Twitter messages was analysed by the computer-aided text-analysis software: T-LAB [6–9].

Figure 9.1 represents the general methodology of text mining with this solution. The procedure starts with a text gathering of the corpus (in our case, the Tweets of Barack Obama). Next, this corpus is formatted to make the dataset usable by the application. After importing the corpus to the application, we select the lexical tools to be used and the most representative key words, if appropriate. Then, thanks to the analysis tools, we obtain an output report that serves as a basis for interpretation.

In order to identify the main representational contents that characterise the Twitter messages collected, we submitted the messages corpus to cluster analysis. This cluster analysis provides a statistical classification, specifically, a *"grouping"*

**Fig. 9.1** Text mining
methodology with T-LAB

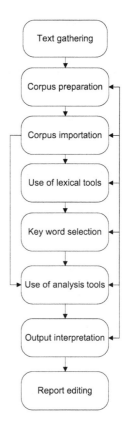

of certain *"objects"* into classes, on the basis of the properties of the objects being classified. The objects in each group are considered members of the same class (the parts forming a same theme), but from a complementary point of view, these parts are defined by the equality of the whole theme, an equality that creates the bonds between the parts. Because of that, the words composing the sentences of a theme (may) change, but the composite *"thematic whole"* still remains the same.

In the present case, cluster analysis assembled the sentences of the text according to a criterion of maximal internal homogeneity and, correspondingly, maximal external differentiation.

Each cluster is thus marked by a specific set of words that tend to occur together in similar sentences, while each of these words tends not to occur with other words: this means that it is not the frequency of a certain word itself which is significant, but the recurring combination of that word with some other words throughout the text messages. According to our methodology, we conceptualise each cluster as the expression of a correspondent set of meanings highlighted by the combination of the Tweets. Each set of meanings enucleated a specific content that emerges as the by-product of the discursive chain produced by the messages. We interpret this discursive chain as a theme characterising parts of the messages, which differs from any other theme emerging through the analysis.

In consideration of this, to perform text analysis, the corpus, first of all, was transformed in a digital *"presence/absence"* matrix. To do that, each Twitter message was considered as a segment of the corpus (namely, a context unit). Each message, thus, represents a row of the matrix. All of the words present in the corpus represent the columns of the matrix. Each cell of the matrix might then assume one of the two levels of a binary code, *"1"* for *"presence"*, of the given lemma in the chosen message, *"0"* for *"absence"*.

Data was analysed according to a two-step procedure:

1. The cluster analysis algorithm was applied to the *"messages x words"* matrix. This analysis allows us to obtain a representation of the corpus contents through few and significant thematic clusters, each one characterised by the co-occurrences of peculiar semantic traits.
2. As the analysis also allows the identification of a *"meaning map"* (given by the relationships among the clusters and between the clusters, the words and the variables present in the corpus), we studied the association between the theme distribution over time and according to specific periods of time.

The threshold value, according to corpus sizes, usually corresponds to the minimum value in the first and in the second range decile (10% or 20%). Anyway, in order to guarantee the reliability of all statistical computations, the minimum T-LAB threshold is fixed to "4".

## Experiment and Results

This section introduces the carrying out of the experiment, as well as the result that arose with it. We describe the dataset and the elementary contexts and then analyse the cluster results.

### *Dataset Description*

The corpus in analysis is composed of 895 Twitter messages or posts (also known as Tweets), all of which displayed in the period between April 29, 2007 (when Senator Barack Obama decided to enter the American presidential scenario), and September 6, 2010 (the moment in which we stopped collecting the Tweets, in order to analyse them). The corpus composes a text document more than 50 pages long and collects up to almost 16,000 occurrences (tokens) and fairly 3,000 different lexical forms. Table 9.1 summarises the dataset description.

We decided to hyphenate those multi-words that in the English *"natural"* language are considered to be single words (such as *"New_York"* and not *"New"* and *"York"* separately) or, for instance, web addresses (e.g. "http_www_barackobama_com" and not *"http"*, *"www"*, *"barackobama"* and *"com"*, all separately as it is encoded in the text-analysis system). By this intervention on the corpus, we

| Element | Amount |
|---------|--------|
| Tweets present in the corpus | 895 |
| Elementary contexts analysed | 895 |
| Tokens in the text | 15,988 |
| Lexical forms present in the text | 2,970 |
| Threshold frequency | 4 |
| Words used in the analysis | 475 |

**Table 9.1** Dataset description

reduced the presence of single words (meaningless by themselves), such as *"http"*, or recovered the original meaning of some other (for instance, the use of the word *"new"*, when it is referred to a substantive – e.g. *"new health reform"* – or when it is part of a proper name, *"New_Hampshire"*). Nevertheless, we maintained the original corpus as much as possible.

Tweets are formed by three main attributes. The first attribute is a unique ID that identifies each Tweet post. The second attribute is the text of the post itself. The third and final attribute indicates the creation date and time of the Tweet posting. There are also other attributes, such as the origin of the Tweet, geographic coordinates, information about replies to other posts and absolute time.

For the purpose of our experiment, we consider that only the text and the creation date and time are relevant. Furthermore, as in this dataset each Tweet has a different date and time, we decided to group Tweet posts by creating a new variable that replaced these data with periods.

These periods correspond to the most relevant moments of Barack Obama's career over the last few years. Table 9.2 represents the time ranges of the grouping. This correlation is structured as follows: the Democratic Party presidential primaries, the general election campaign, the first half of the first year of presidency, the second half of first year of presidency, the first half of second year of presidency and the second half of second year of presidency. We think that this organisation of the dataset is most representative, as the Tweets are balanced through the period, augmenting the data representativeness.

## *Elementary Contexts*

This section introduces the elementary contexts gathered in each of the clusters that were obtained.

Table 9.3 shows the results of the analysis. It represents the instance distribution per clusters detected. We also calculated the summation, the average deviation, the median and the standard deviation in order to validate the distribution of the dataset among the clusters. The total variance between cluster variances is 0.14.

There is a difference between the total number of instances of the dataset (895) and the analysed elementary context instances (887). As we defined a threshold of four occurrences in the text, the instances that do not enclose words reaching this threshold (8, corresponding to 0.89% of the sentences of the text) are not considered.

**Table 9.2** Dataset periods

| Period | Dates | Description |
|---|---|---|
| Democratic party presidential | February 10, 2007 | Obama announced his candidacy |
| | June 7, 2008 | Clinton ended her campaign |
| General election campaign | June 7, 2008 | Obama won the presidency |
| | November 4, 2008 | |
| First semester of presidency | November 4, 2008 | First half of first year of presidency |
| | May 4, 2009 | Obama starts to govern |
| Second semester of presidency | May 4, 2009 | Second half of first year of presidency |
| | November 4, 2009 | |
| Third semester of presidency | November 4, 2009 | First half of second year of presidency |
| | May 4, 2010 | |
| Fourth semester of presidency | May 4, 2010 | Second half of second year of presidency |
| | September 06, 2010 | End of the dataset |

**Table 9.3** Instance distribution per cluster and validation load

| | Elementary contexts | Percentage |
|---|---|---|
| Cluster 1 | 130 | 14.66% |
| Cluster 2 | 189 | 21.31% |
| Cluster 3 | 261 | 29.43% |
| Cluster 4 | 144 | 16.23% |
| Cluster 5 | 163 | 18.38% |
| SUM | 887 | 100 |
| AVEDEV | 38.08 | 4.29 |
| MEDIAN | 163 | 18.38 |
| STDEV | 51.70 | 5.83 |

## *Elementary Context in Each Cluster*

The results of a thematic analysis of the elementary contexts were performed from the analysis of the period variable in the dataset.

T-LAB, obviously, does not interpret the clustered contents in a proper sense; it rather presents a complex output in which the *"most significant"* sentences and words are displayed. Of course, the *"significance"* we are referring to is statistical, which is measured by a metrical index called test value. So far, the higher the test value (either for a sentence or a word), the stronger the association of that sentence or word for a cluster and, consequently, the more important that sentence/word is for the meaning interpretation of the cluster. Table 9.4 shows cluster distribution over the six periods of time in percentages. Figure 9.2 represents the data of the previous table with a broken line plot graphic, and Fig. 9.3 represents the same data with a bar graph plot graphic.

Nonetheless, it is not the presence of a certain theme itself that shapes the overall meaning of the cluster. It is rather the redundancy of that theme across the sentences of the corpus to allow the identification of a certain categorisation in a certain cluster. For instance, in the case of the Tweet messages, the repetition of the health-care reform theme shapes the "health reform" meaning we assigned to cluster 3. So far,

**Table 9.4** Cluster distribution over the six periods before interpretation

| Period | Theme 1 (%) | Theme 2 (%) | Theme 3 (%) | Theme 4 (%) | Theme 5 (%) |
|---|---|---|---|---|---|
| Democratic Party presidential primaries | 13.95 | 6.20 | 0.78 | 5.43 | 73.64 |
| General election campaign | 75.00 | 1.52 | 0 | 0.76 | 22.73 |
| First semester of presidency | 0 | 57.14 | 0 | 0 | 42.86 |
| Second semester of presidency | 2.36 | 25.20 | 60.63 | 7.87 | 3.94 |
| Third semester of presidency | 2.13 | 25.53 | 46.10 | 19.86 | 6.38 |
| Fourth semester of presidency | 1.90 | 33.81 | 25.24 | 33.33 | 5.71 |
| Total | 14.66 | 21.31 | 29.43 | 16.23 | 18.38 |

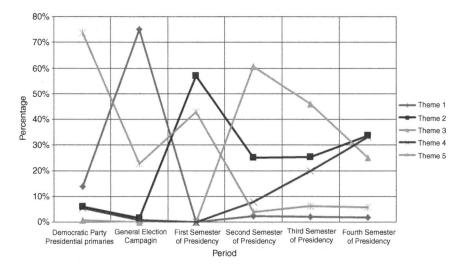

**Fig. 9.2** Clusters distribution over the six periods before interpretation (*broken line* plot)

it is not an objective meaning-making process produced in the categorization of the themes, but an inference process guided by the interpretation of the redundancy of certain words in different sentences. To summarise what was said above, we could define two interpretation criteria:

1. One dealing with the association of a certain theme to a cluster and not to another. The meaning assigned to a cluster is the fruit of the interpretation of the different *"signs"* (sentences and words) it collects: certain signs are more associated (i.e. more important and central) than others (less important and more peripheral) in the construction of the hypotheses about the meaning recalled in a cluster.
2. The other referring to the redundancy of the thematic association displayed in the cluster.

It is by an *"abduction process"* [9, 14] that we interpreted thematic clustering. The themes are a hypothetical interpretation that we provided based on the analysis of the lemmas that each cluster encloses and refers to. Note that the themes are not

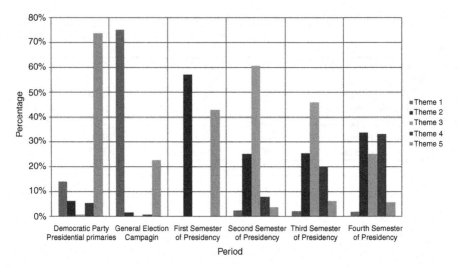

**Fig. 9.3** Clusters distribution over the six periods before interpretation (*bar graph* plot)

to be intended as fixed nor should the themes each cluster refers to be interpreted as fixed. Nevertheless, they help us generalise and interpret the results of Tweets clustering.

## Cluster Analysis Results

This section aims to illustrate the theme interpretation. The interpretation is based on the analysis of the lemmas and the distribution of the Tweets among the clusters.

Cluster analysis shaped five different ways to represent the political context displayed by Barack Obama and his staff since the moment of his presentation until nowadays. As we already said, each cluster corresponds to a certain theme conveyed by a different number of segments/messages sent by Twitter.

Table 9.5 introduces the listing of the first 20 words ordered by descending *Chi-square* value and organised by theme and the given interpretation. These data were essential to perform the analysis.

### Theme 1. Promote Change

The first theme emerging through the analysis identifies two main elements that could be synthesised as follows:

On one hand, it is the proposal itself to be highlighted, and in this case, Obama's proposal is identified first of all concerned with the political change (Change We Need, Vote for Change) according to the previous situation and according to a few central issues (Economic, Energy).

**Table 9.5** Listing of the first 20 words ordered by descending Chi-square value and organised by theme

| Theme 1 | Theme 2 | Theme 3 | Theme 4 | Theme 5 |
|---------|---------|---------|---------|---------|
| Livestream | American | Reform | http://wh.gov | Visit |
| http://my.barackobama.com | People | Health | Watch live | Head |
| Watch it live | Work | http://bit.ly | Live | Info |
| Rally | President | Congress | Speak | Iowa |
| Change we need | Obama | Call | Question | Debate |
| Hold | Commitment | Insurance | Forward | Tonight |
| Town hall | Gulf | Wall street | Answer | Text |
| Discussion | Clean energy | Hear | Move | http://barackobama.com |
| Early | Pass | OFA (Organizing for America) | Education | Change |
| Vote for change | Coast | Member | Nuclear | http://tinyurl.com |
| Watch the event | Lose | Yesterday | Arne | Presidential |
| Event | Future | Final | Duncan | City |
| Stream | Mission | Consumer | Listen live | Campaign |
| Joe | Historic | Senate | White house | Poll |
| Economic | Pay | Law | Economy | Full |
| Energy | Rights | Protection | Innovation | Today |
| Clinton | Combat | Spread | Job | Msnbc |
| Conference | Freedom | Organise | National | Thought |
| Reno | Create | Video | Best | Look |
| Meet | Recovery | Important | Tune | Ask |
| Promote change | US priorities | Health reform | Social issues | Build participation |

On the other hand, the encouragement sent to the citizens through the Tweets helped them to get to know, get used to and participate to Obama's proposal of a new political strategy. This element is underlined by the explicit reference to follow public debates live (Watch, Livestream, Watch it live, Watch the event) and interventions as well (Rally, Town Hall, Discussion, Event, Conference, Meet) or to connect to Internet pages (http://my.barackobama.com) to deepen the issues presented.

According to these two elements, the first theme shapes the idea of a proposal intending to promote change in the citizen to whom the messages are addressed: they are entailed in a change suggestion in which they are also invited to explore and get to know.

Numbered list of the most relevant Tweets by descending order of the *"Promote Change"* theme:

1. In Fredericksburg VA. At a "Change We Need" rally with Joe Biden. Watch it live at http://my.barackobama.com/livestream
2. In Lebanon VA. Holding a "Change We Need" Town Hall. Watch it live at http://my.barackobama.com/livestream

3. In Farmington Hills, MI. Holding a "Change_We_Need" Town_Hall. Watch_it_live at http://my_barackobama_com/livestream
4. In Dunedin FL. Speaking at a Change_We_Need rally. Watch_it_live now at http://my_barackobama_com/livestream
5. In Reno NV. At a "Change_We_Need" rally. Watch_it_live at http://my_barackobama_com/livestream

## Theme 2. US Priorities

The second theme highlighted mainly refers to the political strategy to-be (Future) that the president (President, Obama) presents the American nation (American, People) in order to commit (Commitment) to these topics. The questions highlighted refer to some relevant political topics, such as Work, Gulf, Mission, Combat, Clean Energy, Rights, etc.

In this thematic nucleus, it seems that the Tweets associated highlight the political agenda president Obama is pointing out to the Americans in order to underline the priorities of his politics and, consequently, to illustrate the priorities the nation has to follow.

Numbered list of the most relevant Tweets by descending order of the *"US Priorities"* theme:

1. This Labor Day know that I'm going to keep fighting to turn this economy around put our people back to work and renew the American Dream.
2. I made a pledge to the American people as a candidate for this office – and tonight the American combat mission in Iraq has ended.
3. On Labor Day we honor the American worker and reaffirm our commitment to the great American middle class. http://j.mp/a3RjbF
4. While making progress today we renew our commitment to ensuring that women receive equal pay for equal work. http://j.mp/akQWEj
5. Stand with me in backing Clean Energy. Send a clear message that the American people are ready for a clean-energy future. http://j.mp/cKspy5

## Theme 3. Health Reform

The third theme, different from the two previous ones, expresses a specific topic (that of Health Reform) to which the different co-occurring words give form. In this case, the political reformist direction that Obama submits seems protective (Protection) and innovative to all the people this reform is addressed to (Consumer). Despite of its apparent reformist and protective content, the words co-occurring in the cluster underline how this reform does not appear to be linearly welcomed: it rather appears much debated in the political centres (Congress, Senate) and also strongly opposed and contrasted within other constituted economical power centres (Wall Street).

In this cluster, thus, the health-care reform shapes up as a very controversial topic, strongly wished by some (those who take part to the presidential policy), as well as powerfully disliked and fought by rivals (in particular, within the economic circles). If the presidential Twitter messages underline the importance (important) to sustain the reformist actions in terms of a response/action of participation (called *"Organizing for America"*), this call also highlights the presence of a clear opposition between opposed factions in the political field. This is why the third theme appears to be the most radicalised and the most emotionally charged, and at the same time, the theme in which the enthusiastic request to contribute to the political demand by an action of participation is most present.

Numbered list of the most relevant Tweets by descending order of the *"Health Reform"* theme:

1. Have video skills? Want to help pass health reform? Enter OFA's Health Reform Video Challenge: http://bit.ly/SHdr3#hc09
2. Since August OFA supporters have made over 800k calls to Congress to support health reform. Help break one million today: http://bit.ly/5-b
3. Health reform just took a huge step – but the insurance lobby is working hard to stop it. Urge Congress to pass real reform: http://u.nu/6jhi3
4. As Congress prepares for final votes on Wall Street reform tell your member of Congress that you support reform. http://j.mp/bhyaXG
5. Health reform debate moving soon to the full Congress. it s time to be heard. Help OFA reach 100,000 calls on 10/20: http://bit.ly/10-20

**Theme 4. Social Issues**

The Tweets associated to the fourth theme, similarly to the second cluster enucleated by the analysis, encourage citizens to get to know and take part in Obama's presidential strategy, mainly by identifying the most important and problematic Social Issues of his political agenda. These issues concern the four most important national elements: economical (Economy, Innovation, Job – and not comprehended in the first 20 words: Growth and Business), educational (Education, update), environmental (Nuclear, Plant, and not in the first 20 words: Oil and Spill) and security elements (Terrorist, Security). These social issues seem to be concerned with two more elements: on one hand, they are not limited to the US nation (as in the second theme) but entail the entire world (world), and, on the other hand, they are presented as related to the urge (urgent) to respond to the crisis that president Obama has to face. Furthermore, the theme explicitly recalls the invitation to follow (Watch Live, Listen live) official (White House) speeches, meetings and interventions (Speak, Question, Answer) live.

Numbered list of the most relevant Tweets by descending order of the *"Social Issues"* theme:

1. Speaking about education reform at the National Urban League 100th Anniversary Convention. Watch live at 10:05 a.m. ET. http://wh.gov/live

2. Speaking about today's monthly job numbers report the best in 4 years at 11 a.m. ET. Watch live: http://wh.gov/live

3. Speaking from the White House Rose Garden on the urgent need to extend unemployment benefits. Watch live at 10:30 a.m. ET. http://wh.gov/live

4. Hosting small-business owners & speaking on the importance of small businesses in our economy. Watch live at 11:15 a.m. ET: http://wh.gov/live

5. Taking questions from young African leaders from 47 nations at a White House Town Hall meeting. Watch live at 2 p.m. ET. http://wh.gov/live

## Theme 5. Build Participation

The fifth and final theme refers to the need to present Senator Obama as a potential future president, running for the electoral campaign, and highlights the main topic he is concerned about, that of the commitment to change. The presentation of Barack Obama's campaign (Campaign) is made by the encouragement (Encourage) to attend, participate and listen to his presidential campaign, either locally (Iowa, City, Location) or daily (Today, Tonight), to follow (Look) his talks (Visit, Debate) or to watch what is presented on the Internet or on TV (Info, Text, http://barackobama.com,http://barackobama.com,Msnbc).

Thus, this theme mainly organises itself on the need to make the population feel the wish to participate in the presentation of this presidential candidate, in order to support him in his electoral campaign.

Numbered list of the most relevant Tweets by descending order of the *"Build Participation"* theme:

1. In Myrtle Beach heading to tonight's debate at 8 p.m. on CNN. Please visit http://barackobama.com to watch my speech from Dr. King's church.

2. Watch the VP debate at 9 p.m. ET tonight and cheer on Joe. Also remind your friends to visit http://voteforchange.com & register to vote.

3. In Iowa and heading to today's NPR/Iowa Public Radio Presidential Debate. Watch it live at 2 p.m. ET by visiting http://www.npr.org

4. Asking for your vote today. For polling location info visit http://VoteForChange.com or call 877-874-6226. Make sure everyone votes!

5. In Iowa this week and heading to the Iowa State Fair later this afternoon – Visit http://iowa_barackobama_com/roadtochange for full schedule.

## Distribution of the Cluster Percentages in the Different Periods

Table 9.6 shows the distribution of the Tweet dataset among the categories and the time periods in terms of absolute number of Tweets and in terms of percentages. If we analyse which period has the most relevance per category, we find out the following correspondence:

**Table 9.6** Distribution of the Tweets dataset among the categories and the time periods with theme interpretation, indicating the absolute number of Tweets (N) and the percentages (%)

| Period\Category | Promote change | | US priorities | | Health reform | | Social issues | | Build participation | | Total | |
|---|---|---|---|---|---|---|---|---|---|---|---|---|
| | N | % | N | % | N | % | N | % | N | % | N | % |
| Democratic Party presidential primaries | 18 | 13.95 | 8 | 6.20 | 1 | 0.78 | 7 | 5.43 | 95 | 73.64 | 129 | 100 |
| General election campaign | 99 | 75.00 | 2 | 1.52 | 0 | 0.00 | 1 | 0.76 | 30 | 22.73 | 132 | 100 |
| First semester of presidency | 0 | 0.00 | 4 | 57.14 | 0 | 0.00 | 0 | 0.00 | 3 | 42.86 | 7 | 100 |
| Second semester of presidency | 3 | 2.36 | 32 | 25.20 | 77 | 60.63 | 10 | 7.87 | 5 | 3.94 | 127 | 100 |
| Third semester of presidency | 6 | 2.13 | 72 | 25.53 | 130 | 46.10 | 56 | 19.86 | 18 | 6.38 | 282 | 100 |
| Fourth semester of presidency | 4 | 1.90 | 71 | 33.81 | 53 | 25.24 | 70 | 33.33 | 12 | 5.71 | 210 | 100 |
| General | 130 | 14.66 | 189 | 21.31 | 261 | 29.43 | 144 | 16.23 | 163 | 18.38 | 887 | 100 |

- Promote change was more relevant on the general election campaign.
- US Priorities was more relevant on the first semester of presidency.
- Health Reform was more relevant on the second and third semester of presidency.
- Social Issues was more relevant on the fourth semester of presidency.
- Build Participation was more relevant on the Democratic Party presidential primaries.

In order to provide a validation to this correspondence, we submitted the data to a Pearson's Chi-square test. Results confirm our previous considerations, highlighting statistically significant relationships between periods and themes (chi-square = 951.730, d.f. = 20, P = 0.000).

## Conclusion

In this chapter, we put together the word of meaning-making and the need for improving the analysis of the political communication process in the domain of social networks. Specifically, we focused on the political communication of Barack Obama in the Twitter social network service extracting knowledge forms from his Tweet messages.

We introduced a general methodology to analyse the messages of the Twitter social network users and performed an experiment with it. The results represent the mined knowledge from Barack Obama's Tweets.

The results seem to show an evident relationship between the political agenda of Barack Obama in each period of time and the Tweet posts that were shared on the Twitter social network. These results appear to indicate that there is a relation between users' behaviour on the social networks and their real-life chores. Furthermore, we demonstrated that the proposed method is able to extract and represent knowledge from the Twitter social network by extracting valuable information.

We consider that the proposed methodology may be applied to other research areas among the meaning-making process. It could help new issues, related to social networks (such as marketing, user profiling or trend analysis), to emerge.

Future work will focus on applying the proposed methodology to other representative users of Twitter and other social networks data.

## References

1. Bosio, A., Graffigna, G., Lozza, E.: Online Focus Groups: Toward a Theory of Technique, pp. 192–212. Idea Group, Hershey (2008)
2. Gatti, F., Graffigna, G.: Due Software per l'analisi Testuale: Atlas.TI e T-LAB [Two Software for Text Analysis: Atlas.TI and T-Lab], pp. 183–192. Franco Angeli, Milano (2009)
3. Greener, I.: Who Choosing What? The Evolution of 'Choice' in the NHS, and Its Implications for New Labour, 15th edn., pp. 49–68. Policy, Bristol (2003)

4. Harré, R., Gillett, G.: The Discursive Mind. Sage, London (1994)
5. Kaid, L.L.: Handbook of Political Communication Research. Lawrence Erlbaum, Mahwah (2004)
6. Lancia, F.: The logic of a text-scope. http://www.tlab.it/en/bibliography.php (2002)
7. Lancia, F.: The logic of a text-scope. http://www.mytlab.com/textscope.pdf (2002). Retrieved 13 Nov 2007
8. Lancia, F.: Strumenti per l'analisi dei testi. Introduzione all'uso di T-LAB [Tools for Text Analysis. Introduction to the Use of T-LAB]. Franco Angeli, Milano (2004)
9. Lancia, F.: Mind as Infinite Dimensionality, Chap. Word Co-occurrence and Similarity in Meaning. Firera, Roma (2008)
10. Lauro-Grotto, R., Salvatore, S., Gennaro, A., Gelo, O.: The unbearable dynamicity of psychological processes: highlights of the psychodynamic theories. In: Valsiner, J., Molenaar, P.C.M., Lyra, M.C., Chaudhary, N. (eds.) Dynamic Process Methodology in the Social and Developmental Sciences, pp. 1–30. Springer, New York (2009)
11. Mazzara, B.: I discorsi dei media e la psicologia sociale. Ambiti e strumenti di indagine [Media Discourses and Social Psychology. Fields and Survey Tools]. Carocci, Roma (2008)
12. Montali, L., Colombo, M., Camussi, E., Maglietta, A., Riva, P.: Xenophobia in political discourse: an analysis of Italian parliamentary debates on immigration. The Fourth ECPR Conference. Unpublished paper. http://www.tlab.it/en/bibliography.php (2007). Retrieved 23 Sept 2010
13. Murphy, D.: Twitter: On-track for 200 million users by year's end. PCMAG. http://www.pcmag.com/article2/0,2817,2371826,00.asp (2010). Retrieved 13 Nov 2007
14. Peirce, C.: Abduction and induction. Philosophical Writings of Peirce, pp. 150–156. Dover, New York (1955)
15. Pugliese, A.C., Serino, C.: Using superordinate categories to enlarge consensus: an analysis of Italian politicians' speeches (2003)
16. Salvatore, S., Tebaldi, C., Potì, S.: YIS: Yearbook of Idiographic Science, vol. 1, pp. 39–72. Firera, Roma (2008). First published 2006, in international journal of idiographic science [On Line Journal], Article 3. http://www.valsiner.com/articles/salvatore.htm. Retrieved 20 Sept 2008
17. Valsiner, J.: Processes structure of semiotic mediation in human development. Hum. Dev. **44**, 84–97 (2001)
18. Valsiner, J.: Beyond social representations: a theory of enablement. Pap. Soc. Represent. **12**(7), 7.1–7.16 (2003)
19. Venuleo, C., Salvatore, S.: Linguaggi e dispositivi comunicativi. I Faccia a Faccia televisivi [Language and Communication Devices. Face to Face Television Debates], pp. 151–189. Besa Editrice, Nardò (LE) (2006)
20. Venuleo, C., Salvatore, S., Mossi, P., Grassi, R., Ruggeri, R.: The didactic relationship in the changing world. Outlines for a theory of the reframing setting. Eur. J. Sch. Psychol. **5**(2), 151–180 (2008)

# Part II
# Visualization

# Chapter 10
# Mining and Visualizing Research Networks Using the Artefact-Actor-Network Approach

**Wolfgang Reinhardt, Adrian Wilke, Matthias Moi, Hendrik Drachsler, and Peter Sloep**

**Abstract** Virtual communities are increasingly relying on technologies and tools of the so-called Web 2.0. In the context of scientific events and topical Research Networks, researchers use Social Media as one main communication channel. This raises the question how to monitor and analyze such Research Networks. In this chapter, we argue that Artefact-Actor-Networks (AANs) serve well for modeling, storing, and mining the social interactions around digital learning resources originating from various learning services. In order to deepen the model of AANs and its application to Research Networks, a relevant theoretical background as well as clues for a prototypical reference implementation are provided. This is followed by the analysis of six Research Networks and a detailed inspection of the results. Moreover, selected networks are visualized. Research Networks of the same type show similar descriptive measures while different types are not directly comparable to each other. Further, our analysis shows that narrowness of a Research Network's subject area can be predicted using the connectedness of semantic similarity networks. Finally, conclusions are drawn and implications for future research are discussed.

W. Reinhardt (✉) • A. Wilke
Department of Computer Science, Computer Science Education Group, University of Paderborn,
Fuerstenallee 11, 33012 Paderborn, Germany
e-mail: wolle@upb.de; wilke@mail.upb.de

M. Moi
Faculty of Mechanical Engineering, Computer Application and Integration in Design
and Planning, University of Paderborn, Pohlweg 47-49, 33098 Paderborn, Germany
e-mail: moi@cik.upb.de

H. Drachsler • P. Sloep
Centre for Learning Sciences and Technologies, Open University of the Netherlands,
6401 DL Heerlen, The Netherlands
e-mail: hendrik.drachsler@ou.nl; peter.sloep@ou.nl

A. Abraham (ed.), *Computational Social Networks: Mining and Visualization*,
DOI 10.1007/978-1-4471-4054-2_10, © Springer-Verlag London 2012

## Introduction

With the recent rise of Social Media tools like Twitter and Facebook, the Web-based interaction in virtual communities of like-minded people keeps growing. Lately, Learning Networks and research communities make use of the communication and collaboration features of Social Media platforms. This increases the productivity of the involved participants, enhances mutual awareness, and increases a community's nexus. In recent years we have witnessed the wide application of Social Media to higher education courses and scientific conferences, the discussion about political and environmental phenomena, as well as the usage in research communities and enterprises. The analysis of such online activities enables researchers to reveal patterns in communication, detect and visualize cliques of people, or trace the trails of discussions in a community. Most of these analyses, however, only reflect the social part of the interactions and thus are able to make claims about the structure of a virtual community but not about the respective digital objects.

In this chapter, we present the derivation of the concept of Research Networks (section "Research Networks and Levels of Member Participation") and put the concept in the context of Research 2.0 in section "Research Networks and Research 2.0." Following we present the model of Artefact-Actor-Networks and its reference implementation in section "The AAN Approach for Research Network Mining" that was used for mining different types of Research Networks: conferences, university courses, and hashtag communities (section "Research Networks Analyzed in This Article"). In addition, we give an insight into data storage with Semantic Web technologies. We explore the artefacts and their relations to online actors in three learning services (Delicious, SlideShare, and Twitter). Besides the descriptive analysis of the communities, we apply metrics from Social Network Analysis (SNA) and visualize the networks based on different factors such as semantic similarity (section "Mining of Selected Research Networks"). From the analysis of the networks, we aim at bridging the gap between the use of Social Media tools, as a mean for communication and exchange, and the missing awareness for one's own and activities of others in such settings. Furthermore, we will show the strengths of the Artefact-Actor-Network approach for identifying interesting relations between activities of users, the artefacts they generate, and the larger image those activities produce towards pattern recognition in Learning Networks' activities. The chapter closes with the discussion of the results of the Research Network mining in section "Discussion and Outlook" and gives an outlook how they could be used in future research towards awareness-support for participants in Research Networks.

## Research Networks and Levels of Member Participation

An online community, e-community, virtual community, or online social network is to be understood as a group of people that interact using electronic means of cooperation. Examples of such cooperation media are email, telephone, instant messaging services, and more recently Social Software. Lately, online communities have become a valuable and widespread used supplement for groups that work together in face-to-face contexts but they are also existing exclusively in the online world. Online communities may be centered around professional, educational, recreational, political topics; they may be organizational, topical or regional and most often assemble people around specific objects (also see [6, 10]).

Rheingold coined the term virtual communities and claims that they form "when enough people carry on those public discussions long enough, with sufficient human feeling, to form webs of personal relationships in cyberspace" [39]. Kim adds that web communities are "a group of people who share a common interest or purpose; who have the ability to get to know each other better over time. There are two pieces to that definition. That second piece getting to know each other better over time means that there needs to be some mechanism of identity and communication" [22]. The mere existence of an online community does not mean that there are any strong personal relations between its participants; uncovering the very liberal use of the term community and the term of virtual communities as such [20, 31]. Wellman on the other hand defines community as "networks of interpersonal ties that provide sociability, support, information, a sense of belonging, and social identity. I do not limit my thinking about community to neighbourhoods and villages. This is good advice for any epoch and especially pertinent for the twenty-first century" and further elaborates that "we find community in networks, not groups. Although people often view the world in terms of groups (Freeman 1992), they function in networks. In networked societies: boundaries are permeable, interactions are with diverse others, connections switch between multiple networks, and hierarchies can be flatter and recursive" [54].

In blended learning, classroom learning is combined with web-based learning that may use organizational learning management systems (LMS) or more open approaches with which the learners may decide on the tools they want to use. The learner's Personal Learning Environment (PLE, [55]) provides access to all learning resources, useful people and learning services he might need for pursuing his learning goals. Recently, the term *Learning Networks* has been coined for such online communities of learners. According to Koper et al. [23], Learning Networks (LNs) are online communities in which users share existing information and cooperatively create new knowledge. This way, Learning Networks help participants to develop their skills and competences in rather non-formal, unplanned, and ad hoc learning situations and educational contexts. Different from formal education, there are little learning goals for the whole Learning Network as well as diffuse, hard-to-phrase individual ones. As Koper points out [24], the participants of a Learning Network could:

- Exchange experience and knowledge with each other
- Collaborate on common research questions and tasks
- Offer and get support to/from other participants in the Learning Network (e.g. questions, answers, remarks)
- Set up focussed working groups

- Support each other when encountering learning problems
- Use tools and services to create, share, find, and access learning resources.

Each Learning Network – being a social network – is composed of people that share a similar interest or follow a similar goal. The commitment to the common interest or goal, the timeframe of the Learning Network's existence, the size of the networks and other properties vary between Learning Networks but for all that Learning Networks are providing their participants with resources, services and agents to support their learning purposes. The *participants* in Learning Networks have clearly defined or rather blurred learning goals; they could help seekers as well as mentors, coaches, teachers, or lurking bystanders. The *resources* in a Learning Network are all digital artefacts that might help the participants to accomplish their learning goal or that make them aware of a lack of personal competence that they want to eliminate. Learning resources may include any audio or video file, blog post, wiki page, or learning resources as well as entire courses in LMS. Part of those resources were already existing before the nascency of the Learning Network, others are created by the participants, and all of those resources can be used by several LNs at a time. Sloep elaborates that *learning services* are software tools that increase a Learning Network's viability [44]. Koper adds that such web services are designed to facilitate the participants to exchange experience and knowledge, to stimulate active participation in the Learning Network, to assess and develop the participants' competences, to find relevant peers and experts that could offer support in solving a certain problem, and to facilitate ubiquitous learning [24]. According to Koper, examples of Learning Networks are [23]:

- Communities of teachers who exchange experience on how to handle certain pedagogical issues in the classroom.
- Employees of a company that need to update themselves about the functions of a new product their company released recently.
- Students who cooperatively write a composition on a given topic.
- Lawyers who exchange experience and knowledge when a new law is introduced within their field.
- Researchers that exchange information to find solutions for a specific problem. They update each other with new findings and cooperatively solve problems, co-author documents, attend face-to-face events, and carry out joint projects in a geographically and timely separated manner.

As a matter of course, there exist a range of other Learning Networks with different participants, resources, and services. If the participants in a Learning Network are scholars, the resources used and services in place are related to their research activities or the execution of research projects we call such Learning Networks *Research Learning Networks* or briefly Research Networks (RNs). It is common to all of those Learning Networks that we find differing levels of member participation.

## *Levels of Interaction*

As Kim [22] elaborates, we find differences in the interactions in Research Networks that make use of structured means of communication (such as bulletin boards, mailing lists, or chat rooms) and such Research Networks where interactions are mediated through bottom-up, individual-centred tools (e.g. blogs, microblogs or social networking sites). In almost all Research Networks, there are patterns of social interaction and user contributions. It does not matter if the participation in the Research Network includes posing questions and answering some, tagging resources or creating own learning resources, creating discussion threads or linking online learning repositories; it is a rule-of-thumb that only 1% of the participants create new content, 10% interact with this content, and 89% will just consume the content that is there [2]. This inequality pattern is even worse within Wikipedia, the most well-known Research Network where participants jointly create a high-quality online encyclopaedia. In September 2010, the English version of Wikipedia had 35,222 active users[1] which is only 0.027% of the 130 million unique visitors it has worldwide (it is 0.07% of the 45 million unique visitors it has in the USA alone) [14, 56].

This unbalanced participation patterns can be found in most Research Networks and Social Networking Services (SNS) and can be explained by technical and motivational reasons. If there are technical hurdles that hinder the learner to participate in the Research Network's activities or if the participants sense a lack of compensation for their work, the participation in the Research Network will probably not set up. As the reasons for a learner's participation is both varying and not singular, Research Networks should incentivize participants with multiple types of motivation in order to engage them and keep them engaged. Lately Wikipedia undermined the sovereignty of its users and demotivated some of them with the ongoing controversy around Deletionism versus Inclusionism [7] and the force of producing higher quality articles with a range of external references. This, together with increasing administrative processes needed to edit articles, resulted in a decline of active users in the Learning Network by 12.3% (11,170 users) between January and September 2010. Many Wikipedians lost their feeling of belonging to a community of equivalents, thus trashing their identity in the Learning Network.

Another explanation approach for those participation patterns comes from a more sociological point of view. Kim suggested that there is a membership life cycle [22] and Lave and Wenger presented the model of Legitimate Peripheral Participation (LPP) [26], both claiming that there is a participation life cycle for participants in communities such as Research Networks. Table 10.1 synthesizes the ideas whereupon participants start their life in a Research Network as a visitor or lurker that are only watching interactions and consuming existing content but are not directly adding new content. At some point learners start participating in the

---

[1] A Wikipedian is counted as being active, if he contributed to Wikipedia articles at least five times in a month.

**Table 10.1** Levels of participation in Research Networks (Based on [18])

| Participation | Status | Life cycle |
|---|---|---|
| Peripheral | Visitor | The participant is an outsider and has little or no structured participation in the Research Network (he is lurking) |
| Inbound | Novice | The participant is introduced as newcomer to the Research Network and heading toward full participation in the Network's activities |
| Insider | Regular | The participant is a fully committed inhabitant of the Learning Network |
| Boundary | Leader | The participant is a leader in the Research Network sustaining his membership with active participation and the brokering of information and interactions |
| Peripheral | Elder | The participant is about to leave the Research Network because of new goals, extended relationships to new Research Networks and new positions |

Learning Network's activities and become novices. After having contributed to the RN with both active social and content interaction, the learner becomes a regular participant. If a learner further engages in the RN's activities, he might become a leader that sustains his membership through multifaceted activities. After being in a Research Network for some time, a participant might become an elder that is about to leave the network because of new learning goals or matured knowledge in the domain. It needs to be pointed out that a learner can always be part of many Research Networks at a time; so while he is a leader in one, he might be visitor in another one and regular participant in a third Research Network. At each time and in any Research Network, participants on a lower level of participation must feel engaged and motivated by the fellow participants and be technically empowered to 'graduate' to a higher level.

## Research Networks and Research 2.0

Lately, Research Networks are increasingly dependent on Web 2.0 tools, technologies and techniques to their daily practices. In Technology Enhanced Learning (TEL), the adoption of Web 2.0 is already actively researched under such notations as Learning 2.0 [34], Personal Learning Environments [55], Open Learning Environments [16, 28] or Learning Networks [25]. The application of Web 2.0 to Research Networks is often squired with the terms Research 2.0 or Science 2.0 and aims at leveraging the same opportunities for research. Research 2.0 is a rather young concept but there are already numerous controversial positions, oscillating between new tools and technologies, methods and practices (cf. [47]). Waldrop [52], for example, relates Science 2.0 to "new practices of scientists who post raw experimental results, nascent theories, claims of discovery and draft papers on the Web for other to see and comment on" and Shneiderman [43] comprehends the term as "new technologies [that] continue to reorder whole disciplines [... as ...] increased collaboration [is stimulated] through these socio-technical systems."

Focusing on the change of practices mentioned in Waldrop's definition, Kieslinger and Lindstaedt [21] are underlining the Science 2.0 focus on "improving, enhancing [and] speeding up feedback cycles." Underwood et al. [48] postulate even further that Research 2.0 offers more potential that the mere optimization of science efficiency: participation in research can be broadened beyond existing scientific communities. Research 2.0 as "technology enhanced participatory science" [48] could then unbolt science allowing 'everyday scientists' [40] to participate globally and pervasively in research and collaboration. Butler [5] sees a key feature of Research 2.0 in "dynamic interactions between [scholars] in real time" at the same time criticizing the slow adoption of these new technologies and practices in the scholarly daily routines. Waldrop also claims that Science 2.0 allows for a richer dialogue in Research Networks such as collaborative brainstorming, meta conversations, or an open discourse of "critiquing, suggesting, sharing of ideas and data" among previously unknown parties [52]. Ullmann et al. point out that this way, "Science 2.0 is supposed to enable efficient crowd-sourcing of ideas and refinement of knowledge through open debate." [47]. As Nielsen remarks, the scholarly system has hardly changed since the creation of the first scientific journal in the seventeenth century. With the Internet, WWW and Research 2.0 becoming mainstream, science will "change more over the next 20 years than in the past 300 years" [27]. He goes on and elaborates that Research 2.0 is the "first major opportunity to improve this collective long-term memory [the scientific journal system], and to create a collective short-term working memory, a conversational commons for the rapid collaborative development of ideas."

There is some controversy about whether Research Networks are driven by new technologies or new practices and the reciprocal relationship between those two aspects. Where understanding new practices allows for their implementation into tools, the existence of new tools reshape existing practices and often allow for the appropriation of new practices not foreseen in their design. Finally, Shneiderman controversially asserts Science 2.0 a change in research methodology that would be complementary to the Science 1.0 focus on predictive models and laboratory controlled testing (see also Gillet's elaborations on the transition from Science 1.0 to Science 2.0 in [13]). Research 2.0 would therefore take place embedded in the real world through large-scale, rigorous observations and their validity would be empirically investigated using qualitative and quantitative analysis. Objectors of this understanding point out that many scientific fields including social sciences or natural sciences already rely on this scientific methodology. In spite of that, there seems to be an agreement amongst scholars that Research 2.0 and its new socio-technical systems are more cooperative, more efficient, productive, and open, are fostering engagement and focussing on the sharing of new ideas.

Despite the many undoubted advantages of Research 2.0, many authors mention a reluctant adoption of the new learning services by researchers. In some disciplines, the revolution of Research 2.0 is even passing by without researchers noticing the changes [5]. A recent study conducted by Procter et al. [33] with 1,477 UK researchers reveals that the adoption of Research 2.0 in scholarly communications "has reached only modest levels so far," whereas there are certain learning services that have been rapidly adopted. Especially in the context of scientific events and higher education courses, services like Twitter and SlideShare have proven to be heavily used to share messages and learning resources with a wider public [17, 35]. Duval even says that "In fact, Twitter is more relevant to me now than any [other] research2.0 application" [8]. Another category of learning service that is widely adopted within the scholarly practice are social bookmarking systems such as Delicious or Diigo [53]. What is common to those learning services is the fact that they are built around clearly defined digital social objects [10] and not intended for the usage in the scholarly system in the first place. Instead, researchers adopted and reshaped the learning services in order to make them better suited to the scholarly routines of work.

Summing up, it can be stated that participants in Research Networks use learning services in varying intensity with the goal to open up the previously closed world or research. They share ideas and learning resources with each other and cooperatively create new knowledge that becomes part of the collective memory. Not all learning services are used equally and not all researchers use all existing learning services. In fact, we even observe different usage of different services with one person, meaning that they differentially behave in different learning services. In order to mine Research Networks and the respective learning services, we therefore should differentiate between the different handles of a person in the learning services, allowing for the separated inspection of a user's behavior. Also, we should be able to distinguish between the single learning services like Twitter or Delicious within a Research Network in order to recognize pattern that might exist in one service but not within the other. This will also allow us to compare the usage of learning services in different Research Networks.

The overall goals of Research Network mining are thus: expert finding and recommendation, learning resource clustering and recommendation, pattern recognition within and across Research Networks, community detection within Research Networks, awareness raising about a network's behavior and structure, and the analysis of a participant's research network trajectory. In the following section, we introduce the approach of Artefact-Actor-Networks (AANs) to support these Research Network mining goals.

## The AAN Approach for Research Network Mining

Artefact-Actor-Networks are an approach for mining resources of various kinds of source networks. It comprises two main parts: the theoretical foundation and a reference implementation. In the theoretical part, a concept for a consolidation of social networks and artefact networks of documents is explained. Resources of mined networks are stored by a distinction between artefacts, actors, and keywords. The practical implementation of this concept was put into practice using Semantic

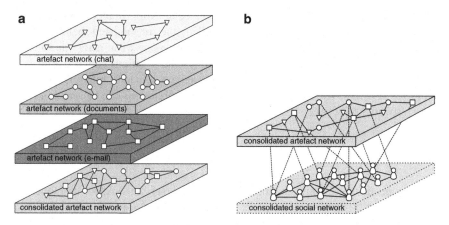

**Fig. 10.1** Schematic assembling of an AAN. (**a**) Consolidated artefact network resulting from three layers. (**b**) Artefact-Actor-Network with semantic relations between artefacts and actors

Web technologies. Section "Theoretical Approach" introduces the fundamentals for a system for finding experts and communities, retrieving information, analyzing and visualizing Research Networks. The reference implementation of this system is introduced in section "AAN Reference Implementation."

## Theoretical Approach

Artefact-Actor-Networks (AANs) were first introduced by Reinhardt, Moi, and Varlemann in 2009 [36] and serve as an approach to semantically intertwine social networks with so-called artefact networks. We distinguish two general types of layers – the artefact and actor layers. Both types can have arbitrary sub-layers to specialize the type of an artefact or actor. This can be understood like the hierarchy concept of higher level programming languages. Furthermore, artefacts and actors can be connected trough typed relations, so-called semantic relations to manifest the semantic context. Examples for semantic relations are *isCoWorker* to connect actors, *references* to connect artefacts, and *isAuthor* to connect artefacts with actors.

### Layer in Artefact-Actor-Networks

Using Artefact-Actor-Networks an actor's participation in the life cycle of artefacts as well as significant connections to other actors will be outlined. Artefact-Actor-Networks consolidate multilayered social networks and artefact networks in an integrated network. Therefore, we consider the communication and collaboration with each learning service or artefact supply (e.g. Twitter, chats, email or scientific documents) as a single layer of the respective network. We unite these single layers in both social and artefact networks to consolidated networks that contain all actors and artefacts, respectively (cf. Fig. 10.1a). While in the consolidated social network we can only make statements concerning the relations between actors and in the consolidated artefact network, we can only analyze the relations between artefacts, Artefact-Actor-Networks (cf. Fig. 10.1b) also contain semantic relations between actors and artefacts. The recently discussed semantic relations can be found in each layer, respectively, between each layers.

## Use of Ontologies

As introduced, we distinguish different types of layers in AANs. To model an Artefact-Actor-Network with its layers we use ontologies to specify semantical and hierarchical relations. Using current techniques like OWL [50] and RDF(S) [51], the inheritance of classes and relations can be accomplished. Every class represents a special type of artefact and actor, which are the base classes. By following this approach, querying specialized information becomes possible and allows to change between different abstraction levels. On the base level, there are only artefacts and actors without further specialization. If we were interested in an aggregated analysis of all artefacts or actors, we would simply query the base class, whereas querying specific classes allows for more focused analyses. Figure 10.2 depicts the ontologies used in the AAN reference implementation.

AANBase and Co.

All our ontologies inherit from the *AANBase* ontology. It holds the base classes *artefact*, *actor*, and *keyword*, which are the most general classes in any Artefact-Actor-Network. An artefact can have arbitrary many keywords. Each keyword can be specialized as a category or tag class.

Figure 10.2 also shows the *AANOnline* ontology, which describes artefacts and actors of the WWW. "Between" the *AANTwitter* and *AANOnline* ontology, there is the *AANMicroblog* ontology which abstracts from the various microblog services and allows to extent the whole ontology in the future. The same holds true for the other most specialized ontologies like *AANMediaWiki* or *AANDeliciousBookmarks*.

Using all ontologies in place, the layers of the Artefact-Actor-Network can be described and distinguished. The *AANBase* ontology represents the consolidated artefact and actor layer. More special layers are *AANMicroblog* or *AANWiki*. The most specialized layers *AANSlideShare*, *AANMediaWiki*, *AANTwitter*, and *AANDeliciousBookmarks* can be inferenced to get a more aggregated view of the network.

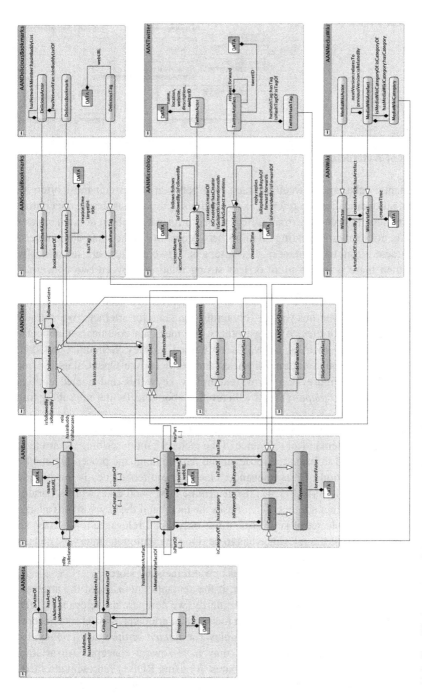

**Fig. 10.2** Simplified overview of the ontologies available in the AAN reference implementation

**Fig. 10.3** Relevant keywords
and named entities for a wiki
artefact about Twitter

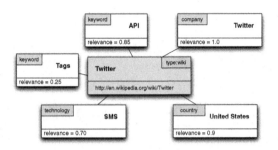

### Analysis of Artefacts

The semantic relations between artefacts and between actors can most often be extracted automatically, like references or citations without considering the content of the artefacts. In order to extract differentiated information about domain experts or the like, not explicitly existing relations between actors in the same domain need to be extracted from the content of their artefacts. If two artefacts are semantically similar, then there is also a more or less strong relation between two concerned actors.

To determine the semantic similarity of two artefacts, we need metadata of the objects. There are numerous ways of obtaining metadata for artefacts. We will not cover all these possibilities. Amongst others, the metadata contains semantically relevant information such as keywords or named entities. Semantic metadata can be extracted through external libraries and services like OpenCalais [38] or AlchemyAPI [29]. Figure 10.3 shows exemplary keywords and named entities (*technology*, *country*, *company*) for a wiki artefact about the Twitter microblogging service.

We have to calculate the relevance for every extracted keyword and named entity, which describes the semantical relevance of the metadata for describing the artefact. Several techniques of information retrieval and natural language processing can be used for the calculation of this relevance. One of these techniques is the inverse document frequency (tf-idf) [41, 42], to determine how good a keyword separates an artefact from all other artefacts. Tf-idf uses the fact that if the keyword has a large frequency in the whole set of keywords, it has only small relevance to describe an artefact. Processing of the relevance has to be done in continuous intervals, caused by the fact that tf-idf is based on the existing keyword corpus from the set of artefacts and thus has to be re-calculated as soon as new artefacts are stored.

Two artefacts are semantically similar, if the semantic metadata of the artefacts are similar. To determine the semantic similarity, we compare the relevance of the metadata of two artefacts. We distinguish metadata of artefacts in different concepts like *keywords* or *named entities*. Examples for *named entities* are *companies*, *technologies* or *persons*. Every artefact may have several concepts. An artefact interprets its referenced concepts as attributes. By using RDF to represent artefacts, we have no redundantly stored concepts. A concept may be referenced by many artefacts in the network. To compute the similarity between two artefacts, there must exist at least one equal concept between them. Otherwise the semantic similarity is zero. For a better understanding of our concept, we divide the process to calculate the semantic similarity into short steps.

## Relevance of Concepts for an Artefact

As discussed previously, an artefact may have arbitrary many concepts with specified relevances. Services like OpenCalais [38] and AlchemyAPI [29] deliver information about keywords and named entities with their respective relevance for the artefact. Directly extracted keywords can be weighted through information retrieval methods like tf-idf.

## Normalizing of Relevances

The relevance of the attributes are absolute values with no respect to other attributes. But to compute the semantic similarity between two artefacts, it is necessary to normalize the values to get the weight of one relevance in respect to all others. In our approach, we normalize the attributes to the value 1. Denote that all relevance factors are mapped into the continuous interval $(0, 1]$. The sum of all relevances is at most one.

## Computation of Semantic Similarity

To compute the similarity between two artefacts, we take into account all common attributes of the artefacts. Pairwise, the difference between the normalized values is calculated and weighted by the minimum of the normalized values of both attributes. Then all pairs will be summed up. The resulting value is the similarity of both artefacts with respect to the weight of their attributes. Hereafter, we present some definitions which are necessary to calculate the semantic similarity in AANs. Let $A$ be an artefact, then $C_A$ denotes the set over all concepts of the artefact $A$ whose relevance $r_A(c)$ is greater than 0. Let $A$ and $B$ be artefacts, then $C_{A,B} = C_A \cap C_B$ denotes the set of the common concepts.

Let $A$ be an artefact and $c \in C_A$ a concept of this artefact, then $r_A(c)$ denotes the relevance of the concept $c$ referred to artefact $A$. The normalized relevance of the concept $c$ referred to artefact $A$ will be calculated as follows:

$$n_A(c) = \frac{r_A(c)}{\sum_{i \in C_A} r_A(i)} \tag{10.1}$$

To calculate the semantic similarity between two artefacts $A$ and $B$, we iterate over all common concepts $C_{A,B}$. At every iteration step, the semantic similarity with respect to the current concept is calculated and summed up. The semantic similarity between two artefacts is then given by

$$\text{SemSim}_{A,B} = \sum_{c \in C_{A,B}} \left( \min\left(n_A(c), n_B(c)\right) \cdot \text{ConSim}_{A,B}(c)^2 \right). \qquad (10.2)$$

with

$$\text{ConSim}_{A,B}(c) = 1 - |n_A(c) - n_B(c)| \qquad (10.3)$$

The function $\text{ConSim}_{A,B}(c)$ (ConceptSimilarity) calculates the semantic similarity between two artefacts $A$ and $B$ with respect to concept $c$ by subtracting the absolute value of the difference of the relevances from 1. The greater the difference of the relevances of a common concept, the lesser the semantic similarity by the concept $c$.

$\text{SemSim}_{A,B}$ is a linear function (cf. Fig. 10.4). For a common concept between two artefacts $A$ and $B$, the relevancies are on the x- and y-axis. The value of the semantic similarity is represented by the z-axis. If the relevance $x$ equals $y$, the semantic similarity is maximal for a given concept.

For example, a common concept *SMS* which is a technology, the relevance of this concept must not necessarily be equal to both artefacts. If the relevancies are same, then ConSim returns 1, which means that the semantic similarity value will not be weakened, because the current concept is identically important to both artefacts. The minimum of the normalized relevancies in the first part of the formula guarantees, that the semantic similarity value in every iteration is not greater than the smallest relevance. If two artefacts have the same concepts and for every concept equal relevance, then it must be that the semantic similarity is exactly 1. Differences on relevancies for common concepts affect alleviative to the semantic similarity between two artefacts. In an evaluation process, we decided to square ConSim which means that a small difference of the relevance will affect less alleviative.

## AAN Reference Implementation

The different requirements of the AAN concept makes various demands on an implementation. With regard to a pool of possible data sources, the storage of semantic relations, and various goals of analysis by different components, there is a need for a dynamic system. Such a dynamic system can be designed with the OSGi Service Platform [30], which is a specification to develop modularized architectures with the Java programming language. With this basis, modularized components, called bundles, can be defined. A bundle consists of executable code and additional resources. Its functionality is offered by services, which are defined by interfaces. In this way a service can be provided by different bundles. This means that a specific task can be executed by several bundles, e.g. the analysis of a resource can be done by different specialized components. Another advantage of the OSGi

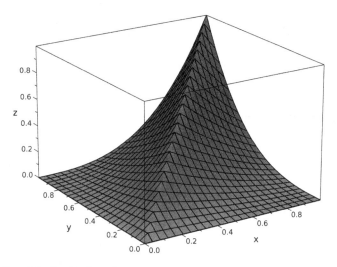

**Fig. 10.4** Plot of the *SemSim* formula

Service Platform is the dynamic treatment at runtime. Bundles can be in different states, they can be installed, started, and stopped at runtime. Thus it is possible to add a more recent version of a bundle without restarting the system.

The architecture of the reference implementation is divided into three main blocks of bundles, in which tasks of the fields data acquisition, data storage, and analysis are performed. Figure 10.5 shows the main parts of bundles and interfaces for the data flow. A more detailed insight is given in [37].

Bundles in the crawling block are responsible for the data acquisition. This block comprises three main types of bundles: CrawlerManager, Crawler, and Parser. The purpose of CrawlerManagers is to define tasks, by which resources of given URIs are processed. The first URI and additional parameters of an overall job can be given by users. This is why CrawlerManagers are accessible by web services. Beside an URI, a user can define when a job is started, if a job has to be repeated after some time, and how deep a network has to be accessed. General jobs, like of simple websites, can be executed by the GeneralCrawlerManager. If a network requires special handling, there is the possibility to define adapted CrawlerManagers, e.g. the DeliciousCrawlerManager, which was implemented to fit the requirements of Delicious feeds. With this component, it is possible to define, if resources of an actor or a keyword is of interest. After an overall crawling job is started, the Crawler component works through the job by a working chain, consisting of Accessor, MimeTyper, and Parser. The Accessor component accesses the resource given by an URI and temporarily stores the data of the URI locally. In the next step, the MimeTyper component determines the MIME type of the resource. Finally, a fitting Parser component is extracting relevant data. A suitable parser is chosen by the MIME type and the URI of a resource. There are two types of parsers, general and special parsers. General parsers are built up to handle resources like conventional

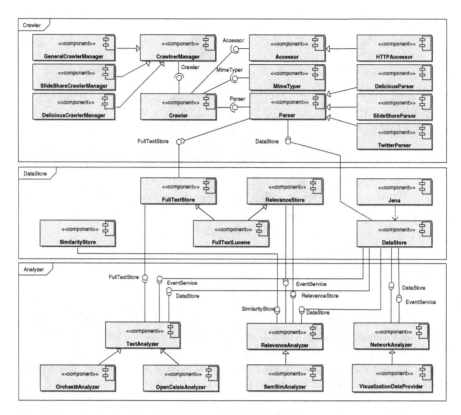

**Fig. 10.5** Architecture of the AAN reference implementation

websites. A general parser extracts hyperlinks and sub-documents like images and adds additional tasks for the extracted links. A specific parser is specialized to extract characteristic metadata of different interfaces, e.g. structured XML contents. Extracted data is handed over to bundles of the DataStore block. After a parser finishes work on a resource, a task is completed.

There are three types of data which are stored by bundles of the DataStore block: full texts, semantic data, and data describing the similarity of resources. The first two types are handed over by parsers. Full texts can be the main content of a website, a presentation, a microblog entry or other artefacts. The FullTextStore is realized using Apache Lucene, a Java-based indexing and search implementation. With this component, URIs and their related full texts can be stored and loaded again. Stored full text can be used for further analysis, e.g. clustering or keyword extraction to classify artefacts. Another exciting matter is the storage of semantic data. Objects, their semantic relations, and additional metadata can be stored by the DataStore bundle. The Semantic Web framework Jena [19] serves as the basis of this component. It provides a model, whose schema is specified by the AAN ontology. By the use of this model, statements in the form of triples can be stored (e.g. an actor is the creatorOf an artefact). Further, it is possible to make queries, written in the RDF query language SPARQL [49]. This offers various opportunities for defining specialized requests. For example, some metadata properties for all artefacts of a special class, reduced to a set of related authors and keywords can be queried. Such requests can be used for selecting data of interest and to analyze the data or visualize relations between requested objects. The third type of stored data is used indirectly by the analyzing component SemSim to store data about semantic similarity between artefacts.

Based on the harvested data, there are various opportunities for analysis. The first two developed components in the Analyzer block are bundles of the type TextAnalyzer, with which relevant entities (like describing keywords) for representing a full text can be extracted. The developed bundles are listening on upcoming events, which are fired in the DataStore block. These events occur every time a new resource is stored. The bundles OpenCalaisAnalyzer and Orchestr8Analyzer are based on the web services of OpenCalais [38] and the Orchestr8 AlchemiAPI [29]. Their functionality, efficiency, and accuracy are described in detail in [4]. The returned metadata is stored within the semantic model and provides describing data for further analysis. Another bundle of the type RelevanceAnalyzer is the SemSimAnalyzer, which translates an approach of computing semantic similarity into practice. Like presented in [36], the SemSimAnalyzer computes the similarity of artefacts in pairs. Therefore, all common attributes of two artefacts are taken into account pairwise. By the minimum of the normalized values of two attributes, the difference between the normalized values is calculated and weighted. The resulting values form the basis of the semantic similarity presented in this chapter. Finally, the harvested and calculated data have to be extracted and transformed for further analysis. This is done by the VisualizationDataProvider. With this bundle it is possible to extract subnetworks in form of data describing graphs. Subgraphs consist of edges and nodes. Nodes represent resources, like artefacts or actors, of the different network sources. Edges either represent semantic similarity or relations describing the relationships in the networks themselves. By web services, artefact and actor classes of interest, which have to be defined in the ontology, can be requested. Further, context keywords (e.g. a keyword or tag) can be given. Resources, described by these context keywords, are extracted and exported in the Graph Exchange XML Format (GEXF). Such files can be opened, analyzed, and visualized by software like Gephi [12].

## Research Networks Analyzed in This Article

In this chapter, we analyzed six different Research Networks using the Artefact-Actor-Networks approach as described in the previous sections. The Research Networks were chosen because of their widespread adoption of Research 2.0 services and established practices within the particular communities. In our exploration, we focused on the analysis of three types of learning services: (1) Twitter,[2] (2) SlideShare,[3] and (3) Delicious.[4] As described in [33, 46, 53], those services are especially good adopted by researchers for supporting scholarly communications. In our analysis, we incorporated three types of Research Networks: (a) such networks that are formed around a scientific event like conferences or workshops, (b) such networks that arise in the context of higher education courses and (c) networks that accrue from the usage of a common tag.[5] In detail we analyzed four scientific conferences, one university seminar, and one hashtag community. Those Research Networks differ in context, size, structure, voluntariness of participation, and their age. Table 10.2 presents an aggregated overview about the data we used for our analysis (labeled with 'analyzed'). The table shows that there are differences in the number of analyzable and analyzed data. For the case of Delicious we compared the number of bookmarks in the system ('Web') with those that are accessible via publicly available interfaces. The reasons for the partially significant differences are to be explained with restrictions in the Delicious API limiting the number of bookmarks you can access. For the learning service Twitter, we compared the number of tweets that were accessible directly via Twitter's search interface ('Web'), a third-party Twitter archive called TwapperKeeper[6] ('TwK') and those crawled using the AAN reference implementation. Finally, we show the number of artefacts available in the learning service SlideShare for each of the Research Networks.

Following, we briefly introduce the selected Research Networks and name the hashtags that were used by the participants of the network in order to identify their output as belonging to the Research Network.

The selected conferences were chosen because they dealt with topical themes in the context of Research 2.0 and personalized learning. The conferences attracted many well-known researchers and provided a broad range of social networking opportunities. Moreover, the participants of the conferences were affine with the usage of various learning services in scientific events.

In detail we analyzed the 1st PLE Conference 2010, the 17th international conference of the Association for Learning Technology (ALT-C), the 2010 Science Online London conference, and the ED-MEDIA conferences 2009 and 2010.

---

[2]http://www.twitter.com

[3]http://www.slideshare.net/

[4]http://www.delicious.com/

[5]Such Learning Networks are also known as *hashtag communities* as they spring up around the accidental or planned usage of a tag, meaning a keyword or term associated with a piece of digital information. Some authors use the term *Communities of Interest* for describing such virtual communities with shared problems and goals [11].

[6]In TwapperKeeper (http://www.twapperkeeper.com/), someone has to manually create an archive for a hashtag. The software then stores all the tweets associated with that hashtag and makes them accessible via an open interface. As of 20.03.2011 the API capabilities have been removed from TwapperKeeper. The same functionality can be achieved with an Open Source version of TwapperKeeper (yourTwapperKeeper) that can be installed on a local web server.

**Table 10.2** Research Networks investigated in this article (Data as of 22.09.2010)

| | Type | Tag(s) | Delicious | | Twitter | | SlideShare | |
|---|---|---|---|---|---|---|---|---|
| PLE 2010 | Conference | ple_bcn | Web | 196 | Web | 1 | Web | 20 |
| | | plebcn | | | TwK | 6,772 | | |
| | | | Analyzed | 181 | analyzed | 6,542 | analyzed | 0 |
| ALT-C 2010 | Conference | altc2010 | Web | 345 | Web | 1 | Web | 5 |
| | | | | | TwK | 6,723 | | |
| | | | Analyzed | 245 | analyzed | 6,679 | analyzed | 5 |
| FSLN 2010 | Seminar | fsln10 | Web | 384 | Web | 0 | Web | 17 |
| | | | | | TwK | 768 | | |
| | | | Analyzed | 383 | analyzed | 689 | analyzed | 17 |
| SOLO 2010 | Conference | solo2010 | Web | 124 | Web | 28 | Web | 4 |
| | | solo10 | | | TwK | 4,925 | | |
| | | | Analyzed | 118 | analyzed | 4,635 | analyzed | 4 |
| PLE | Hashtag community | ple | Web | 22,599 | Web | 76 | Web | 595 |
| | | | | | TwK | 71,761 | | |
| | | | Analyzed | 2,314 | analyzed | 2,908 | analyzed | 595 |
| ED-MEDIA | Conference | edmedia | Web | 190 | Web | 0 | Web | 14 |
| | | | | | TwK | 2,120 | | |
| | | | Analyzed | 128 | analyzed | 1,993 | analyzed | 14 |

Due to a problem accessing SlideShare contents, the artefacts for PLE 2010 were not analyzed in this chapter

*Web* artefacts available on the websites, *TwK* TwapperKeeper

The 1st PLE Conference (used hashtags were #ple_bcn and #plebcn) took place on July 7–9, 2010 in Barcelona, Spain, and was intended "to produce a space for researchers and practitioners to exchange ideas, experience and research around the development and implementation of Personal Learning Environments (PLEs) including the design of environments, sociological and educational issues and their effectiveness and desirability as (informal) learning spaces" [32]. The conference provided opportunities for unconferencing events [15] and was squired by a rich range of Social Media offers such as a YouTube channel,[7] a Twitter account for the conference, and a dedicated Crowdvine[8] site with 116 registered participants.

The 17th international conference of the Association for Learning Technology (ALT-C) was held in Nottingham, UK, from September 7–9, 2010. The participants of this Research Network used the hashtag altc2010 and were also supported with a Crowdvine site to extend social interaction amongst more than 400 registered participants. ALT-C 2010 was targeted towards "practitioners, researchers and policy-makers from all sectors to explore, reflect, and learn" [1].

[7]http://www.youtube.com/

[8]http://www.crowdvine.com/

The 2010 Science Online London (hashtags were solo2010 and solo10) conference took place September 3–4, 2010 in London, UK, and was amongst others hosted by the popular reference management maker and scientific social network provider Mendeley.[9] The organizers of the conference were asking "How is the web changing the way we conduct, communicate, share, and evaluate research? How can we employ these trends for the greater good?" and answered "This September, a brilliant group of scientists, bloggers, web entrepreneurs, and publishers will be meeting for two days to address these very questions." [45]. The event was promoted and transacted using the social event management software Eventbrite,[10] accompanied with a dedicated Twitter account and pictures on Flickr.[11]

The Research Network that uses the hashtag *edmedia* is made up of participants of the ED-MEDIA conference series, run by the Association for the Advancement of Computing in Education. "This annual conference serves as a multi-disciplinary forum for the discussion and exchange of information on the research, development, and applications on all topics related to multimedia, hypermedia and telecommunications/distance education" [3]. In particular, we investigated learning resources that were published in the context of the 2009 and 2010 conferences. ED-MEDIA attracts participants from all over the world and encourages online interactions with the providence of a group blog, a dedicated Twitter account, a conference group on Ning,[12] and a Flickr account.

Besides the four scientific conferences, we also analyzed an interdisciplinary seminar that took place in two geographically separated German Universities. The educational design of the seminar entitled *Future Social Learning Networks* demanded to cooperate in teams of two using mainly Social Media as means for sharing and communication. The usage of Twitter and Delicious was mandatory for all participants in the seminar, whereas the students could additionally use any other Social Media services that would support them in achieving their learning goals [17].

Finally, we analyzed the hashtag community that formed around the usage of the tag PLE. We chose this tag as it is the acronym for a term widely discussed in the domain of technology enhanced learning: Personal Learning Environments [9, 55].

## Mining of Selected Research Networks

In this section, we describe the process of mining the selected Research Networks. This comprises the description of our hypotheses, the analysis procedure, and the data mining of artefact- and actor-level data. Finally, the most important results of

---

[9]http://www.mendeley.com/

[10]http://www.eventbrite.com

[11]http://www.flickr.com/

[12]http://www.ning.com/

the analysis of the mined data is presented. During the analysis of the Research Networks, we use descriptive measures about the structure of Artefact-Actor-Networks and the networks that stem from semantic similarity between artefacts and actors. Those measures are defined as follows:

*Bookmark ratio*   The bookmark ratio describes the quantitative relation how often a web resource has been bookmarked in the learning service Delicious from different participants of a Research Network.

*Artefact/actor ratio*   The artefact/actor ratio describes the quantitative relation how many artefacts an actor has a relation to.

*Density*   The density of a network measures how close the network is to complete. A complete network has all possible edges and the density equals to 1.

*Connectedness*   The connectedness denoted the average degree of an artefact or actor in the respective network and thus measures the number of relations to other artefacts or actors.

## *Hypotheses and Procedure*

Our analysis of Research Networks using Artefact-Actor-Network theory was led by the following hypotheses:

H1:  The analysis of all Research Networks will show similar results based on the descriptive metrics.

H2:  The analysis of all Research Networks of the same type (e.g. conferences) will show similar results based on the descriptive metrics.

H3:  The hashtag community will have the lowest density of all Research Networks on the artefact level.

H4:  The narrower the subject of a Research Network, the higher the semantic similarity of the associated artefacts will be.

H5:  The similarity of artefacts and actors of a Research Network is independent of a vivid social interaction within the Research Network.

In order to test the above hypotheses, we obtained the data using the AAN reference implementation as described in section "AAN Reference Implementation," selected the relevant subsets of the data and exported them for visual analytics to the Graph Exchange XML Format.[13] We then used Gephi [12] to visually explore the resulting visualizations, calculated the descriptive measures, and tested the hypotheses.

---

[13] Altogether, we exported 144 subsets, containing data of the six Research Networks, the three learning services (Delicious, SlideShare, Twitter) and a consolidated set, the three levels (artefact-, actor-, and combined Artefact-Actor-Networks), and two different graph types (semantic similarity of objects and the networks themselves).

**Table 10.3** Measures for network structure of artefact networks

|  |  | PLE 2010 | ALT-C 2010 | FSLN 2010 | SOLO 2010 | PLE | ED-MEDIA |
|---|---|---|---|---|---|---|---|
| Delicious | Artefacts | 314 | 437 | 733 | 203 | 4,001 | 245 |
|  | Bookmark ratio | 2.38 | 2.27 | 2.09 | 2.39 | 2.37 | 2.09 |
|  | Edges | 540 | 840 | 993 | 424 | 7,643 | 334 |
|  | Connectedness | 3.44 | 3.84 | 2.71 | 4.18 | 3.82 | 2.73 |
|  | Density | 0.0054944 | 0.0044087 | 0.0018507 | 0.0103400 | 0.0004776 | 0.0055872 |
| SlideShare | Artefacts | 0 | 5 | 17 | 4 | 595 | 14 |
|  | Edges | 0 | 0 | 0 | 0 | 0 | 0 |
|  | Connectedness | 0 | 0 | 0 | 0 | 0 | 0 |
|  | Density | 0 | 0 | 0 | 0 | 0 | 0 |
| Twitter | Artefacts | 6,542 | 6,679 | 689 | 4,635 | 2,908 | 1,993 |
|  | Edges | 1,174 | 1,276 | 108 | 736 | 142 | 440 |
|  | Connectedness | 0.36 | 0.38 | 0.31 | 0.32 | 0.10 | 0.44 |
|  | Density | 0.0000274 | 0.0000286 | 0.0002278 | 0.0000343 | 0.0000168 | 0.0001108 |
| Consolidated | Artefacts | 6,856 | 7,121 | 1,435 | 4,841 | 7,456 | 2,251 |
|  | Edges | 3,586 | 3,528 | 1,337 | 2,148 | 8,923 | 832 |
|  | Connectedness | 1.05 | 0.99 | 1.86 | 0.89 | 2.39 | 0.74 |
|  | Density | 0.0000763 | 0.0000696 | 0.0006497 | 0.0000917 | 0.0001605 | 0.0001643 |

The number of Delicious nodes is the sum of the bookmarks and the bookmarked resources

## Results

The result section presents findings regarding our hypotheses for the six Research Networks and the learning services Twitter, SlideShare, and Delicious.

### Network Structure

In this analysis, we consider the network structure for all learning services only on the artefact level. An overview of the calculated measures for the network structure of the 24 extracted artefact networks can be found in Table 10.3. The analysis of the artefact/actor ratio is presented in Table 10.4. In order to support the descriptive analysis and to compare the structure of the artefact networks that form in the different learning services, we exemplarily created visualizations for the conference ED-MEDIA. The visualizations of Twitter, Delicious, and the consolidated artefact network are shown in Figs. 10.6f and 10.7. Table 10.5 shows an overview of the calculated measures for the Research Networks.

First, we explore how comparable Research Networks are based on the analysis of descriptive measures (H1 and H2). In Table 10.3, the high frequency of zeros in the social media network SlideShare is noticeable. In SlideShare, there are no direct links between two presentations (unless there are HTML links in the text of the presentation) what explains the zeros in the appropriate rows. It is in the

**Table 10.4** Artefact/actor ratio for the analyzed learning services

|  |  | PLE 2010 | ALT-C 2010 | FSLN 2010 | SOLO 2010 | PLE | ED-MEDIA |
|---|---|---|---|---|---|---|---|
| Delicious | Artefacts | 182 | 245 | 383 | 118 | 2,314 | 128 |
|  | Actors | 37 | 25 | 10 | 29 | 147 | 51 |
|  | Artefact/actor ratio | 4.91 | 9.80 | 38.30 | 4.07 | 15.74 | 2.51 |
| SlideShare | Artefacts | 0 | 5 | 17 | 4 | 595 | 14 |
|  | Actors | 0 | 5 | 13 | 4 | 308 | 12 |
|  | Artefact/actor ratio | 0.00 | 1.00 | 1.31 | 1.00 | 1.93 | 1.17 |
| Twitter | Artefacts | 6,542 | 6,679 | 689 | 4,635 | 2,908 | 1,993 |
|  | Actors | 735 | 847 | 82 | 782 | 1,551 | 411 |
|  | Artefact/actor ratio | 8.90 | 7.89 | 8.40 | 5.93 | 1.87 | 4.85 |
| Consolidated | Artefacts | 6,724 | 6,929 | 1,089 | 4,757 | 5,817 | 2,135 |
|  | Actors | 772 | 877 | 106 | 815 | 2,006 | 474 |
|  | Artefact/actor ratio | 8.71 | 7.90 | 10.27 | 5.83 | 2.90 | 4.50 |

The number of Delicious nodes is the number of bookmarks in the service

nature of bookmarking services and microblogs that their artefacts have more links between them. A comparison of the Delicious and Twitter networks shows that the average degree of Delicious nodes (3.45) is clearly larger than the degree of Twitter nodes (0.32). One reason for this can be found in the data gathering process: in Delicious – being a bookmarking service – for each bookmark a referenced website was extracted. As a result, each node is connected to at least one other node. The referenced website then can contain references to other websites again or can be bookmarked more then once. The bookmark ratio in the analyzed Research Networks ranges from 2.09 to 2.39 meaning that each resource was bookmarked about two times. The connectedness in the learning service Delicious is between 2.71 and 4.18. For the learning service Twitter, we see that the hashtag community has a clearly worse connectedness than the ED-MEDIA conference. Thus, we need to reject hypothesis H1. Testing hypothesis H2, we showed for all measures significant lower standard deviations when only Research Networks of the type 'conference' are compared. Thus, with the descriptive measures in Table 10.5 we can confirm hypothesis H2.

To exemplarily compare the use of learning services for different Research Networks, we visualized the respective Twitter graphs. Figure 10.6 shows the artefact networks for the learning service Twitter where only nodes with a degree of at least 1 were drawn. The depicted edges represent replies of Twitter artefacts (tweets) to previous tweets. The graphs of PLE 2010 Fig. 10.6a and FSLN 2010 Fig. 10.6c show chains of related tweets, pointing to ongoing discussions in the Research Network. For the conference ED-MEDIA, Fig. 10.6f shows a star-like accumulation of tweets. In the center of the star is a tweet with the text: *Giving a prez at #edmedia. Please say hi, tell us where u're from, why u use social media in teaching/learning/pd. Pls use #edmedia tag.* More than 20 participants in Research Network replied to this tweet and thus enhanced the connectedness of the whole Research Network (cf. Table 10.3). The accumulation of edges in Fig. 10.7a is a set

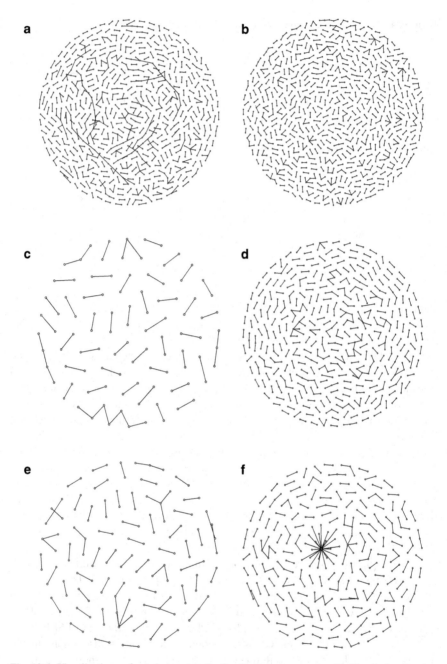

**Fig. 10.6** Visualizations of artefact networks for the learning service Twitter (only showing artefacts with at least one relation to another artefact). (**a**) PLE 2010. (**b**) ALT-C 2010. (**c**) FSLN 2010. (**d**) SOLO 2010. (**e**) PLE. (**f**) ED-MEDIA

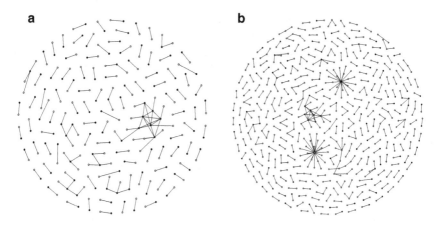

**Fig. 10.7** Artefact-level visualizations of ED-MEDIA learning networks. (**a**) Delicious. (**b**) Consolidated

**Table 10.5** Overview of the calculated measures, means, and standard deviations

|  | All RN | | Conference RN | |
|---|---|---|---|---|
|  | M | SD | M | SD |
| Bookmark ratio | 2.32 | 0.14 | 2.33 | 0.14 |
| Connectedness (Delicious) | 3.63 | 0.61 | 3.64 | 0.62 |
| Connectedness (SlideShare) | 0 | 0 | 0 | 0 |
| Connectedness (Twitter) | 0.34 | 0.12 | 0.37 | 0.05 |
| Connectedness (Consolidated) | 1.02 | 0.65 | 0.94 | 0.14 |
| Density (Delicious) | 0.00495 | 0.00344 | 0.00554 | 0.00264 |
| Density (SlideShare) | 0 | 0 | 0 | 0 |
| Density (Twitter) | 0.00003 | 0.00008 | 0.00003 | 0.00004 |
| Density (Consolidated) | 0.00013 | 0.00022 | 0.00008 | 0.00004 |
| Artefact/actor ratio (Delicious) | 7.36 | 13.50 | 4.49 | 3.17 |
| Artefact/actor ratio (SlideShare) | 1.09 | 0.63 | 1.00 | 0.53 |
| Artefact/actor ratio (Twitter) | 6.91 | 2.67 | 6.91 | 1.87 |
| Artefact/actor ratio (Consolidated) | 6.87 | 2.77 | 6.87 | 1.92 |

*RN* Research Network, *M* mean, *SD* standard deviation

of websites relating each other that are also bookmarked several times by different participants.

While the Twitter network for the hashtag community PLE contains a set of 2,908 tweets, there are much less relations (Fig. 10.6e) and also a distinct worse artefact/actor ratio (cf. Table 10.4). The hashtag community PLE in the learning service Delicious (0.0004776) is less than half as dense as the second smallest value (0.0018507 in the FSLN 2010 seminar). In the learning service Twitter, the PLE hashtag community also has the smallest density (0.0000168). This confirms hypothesis H3. Despite the sparse networks in the single learning services, Table 10.4 also reveals that participants in the hashtag community actively create learning resources in the learning services Delicious and SlideShare but there is

**Table 10.6** Measures for semantic similarity of artefact networks

|  |  | PLE 2010 | ALT-C 2010 | FSLN 2010 | SOLO 2010 | PLE | ED-MEDIA |
|---|---|---|---|---|---|---|---|
| Delicious | Artefacts | 132 | 192 | 350 | 85 | 1,687 | 117 |
|  | Edges | 374 | 242 | 622 | 124 | 11,002 | 510 |
|  | Connected-ness | 5.66 | 2.52 | 3.55 | 2.92 | 13.04 | 8.72 |
|  | Density | 0.0216285 | 0.0065990 | 0.0050921 | 0.0173669 | 0.0038681 | 0.0375774 |
| SlideShare | Artefacts | 0 | 5 | 17 | 4 | 595 | 14 |
|  | Edges | 0 | 0 | 70 | 0 | 4,868 | 36 |
|  | Connected-ness | 0 | 0 | 8.24 | 0 | 16.36 | 5.14 |
|  | Density | 0 | 0 | 0.2573529 | 0 | 0.0137736 | 0.1978022 |
| Twitter | Artefacts | 6,542 | 6,679 | 689 | 4,635 | 2,908 | 1,993 |
|  | Edges | 361,876 | 37,206 | 3,768 | 78,722 | 438,924 | 1,314 |
|  | Connected-ness | 110.63 | 11.14 | 10.94 | 33.97 | 301.87 | 1.32 |
|  | Density | 0.0084568 | 0.0008342 | 0.0079488 | 0.0036651 | 0.0519218 | 0.0003310 |
| Consolidated | Artefacts | 6,674 | 6,876 | 1,052 | 4,723 | 5,142 | 2,123 |
|  | Edges | 373,376 | 37,522 | 5,254 | 79,010 | 480,776 | 2,232 |
|  | Connected-ness | 111.89 | 10.91 | 9.99 | 33.46 | 187.00 | 2.10 |
|  | Density | 0.0083838 | 0.0007937 | 0.0047519 | 0.0035427 | 0.0181871 | 0.0004954 |

The number of Delicious nodes is the number of bookmarked resources

only very little interaction between them. In the learning service Twitter, only every tenth artefact (see Table 10.3) has a relation to another artefact. Since Twitter relies on the vivid interactions between its users, this is a remarkable finding.

## Semantic Similarity

The semantic similarity of the Research Networks is analyzed for all learning services on both artefact and actor level. The measures for the 24 artefact networks based on semantic similarity are presented in Table 10.6. The number of contemplated artefacts from the learning service Delicious is smaller than in Table 10.3, as not the bookmarks themselves have analyzable full texts but the bookmarked resources. Thus, we analyzed the accessible full texts of the bookmarked resources. As for the other learning services, the full texts of the artefacts have been analyzed. With this data we can compare the artefact networks stemming from the different learning services based on semantic similarity.

The density in the artefact networks based on semantic similarity (cf. Table 10.6) ranges from 0.0038681 (PLE hashtag community) to 0.0375774 (ED-MEDIA conference) for the learning service Delicious, in SlideShare the range is from

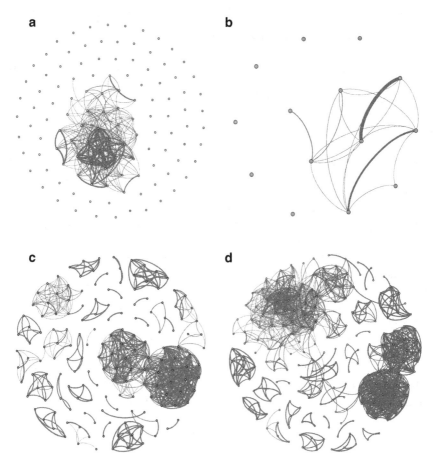

**Fig. 10.8** Visualizations of semantic similarity in the artefact networks for the Research Network ED-MEDIA. (**a**) Delicious. (**b**) SlideShare. (**c**) Twitter. (**d**) Consolidated

0 to 0.2573529, and in Twitter from 0.0003310 to 0.0519218. Apart from the three Research Networks with a density of 0, SlideShare artefacts have the highest semantic similarity with about 0.01, 0.20, and 0.26. The reason for this can be found in the more extensive full texts, which provide a better basis for extracting relevant keywords. Based on our measures, the artefacts in the learning service Twitter seem less similar to each other. This is mainly due to shortness of text per artefact. We visualized the semantic similarity for a set of artefact networks. Figure 10.8 shows the similarity for the conference ED-MEDIA and the learning services Delicious, SlideShare, Twitter, and a consolidated network. A strong edge strength represents a large semantic similarity. In Fig. 10.8c, a formation of clusters is discernible that correlates to the star subnetwork from Fig. 10.6f. The second cluster cannot be explained with structural properties, but is a similarity cluster in the analyzed tweets.

In order to test hypothesis H4, we need to take a look at the thematic priorities of the selected Research Networks. The hashtag community PLE deals with all aspects of the design, development, application, and definition of Personal Learning Environments. The Research Network that formed around the seminar FSLN 2010 dealt with topics of Social Networking and new media for improving individual and group learning. In the course of this, the participants touch many diverse topics ranging from interactive learning resources to game-based learning. The foci of the selected Research Networks of the type conference were described on the according web pages and in the calls for participation. Thus, the thematic priorities can be defined more precisely.

The 1st PLE Conference was intended to be a place "to exchange ideas, experience and research around the development and implementation of Personal Learning Environments (PLEs) including the design of environments, sociological and educational issues and their effectiveness and desirability as (informal) learning spaces" [32]. The ED-MEDIA "conference serves as a multi-disciplinary forum for the discussion and exchange of information on the research, development, and applications on all topics related to multimedia, hypermedia and telecommunications/distance education" [3]. The SOLO 2010 conference was aiming at answering the question "How is the web changing the way we conduct, communicate, share, and evaluate research?" [45] and the ALT-C 2010 conference was targeted towards "practitioners, researchers and policy-makers from all sectors to explore, reflect, and learn" [1].

From those descriptions, we realize that both the hashtag community and the PLE 2010 conference deal with a very specialized topic. The SOLO 2010 conference also had a clearly defined, yet broader topic. The FSLN 2010 seminar and the ALT-C 2010 conference have a clearly defined topical boundary whereas the ED-MEDIA conference is very broad in its topics. Exemplarily, we visualized the actor networks in the learning service Twitter based on the semantic similarity between two actors in Fig. 10.9 as well as the actor networks from all learning services in ED-MEDIA in Fig. 10.10. A relation between two actors exist, if there are at least two artefacts related to those actors, which have a semantic similarity greater than zero. The strength of a similarity relation is totalized by the similarity values between the actors. If the two actors share many similar artefacts, there is a stronger binding between them.

The analysis of the connectedness measure in both artefact and actor networks based on semantic similarity shows exactly those differences. The PLE hashtag community and the PLE 2010 conference have by far higher values of connectedness in all learning services and in the consolidated artefact network (cf. Table 10.6). The narrower topic of the SOLO 2010 conference is clearly observable in the learning service Twitter as well as in the consolidated artefact network. The analysis of the semantic similarity of artefacts for ED-MEDIA on the other hand reveals the very broad thematic catalog in a connectedness that is 89 times smaller than that in the PLE hashtag community. The same holds true when looking at the semantic similarity of the actor networks in Table 10.7. This confirms hypothesis H4.

The connectedness of the artefact networks stemming from the learning service Twitter is an indicator for the interaction between participants of a Research

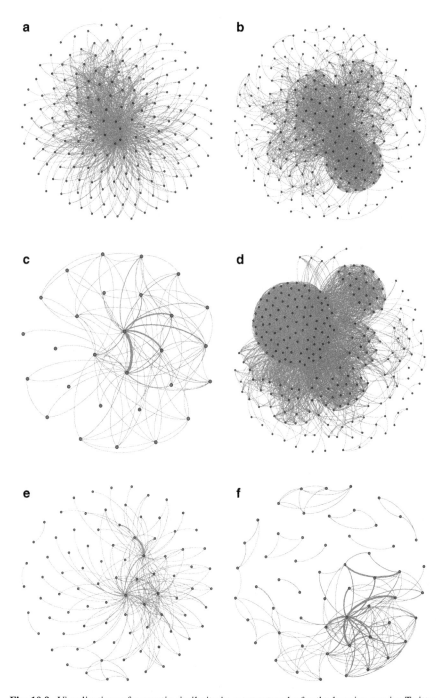

**Fig. 10.9** Visualizations of semantic similarity in actor networks for the learning service Twitter. (**a**) PLE 2010. (**b**) ALT-C 2010. (**c**) FSLN 2010. (**d**) SOLO 2010. (**e**) PLE. (**f**) ED-MEDIA

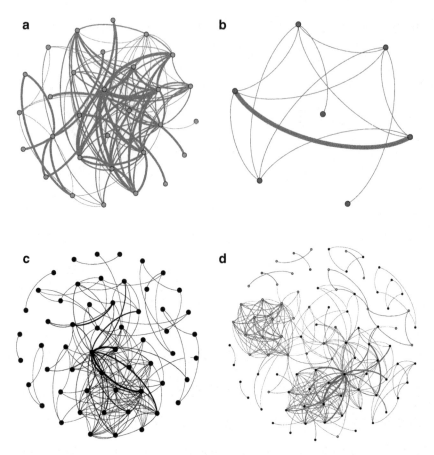

**Fig. 10.10** Visualizations of semantic similarity in the actor networks for the Research Network ED-MEDIA. (**a**) Delicious. (**b**) SlideShare. (**c**) Twitter. (**d**) Consolidated

Network. The higher the value, the more direct interactions between participants take place. Even though the according values are larger by factor 3–4 for all other analyzed Research Networks (Table 10.6), the semantic similarity for both artefacts and actors is considerably higher in the PLE hashtag community than in all other Research Networks (cf. Tables 10.6 and 10.7). This confirms hypothesis H5.

## Limitations

With the presented research, we face some limitations: (1) only a small set of Research Networks was analyzed, (2) not all artefacts of the learning services could be accessed, and (3) the semantic analysis of artefacts from the learning service Twitter provides only little amount of usable keywords.

**Table 10.7** Measures for semantic similarity of actor networks

|  |  | PLE 2010 | ALT-C 2010 | FSLN 2010 | SOLO 2010 | PLE | ED-MEDIA |
|---|---|---|---|---|---|---|---|
| Delicious | Actors | 37 | 25 | 10 | 28 | 146 | 51 |
|  | Edges | 142 | 63 | 21 | 101 | 3029 | 139 |
|  | Connectedness | 7.676 | 5.04 | 4.2 | 7.214 | 41.493 | 5.451 |
|  | Density | 0.213 | 0.21 | 0.467 | 0.267 | 0.286 | 0.109 |
| SlideShare | Actors | 0 | 5 | 13 | 4 | 308 | 12 |
|  | Edges | 0 | 0 | 21 | 0 | 1056 | 12 |
|  | Connectedness | 0 | 0 | 3.23 | 0 | 6.86 | 2 |
|  | Density | 0 | 0 | 0.269 | 0 | 0,022 | 0.182 |
| Twitter | Actors | 581 | 719 | 52 | 683 | 1,225 | 348 |
|  | Edges | 13,384 | 2,129 | 106 | 6,270 | 21,781 | 164 |
|  | Connectedness | 46.07 | 5.92 | 4.08 | 18.36 | 35.561 | 0.943 |
|  | Density | 0.079 | 0.008 | 0.08 | 0.027 | 0.029 | 0.003 |
| Consolidated | Actors | 623 | 749 | 75 | 715 | 1,679 | 411 |
|  | Edges | 15,249 | 2,228 | 253 | 6,432 | 36,954 | 472 |
|  | Connectedness | 48.953 | 5.949 | 6.747 | 17.992 | 44.019 | 2.297 |
|  | Density | 0.079 | 0.008 | 0.091 | 0.025 | 0.026 | 0.006 |

Regarding 1, we have to expand our analyses in the future and test our hypotheses with more different and diverse Research Networks. Particularly, we have to investigate more hashtag communities in order to see if the findings (especially H4 and H5) are also existing there. Regarding 2, we face technical limitations with the service providers. For example, the API of the learning service Delicious is very restrictive making it impossible of analyzing all artefacts of large Research Networks. In spite of that we will go on improving the accuracy and efficiency of the AAN crawling process. Regarding 3, the short texts in Twitter are hardly analyzable with established methods. We have to stress how and where improvements for the analysis can be done.

## Discussion and Outlook

In this chapter, we have introduced the notation of Research Networks as being special Learning Networks of scholars pursuing their individual learning goals (section "Research Networks and Levels of Member Participation"). The participants in Research Networks use different learning services to exchange experience, collaboratively elaborate common research questions, offer each other support in solving tasks and to create, share and find learning resources. We have given an overview about the different levels of interaction in Research Networks (section "Levels of Interaction") and discussed the possible learning trajectories of participants in Research Networks. We have further explored the application of Web 2.0 tools, technologies, and techniques in Research Networks (under the umbrella of terms

like Research 2.0 or Science 2.0). We discussed the fact that Research Networks
now are driven by new technologies, practices, and methods and presented overall
goals for mining Research Networks.

In section "The AAN Approach for Research Network Mining," we introduced
the approach of Artefact-Actor-Networks (AANs) for mining Research Networks.
AANs semantically intertwine social networks with artefact networks. Both network
types have multiple layers for each learning service used in the Research Network
what allows the layer-wise analysis as well as the consolidated one. Objects in
the networks are artefacts and actors that are connected via semantic relations.
Moreover, we presented a reference implementation for AANs that was developed
as modular application in Java using the OSGi Service Platform. We used the
reference application for analyzing six Research Networks. They were introduced
in section "Research Networks Analyzed in This Article" and classified according
to their type. We described the mining of the Research Networks in section
"Results" and showed that Research Networks of the same type are comparable
based on descriptive statistics. We found that hashtag communities are least dense
on the artefact level but best connected when comparing the semantic similarity of
artefacts. Further, our analysis showed that the narrower the subject of a Research
Network, the higher the semantic similarity of the associated artefacts will be no
matter if there are vivid social interactions between the participants in the Research
Network.

The results of the research presented here will have to be further validated in
prospective experiments. Future experiments should try to mine learning trajectories
of participants and to identify boundary objects that connect various Research
Networks. Moreover, we should extend the possible data sources to incorporate
more learning services; for conferences, for example, we will consider publications
as another type of artefact in the future. The analyses in this chapter took place
subsequent to the happenings in the selected Research Networks. In order to
better support the awareness of participants in Research Networks, we should
prospectively provide them with real-time analyses that help them better assessing
their knowledge, recognizing competence deficits, and being aware about the
network structure and evolvement. For future research, we will explore how the
presented results can be applied to the context of scientific events in order to
raise awareness about the topical narrowness of an event and to predict discussed
themes.

# References

1. ALT-C 2010 Organizing Committee: ALT-C 2010: Into something rich and strange. Available
online http://www.alt.ac.uk/altc2010/index.html (2010). Accessed 31 Dec 2010
2. Arthur, C.: Free our data debate goes public, hydrogen-powered London buses, US and
ICANN, ISPs and file sharing, the 1% rule and much more . . ... Available online http://www.
guardian.co.uk/technology/blog/2006/jul/20/freeourdatad (2006). Accessed 31 Dec 2010
3. Association for the Advancement of Computing in Education: AACE - ED-MEDIA. Available
online http://www.aace.org/conf/edmedia/ (2010). Accessed 31 Dec 2010

4. Bosnic, I., Verbert, K., Duval, E.: Automatic keywords extraction – a basis for content recommendation. In: Proceedings of the Fourth International Workshop on Search and Exchange of e-le@rning Materials 2010 (SE@M10), Barcelona, pp. 51–60, (2010). URL http://sunsite.informatik.rwth-aachen.de/Publications/CEUR-WS/Vol-681/paper07.pdf
5. Butler, D.: Science in the web age: joint efforts. Nature **438**, 548–549 (2005)
6. Cetina, K.K.: Sociality with objects: social relations in postsocial knowledge societies. Theory Cult. Soc. **14**(4), 1–30 (1997)
7. Crowdsourced: Deletionism and inclusionism in Wikipedia. Available online http://en.wikipedia.org/w/index.php?title=Deletionism_and_inclusionism_in_Wikipedia&oldid=392147959 (2010). Accessed 31 Dec 2010
8. Duval, E.: Science 2.0 approach to research. Available online http://erikduval.wordpress.com/2010/06/10/science-2-0-approach-to-research/ (2010). Accessed 31 Dec 2010
9. EDUCAUSE: 7 things you should know about personal learning environments. Report, available online http://net.educause.edu/ir/library/pdf/ELI7049.pdf (2009). Accessed 31 Dec 2010, EDUCAUSE Learning Initiative
10. Engeström, J.: Why some social network services work and others don't – or: the case for object-centered sociality. Available online http://bit.ly/eJA7OQ (2005). Accessed 31 Dec 2010
11. Fischer, G.: Communities of interest: learning through the interaction of multiple knowledge systems. In: 24th Annual Information Systems Research Seminar In Scandinavia (IRIS'24), pp. 1–14 (2001)
12. Gephi NGO: Gephi – the open graph viz platform. Available online http://gephi.org (2010). Accessed 31 Dec 2010
13. Gillet, D.: eResearch: community of practice and social media for PhD students. Available online http://www.slideshare.net/dgillet/eresearch-4693039 (2010). Accessed 31 Dec 2010
14. Google Inc.: Doubleclick ad planner by google (for en.wikipedia.org). Available online https://www.google.com/adplanner/planning/site_profile?identifier=en.wikipedia.org (2010). Accessed 31 Dec 2010
15. Hamlin, K.: Unconferencing. Available online http://www.kaliyasblogs.net/Files/unconferencing.pdf (2008). Accessed 31 Dec 2010
16. Hannafin, M., Land, S., Oliver, K.: Open learning environments: foundations, methods, and models. In: Instructional design theories and models: a new paradigm of instructional theory, pp. 115–140. Lawrence Erlbaum Associates, Mahwah (1999)
17. Heinze, N., Reinhardt, W.: Future social learning networks at universities – an exploratory seminar setting. In: Educating Educators with Social Media. Cutting-Edge Technologies in Higher Education, vol. 1, pp. 153–170. Emerald Publishing Group, Bingley (2011)
18. Hughes, J. (ed.): Communities of sharing (chapter 29). In: Teacher's Aids on Creating Content for Learning Environments – The E-learning Handbook for Classroom Teachers. Go! Onderwijs Van De Vlaamse Gemeenschap, Brussel (2009)
19. Jena team: Jena – A semantic web framework for Java. Available online http://openjena.org (2010). Accessed 31 Dec 2010
20. Jones, S.: Understanding community in the information age. In: Cybersociety: Computer-Mediated Communication and Community, pp. 10–35. Sage, Thousand Oaks (1995)
21. Kieslinger, B., Lindstaedt, S.: Science 2.0 practices in the field of technology enhanced learning. In: Proceedings of the 1st International Workshop on Science 2.0 for TEL at the 4th European Conference on Technology Enhanced Learning (EC-TEL'09). Springer, Berlin/Heidelberg, (2009)
22. Kim, A.J.: Community Building on the Web: Secret Strategies for Successful Online Communities, 1st edn. Wesley, Boston (2000)
23. Koper, R. (ed.): Learning Network Services for Professional Development. Springer, Berlin/Heidelberg (2009)
24. Koper, R.: Introduction. In: Learning Network Services for Professional Development, pp. 3–11. Springer, Berlin/Heidelberg (2009)
25. Koper, R., Sloep, P.: Learning networks – connecting people, organizations, autonomous agents and learning resources to establish the emergence of effective lifelong learning. Programme plan, Open University of the Netherlands (2003)

26. Lave, J., Wenger, E.: Situated Learning: Legitimate Peripheral Participation. Cambridge University Press, Cambridge/New York (1991)
27. Nielsen, M.: The future of science: building a better collective memory. Available online http://michaelnielsen.org/blog/the-future-of-science-2/ (2008). Accessed 31 Dec 2010
28. Oliver, K., Hannafin, M.: Developing and refining mental models in open-ended learning environments: a case study. Edu. Technol. Res. Dev. **49**(4), 5–32 (2001)
29. Orchestr8 LLC: Alchemyapi. Available online http://www.alchemyapi.com/ (2009). Accessed 31 Dec 2010
30. OSGi Alliance: OSGi alliance. Available online http://www.osgi.org/ (2010). Accessed 31 Dec 2010
31. Paccagnella, L.: Getting the seats of your pants dirty: strategies for ethnographic research on virtual communities. J. Comput. Mediat. Commun. **3**(1), (1997)
32. PLE conference organizing committee: PLE conference. Available online http://pleconference. citilab.eu/ (2010). Accessed 31 Dec 2010
33. Procter, R., Williams, R., Stewart, J., Poschen, M., Snee, H., Voss, A., Asgari-Targhi, M.: Adoption and use of web 2.0 in scholarly communications. Phil. Trans. R. Soc. A **368**, 4039–4056 (2010)
34. Redecker, C., Ala-Mutka, K., Bacigalupo, M., Ferrari, A., Punie, Y.: Learning 2.0: the impact of web 2.0 innovations on education and training in Europe. Jcr scientific and technical report, European Commission, Joint Research Centre (JRC), (2009)
35. Reinhardt, W., Ebner, M., Beham, G., Costa, C.: How people are using Twitter during conferences. In: Hornung-Prähauser, V., Luckmann, M. (eds.) Creativity and Innovation Competencies on the Web. Proceedings of the 5th EduMedia 2009, Salzburg, pp. 145–156, (2009)
36. Reinhardt, W., Moi, M., Varlemann, T.: Artefact-Actor-Networks as tie between social networks and artefact networks. In: Proceedings of CollaborateCom, Washington, DC, USA (2009)
37. Reinhardt, W., Varlemann, T., Moi, M., Wilke, A.: Modeling, obtaining and storing data from social media tools with Artefact-Actor-Networks. In: Atzmueller, M., Benz, D., Hotho, A., Stumme, G. (eds.) LWA 2010 Workshop Proceedings, Kassel, pp. 323–330 (2010)
38. Reuters, T.: Calais: connect. Everything. Available online http://www.opencalais.com/about (2009). Accessed 31 Dec 2010
39. Rheingold, H.: The virtual community: homesteading on the electronic frontier. Wesley, Reading (1993)
40. Roure, D.D.: The new e-science. Available online http://www.slideshare.net/dder/new-escience-edinburgh-late-edition-presentation (2007). Accessed 31 Dec 2010
41. Salton, G., Buckley, C.: Term-weighting approaches in automatic text retrieval. Inf. Proc. Manag. **24**(5), 513–523 (1988)
42. Salton, G., McGill, M.J.: Introduction to Modern Information Retrieval. McGraw-Hill, New York (1983)
43. Shneiderman, B.: Science 2.0. Science **319**(5868), 1349–1350 (2008)
44. Sloep, P.: Social interaction in learning networks. In: Learning Network Services for Professional Development, pp. 13–16. Springer, Berlin/Heidelberg (2009)
45. Solo 2010 Organizing Committee: Science online London 2010. Available online http://scienceonlinelondon.org/ (2010). Accessed 31 Dec 2010
46. Tacke, O.: Open science 2.0: how research and education can benefit from open innovation and web 2.0. In: Proceedings of the 1st Symposium on Collective Intelligence (COLLIN 2010), Braunschweig, (2010)
47. Ullmann, T.D., Wild, F., Scott, P., Duval, E., Vandeputte, B., Parra, G., Reinhardt, W., Heinze, N., Kraker, P., Fessl, A., Lindstaedt, S., Nagel, T., Gillet, D.: Components of a research 2.0 infrastructure. In: Wolpers, M., Kirschner, P.A., Scheffel, M., Lindstaedt, S., Dimitrova, V. (eds.) Sustaining TEL: From Innovation to Learning and Practice (EC-TEL 2010). Springer, Berlin (2010)

48. Underwood, J., Luckin, R., Smith, H., Walker, K., Rowland, D., Fitzpatrick, G., Good, J., Benford, S.: Reflections on participatory science for telsci2.0. In: Proceedings of the 1st International Workshop on Science 2.0 for TEL at the 4th European Conference on Technology Enhanced Learning (EC-TEL'09). Springer, Berlin/Heidelberg (2009)
49. W3C, World Wide Web Consortium: SPARQL query language for RDF. Available online http://www.w3.org/TR/rdf-sparql-query/ (2008). Accessed 31 Dec 2010
50. W3C, World Wide Web Consortium: Owl web ontology language. Available online http://www.w3.org/TR/2004/REC-owl-features-20040210/ (2010). Accessed 31 Dec 2010
51. W3C, World Wide Web Consortium: RDF vocabulary description language 1.0: RDF schema. Available online http://www.w3.org/TR/2004/REC-rdf-schema-20040210/ (2010). Accessed 31 Dec 2010
52. Waldrop, M.: Science 2.0. Scientific Am. **298**(5), 68–73 (2008)
53. Weller, K., Dornstädter, R., Freimanis, R., Klein, R.N., Perez, M.: Social software in academia: three studies on users' acceptance of web 2.0 services. In: Proceedings of the WebSci10: Extending the Frontiers of Society On-Line, Raleigh, (2010)
54. Wellman, B.: Physical place and cyberplace: the rise of personalized networking. Int. J. Urb. Reg. Res. **25**, 227–252 (2001)
55. Wilson, S., Liber, O., Johnson, M., Beauvoir, P., Sharples, P., Milligan, C.: Personal learning environments: challenging the dominant design of educational systems. J. e-Learn. Knowl. Soc. **2**, (2007)
56. Zachte, E.: Wikipedia statistics. Available online http://stats.wikimedia.org/EN/TablesWikipediansEditsGt5.htm (2010). Accessed 31 Dec 2010

# Chapter 11
# Intelligent-Based Visual Pattern Clustering for Storage Layouts in Virtual Environments

Shao-Shin Hung, Chih-Ming Chiu, Tsou Tsun Fu, Jung Tzung Chen, and Jyh-Jong Tsay

**Abstract** There has been an increased demand for characterizing user access patterns using data mining techniques since the informative knowledge extracted from 3D server log files cannot only offer benefits for web site structure improvement but also for better understanding of user navigational behavior. In this paper, we present hypergraph-based clustering method, which utilize 3D user usage and traversal pattern information to capture user access pattern based on data mining model. This study presents a storage solution called Object-oriented HyperGraph-based Clustering (OHGC) approach, which employs hidden hinting among objects in virtual environments (VE). The OHGC takes frequent patterns for input that are discovered in the traversal databases, but with more efficient data management to assist in performance improvement. Analytical results reveal that the proposed approach for VE-based application hint clustering produces efficiency savings of up to 30% or more over conventional non-OHGC storage solutions, whereas the non-OHGC schemes for retrieve only achieve savings about 20% over conventional storage systems.

S.-S. Hung (✉)
Department of Computer Science and Information Engineering, WuFeng University,
Taiwan, China
e-mail: hss@cs.ccu.edu.tw

C.-M. Chiu • J.-J. Tsay
Department of Computer Science and Information Engineering, National Chung Cheng
University, Chiayi, Taiwan

T.T. Fu
Department of Applied Digital Media, WuFeng University, Chiayi, Taiwan

J.T. Chen
Department of Applied Game Technology, WuFeng University, Chiayi, Taiwan

A. Abraham (ed.), *Computational Social Networks: Mining and Visualization*,
DOI 10.1007/978-1-4471-4054-2_11, © Springer-Verlag London 2012

# Introduction

MMOG (Massively Multiplayer Online Game) [1–7] has become very popular in last decades and brought us a powerful platform to disseminate information and retrieve information as well as analyze information, and nowadays the MMOG has been known as a big social interaction of data repository consisting of a variety of interaction/visualization types, as well as a knowledge base, in which informative MMOG knowledge is hidden. However, users are often facing the problems of information overload and drowning due to the significant and rapid growth in amount of information and the number of users. Particularly, in MMOG, users usually suffer from the difficulties in finding desirable and accurate information on the MMOG due to two problems of low fidelity and more lag caused by above reasons. For example, if a user wants to navigate the desired scene by utilizing a navigation tool such as mouse, the 3D scene management system will provide not only scenic contents related to the query topic, but also a large amount of irrelevant contents, which results in difficulties for users to obtain their exactly needed scenic contents. Thus, these bring forward a great deal of challenges for MMOG researchers to address the challenging research issues of effective and efficient 3D content-based information management and retrieval. On the other hand, for the data on the MMOG, it has its own distinctive features from the data in conventional database management systems. MMOG data usually exhibits the following characteristics: the data on the MMOG is huge in amount, distributed, heterogeneous, unstructured, real-time, on-line and dynamic. To deal with the heterogeneity and complexity characteristics of MMOG data, MMOG community has emerged as a new efficient 3D game data management means to model MMOG objects. Unlike the conventional database management, in which data models and schemas are well defined, MMOG community, which is a set of Game-based objects (3D objects and users) has its own logical/geometric structures. MMOG communities could be modeled as 3D game groups, user clusters and co-clusters of 3D contents and users. MMOG community construction is realized via various approaches on Computer graphics—textual, scenes, navigation, rendering or semantic-based analysis. Recently, the research of Social Network Analysis in the MMOG has become a newly active topic due to the prevalence of Web 2.0 technologies, which results in an inter-disciplinary research area of Social Networking. Social networking refers to the process of capturing the social and societal characteristics of networked structures or communities over the MMOG. Social networking research involves in the combination of a variety of research paradigms, such as data mining, MMOG communities, social network analysis and behavioral and cognitive modeling and so on.

However, quantification of collective human behavior or MMOG/social dynamics collecting is a difficult challenge [5, 6, 8, 9]. It is remarkable to some extent that human knows more than dynamics of atomic particles than it knows about the dynamics of human groups. The reason for this situation is that the establishment of a fully experimental and falsifiable social science of group dynamics is tremendously complicated by the following factors. First, unlike other problems in the social/natural sciences, dynamics of the social behaviors constitute a complex system, characterized by implicit/explicit and short/long-range interactions, which are in general not treatable by traditional mathematical methods and other concepts. Second, data is seldom available and of poor quality [8, 10–13]. It is apparent that availability of these social interaction data from social systems is much harder than those data from other scientific systems. On the other side, many complex systems cannot be understood without their surroundings, contexts or boundaries, together with the interactions between these boundaries and the system itself. This is obviously necessary for measuring large-scale dynamics of human groups. Regarding data acquisition it is therefore essential not only to record decisions of individual humans but also the simultaneous state of their surroundings. Further, in any data-driven science the observed system should not be significantly perturbed through the act of measurement. In social science experiments subjects usually are fully aware of being observed—a fact that might strongly influence their behavior. Finally, data acquisition in the social sciences becomes especially tiresome on group levels, see, e.g. [4, 14]. Traditional methods of social science such as interviews and questionnaires do not only need a lot of time and resources to deliver statistically meaningful assertions, but may introduce well-known biases [8]. To many it might seem clear that social sciences cannot overcome these problems, and that therefore social sciences would always remain on a lower quantitative and qualitative level than the natural sciences.

In these different modeling for social behaviors and interactions with other people, the virtual environment or walkthrough system may be a better but more practical choice. From a scientific point of view online games provide a tool for understanding collective human phenomena and social dynamics on an entirely different scale [5, 6]. In these games all information about all actions taken by all players can be easily recorded and stored in log-files at practically no cost. This quantity of data has been unthinkable in the traditional social sciences where sample sizes often do not exceed several dozens of questionnaires, school classes or students in behavioral experiments. In MMOGs on the other hand, the number of subjects can reach several hundred thousands, with millions of recorded actions. These actions of individual players are known in conjunction with their surroundings, i.e. the circumstances under which particular actions or decisions were taken. This offers the unique opportunity to study a complex social system: conditions under which individuals take decisions can in principle be controlled, the specific outcomes of decisions can be measured. In this respect social science is on the verge of becoming a fully experimental science [10] which should increasingly become capable of making a great number of repeatable and eventually falsifiable statements about collective human behavior, both in a social and economical context.

Another advantage over traditional ways of data acquisition in the social sciences is that players of MMOGs do not consciously notice the measurement process 1. These "social experiments" practically do not perturb or influence the sample. Moreover MMOGs not only open ways to explore sociological questions, but— if economic aspects are part of the game (as it is in many MMOGs)—also to study economical behavior of groups. Here again economical actions and decisions can be monitored for a huge number of individual players within their social and economical contexts. This means that MMOGs offer a natural environment to conduct behavioral economics experiments, which have been of great interest in numerous small-scale surveys, see, e.g. [4–7, 9]. It becomes possible to study the socioeconomic unit of large online game societies. Based on the above discussions, we adopt and build a walkthrough system to simulate interactions between the users and 3D scenes and explore the hidden knowledge for predicting the future behavior of users.

Recent advances in storage technology make it possible to store and keep a series of large Web archives. It is now an exciting challenge for us to observe evolution of the Web, since it has experienced dramatic growth and dynamic changes in its structure. We could see a lot of phenomena in the Web, which correspond to social activities in the real world. For example, if some topic becomes popular in the real world, many games about the topic are created, then good quality web pages are pointed to by public bookmarks or link lists for that topic, and these games become densely connected.

In the last decades, there is an increasing interest in developing techniques to deal with different 3D applications like MMOG models, 3D walkthrough. Many query processing techniques are proposed [15–17] to overcome the problems faced within the extensive scale of 3D applications. Most researches on 3D spatial databases focused on the Euclidean space, where the distances between the objects are determined by the relative positions of the objects in space. However, the operations in 3D spatial data, where the data has an underlying shape topology, do not solely rely on geographical locations. In WT, both the topological and geographical properties of the underlying network are important. The topological properties are usually represented as a finite collection of points, lines and surfaces. Due to serious transfer bottleneck of massive data from hard-disk to the main memory, the current researches mainly focus on the out-of-core rendering systems, in addition to their implementation of sophisticated techniques for culling, simplification, GPU-based rendering, etc., have to work on cache management of data for interactive out-of-core processing of massive data. On the other hand, efforts devoted for data layout on disks for efficient access have been proposed seldom. Especially, the layout can reflect semantic property is neglected and draw little attractions.

The remainder of this paper is organized as follows. Related works are discussed in section "Related Works." Section "Motivating Examples," describes the proposed hypergraph model and problem formulation. Sections "Problem Formulation and Graph-Based Model" and "Data Layout Algorithm Based on Hypergraph Structure" explain the recommended clustering mechanism with illustrative examples. Section "Experimental Evolution" then presents the experiment results. Conclusions are finally, drawn in section "Conclusions and Future Works," along with future research.

## Related Works

In this subsection, we will briefly describe related works about virtual environments, sequential pattern mining and pattern clustering, respectively.

### *Prefetching and Caching Methods Based on Spatial Access Models*

Most of the earlier researches have assumed that WT are memory resident. It is not until recently that managing large WT has become an active area [15–17]. Most of the works have adopted spatial indexes to organize, manipulate and retrieve the data in large WT.

The related work of prefetching and caching method involves in four aspects. First, *data-related*: it is concerned with the organization of objects, such as object partitioning, connectivity and block size. Like the level-of-detail (LOD) management [18–20], hierarchical view-frustum and occlusion culling, working-set management (geometry caching) [20–25] are these examples; Second, *traversal-related*: this focus on reduction of access times for objects. Traditional *cache-efficient* layouts [15, 20, 21, 26] (also called *cache-aware*), based on the knowledge of cache parameters, utilize the different localities to reduce the number of cache misses and the size of the working set; Finally, another variation is *cache-oblivious* algorithms [15, 20, 26]. Instead, they do not require any knowledge of cache parameters or block sizes of the memory hierarchy involved in the computation. In addition, large polygons of such highly complex scenes require a lot of hard disk space so that the additional data could exceed the available capacities [20, 21, 26, 27]. Moreover, the *semantics of data access* is more important in defining the placement policy [16, 17, 28–30]. To meet these requirements, an appropriate data structure and an efficient technique should be developed with the constraints of memory consumption.

### *Hypergraph-Based Pattern Clustering Methods*

The fundamental clustering problem is to partition a given data set into groups (clusters), such that data points in a cluster are more similar to each other (i.e., *intra-similar property*) than points in different clusters (i.e., *inter-similar property*) [31]. These discovered clusters are used to explain the characteristics of the data distribution [31]. However, these schemes fail to produce meaningful clusters, if the number of objects is large or the dimensionalities of the WT (i.e., the number of different features) are diverse and relatively large.

# Motivating Examples

Well known drawbacks of traditional geometric scene modelers make it difficult, and even sometimes impossible, intuitive design of 3D scenes [16–18, 20, 21, 26, 31]. In this section we will discuss on intelligent storage layout modeling, that is modeling using intelligent techniques during the designing process and thus allowing intuitive storage layout design. Based on the above discussions, the following subsections will explain our observations and motivations.

## *Motivations on Theoretical Foundations*

Data mining [16, 17, 19, 32], in artificial intelligence area, deals with finding hidden or unexpected relationships among data items and grouping the related items together. The two basic relationships that are of particular concern to us are:

- *Association*: states when one object occurs, it is highly probable that the other will also occur in.
- *Sequence*: where the data items are associated and, in addition to that, we know the order of occurrence as well.

Association rule mining [19, 32] aims to extract interesting *correlations, frequent patterns*, *associations* or *casual* structures among sets of items in the transaction databases or other data repositories. Especially, a significant hidden relationship is the concept of *association*. More formally, let $I = i_1, i_2, \ldots, i_n$ denote a set of literals, called items, where a transaction $T$ contains a set of items $X$ if $X \subseteq T$. Let $D$ represents a set of transactions such that $\forall T \in D$, $T \subseteq I$. A set $X \subseteq I$ is also called an *itemset*. An itemset with $k$ items is called a $k$-itemset. An *association rule* is indicated by an implication of the form $X \Rightarrow Y$, where $X \subseteq I$, $Y \subseteq I$, and $X \cap Y = \emptyset$. A $X \Rightarrow Y$ is said to hold in transaction set $D$ with *support s* in the transaction set $D$ if $s$-% of transactions in $D$ contain $X \cup Y$. The rule $X \Rightarrow Y$ has *confidence c* if $c$-% of the transactions in $D$ containing $X$ also contain $Y$. The thresholds for support and confidence are called *minsup* and *minconf*, respectively. The *support* of an itemset $X$, denoted $\sigma(X)$, is the number of transactions in which that itemset arises as a subset. Thus $\sigma(X) = |t(X)|$. An itemset is called a *frequent pattern* [19, 32] if its support is greater than or equal to some threshold *minimum support* (*min sup*) value, i.e., if $\sigma(X) \geqq min\ sup$.

## *Motivations on Practical Demands*

Suppose that we have a set of data items $\{a, b, c, d, e, f, g\}$. A sample access history over these items consisting of five sessions is shown in Table 11.1. The request sequences extracted from this history with minimum support 40% are $(a, f)$ and

**Table 11.1** Sample database of user requests

| Session no | Accessed request |
| --- | --- |
| 1 | $e, a, f$ |
| 2 | $b, d$ |
| 3 | $c, d, a, f, g$ |
| 4 | $b, a, f, g$ |
| 5 | $c, d, a, f$ |

**Table 11.2** Sample association rules

| Rule | Support | Confidence |
| --- | --- | --- |
| $a \Longrightarrow f$ | 80% | 100% |
| $c \Longrightarrow d$ | 40% | 100% |

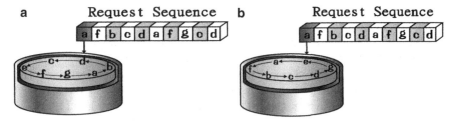

**Fig. 11.1** Effects on accessed objects organization in disk. (**a**): without association rules; (**b**) with association rules

$(c, d)$. The rules obtained out of these sequences with 100% minimum confidence are $a \Rightarrow f$ and $c \Rightarrow d$, as shown in Table 11.2. Two accessed data organizations are depicted in Fig. 11.1. An accessed schedule without any intelligent preprocessing is shown in Fig. 11.1a. A schedule where related items are grouped together and sorted with respect to the order of reference is shown in Fig. 11.1b. Assume that the disk is spinning counterclockwise and consider the following client request sequence, $a$, $f, b, c, d, a, f, g, e, c, d$, shown in Fig. 11.1. Note that dashed lines mean that the first element in the request sequence (counted from left to right) would like to fetch the first item supplied by disk. And directed graph denotes the rotation of disk layout in counterclockwise way. For this request, if we have the access schedule ($a, b, c, d, e$, $f, g$), which dose not take into account the rules, the total I/O access times for the client will be $a{:}5, f{:}5, b{:}3, c{:}2, d{:}6, a{:}5, f{:}5, g{:}1, e{:}5, c{:}6, d{:}6$. The total access times is 49 and the average latency will be $49/11 = 4.454$. However, if we partition the items to be accessed into two groups with respect to the sequential patterns obtained after mining, then we will have $\{a, b, f\}$ and $\{c, d, e, g\}$. Note that data items that appear in the same sequential pattern are placed in the same group. When we sort the data items in the same group with respect to the rules $a \Rightarrow f$ and $c \Rightarrow d$, we will have the sequences $(a, f, b)$ and $(c, d, g, e)$. If we organize the data items to be accessed with respect to these sorted groups of items, we will have the access schedule presented in Fig. 11.1b.In this case, the total access times for the client for

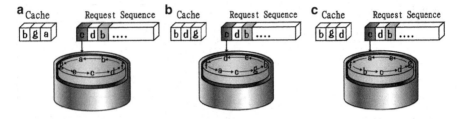

**Fig. 11.2** Effects of prefetching

the same request pattern will be $a{:}1, f{:}1, b{:}1, c{:}1, d{:}1, a{:}3, f{:}1, g{:}4, e{:}1, c{:}4, d{:}1$. The total access times is 19 and the average latency will be $19/11 = 1.727$, which is much lower than 4.454.

Another example that demonstrates the benefits of rule-based prefetching is shown in Fig. 11.2. We demonstrate three different requests of a client for consideration. Based on the obtained association rules, the prediction can be achieved. The current request is $c$ and these is a rule stating that, if data items $c$ is requested, then data items $d$ will be also be requested (i.e., association rule $c \Rightarrow d$). In Fig. 11.2a, data item $d$ is absent in the cache and the client must spend more waiting time for item $d$. In Fig. 11.2b, although the item $d$ is also absent in the cache, the client still spend one disk latency time for item $d$. In Fig. 11.2c, the cache can supply the item $d$ and no disk latency time is needed.

Instead, methods essentially exploit the *semantic* information about whether a data is cached or not given a cache and sort patterns depending on the data access pattern during the scene traversal. This kind of approach cannot only reduce the number of expensive disk I/O accesses but also achieve high system performance. In the following sections, we will explain how we cluster data items with respect to frequent patterns.

## Motivations on Intertwined Relationship Demands

In essence, this can be classified into two different relationships. Under the concern of *intra-similarity*, every *object* represents some importance [32]. For example, the support for frequent pattern *abcd* is 5, but the supports for the object $a$, $b$, $c$, $d$ are 5, 6, 7, 8, respectively. Under the concern of *inter-similarity*, shown in Fig. 11.3, every *frequent pattern* represents some importance. For example, the support for frequent pattern *abcd* is 5, but the supports for the object *abe*, *abcde*, *cd*, *df* are 5, 4, 6, 8, respectively. From the above observations, these patterns are intertwined with the relationships and should be properly and efficiently managed. Therefore, those observations also motivate us to adopt the HG model for representing the relationships.

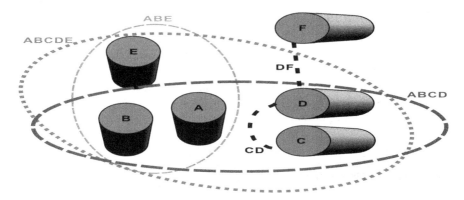

**Fig. 11.3** Demonstration for intra-/inter-relationships among the frequent patterns

## Problem Formulation and Graph-Based Model

In this section, we present a novel application of hypergraph partitioning to automatically determine the computation and I/O schedule. We begin with a definition of the problem and explain the hypergraph partitioning problem. We then present an alternative formulation that better solves our problem of interest.

Clustering is a good candidate for inferring object correlations in storage systems. As the previous sections mentioned, object correlations can be exploited to improve storage system performance. First, correlations can be used to direct prefetching. For example, if a strong correlation exists between objects $a$ and $b$, these two objects can be fetched together from disks whenever one of them is accessed. The disk read-ahead optimization is an example of exploiting the simple data correlations by prefetching subsequent disk blocks ahead of time. Several studies [10, 33] have shown that using these correlations can significantly improve the storage system performance. Our results demonstrate that prefetching based on object correlations can improve the performance much better than that of non-correlation layout in all cases.

A storage system can also lay out data is disks according to object correlations. For example, an object can be collocated with its correlated objects so that they can be fetched together using just one disk access. This optimization can reduce the number of disk seeks and rotations, which dominate the average disk access latency. With correlation-directed disk layouts, the system only needs to pay a one-time seek and rotational delay to get multiple objects that are likely to be accessed soon. Previous studies [31, 34] have shown promising results in allocating correlated file blocks on the same track to avoid track-switching costs.

## *Problem Definition*

Suppose that a user-based traversal database consists of a set of visible patterns, with each pattern accessing a set of data objects. The data objects are often in secondary storage and each data object is always potentially accessed or requested by more than one patterns. The objective is to determine a storage access schedule, so as to minimize the total disk I/O cost.

## *Hypergarph Partitioning Problem*

A *hypergraph HG* $= (V, N)$ [34, 35] is defined as a set of *vertices V* and a set of *nets* (*hyper-edges*) $N$ among those vertices. Every net $n_j \in N$ is a subset of vertices, i.e., $n_j \subseteq V$. The size of a net $n_j$ is equal to the number of vertices it has, i.e., $s_j = | n_j |$. Weight ($w_j$) and cost ($c_j$) can be assigned to the vertices ($v_j \in V$) and edges ($n_j \in N$) of the HG, respectively. $\prod = \{V_1, V_2, \ldots, V_n\}$ is a $n$-way partition of *HG* and satisfies the following conditions: (1) each partition is a nonempty subset of $V$, (2) partitions are pairwise disjoint, and (3) union of $K$ partitions is equal to $V$.

In our model, we assign every object to one vertex, and every frequent pattern is represented by one hyper-edge (net). As shown in Fig. 11.3, according to how many objects involved, object $a$, $b$, $c$, $d$, $e$, and $f$ are circled together in different line form, respectively. Since there are five different patterns, we plot five different nets for demonstration.

Finally, we will define our problem in two phases. Phase I: given a frequent pattern set $P = \{p_1, p_2, \ldots, p_n\}$, we design a efficient formulation scheme to bridge two different domain knowledge (i.e., $P$ and HG model); phase II: in order to reduce the disk access time, we distribute $P$ into a set of clusters, such that minimize inter-cluster similarity and maximize intra-cluster similarity.

## Data Layout Algorithm Based on Hypergraph Structure

Several studies [32–35] have shown that using these correlations can significantly improve the storage system performance. In this section, we describe a direct application of hypergraph partitioning to the disk I/O minimization problem. The construction of the hypergraph is described, followed by the partitioning procedure to derive a valid object layout and I/O schedule.

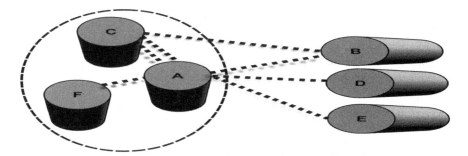

**Fig. 11.4**  The initial condition

## Object-Centric Clustering Scheme

First, as mentioned previously, let the object corresponds to a vertex, and a frequent pattern also corresponds to a hyperedge. The weight $\psi_e$ of a hyperedge $e$ is defined as $1/|e|$, which is inversely proportional to the number of objects that are incident to the hyperedge. Inspired by the main concepts of [35–37], we propose our semantic-based hypergraph clustering scheme. Let two objects $u$ and $v$ are given, the similarity score $d\,(u,v)$ for between $u$ and $v$ is defined as

$$d(u, v) = \sum_{e \in E \mid u,v \in e} \frac{\psi_e}{(m(u) + m(v))} \tag{11.1}$$

Where $e$ is a hyperedge connecting objects $u$ and $v$. $\psi_e$ is a corresponding edge weight, and $m(u)$ and $m(v)$ are the some interesting measures of $u$ and $v$, respectively. As Han et al. [31] cited that the support measure is not a proper measure used in a hypergraph model. Therefore, in our experiments, shown in next section, the confidence measure was used. The similarity score of two objects is directly proportional to the total sum of edge weights connecting them and is inversely proportional to the sum of their measures. Suppose $N_u$ is the set of neighboring objects to a given object $u$. We define the *closest* object to $u$, denoted $c(u)$, as the neighbor object with the *highest similarity score* to $u$, i.e., $c(u) = v$ such that $d\,(u,v) = \text{Max}\,\{d\,(u,z)\mid z \in N_u\}$.

In Fig. 11.4, the dot lines denote which vertexes are connected in the hyperedges. The circle is especially for represented one hyperedge $\{A, C, F\}$. Since the multiplicity of hyperedge $\{A, C\}$ is two. Therefore, there are two hyperedges between vertex $A$ and $C$. The following is the pseudo codes of object-based hypergraph clustering algorithm.

### Object-Oriented Hypergraph-Based Clustering(OHGC)Algorithm
*//D* is the database. $P$ is the set of frequent patterns. *Obj* is the set of frequent patterns. $T$ is the set of clusters, and is set to empty initially.

**Input**: *D*, *P*, *Obj*, and *T*.
**Output**: *T*
**Begin**
// **Phase 1**: Initialization step for *Priority_Queue* (*PQ*)
1. **While** (let each object $u \in Obj$ and *Obj* is not empty) **do**
2. **Begin**
3.      Find closest object *v*, and its associated similarity score *d*;
4.          Insert the tuple (*u*, *v*, *d*) into *PQ* with *d* as key;
5. **End**;   // while in Phase 1.
// **Phase 2**: Hypergraph Clustering based on *PQ*
6. **While** (user-defined cluster number is not reached or top tuple's score *d* >0) **do**
7.          Pick top tuple (*u*, *v*, *d*) from *PQ*;
8.          Cluster *u* and *v* into new object *u'* and update the *T*;
9.          Find closest object *v'* to *u'* its associated similarity score *d'*;
10.          Insert the tuple (*u'*, *v'*, *d'*) into *PQ* with *d'* as key;
11.          Update similarity scores of neighbor of *u*;
12. **End**;   // while in Phase 2.

Now, we will explain our clustering algorithms. The main ideas come from both *object-based* and *HG-based* mechanisms. Since there are multiple relationships exist in object-to-object and pattern-to-pattern formats. Using the ordinary graph models are not sufficient to represent such relationships. This is our main motivation for HG-model.

In order to identify the globally closest pair of objects with the highest score, a data structure with *priority-queue* (*PQ*) mechanism is implemented. There are two phases in our algorithm. Phase 1: we would like to build the *PQ* structure initially. First, for each object *u* in the *Obj* (Object Set), the closest object *v* and its associated similarity score are found, and inserted into the *PQ* with the key *d*. Note that for each object *u*, only one tuple with the closest object v is inserted and maintained. Due to the less complexity in computation, this vertex-oriented *PQ* is more efficient than methods of edge-based. Phase 2: First, we pick up the top tuple (*u*, *v*, *d*) in the *PQ* (step 7). If conditions are satisfied, the pair of objects (*u*, *v*) is clustered and created a new object *u'* (step 8). In step 9 and 10, the new closest object *v'* is found and the *T* set is updated. Therefore, a new tuple (*u'*, *v'*, *d'*) is inserted into *PQ* with *d'* as the new key. Since the clustering changes the vertex-connectivity of HG, some of previously calculated similarity scores might become invalid. Thus, the similarity scores of the neighbors of the new object *u'* need to be re-calculated, and the *PQ* is adjusted accordingly. Demonstration example will be given later. The following is the pseudo codes of object-based hypergraph clustering algorithm.

*Example 1 (OHGC)* Assume that the system has 6 objects and 8 frequent patterns. Let *Obj* = {*A*, *B*, *C*, *D*, *E*, *F*, *G*} and frequent patterns ser $P = \{P_1 = AB; P_2 = AC; P_3 = AD; P_4 = AE; P_5 = AF, P_6 = AC, P_7 = BC, and P_8 = ACF\}$. Note that the multiplicity of hyperedge {*A*,*C*} is two. This is one of main differences between other methods and ours. We set up the *level-wise threshold* for the *multiplicity* of frequent patterns. For example, if the support of $P_i$ is less than some fixed constant, say $\alpha$, then the multiplicy of $Pi$ is set up to be 1; otherwise if the support of $P_i$ is less than or equal to some fixed constant $2\alpha$ but great than $\alpha$, then the multiplicy of $P_i$ is set up to be 2. This idea will alleviate the complexity of HG-model for future partitioning. Therefore, the above initial conditions are shown in Fig. 11.4.

*Step1*. Initially, we start to calculating the similarity score of $A$ and its neighbors. Let the size of each object is 1. Now consider the vertex $B, D$, and $E$.

Since only *one* hyperedge contains vertex $A$ and $B$, its Weight $W_e = 1/|e|$
$= 1/(A + B) = 1/(1 + 1) = 1/2 = 0.5;$
$d\ (A, B) = (W_e)/(A + B) = [1/2]/(1 + 1) = 1/4 = 0.25;$
Similarly, both $d\ (A, D)$ and $d\ (A, E)$ also have the same value (i.e., 0.25).

*Step2*. We still calculate the similarity score of $A$ and its neighbors continuously. Now consider the vertex $F$.

Since only *two* hyperedges contains vertex $A$ and $F$, (i.e., **1**\* $\{A, F\}$ and **1**\*$\{A, C, F\}$).
Case 1: for $\{A, F\}$ is concerned,
its Weight $W_e = 1/|e| = 1/2;$ therefore, $d\ (A,\ F) = (W_e)/(A + F) = \mathbf{1}*[(1/2)/(1 + 1)] = 1/4 = 0.25;$
Case 2: for $\{A, C, F\}$ is concerned,
its Weight $W_e = 1/|e| = 1/(1 + 1 + 1) = 1/3;$ therefore, $d\ (A,F) = (W_e)/(A + F) = \mathbf{1}*[(1/3)/(1 + 1)] = 1/6 = 0.25;$
To sum up, the $d\ (A, F) = 1/4 + 1/6 = 5/12 = 0.416;$

*Step3*. We still calculate the similarity score of $A$ and its neighbors continuously. Now consider the vertex $C$.

Since only *three* hyperedges contains vertex $A$ and $C$ (i.e., **2**\* $\{A, F\}$ and **1**\*$\{A, C, F\}$).
Case 1: for **2**\* $\{A, F\}$ is concerned,
its Weight $W_e = 1/|e| = 1/2;$ therefore,
$d\ (A, F) = \mathbf{2}* (W_e)/(A + F) = \mathbf{2}*[(1/2)/(1 + 1)] = \mathbf{2}*\ 1/4 = 1/2 = 0.5;$
Case 2: for **1**\*$\{A, C, F\}$ is concerned,
its Weight $W_e = 1/|e| = 1/(1 + 1 + 1) = 1/3;$ therefore, $d\ (A,F) = (W_e)/(A + F) = \mathbf{1}*[(1/3)/ (1 + 1)] = 1/6 = 0.25;$
To sum up, the $d\ (A, F) = 1/2 + 1/6 = 4/6 = 0.667;$

*Step4*. From the above steps, we have the following similarity scores among vertex $A$ and its neighbors.

$d\ (A, B) = d\ (A, D) = d\ (A, F) = 0.25;$
$d\ (A, F) = 5/12 = 0.416;$
$d\ (A, C) = 2/3 = \mathbf{0.667};$
Since $d\ (A, C)$ has the highest similarity score, vertex $C$ is declared as the closest object to $A$. The result is shown in Fig. 11.5.

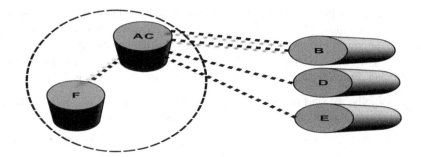

**Fig. 11.5** After the computation of step1 to step 4, the vertex *C* was chosen and merged with vertex *A*

*Step5*. The following steps are shown how to update the similarity scores of neighbors of vertex *A*. As Fig. 11.5 shown, we want to update the related similarity values after the vertex *A* and vertex *C* were merged (i.e., vertex *A* and vertex *C* were considered as only one vertex). Now consider the vertex ***D***.

Since only *one* hyperedge contains vertex *AC* and *D*, (i.e., **1**\*{*AC*, *D*}).
For {*AC*, *D*} is concerned,
its Weight $W_e = 1/|e| = 1/(1 + 1 + 1) = 1/3$; therefore, $d\ (AC, D) = (W_e)/(AC+D)$
   $= \mathbf{1}*[(1/3)/(1 + 1)] = 1/6 = 0.167$;
Similarly, $d\ (AC, E)$ has the same value (i.e., 0.167).

*Step6*. Now consider the vertex ***B***. Since there are *two* hyperedges contain vertex *AC* and *B*, (i.e., **2**\*{*AC*, *B*}).

For {*AC*, *B*} is concerned,
its Weight $W_e = 1/|e| = 1/(1 + 1 + 1) = 1/3$; therefore, $d\ (AC, B) = (W_e)/(AC + B)$
   $= \mathbf{2}*[(1/3)/(1 + 1)] = 1/3 = 0.333$;

*Step7*. Now consider the vertex ***F***. Since there are *two* hyperedges contain vertex *AC* and *B*, (i.e., **1**\*{*AC*, *F*} and **1**\*{*A*, *C*, *F*}).

Case 1: for {*AC*, *F*} is concerned,
its Weight $W_e = 1/|e| = 1/3$; therefore, $d\ (AC,\ F) = (W_e)/(AC + F) = \mathbf{1}*[(1/3)/(1 + 1)] = 1/6$;
Case 2: for {*A*, *C*, *F*} is concerned,
its Weight $W_e = 1/|e| = 1/(1 + 1 + 1) = 1/3$; therefore, $d\ (AC, F) = (W_e)/(AC + F)$
   $= \mathbf{1}*[(1/3)/(1 + 1)] = 1/6$;
To sum up, the $d\ (AC, F) = 1/6 + 1/6 = 2/3 = 0.333$;

This idea will alleviate the complexity of HG-model for future partitioning. The initial conditions are shown in Fig. 11.4 and final result was shown in Fig. 11.5.

$$P_1=\{5A, 6B, C\}, \ P_2=\{3A,2B, 5C, 8D\}, \ P_3=\{5C, 8D\}$$

| New–Jaccard($P_1$,$P_2$) | New–Jaccard($P_1$,$P_3$) | New–Jaccard($P_2$,$P_3$) |
|---|---|---|
| $=\dfrac{\lvert\{3A,2B,1C\}\rvert}{\lvert\{5A,6B,5C,8D\}\rvert}$ | $=\dfrac{\lvert\{1C\}\rvert}{\lvert\{5A,6B,5C,8D\}\rvert}$ | $=\dfrac{\lvert\{5C,8D\}\rvert}{\lvert\{3A,2B,5C,8D\}\rvert}$ |
| $=\dfrac{6}{24}=\dfrac{1}{4}=0.25$ | $=\dfrac{1}{24}=0.04$ | $=\dfrac{13}{18}=0.72$ |
| Old–Jaccard($P_1$,$P_2$) | Old–Jaccard($P_1$,$P_3$) | Old–Jaccard($P_2$,$P_3$) |
| $=\dfrac{\lvert\{A,B,C\}\rvert}{\lvert\{A,B,C,D\}\rvert}$ | $=\dfrac{\lvert\{C,D\}\rvert}{\lvert\{A,B,C,D\}\rvert}$ | $=\dfrac{\lvert\{C,D\}\rvert}{\lvert\{A,B,C,D\}\rvert}$ |
| $=\dfrac{3}{4}=0.75$ | $=\dfrac{2}{4}=0.50$ | $=\dfrac{2}{4}=0.50$ |

**Fig. 11.6** Illustration between two different concerns about the Jaccard mechanisms

## Quantity-Based Jaccard Function

The Jaccard index [38], also known as the Jaccard similarity coefficient, is a statistic used for comparing the similarity and diversity of sample sets. However, if the quantity for each element involved, this similarity can not reflect the following conditions. Let us consider three different frequent patterns, $P_1$, $P_2$, and $P_3$: $P_1 = \{5A, 6B, C\}$, $P_2 = \{3A, 2B, 5C, 8D\}$, $P_3 = \{5C, 8D\}$. Here take $P_1$ for an example, *5A* means there are *five* elements for object with type *A*. Similarly, *6B* means there are *six* elements for object with type *B*, and *1C* means there is *one* element for object with type *C*.

As shown in Fig. 11.6, the new jaccard similarity mechanism (i.e., *quantity-based Jaccard similarity* formula) can capture more semantic meanings than the old one.

**Definition 1: Intra-distance measure (Co-occurrence)** Let $P_1$ and $P_2$ be two frequent patterns. We can represent $D(P_1, P_2)$ as the normalized difference between the cardinality of their union and the cardinality of their intersection:

$$D(P_1, P_2) = 1 - \frac{\lvert P_1 \cap P_2 \rvert}{\lvert P_1 \cup P_2 \rvert} \tag{11.2}$$

## Quantity-Based Jaccard Clustering Approach

Based on the above discussions, the following is our Jaccard-based clustering algorithm.

**Table 11.3** Information on radius and average number of objects in one view

| View radius | Average objects in one view |
|---|---|
| 2,000 | 15 |
| 4,000 | 26 |
| 6,000 | 46 |
| 8,000 | 63 |
| 10,000 | 81 |
| 12,000 | 114 |

### Pattern Clustering Algorithm for Jaccard Function

// $P$ is the set of frequent patterns. $T$ is the set of clusters, and is set to empty initially.

**Input**: $P$ and $T$.
**Output**: $T$
**Begin**
1. $FreqTable = \{ft_{ij}|$ the frequency of $pattern_i$ and $pattern_j$ co-existing in the database $D\}$;
2. $DistTable = \{dt_{ij} \mid$ the distance between of $pattern_i$ and $pattern_j$ in the database $D\}$;
3.     $C_1 = \{C_i \mid$ At the beginning each pattern to be a single cluster$\}$
4.     // Set up the Extra-Similarity Table for evaluation
5.     $M_1 =$ Intra-Similar $(C_1, \varnothing)$;
6.     $k = 1$;
7.  **while**$|C_k| > n$ do **Begin**
8.     $C_{k+1} =$ PatternCluster $(C_k, M_k, FreqTable, DistTable)$;
9.         $M_{k+1} =$ Intra-Similar $(C_{k+1}, M_k)$;
10.        $k = k + 1$;
11. **End;**
12. return $C_k$;
13. **End;**

**Definition 2: View-radius** Inspired by the idea of *view importance* [33], Firstly, to obtain the efficient computation cost, we propose a simple but effective distance to measure the number of observable objects. Secondly, according to the distance threshold given by users, we define *view radius* in order to choose representative objects. For the comparison purposes, we divide the different intervals among the view-radius. The detailed data was shown in Table 11.3.

# Experimental Evaluation

This section presents a progression of experiments for the effectiveness of predictive-prefetching mechanism in the storage systems. We begin by explaining the set-ups for experimental environments, included the experimental setups.

Next, under different constraints, we show that HG-based clustering approach can outperform the other schemes. Besides, in order to compare with knowledge-based tree-like data structures [21], the mechanism of *Access Path Predictor* (APP) was implemented for performance comparisons.

Since the APP scheme share some similar properties with our approaches. For examples, APP claims that the most common access pattern within a dataset is the *frequent appearance* of the same *predecessor-current-successor* patterns [21]. This pattern represents a section of a *path* along which one application *navigates* through its data. As far as the intra-relationship be concerned, this type of patterns are similar our frequent sequential patterns. However, some significant limitation was posed on the APP scheme. Because the *correlated relationships* cover both the intra-relationship and inter-relationship [21, 30]. The APP scheme only considered their pattern inferred by intra-relationship only hidden in the same path. In other words, the inter-relationships across the different paths were neglected in the APP scheme. On the contrary, both of them were considered in our HG-based clustering approach. Based on the above discussions, we adopt the APP scheme for performance evaluation.

## Implementation Setup

The experiments were conducted on a machine with a 1.6 GHz Pentium 4 processor, 1 GB main memory, running Microsoft Windows 2003 server. All algorithms were implemented in Java.

## Results and Performance

We conduct several experiments to determine the performance of our proposed OHCG approach. In all four experiments, we test the performance of proposed technique for our traversal trace data using the mentioned clustering measures, Hypergraph and quantity-based Jaccard similarity.

Furthermore, we perform the same set of experiments for three other prediction techniques namely, Without-Clustering approach, APP approach, and quantity-based Jaccard approach. Without-Clustering approach is monitored and managed by operation system, where the prediction computation is deferred until LRU-like mechanism works. The APP approach uses tree-like data structure, a mechanism that calculates a probability by counting the frequency of values and combinations of values in the historical data. On the other side, quantity-based Jaccard approach focuses on selecting the most similar frequent patterns for a given patterns by combing both the co-occurrence and quantity principles. The final output of the hypergraph-based clustering is partitioned via pattern-based hypergraph model,

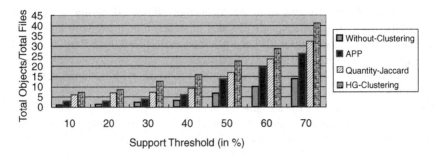

**Fig. 11.7** Comparison of different algorithms on the number of objects retrieved

where OHGC determines the best partition to place objects into the storage system for future accesses. This helps to explore the hidden relationships and estimate future fine-grained placements, leveraging the most effective predictive mechanism for each situation. Note that HG-Clustering represents our OHGC clustering scheme.

In particular, we focused on the following metrics, namely *demanded total objects*, *response time (in ms)*, and *number of retrieval files*. The demanded total objects indicates that the percentage of request which can be met without accessing the out-of-core storage. The response time metric is the time interval elapsed that a clustering algorithm was required to load data form the disk. The number of retrieval files metric indicates that the effect of correlated relationships.

We carry out our experiments to compare four algorithms in the traversal database mainly on total objects/total files, response time, and number of retrieval files. Moreover, we vary the support threshold (between 70% and 10%). Similarly, we also vary the view radius threshold (between 2,000 and 12,000).

In the experiments of *total objects/total files*, as the Fig. 11.7 shown, it represents demanded total objects for the algorithms comprising points in a spherical volume. Besides, we have the following observations: firstly, the number of representative semantic patterns by OHCG is much more than those of the other three algorithms. It implies there are huge access time reductions during the retrieval of objects; secondly, in the algorithm of OHCG, we can obtain the dominating clusters which include the most representative sequential patterns. In addition, to verify the effectiveness of OHCG we proposed in our work, we also make the experiments on number of retrieval files which are shown in Figs. 11.8–11.10. Moreover, in the experiments of response time, as the Figs. 11.8 and 11.10 shown, the response time of OHCG is much less than the other three algorithms, and APP is very close to the time of quantity-Jaccard. This is because that the clustering mechanism can accurately support prefetching objects for future usage. Not only the access time is cut down but also the I/O efficiency is improved.

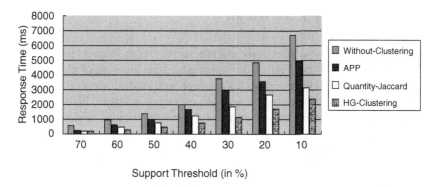

**Fig. 11.8** Comparison of different algorithms on system response time under different support threshold

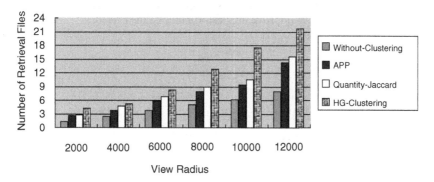

**Fig. 11.9** Comparison of different algorithms on the number of files retrieved

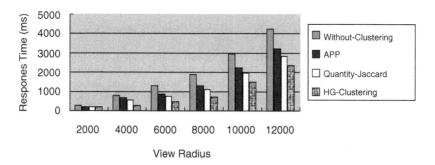

**Fig. 11.10** Comparison of different algorithms on system response time under different view radius

## Conclusions and Future Works

This paper studies how to effectively and efficiently cluster frequent patterns from traversal database. To the best of our knowledge, the problem of clustering the semantic objects in 3D walkthrough has not been well studied in existing work.

Inspired by ideas of speedup of accessing semantic patterns, firstly, to obtain the high-quality clustering, we design a novel hypergraph-based model to measure the associations which shows the similarity between frequent patterns. Besides, the quantity-Jaccard distance is also presented. Secondly, according to the distance threshold, we define meaningful clustering in order to choose representative frequent patterns. Finally, since the problem of retrieving 3D objects is equivalent to minimizing the number of frequencies for accessing 3D objects, we develop an algorithm, OHCG, including an efficient partitioning strategy. On the other side, Quantity-Jaccard is more flexible, due to its easy adaptation and implementation. This opens a new era for inducing the concepts of data mining to discover the hidden but valuable knowledge to improve the performance of the system.

## References

1. Golder, S., Wilkinson, D., Huberman, B.: Rhythms of social interaction: messaging within a massive online network. In: Communities and Technologies 2007: Proceedings of the Third Communities and Technologies Conference, Michigan State University. Springer, London (2007)
2. Hamasaki, M., Takeda, H., Hope, T., Nishimura, T.: Network analysis of an emergent massively collaborative creation community. In: Proceedings of the Third International ICWSM Conference, San Jose, pp. 222–225, 17–20 May 2009
3. Jiang, Z., Zhou, W., Tan, Q.: Online-offline activities and game-playing behaviors of avatars. Europhys. Lett. **88**, 48007 (2009)
4. Szell, M., Thurnrt, S.: Measuring social dynamics in a massive multiplayers online game. Soc. Netw. **32**, 313–329 (2010)
5. Bainbridge, W.: The scientific research potential of virtual worlds. Science **317**(5837), 472 (2007)
6. Castronova, E.: On the research value of large games. Games Cult. **1**, 163–186 (2006)
7. Henrich, J., Boyd, R., Bowles, S., Camerer, C., Fehr, E., Gintis, H., McElreath, R., Alvard, M., Barr, A., Ensminger, J., et al.: "Economic man" in cross-cultural perspective: behavioral experiments in 15 small-scale societies. Behav. Brain Sci. **28**(6), 795–815 (2005)
8. Carrington, P., Scott, J., Wasserman, S.: Models and Methods in Social Network Analysis. Cambridge University Press, Cambridge (2005)
9. Gachter, S., Fehr, E.: Collective action as a social exchange. J. Econ. Behav. Organ. **39**(4), 341–369 (1999)
10. Lazer, D., Pentland, A., Adamic, L., Aral, S., Barabasi, A., Brewer, D., Christakis, N., Contractor, N., Fowler, J., Gutmann, M., et al.: Computational social science. Science **323**(5915), 721 (2009)
11. Watts, D.: A twenty-first century science. Nature **445**(7127), 489 (2007)
12. Johnson, N., Xu, C., Zhao, Z., Ducheneaut, N., Yee, N., Tita, G., Hui, P.: Human group formation in online guilds and offline gangs driven by a common team dynamic. Phys. Rev. **79**(6), 66117 (2009)

13. Labianca, G., Brass, D.: Exploring the social ledger: negative relationships and negative asymmetry in social networks in organizations. Acad. Manage. Rev. **31**(3), 596–614 (2006)
14. Newcomb, T.: The Acquaintance Process. Holt, Rinehart and Winston, New York (1961)
15. Sajadi, B., et. al.: A novel page-based data structure for interactive walkthroughs. In: ACM SIGGRAPH Symposium on Interactive 3D Graphics and Games (I3D), 18 Dec 2009
16. Bertini, E., Lalanne, D.: Investigating and reflecting on the integration of automatic data analysis and visualization in knowledge discovery. ACM SIGKDD Explor. **11**(2), 9–18 (2009)
17. Plemenos, D., Miaoulis, G.: Visual Complexity and Intelligent Computer Graphics Techniques Enhancements. Springer, New York (2009)
18. Zhu, Y.: Uniform remeshing with an adaptive domain: a new scheme for view-dependent level-of-detail rendering of meshes. IEEE Trans. Vis. Comput. Graph. **11**(3), 306–316 (2005)
19. Agrawal, R., Imielinski, T., Swami, A.N.: Mining association rules between sets of items in large databases. In: Proceedings of the ACM SIGMOD International Conference on Management of Data, pp 207–216, May 1993
20. Yoon, S.E., Manocha, D.: Cache-efficient layouts of bounding volume hierarchies. Eurographics **25**(3), 507–516 (2006)
21. Chisnall, D., Chen, M., Hansen, C.: Knowledge-based out-of-core algorithms for data management in visualization. In: Eurographics/IEEE-VGTC Symposium on Visualization, Lisbon, 8–10 May 2006
22. Correa, W.T., Klosowaki, J.T., Silva, C.T.: Visibility-based prefetching for interactive out-of-core rendering. In: Proceedings of the 2003 IEEE Symposium on Parallel and Large-Data Visualization and Graphics (PVG'03), Seattle, pp 2–8, 20–21 Oct 2003
23. Ng, C.-M., Nguyen, C.-T., Tran, D.-N., Yeow, S.-W., Tan, T.-S.: Prefetching in visual simulation. In: Proceedings of the 14th IEEE Visualization 2003 (VIS'03), Seattle, pp 98–99, 19–24 Oct 2003
24. Rhodes, P.J., Tang, X., Bergeron, R., Sparr, T.M.: Out of core visualization using iterator aware multidimensional prefetching. In: Proceedings SPIE, vol 5669, Visualization and Data Analysis, San Jose, CA, pp 295–306, Jan 2005
25. Khanna, G., Catalyurek, U., Kurc, T.K, Sadayappan, P., Saltz, J.: A data locality aware online scheduling approach for I/O-intensive jobs with file sharing. In: Proceedings of the 12th International Workshop on Job Scheduling Strategies for Parallel Processing (JSSPP 2006), in Conjunction with SIGMETRICS 2006, Saint-Malo, France, June 2006
26. Yoon, S.-E., Lindstrom, P., Pascucci, V., Manocha, D.: Cache-oblivious mesh layouts. ACM Trans. Gr. **24**(3), 886–893 (2005)
27. Sivathanu M., et al.: Semantically-smart disk systems. In: Proceedings of the Second USENIX Conference on File and Storage Technologies, San Francisco, 31 Mar–2 Apr 2003
28. Li, J., Prabhakar, S.: Data placement for tertiary storage. In: Proceedings of the 10th NASA Goddard Conference on Mass Storage Systems and Technologies/19th IEEE Symposium on Mass Storage Systems (MMS 2002), 193–207, Apr 2002
29. Domenech, J., Pont, A., Sahuquillo, J., Gil J.A..: Giving facilities for the design and test of web prefetching techniques. In: Proceedings of the Second International Working Conference Performance Modelling and Evaluation of Heterogeneous Networks, Ilkley, UK, July 2004
30. Hu, B., Sadowaks, M.M.: Fine granularity clustering-based placement. IEEE Trans. Comput-Aid Des. Integr. Circuit Syst. **23**(4), 527–536 (2004)
31. Han, E.-H., Karypis, G., Kumar, V., Mobasher, B.: Clustering based on association rule hypergraph. In: Workshop on Research Issues on Data Mining and Knowledge Discovery, May 1997
32. Hung, S.S., Liu, D.S.M.: Using predictive prefetching to improve interactive walkthrough latency. Comput. Anim. Virtual World J. **17**(3–4), 469–478 (2006)
33. Chim, R., Lau, W.H., Leong, H.V., Si, A.: CyberWalk — a web-based distributed virtual walkthrough environment. IEEE Trans. Multimed. **5**(4), 503–515 (2003)
34. Demir, E., Aykanat, C., Cambazoglu, B.B.: Clustering spatial networks for aggregate query processing: a hypergraph approach. Inf. Syst. **33**, 1–17 (2008)

35. Nam, G.-J., et al.: A fast hierarchical quadratic placement algorithm. IEEE Trans. Comput-Aid Des. Integr. Circuit Syst. **25**(4), 678–691 (2006)
36. Karypis, G., Kumar, V.: Multilevel K-way hypergraph partitioning. In: Proceeding of the ACM/IEEE Design Automation Conference, New Orleans, pp 343–348, June 1999
37. Comg, J., Lim, S.K.: Edge separability-based circuit clustering with application to multilevel circuit partitioning. IEEE Trans. Comput-Aid Des. Integr. Circuit Syst. **23**(3), 346–357 (2004)
38. Jaccard, P.: The distribution of The flora of the Alpine zone. New Phytol. **11**, 37–50 (1912)

# Chapter 12
# Extraction and Analysis of Facebook Friendship Relations

**Salvatore Catanese, Pasquale De Meo, Emilio Ferrara, Giacomo Fiumara, and Alessandro Provetti**

**Abstract**  Online social networks (OSNs) are a unique web and social phenomenon, affecting tastes and behaviors of their users and helping them to maintain/create friendships. It is interesting to analyze the growth and evolution of online social networks both from the point of view of marketing and offer of new services and from a scientific viewpoint, since their structure and evolution may share similarities with real-life social networks. In social sciences, several techniques for analyzing (off-line) social networks have been developed, to evaluate quantitative properties (e.g., defining metrics and measures of structural characteristics of the networks) or qualitative aspects (e.g., studying the attachment model for the network evolution, the binary trust relationships, and the link prediction problem). However, OSN analysis poses novel challenges both to computer and Social scientists. We present our long-term research effort in analyzing Facebook, the largest and arguably most successful OSN today: it gathers more than 500 million users. Access to data about Facebook users and their friendship relations is restricted; thus, we acquired the necessary information directly from the front end of the website, in order to reconstruct a subgraph representing anonymous interconnections among a significant subset of users. We describe our ad hoc, privacy-compliant crawler for Facebook data extraction. To minimize bias, we adopt two different graph mining techniques: breadth-first-search (BFS) and rejection sampling. To analyze the structural properties of samples consisting of millions of nodes, we developed a

S. Catanese • P. De Meo • G. Fiumara
Department of Physics, Informatics Section. University of Messina, Messina, Italy

E. Ferrara (✉)
Department of Mathematics, University of Messina, Messina, Italy

A. Provetti
Department of Physics, Informatics Section. University of Messina, Messina, Italy

Oxford-Man Institute, University of Oxford, Oxford, UK

A. Abraham (ed.), *Computational Social Networks: Mining and Visualization*,
DOI 10.1007/978-1-4471-4054-2_12, © Springer-Verlag London 2012

specific tool for analyzing quantitative and qualitative properties of social networks, adopting and improving existing Social Network Analysis (SNA) techniques and algorithms.

## Introduction

The increasing popularity of online social networks (OSNs) is witnessed by the huge number of users that MySpace, Facebook, etc. acquired in a short amount of time. The growing accessibility of the web, through several media, gives to most users a 24/7 online presence and encourages them to build a online mesh of relationships.

As OSNs become the tools of choice for connecting people, we expect that their structure will increasingly mirror real-life society and relationships. At the same time, with an estimated 13 million transactions per second (at peak), Facebook is one of the most challenging computer science artifacts, posing several optimization, scalability, and robustness challenges.

The essential feature of Facebook is the friendship relation between participants. It consists, mainly, in a permission to consult each others' friends list and posted content: news, photos, links, blog posts, etc.; such permission is mutual. In this chapter, we consider the Facebook friendship graph as the (nondirected) graph having FB users as vertices and edges represent their friendship relation.

The analysis of OSN connections is a fascinating topic on multiple levels. First, a complete study of the structure of large *real* (i.e., off-line) communities was impossible or at least very expensive before, even at fractions of the scale considered in OSN analysis. Second, data is clearly defined by some structural constraints, usually provided by the OSN structure itself, w.r.t. real-life relations, often hardly identifiable. The interpretation of these data opens up new fascinating research issues, e.g., is it possible to study OSNs with the tools of traditional Social Network Analysis, as in Wasserman-Faust [89] and [69]? To what extent the behavior of OSN users is comparable to that of people in real-life social networks [39]? What are the topological characteristics of the relationships network (friendship, in the case of FB) of OSN [4]? And what about their structure and evolution [58]?

To address these questions, further computer science research is needed to design and develop the tools to acquire and analyze data from massive OSNs. First, proper social metrics need to be introduced, in order to identify and evaluate properties of the considered OSN. Second, scalability is an issue faced by anyone who wants to study a large OSN independently from the commercial organization that owns and operates it. For instance, last year Gjoka et al. [42] estimated the crawling overhead needed to collect the whole Facebook graph in 44 Tb of data. Moreover, even when such data could be acquired and stored locally (which, however, raises storage issues related to the social network compression [16, 17]), it is nontrivial to devise and implement effective functions that traverse and visit the graph or even evaluate simple metrics. In literature, extensive research has been conducted on sampling techniques for large graphs; only recently, however, studies have shed light on the bias that those methodologies may introduce. That is, depending on the method by which the graph has been explored, certain features may result over/underrepresented w.r.t. the actual graph.

Our long-term research on these topics is presented in this chapter. We describe in detail the architecture and functioning modes of our ad hoc Facebook crawler, by which, even on modest computational resources, we can extract large samples containing several milions of nodes. Two recently collected samples of about eight millions of nodes each are described and analyzed in detail. To comply with the FB end-user licence, data is made anonymous upon extraction, hence we never memorize users' sensible data. Next, we describe our newly developed tool for graph analysis and visualization, called LogAnalysis. LogAnalysis may be used to compute the metrics that are most pertinent to OSN graph analysis, and can be adopted as an open-source, multiplatform alternative to the well-known NodeXL tool.

## Background and Related Literature

The task of extracting and analyzing data from Online Social Networks has attracted the interest of many researchers, e.g., in [7, 39, 93]. In this section, we review some relevant literature directly related to our approach.

In particular, we first discuss techniques to crawl large social networks and collect data from them (see section "Data Collection in OSN"). Collected data are usually mapped onto graph data structures (and sometimes hypergraphs) with the goal of analyzing their structural properties.

The ultimate goal of these efforts is perhaps best laid out by Kleinberg [56]: topological properties of graphs may be *reliable indicators* of human behaviors. For instance, several studies show that node degree distribution follows a power law, both in real and online social networks. That feature points to the fact that most social network participants are often *inactive,* while few key users generate a large portion of data/traffic. As a consequence, many researchers leverage on tools provided from *graph theory* to analyze the social network graph with the goal, among others, of better interpreting personal and collective behaviors on a large scale. The list of potential research questions arising from the analysis of OSN graphs is very long; in the following, we shall focus on three themes which are directly relevant to our research:

1. *Node Similarity Detection*, i.e., the task of assessing the degree of similarity of two users in an OSN (see section "Similarity Detection")
2. *Community Detection*, i.e., the task of of finding groups of users (called *communities*) who frequently interact with each other but seldom with those outside their community (see section "Community Detection")
3. *Influential User Detection*, i.e., the task of identifying users capable of stimulating other users to join activities/discussions in their OSN (see section "Influential User Detection").

## Data Collection in OSN

The most works focusing on data collection adopt techniques of web information extraction [34], to crawl the front end of websites; this is because OSN datasets are usually not publicly accessible; data rests in back-end databases that are accessible only through the web interface.

In [63] the problem of sampling from large graphs adopting several graph mining techniques, in order to establish whether it is possible to avoid bias in acquiring a subset of the whole graph of a social network is discussed. The main outcome of the analysis in [63] is that a sample of size of 15% of the whole graph preserves most of the properties.

In [69], the authors crawled data from large online social networks like Orkut, Flickr, and LiveJournal. They carried out an in-depth analysis of OSN topological properties (e.g., link symmetry, power-law node degrees, groups formation) and discussed challenges arising from large-scale crawling of OSNs.

Ye et al. [93] considered the problem of crawling OSNs analyzing quantitative aspects like the efficiency of the adopted visiting algorithms, and bias of data produced by different crawling approaches.

The work by Gjoka et al. [42] on OSN graphs is perhaps the most similar to our current research, e.g., in [22]. Gjoka et al. have sampled and analyzed the Facebook friendship graph with different visiting algorithms namely, BFS, Random Walk, and Metropolis-Hastings Random Walks. Our objectives differ from those of Gjoka et al. because their goal is to produce a *consistent* sample of the Facebook graph. A sample is defined consistent when some of its key structural properties, i.e., node degree distribution, assortativity and clustering coefficient approximate fairly well the corresponding properties of the original Facebook graph. Vice versa, our work aims at crawling a portion of the Facebook graph and to analytically study the structural properties of the crawled data.

A further difference with [42] is in the strategy for selecting which nodes to visit: Gjoka's strategy requires to know in advance the degree of the considered nodes. Nodes with the highest degree are selected and visited at each stage of the sampling. In the Facebook context, a node's degree represents the number of friends a user has; such information is available in advance by querying the profile of the user. Such an assumption, however, is not applicable if we consider other online social networks. Hence, to know the degree of a node, we should preliminarily perform a complete visit of the graph, which may not be feasible for large-scale OSN graphs.

## Similarity Detection

Finding similar users of a given OSN is a key issue in several research fields like Recommender Systems, especially Collaborative Filtering (CF) Recommender Systems [3]. In the context of social networks, the simplest way to compute user similarities is by means of accepted similarity metrics such as the well-known

Jaccard coefficient [50]. However, the usage of the Jaccard coefficient is often not satisfactory because it considers only the acquaintances of a user in a social network (and, therefore, local information) and does not take global information into account. A further drawback consists of the fact that users with a large number of acquaintances have a higher probability of sharing some of them w.r.t. users with a small number of acquaintances; therefore, they are likely to be regarded as similar even if no real similarity exists between them. Adamic and Adar [1] proposed that the similarity of two users increases if they share acquaintances who, in turn, have a low number of acquaintances themselves.

In order to consider global network properties, many approaches rely on the idea of *regular equivalence*, i.e., on the idea that two users are similar if their acquaintances are similar too. In [13] the problem of computing user similarities is formalized as an optimization problem. Other approaches compute similarities by exploiting matrix-based methods. For instance, the approaches of [27, 61] use a modified version of the Katz coefficient, SimRank [53], provides an iterative fixpoint method. The approach of [14] operates on directed graphs and uses an iterative approach relying on their spectral properties.

Some authors studied computational complexity of social network analysis with an emphasis on the problem of discovering links between social network users [85, 86]. To this purpose, tools like Formal Concept Analysis and Matrix Factorization are described and employed in this chapter.

To describe these approaches, assume to consider a social network and let $G = \langle V, E \rangle$ be the graph representing it; each node in $V$ represents a user, whereas an edge specifies a tie between a pair of users (in particular, the fact that a user *knows* another user).

In the first stage, *Formal Concept Analysis* is applied to map $G$ onto a graph $G'$. The graph $G'$ is more compact than $G$ (i.e., it contains less nodes and edges of $G$) but, however, it is *sparse*, i.e., a node in $G'$ still has few connections with other nodes. As a consequence, the task of predicting if two nodes are similar is quite hard and comparing the number of friends/acquaintances they share is not effective because, in most cases, two users do not share any common friend and, therefore, the similarity degree of an arbitrary pair of users will be close to 0. To alleviate sparsity, *Singular Value Decomposition* [46] (SVD) is applied. Experiments provided in [85] show that the usage of *SVD* is effective in producing a more detailed and refined analysis of social network data.

The *SVD* is a technique from Linear Algebra which has been successfully employed in many fields of computer science like Information Retrieval; in particular, given a matrix $\mathbf{A}$, the *SVD* allows the matrix $\mathbf{A}$ to be decomposed as follows:

$$\mathbf{A} = \mathbf{U} \mathbf{\Sigma} \mathbf{V},$$

being $\mathbf{U}$ and $\mathbf{V}$ two *orthogonal matrices* (i.e., the columns of $U$ and $V$ are pairwise orthogonal); the matrix $\mathbf{\Sigma}$ is a diagonal matrix whose elements coincide with the square roots of the eigenvalues of the matrix $\mathbf{A}\mathbf{A}^T$; as usual, the symbol $\mathbf{A}^T$ denotes the transpose of the matrix $\mathbf{A}$.

The *SVD* allows to decompose a matrix **A** into the product of three matrices and if we would multiply these three matrices, we would reconstruct the original matrix **A**. As a consequence, if **A** is the adjacency matrix of a social network, any operation carried out on **A** can be equivalently performed on the three matrices **U**, **Σ**, and **V** in which **A** has been decomposed.

The main advantage of such a transformation is that matrices **U** and **V** are dense and, then, we can compute the similarity degree of two users even if the number of friends they share is 0.

## Community Detection

The problem of detecting groups of related nodes in a single social network has been largely analyzed in the physics, bioinformatics and computer science literature and is often known as *community detection* [71, 72] and studied, among others, by Borgatti et al. [18].

A number of community detection algorithms are based on the concept of *network modularity*. In particular, if we assume that an OSN $S$ (represented by means of a graph $G$) has been partitioned into $m$ communities, the corresponding network modularity $Q$ is defined as follows:

$$Q = \sum_{s=1}^{m} \left[ \frac{l_s^2}{L} - \frac{d_s^2}{2L} \right] \tag{12.1}$$

where $L$ is the number of edges in $G$, $l_s$ is the number of edges between nodes belonging to the $s$th community, and $d_s$ is the sum of the degrees of the nodes in the $s$th community.

High values of $Q$ reflect a high value of $l_s$ for each identified community; in turn, this implies that detected communities are highly cohesive and weakly coupled. Therefore, it is not surprising that the idea inspiring many community detection algorithms is to maximize the function $Q$. Unfortunately, maximizing $Q$ is NP-hard [20], thus viable heuristics must be considered.

A first heuristics is the Girvan-Newman algorithm (hereafter, GN) [41]. It relies on the concept of *edge betweenness*; in particular, given an edge $e$ of $S$, its edge betweenness $B(e)$ is defined as

$$B(e) = \sum_{n_i \in S} \sum_{n_l \in S} \frac{np_e(n_i, n_l)}{np(n_i, n_l)} \tag{12.2}$$

where $n_i$ and $n_l$ are nodes of $S$, $np(n_i, n_l)$ is the number of distinct shortest paths between $n_i$ and $n_l$, and $np_e(n_i, n_l)$ is the number of distinct shortest paths between $n_i$ and $n_l$ containing $e$ itself.

Intuitively, edges with a high betweenness connect nodes belonging to different communities. As a consequence, their deletion would lead to an increase of $Q$. Algorithm GN relies on this intuition. It first ranks edges on the basis of their betweenness; then it removes the edge with the highest betweenness (Step 1). After this, it recomputes the betweenness of the remaining edges and the value of $Q$ (Step 2). It repeats Steps 1 and 2 until it does not observe any significant increase of $Q$. At each iteration, each connected component of $S$ identifies a community. The computational complexity of GN is $O(N^3)$, $N$ being the number of nodes of $S$. The cubic complexity algorithm may not be scalable enough for the size of online social networks but a more efficient – $O(N \log^2 N)$ – implementation of GN can be found in [25].

Blondel et al. [15] propose to apply GN on the neighborhood of each node rather than on the whole network. Once communities have been identified, the group of nodes associated with a community is replaced by a supernode, thus producing a smaller graph. This process is iterated and, at each iteration, the function $Q$ is recomputed. The algorithm ends when $Q$ does not significantly increase anymore.

Radicchi et al. [80] illustrate an algorithm which strongly resembles GN. In particular, for each edge $e$ of $S$, it computes the so-called *edge clustering coefficient* of $e$, defined as the ratio of the number of cycles containing $e$ to the maximum number of cycles which could potentially contain it. Next, GN is applied with the edge clustering coefficient (rather than edge betweenness) as the parameter of reference. The most important advantage of this approach is that the computational cost of the edge clustering coefficient is significantly smaller than that of edge betweenness.

All approaches described above use the greedy technique to maximize $Q$. In [48], the authors propose a different approach which maximizes $Q$ by means of the simulated annealing technique. That approach achieves a higher accuracy but can be computationally very expensive.

Palla et al. [75] describes *CFinder*, which, to the best of our knowledge, is the first attempt to find overlapping communities, i.e., communities which may share some nodes. In CFinder, communities are detected by finding cliques of size $k$, where $k$ is a parameter provided by the user. Such a problem is computationally expensive, but experiments showed that it scales well on real networks and it achieves a great accuracy.

The approach of [73] uses a Bayesian probabilistic model to represent an online social network. An interesting feature of [73] is the capability of finding *group structures*, i.e., relationships among the users of a social network which go beyond those characterizing conventional communities. For instance, this approach is capable of detecting groups of users who show forms of aversion with each other rather than just users who are willing to interact. Experimental comparisons of various approaches to finding communities in OSNs are reported in [35, 65].

In [55], the authors propose CHRONICLE, an algorithm to find time-evolving communities in a social network. CHRONICLE operates in two stages: in the first one, it considers $T$ "snapshots" of the social network in correspondence of $T$ different timestamps. For each timestamp, it applies a density-based clustering algorithm on each snapshot to find communities in the social network. After this, it builds a $T$-partite graph $G_T$ which consists of $T$ layers each containing the communities of nodes detected in the corresponding timestamp. It adds also some edges linking adjacent layers: they indicate that two communities, detected in correspondence of consecutive timestamps, share some similarities. As a consequence, the edges and the paths in $G_T$ identify similarities among communities over time.

## *Influential User Detection*

A recent trend in OSN analysis is the identification of *influential users* [40, 74]. Influential users are those capable of stimulating others to join OSN activities and/or to actively contribute to them.

In Weblog (blog) analysis, there is a special emphasis on so-called *leader identification*. In particular, Song et al. [87] suggested to model the blogosphere as a graph (whose nodes represent bloggers whereas edges model the fact that a blogger cites another one). In [66], the authors introduce the concept of *starter,* i.e., a user who first generates information that catches the interest of fellow users/readers. Among others, the approach of [66] has deployed the *Random Walk* technique to find starters. Researchers from HP Labs analyzed user behaviors on Twitter [82]; they found that influential users should not only catch attention from other users but they should also overcome the passivity of other users and spur them to get involved in OSN activities. To this purpose, they developed an algorithm (based on the HITS algorithm of [57]) to assess the degree of influence of a user. Experimental results show that high levels of popularity of a user do not necessarily imply high values in the degree of influence.

## Sampling the Facebook Social Graph

Our work on OSN analysis began with the goal to understand the organization of popular OSN, and as of 2010 Facebook was by far the largest and most studied. Facebook gathers more than 500 million active users, and its growth rate has been proved to be the highest among all the other competitors in the last few years. More than 50% of users log on to the platform in any given day. Coarse statistics about the usage of the social network is provided by the company itself.[1] Our study is interested in analyzing the characteristics and the properties of this network on a large scale. In order to reach this goal, first of all we had to acquire data from this platform, and later we proceed to their analysis.

---

[1] Please refer to http://www.facebook.com/press/info.php?statistics

## *The Structure of the Social Network*

The structure of the Facebook social network is simple. Each subscribed user can be connected to others via friendship relationships. The concept of friendship is *bilateral*, this means that users must confirm the relationships among them. Connections among users do not follow any particular hierarchy, thus we define the social network as *unimodal*.

This network can be represented as a graph $G = (V, E)$ whose nodes $V$ represent users and edges $E$ represent friendship connections among them. Because of the assumption on the bilateralness of relationships, the graph is *undirected*. Moreover, the graph we consider is *unweighted*, because all the friendship connections have the same value within the network. However, it could be possible to assign a weight to each friendship relation, for instance, considering the frequency of interaction between each pair of users, or different criteria. Considering the assumption that loops are not allowed, we conclude that in our case it is possible to use a simple unweighted undirected graph to represent the Facebook social network. The adoption of this model has been proved to be optimal for several social networks (see [45]).

Although choosing the model for representing a network could appear to be simple, this phase is important and could not be trivial. Compared to Facebook, the structure of other social networks requires a more complex representative model. For example, Twitter should be represented using a *multiplex* network; this is because it introduces different types of connections among users ("following," "reply to" and "mention") [83]. Similar considerations hold for other OSNs, such as aNobii [5], Flickr, and YouTube [69].

### How to Get Information About the Structure of the Network

One important aspect to be considered for representing the model of a social network is the amount of information about its structure we have access to. The ideal condition would be to have access to the whole network data, for example acquiring them directly from the company which manages the social networking service. For several reasons (see further), most of the time this solution is not viable.

Another option is to obtain data required to reconstruct the model of the network, acquiring them directly from the platform itself, exploiting its public interface. In other words, a viable solution is to collect a representative sample of the network to correctly represent its structure. To this purpose, it is possible to exploit web data mining techniques [34] to extract data from the front-end of the social network websites. This implies that, for very large OSNs, such as Facebook, Twitter, etc., it is hard or even impossible to collect a complete sample of the network. The first limitation is related to the computational overhead of a large-scale web mining task. In the case of Facebook, for example, to crawl the friend-list web page (dimension $\simeq 200$ KB) for the half billion users, it would approximately require to download more than $200\,\text{KB} \cdot 500\,\text{M} = 100\,\text{Tb}$ of HTML data. Even if possible, the acquired sample would be a snapshot of the structure of the graph at the time of the mining process. Moreover, during the sampling process, the structure of the network slightly changes. This is because, even if short, the data mining process requires a nonnegligible time, during which the connections among users evolve, thus the social network, and its structure, changes accordingly. For example, the growth rate of Facebook has been estimated in the order of 0.2% per day [42]. In other words, neither all these efforts could ensure to acquire a perfect sample. For these reasons, a widely adopted approach is to collect small samples of a network, trying to preserve characteristics about its structure. There are several different sampling techniques that can be exploited; each algorithm ensures different performances, bias of data, etc.

For our experimentation we collected two significant samples of the structure of the social network, of a size comparable to other similar studies [24, 42, 92]. In particular, we adopted two different sampling algorithms, namely, "breadth-first-search" and "Uniform." The first is proved to introduce bias in certain conditions (e.g., in incomplete visits) toward high-degree nodes [59]. The latter is proved to be unbiased by construction [42].

Once collected, data are compared and analyzed in order to establish their quality, study their properties and characteristics. We consider two quality criteria to evaluate the samples: (1) coherency with statistical data provided by the social network itself; (2) congruency with results reported by similar studies. Considerations about the characteristics of both the "breadth-first-search" and the "Uniform" samples follow in section "Experimental Work."

## How to Extract Data from Facebook

Companies providing online social networking services, such as Facebook, Twitter, etc., do not have economic interests in sharing their data about users, because their business model mostly relies on advertising. For example, exploiting this information, Facebook provides unique and efficient services to advertising companies. Moreover, questions about the protection of these data have been advanced, for privacy reasons, in particular for Facebook [47, 67].

In this social network, for example, information about users and the interconnections among them, their activities, etc. can only be accessed through the interface of the platform. To preserve this condition some constraints have been implemented. Among others, a limit is imposed to the amount of information accessible from profiles of users not in friendship relations among them. There are also some technical limitations, e.g., the friend list is dispatched through an asynchronous script, so as to prevent naive techniques of crawling. Some web services, such as the "Graph API,"[2] have been provided during the last few months of 2010,

---

[2] Available from http://developers.facebook.com/docs/api

**Fig. 12.1** Architecture of the data mining platform

by the Facebook developers team, but they do not bypass these limitations (and they eventually add even more restrictions). As of 2010, the structure of this social network can be accessed only exploiting techniques typical of web data mining.

## The Sampling Architecture

In order to collect data from the Facebook platform, we designed a web data mining architecture, which is composed of the following elements (see Fig. 12.1): (1) a server running the mining agent(s); (2) a cross-platform Java application, which implements the logic of the agent; and (3) an Apache interface, which manages the information transfer through the web. While running, the agent(s) query the Facebook server(s) obtaining the friend-list web pages of specific requested users (this aspect depends on the implemented sampling algorithm), reconstructing the structure of relationships among them. Collected data are stored on the server and, after a postprocessing step (see section "Data Preparation"), they are delivered (eventually represented using an XML standard format [21]) for further experimentation.

### The Facebook Crawler

The cross-platform Java agent which crawls the Facebook front end is the core of our mining platform. The logic of the developed agent, regardless of the sampling algorithm implemented, is depicted in Fig. 12.2. The first preparative step for the agent execution includes choosing the sampling methodology and configuring some technical parameters, such as termination criterion/a, maximum running time, etc. Thus, the crawling task can start or be resumed from a previous point. During its execution, the crawler visits the friend-list page of a user, following the chosen sampling algorithm directives, for traversing the social graph. Data about new discovered nodes and connections among them are stored in a compact format, in order to save I/O operations. The process of crawling concludes when the termination criterion/a is/are met.

**Fig. 12.2** State diagram of the data mining process

**Table 12.1** HTTP requests flow of the crawler: authentication and mining steps

| Number | Action Protocol Method URL | KB |
|---|---|---|
| 1 | Open the Facebook page | |
| | HTTP    GET    www.facebook.com/ | 242 |
| 2 | Login providing credentials | |
| | HTTPS   POST   login.facebook.com/login.php | 234 |
| | HTTP    GET    /home.php | 87 |
| 3 | Visit the friend-list page of a specific user | |
| | HTTP    GET    /friends/ajax/friends.php?id=#&filter=afp | 224 |

During the data mining step, the platform exploits the Apache HTTP Request Library[3] to communicate with the Facebook server(s). After an authentication phase which uses a secure connection and "cookies" for logging into the Facebook platform, HTML friend-list web pages are obtained via HTTP requests. This process is described in Table 12.1.

## Limitations

During the data mining task we noticed a technical limitation imposed by Facebook on the dimension of the dispatched friend-list web pages, via HTTP requests. To reduce the traffic through its network, Facebook provides shortened friend lists not exceeding 400 friends. During a normal experience of navigation on the website, if the dimension of the friend-list web page exceeds 400 friends, an asynchronous script fills the page with the remaining. This result is not reproducible using an agent based on HTTP requests. This problem can be avoided using a different mining approach, for example adopting visual data extraction techniques [34]. Data can be retrieved directly from the web page using specific scripts designed for a web browser, or alternatively by developing an agent which integrates a web browser for rendering the pages. This approach is not viable for large-scale mining tasks, but we already dealt with this approach in [22] for a smaller experimentation. In section "Degree Distribution," we investigated the impact of this limitation on the samples.

---

[3]http://httpd.apache.org/apreq

## *Breadth-First-Search Sampling*

The breadth-first-search (BFS) is an uninformed traversal algorithm which aims to visit a graph. Starting from a "seed node," it explores its neighborhood; then, for each neighbor, it visits its unexplored neighbors, and so on, until the whole graph is visited (or, alternatively, if a termination criterion is met). This sampling technique shows several advantages: (1) ease of implementation; (2) optimal solution for unweighted graphs; (3) efficiency. For these reasons, it has been adopted in a variety of OSN mining studies, including [22, 24, 42, 69, 92, 93]. In the last year, the hypothesis that the BFS algorithm produces biased data, toward high-degree nodes, if adopted for partial graph traversal, has been advanced by [59]. This is because, in the same (partial) graph, obtained adopting a BFS visiting algorithm, are both represented nodes which have been visited (high-degree nodes) and nodes which have just been discovered, as neighbors of visited ones (low-degree nodes). One important aspect of our experimentation has been to verify this hypothesis, in order to highlight which properties of a partial graph obtained using the BFS sampling are preserved, and which are biased. To do so, we had to acquire a comparable sample which is certainly unbiased by construction (see further).

### Description of the Breadth-First-Search Crawler

The BFS sampling methodology is implemented as one of the possible visiting algorithms in our Facebook crawler, described before. While using this algorithm, the crawler, for first, extracts the friend list of the "seed node," which is represented by the user actually logged on to the Facebook platform. The user-IDs of contacts in its friend-list are stored in a FIFO queue. Then, the friend lists of these users are visited, and so on. In our experimentation, the process continued until two termination criteria have been met: (1) at least the third sublevel of friendship was completely covered; (2) the mining process exceeded 240 h of running time. As discussed before, the time constraint is adopted in order to observe a short mining interval; thus the temporal evolution of the network is minimal (in the order of 2%) and can be ignored. The obtained graph is a partial reconstruction of the Facebook network structure, and its dimension is used as a yardstick for configuring the "Uniform" sampling (see further).

### Characteristics of the Breadth-First-Search Dataset

This crawler has been executed during the first part of August 2010. The acquired sample covers about 12 million friendship connections among about 8 million users. Among these users, we performed the complete visit of about 63.4 thousands of them, thus resulting in an average degree $\overline{d} = \frac{2 \cdot |E|}{|V_v|} \simeq 396.4$, considering $V$ as the number of *visited users*.

**Table 12.2** BFS dataset description (crawling period: 08/2001 to 10/2010)

| No. of visited users | | No. of discovered neighbors | | | No. of edges | |
|---|---|---|---|---|---|---|
| 63.4K | | 8.21M | | | 12.58M | |
| Avg. deg. | Bigg. eigenval. | Eff. diam. | Avg. clust. coef. | | Coverage | Density |
| 396.8 | 68.93 | 8.75 | 0.0789 | | 98.98% | 0.626% |

The overall mean degree, considering $V$ as the number of *total nodes* on the graph (*visited users + discovered neighbors*), is $\bar{o} = \frac{2 \cdot |E|}{|V_t|} \simeq 3.064$. The expected density of the graph is $\Delta = \frac{2 \cdot |E|}{|V_v| \cdot (|V_v|-1)} \simeq 0.006259 \simeq 0.626\%$, considering V as the number of visited nodes. We can combine the previous equations obtaining $\Delta = \frac{\bar{d}}{|V_v|-1}$. It means that the expected density of a graph is the average proportion of edges incident with nodes in the graph.

In our case, the value $\delta = \frac{\bar{o}}{\bar{d}} = \frac{|V_v|}{|V_t|} \simeq 0.007721 \simeq 0.772\%$, which here we introduce, represents the effective density of the obtained graph.

The distance among the effective and the expected density of the graph, which here we introduce, is computed as $\partial = 100 - \frac{\Delta * 100}{\delta} \simeq 18.94\%$.

This result means that the obtained graph is slightly more connected than expected, w.r.t. the number of unique users it contains. This consideration is also compatible with hypothesis advanced in [59]. The effective diameter of this (partial) graph is 8.75, which is compliant with the "six degrees of separation" theory [10, 68, 72, 88].

The coverage of the graph is almost complete (99.98%). The small amount of disconnected nodes can be intuitively adducted due to some collisions caused by the hash function exploited to de-duplicate and anonymize user-IDs adopted during the data cleaning step (see section "Data Preparation"). Some interesting considerations hold for the obtained clustering coefficient result. It lies in the lower part of the interval [0.05, 0.18] reported by [42] and, similarly, [0.05, 0.35] by [92], using the same sampling methodology. The characteristics of the collected sample are summarized in Table 12.2.

## Uniform Sampling

To acquire a comparable sample, unbiased for construction, we exploited a rejection sampling methodology. This technique has been applied to Facebook in [42], where the authors proved its correctness. Its efficiency relies on the following assumptions:

1. It is possible to generate uniform sampling values for the domain of interest.
2. These values are not sparse w.r.t. the dimension of the domain.
3. It is possible to sample these values from the domain.

In Facebook, each user is identified by a 32-bit number user-ID. Considering that user-IDs lie in the interval $[0, 2^{32} - 1]$, the highest possible number of assignable user-IDs using this system is $H \simeq 4.295e9$.

The space for names is currently filling up since the actual number of assigned user-IDs, $R \simeq 5.4e8$ roughly equals to the 540 million of currently subscribed users[4,5], the two domains are comparable and the rejection sampling is viable. We generated an arbitrary number of random 32-bit user-IDs, querying Facebook for their existence (and, eventually, obtaining their friend lists). That sampling methodology shows two advantages: (1) we can statistically estimate the probability $\frac{R}{H} \simeq 12.5\%$ of getting an existing user and (2) we can generate an arbitrary number of user-IDs in order to acquire a sample of the desired dimension. Moreover, the distribution of user-IDs is completely independent w.r.t. the graph structure.

### Description of the "Uniform" Crawler

The "Uniform" sampling is another algorithm implemented in the Facebook crawler we developed. Differently w.r.t. the BFS sampler, if adopting this algorithm, it is possible to parallelize the process of extraction. This is because user-IDs to be requested can be stored in different "queues." We designed the uniform sampling task starting from these assumptions: (1) the number of subscribed users is $2^{29} \simeq 5.368e8$; (2) this value is comparable with the highest possible assignable number of user-IDs, $2^{32} \simeq 4.295e9$, and (3) we can statistically assert that the possibility of querying Facebook for an existing user-ID is $\frac{2^{29}}{2^{32}} = \frac{1}{8}$ (12.5%). For this purpose, we generated eight different queues, each containing $2^{16} \simeq 65.5K \cong 63.4K$ random user-IDs (the number of visited users of the BFS sample), used to feed eight parallel crawlers.

### Characteristics of the "Uniform" Dataset

The uniform sampling process has been executed during the second part of August 2010. The crawler collected a sample which contains almost eight million friendship connections among a similar number of users. The acquired amount of nodes differs from the expected number due to the privacy policy adopted by those users who prevent their friend-lists being visited. The privacy policy aspect is discussed in section "Privacy Settings."

The total number of visited users has been about 48.1 thousand, thus resulting in an average degree of $\overline{d} = \frac{2 \cdot |E|}{|V_v|} \simeq 326.0$, considering $V$ as the number of *visited users*. Same assumptions, the expected density of the graph is $\Delta = \frac{2 \cdot |E|}{|V_v| \cdot (|V_v|-1)} \simeq 0.006777 \simeq 0.678\%$.

---

[4]As of August 2010, http://www.facebook.com/press/info.php?statistics
[5]http://www.google.com/adplanner/static/top1000/

If we consider $V$ as the number of *total nodes* (*visited users* + *discovered neighbors*), the overall mean degree is $\overline{o} = \frac{2 \cdot |E|}{|V_t|} \simeq 2.025$. The effective density of the graph, previously introduced, is $\delta = \frac{|V_v|}{|V_t|} \simeq 0.006214 \simeq 0.621\%$. The distance among the effective and the expected density of the graph, is $\partial = 100 - \frac{\Delta * 100}{\delta} \simeq -9.06\%$. This can be intuitively interpreted as a slight lack of connection of this sample w.r.t. the theoretical expectation.

Some considerations hold, also comparing against the BFS sample: the average degree is slightly less (326.0 vs. 396.8), but the effective diameter is almost the double (16.32 vs. 8.75). We justify this characteristic considering that the sample could be still too small and disconnected to perfectly reflect the structure of the network. Our hypothesis is also supported by the dimension of the largest connected component, which does not contain the 5% of the sample. Finally, the clustering coefficient, less than the BFS sample (0.0471 vs. 0.0789), is still comparable w.r.t. previously considered studies [42, 92].

## Data Preparation

During the data mining process, it could happen to store redundant information. In particular, while extracting friend-lists, a crawler could save multiple instances of the same edge (i.e., a parallel edge), if both the connected users are visited; this is because the graph is undirected. We adopted a hashing-based algorithm which cleans data in $O(N)$ time, removing duplicate edges. Another step, during the data preparation, is the *anonymization*: user-IDs are "encrypted" adopting a 48-bit hybrid rotative and additive hash function [77], to obtain anonymized datasets. The final touch was to verify the integrity and the congruency of data. We found that the usage of the hashing function caused occasional collisions (0.0002%). Finally, some datasets of small sub-graphs (e.g., ego-networks) have been postprocessed and stored using the GraphML format [21].

## Network Analysis Aspects

During the last years, important achievements have been reached in understanding the structural properties of several complex real networks. The availability of large-scale empirical data, on the one hand, and the advances in computational resources, on the other, made it possible to discover and understand interesting statistical properties commonly shared among different real-world social, biological and technological networks. Among others, some important examples are: the World Wide web [6], Internet [32], metabolic networks [54], scientific collaboration networks [11, 70], citation networks [81], etc. Indeed, during the last years, even the social networks are strongly imposing themselves as complex networks described by very specific models and properties. For example, some studies [8, 68, 88] proved the existence of the so-called "small-world" property in complex social networks.

Others [2, 76] assert that the so-called "scale-free" complex networks reflect a "power-law" distribution as model for describing the behavior of node degrees. We can conclude that the topology of the networks usually provides useful information about the dynamics of the network entities and the interaction among them.

In addition to contributing to the advances in *graph theory*, the study of complex networks led to important results also in some specific contexts, such as the *social sciences*. A branch of the network analysis applied to *social sciences* is the *Social Network Analysis* (SNA). From a different perspective w.r.t. the analysis of complex networks, which mainly aims to analyze structural properties of networks, the SNA focuses on studying the nature of relationships among entities of the network and, in the case of social networks, investigating the motivational aspect of these connections.

In this section, we will briefly describe properties and models characterizing the structure of complex networks (see sections "Definitions" and "Networks Models"); then we will focus on defining measures and metrics property of SNA (see section "Social Network Analysis") and, while concluding, we will consider some interesting aspects regarding the visualization of related graphs (see section "Visualizing Social Networks").

## *Definitions*

In this section, we describe some of the common structural properties which are usually observed in several complex networks and define the way they are measured. Then, we describe concepts about the mathematical modeling of networks, including random graph models and their generalizations, the "small-world" model and its variations, and models of growth and evolution of graphs, including the preferential attachment models.

### Shortest Path Lengths, Diameter, and Betweenness

Let $G = (V, E)$ be a graph representing a network; the distance $d_{ij}$ between two nodes, labeled $i$ and $j$, respectively, is defined as the number of edges along the shortest path connecting them. The diameter $D$ of the network represented by $G$, therefore, is defined to be the maximal distance among all distances between any pair of nodes in the network.

A common measure of distance between two nodes of the graph $G$, is given by the *average shortest path length* [90, 91] (also called *characteristic path length*), defined as the mean value of the geodesic distance (i.e., the shortest path) between the all-pairs node of the graph (a.k.a. the "all-pairs-shortest-path problem" [84]):

$$\ell = \frac{1}{N(N-1)} \sum_{i \neq j} d_{ij} \qquad (12.3)$$

The main problem adopting this definition is that $\ell$ diverges if the graph contains disconnected components. A possible solution to this issue is to limit the domain of the summation in Eq. 12.3 only to the pairs of nodes belonging to the largest connected component of the graph.

Several metrics have been defined to compute the centrality of a node within a graph, such as the degree, closeness, and the betweenness centrality. The latter one has been originally introduced to quantitatively evaluate the importance of an individual in a network [60,89] and is recognized to be the most appropriate measure to reflect the concept of centrality in a network. The betweenness centrality of a node was defined by Freeman [36,37] as in Eq. 12.2. Correlations "betweenness-vs.-betweenness" and "betweenness-vs.-degree" have been investigated, respectively, by authors of Refs. [43] and [26, 44, 49]. In section "Betweenness Centrality in Facebook," we will focus on analyzing this metric calculated on the Facebook graph, for reasons further explained.

## Clustering

In several networks, it is shown that if a node $i$ is connected to a node $j$, which in its turn is connected to a node $k$, then there is a heightened probability that node $i$ will be also connected to node $k$. From a social network perspective, a friend of your friend is likely also to be your friend. In terms of network topology, transitivity means the presence of a heightened number of triangles in the network, which constitute sets of three nodes connected to each other [71]. The global clustering coefficient is defined by

$$C_g = \frac{3 \times \text{no. of triangles in } G}{\text{no. of connected triples}} \tag{12.4}$$

where a *connected triple* represents a pair of nodes connected to another node. $C_g$ is the mean probability that two persons who have a common friend are also friends together. An alternative definition of clustering coefficient $C$ has been provided by Watts and Strogatz [91]. During our experimentation, we investigated the clustering effect on the Facebook network (see section "Diameter and Clustering Coefficient").

## The "Small-World" Property

It is well known in literature that most large-scale networks, despite their huge size, show a common property: there exists a relatively short path which connects any pair of nodes within the network. This characteristic, the so-called *small-world* property, is theoretically supported by the average shortest path length, defined by Eq. 12.3, and it scales proportionally to the logarithm of the dimension of the network. The study of this phenomenon is rooted in *social sciences* [68, 88] and is strictly interconnected with the notion of diameter we introduced before. The Facebook social network reflects the "small-world" property as discussed in section "Diameter and Clustering Coefficient."

**Scale-Free Degree Distributions**

On the one hand, in a random graph (see further), the node degree (i.e., the number of edges the node has) is characterized by a distribution function $P(k)$ which defines the probability that a randomly chosen node has exactly $k$ edges. Because the distribution of edges in a random graph is aleatory, most of the nodes have approximately the same node degree, similar to the mean degree $\langle k \rangle$ of the network. Thus, the degree distribution of a random graph is well described by a Poisson distribution law, with a peak in $P(\langle k \rangle)$. On the other hand, recent empirical results show that in most of the real-world networks the degree distribution significantly differs w.r.t. a Poisson distribution. In particular, for several large-scale networks, such as the World Wide web [6], Internet [32], metabolic networks [54], etc., the degree distribution follows a power law:

$$P(k) \sim k^{-\lambda} \tag{12.5}$$

This power-law distribution falls off more gradually than an exponential one, allowing for a few nodes of very large degree to exist. Since these power laws are free of any characteristic scale, such a network with a power-law degree distribution is called a scale-free network [9]. We proved that Facebook is a scale-free network well described by a power-law degree distribution, as discussed in section "Degree Distribution."

## Network Models

Concepts such as the short path length, the clustering, and the scale-free degree distribution have been recently applied to rigorously model the networks. Three main modeling paradigms exist: (1) random graphs, (2) "small-world" networks, and (3) power-law networks. Random graphs represent an evolution of the Erdős-Rényi model, and are widely used in several empirical studies, because of the ease of adoption. After the discovery of the clustering property, a new class of models, namely, "small-world" networks, has been introduced. Similarly, the power-law degree distribution definition led to the modeling of the homonym networks, which are adopted to describe scale-free behaviors, focusing on the dynamics of the network in order to explain phenomena such as the power-law tails and other non-Poisson degree distribution, empirically shown by real-world networks.

## The Erdős-Rényi Model

Erdős and Rényi [30, 31] proposed one of the first models of network, the random graph. They defined two models: the simple one consists of a graph containing $n$ vertices connected randomly. The commonly adopted model, indeed, is defined as a graph $G_{n,p}$ in which each possible edge between two vertices may be included in the graph with the probability $p$ (and may not be included with the probability $(1 - p)$).

Although random graphs have been widely adopted because their properties ease the work of modeling networks (e.g., random graphs have a small diameter), they do not properly reflect the structure of real-world large-scale networks, mainly for two reasons: (1) the degree distribution of random graphs follows a Poisson law, which substantially differs from the power-law distribution shown by empirical data; (2) they do not reflect the clustering phenomenon, considering all the nodes of the network with the same "weight," and reducing, de facto, the network to a giant cluster.

## The Watts-Strogatz Model

The real-world social networks are well connected and have a short average path length like random graphs, but they also have exceptionally large clustering coefficient, which is not reflected by the Erdős-Rényi model or by other random graph models. In [91], Watts and Strogatz proposed a one-parameter model that interpolates between an ordered finite dimensional lattice and a random graph. Starting from a ring lattice with $n$ vertices and $k$ edges per vertex, each edge is rewired at random with probability $p$ [91].

The model has been widely studied since the details have been published. Its role is important in the study of the small-world theory. Some relevant theories, such as Kleinberg's work [56, 57], are based on this model and its variants. The disadvantage of the model, however, is that it is not able to capture the power-law degree distribution as presented in most real-world social networks.

## The Barabási-Albert Model

The two previously discussed theories observe properties of real-world networks and attempt to create models that incorporate those characteristics. However, they do not help in understanding the origin of social networks and how those properties evolve.

The Barabási-Albert model suggests that two main ingredients of self-organization of a network in a scale-free structure are *growth* and *preferential attachment*. These pinpoint to the facts that most of the networks continuously grow by the addition of new nodes which are preferentially attached to existing nodes with large numbers of connections (again, "rich gets richer"). The generation scheme of a Barabási-Albert scale-free model is as follows: (1) *Growth*: let $p_k$ be the fraction of nodes in the undirected network of size $n$ with degree $k$, so that $\sum_k p_k = 1$ and therefore the mean degree $m$ of the network is $\frac{1}{2} \sum_k k p_k$. Starting with a small number of nodes, at each time step, we add a new node with $m$ edges linked to nodes already part of the system; (2) *preferential attachment*: the probability $\prod_i$ that a new node will be connected to the node $i$ (one of the $m$ already existing nodes) depends on the degree $k_i$ of the node $i$, in such a way that $\prod_i = k_i \sum_j k_j$.

Models based on preferential attachment operates in the following way. Nodes are added one at a time. When a new node $u$ has to be added to the network, it creates $m$ edges ($m$ is a parameter and it is constant for all nodes). The edges are not placed uniformly at random but *preferentially*, i.e., probability that a new edge of $u$ is placed to a node $v$ of degree $d(v)$ is proportional to its degree, $p_u(v) \propto d(v)$. This simple behavior leads to power-law degree tails with exponent $\lambda = 3$. Moreover, it also leads to low diameters. While the model captures the power-law tail of the degree distribution, it has other properties that may or may not agree with empirical results in real networks. Recent analytical research on average path length indicates that $\ell \sim ln(N)/lnln(N)$. Thus the model has much shorter $l$ w.r.t. a random graph. The clustering coefficient decreases with the network size, following approximately a power-law $C \sim N^{-0.75}$. Though greater than those of random graphs, it depends on network size, which is not true for real-world social networks.

## Social Network Analysis

In the previous section, we discussed about the network as a complex system: in particular, complex network theory, by its graph theoretical approach, does not explain the network by its elements' behavior, but it deals with a whole organism that evolves by means of its single components. In this section, instead, we approach the study of that components: SNA deals with the study of the actors involved in a network. It is an approach based on the analysis of the behavior of single entities which are part of the network and govern its evolution. The single components have the possibility of choosing their own connections without considering the network as a whole structure but only w.r.t. individual characteristics. Indeed, almost the totality of social network models deals with the external information on the actors. Social network analysts often use these additional information to explain network formation. This is the principal difference between social network analysis and complex network theory. In the latter, we often disregard the additional information on the single nodes because the attention is pointed out toward a more structural method, namely, a *systemic approach*.

**Metrics**

Metrics allow analysts to systematically dissect the social world, creating a basis on which to compare networks, track changes over the time, and determine the relative position of individuals and clusters within the network [51].

One of the primary uses of *graph theory* in social network analysis is the identification of the most important actors in a social network [89]. The *degree centrality* is a measure of the degree of an actor in a network. An actor with a high-degree centrality is "where the action is" in the network. Thus, this measure focuses on the most visible actors in the network. This actor can be recognized by others as a major channel of relational information. In contrast, actors with low degrees are peripheral in the network.

A second view of centrality is based on *closeness* or distance. This measure focuses on how close an actor is to all the other actors in the network. This idea of centrality based on closeness is inversely related to the distance. As a node grows farther apart in distance from other nodes, its centrality will decrease, since there will be more lines in the geodesics linking that node to the rest [33]. Finally, interactions between two non-adjacent actors might depend on the other actors, especially those lying on the paths between them. These other actors potentially might have some control over the interactions between the two nonadjacent actors. The important idea here is that an actor is central if it lies between other actors on their geodesics. This implies that to have a large *betweenness centrality* [36], the actor must be between many of the actors via their geodesics [91]. Although this centrality has gained popularity because of its generality, this index assumes that all geodesics are equally likely when estimating the critical probability that an actor fall on a particular geodesic. It also ignores the fact that if some actors on the geodesics have large degrees, then the geodesics containing these expansive actors are more likely to be used as shortest paths than other geodesics. Also it would be more realistic to consider betweenness counts which focus on paths other than geodesics. Information centrality generalizes the notion of betweenness centrality, so all paths between actors, with weights depending on their lengths, are considered when calculating the betweenness counts.

## *Visualizing Social Networks*

One of the key elements that characterize modern social network analysis is the visual representation. Looking at a network graph may provide an overview of the structure of the network, calling out cliques, communities, and key participants. Drawings of relational structures like social networks are only useful if they "effectively convey information to the people that use them" [19, 28, 29]. Network visualization is often as frustrating as appealing. Network graphs can rapidly get too dense and large to make out any meaningful patterns. Many obstacles like vertex occlusions and edge crossings make creating well-organized and readable network

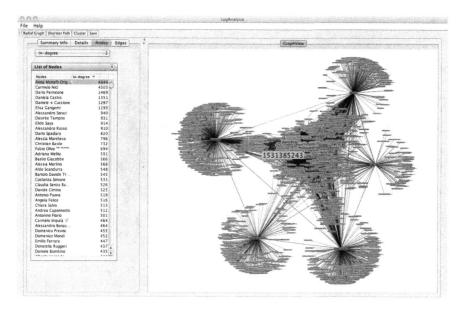

**Fig. 12.3**  N-Body approach with LogAnalysis

graphs challenging. There is an upper limit on the number of vertices and edges that can be displayed in a bounded set of pixels; typically, only a few hundred or thousand vertices can be meaningfully and distinctly represented on average-sized computer screens.

A key reference for better-quality network visualization is the so-called Netviz Nirvana guidelines [79]. Several graph layout algorithms can be used, including variants of the "spring embedder" such as the Harel-Koren [52] fast multi-scale method, the popular Fruchterman-Reingold [38] force-directed algorithm, and more scalable gravitational N-Body approaches (see Figs. 12.3 and 12.4), such as those implemented in *LogAnalysis* [23] and *NodeXL* [51]. The results of applying these algorithms vary depending on the size and topology of the network.

*LogAnalysis* presents social networks using a familiar node-link representation, where nodes represent members of the system and links represent the articulated "friendship" links between them. It integrates statistics proposed by Perer and Shneiderman [78]: overall network metrics (i.e., number of nodes, number of edges, density, diameter), node rankings (i.e., degree, betweenness and closeness centrality), edge rankings (i.e., weight, betweenness centrality), edge rankings in pairs, and cohesive subgroups. Network members are presented using both their self-provided name, ID (e.g., the Facebook user-ID) and, if available, a representative photograph (e.g., the Facebook profile picture). The networks are presented as egocentric networks. Users can expand the display by selecting nodes to make visible others' friends as well. Analysts can also explore a network by focusing on one node, the node's neighbors, and the ties among them and can interactively increase the depth of the neighborhood by dragging a slider bar.

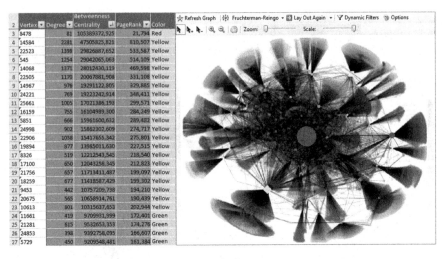

| | Vertex | Degree | Betweenness Centrality | PageRank | Color |
|---|---|---|---|---|---|
| 3 | 8478 | 81 | 105389372,925 | 21,794 | Red |
| 4 | 14584 | 2281 | 47505825,821 | 810,507 | Yellow |
| 5 | 22523 | 1398 | 29826887,652 | 533,587 | Yellow |
| 6 | 545 | 1254 | 29042065,063 | 514,109 | Yellow |
| 7 | 14068 | 1371 | 28012430,119 | 469,598 | Yellow |
| 8 | 22505 | 1170 | 20067881,908 | 331,108 | Yellow |
| 9 | 14967 | 976 | 19291122,805 | 329,885 | Yellow |
| 10 | 24221 | 769 | 19223242,914 | 348,411 | Yellow |
| 11 | 25661 | 1005 | 17021386,193 | 299,571 | Yellow |
| 12 | 16159 | 755 | 16104989,300 | 284,249 | Yellow |
| 13 | 5851 | 666 | 15961600,632 | 289,482 | Yellow |
| 14 | 24998 | 902 | 15862302,609 | 274,717 | Yellow |
| 15 | 22906 | 1038 | 15417655,342 | 275,801 | Yellow |
| 16 | 19894 | 977 | 13985011,630 | 227,515 | Yellow |
| 17 | 8326 | 519 | 12212543,545 | 218,540 | Yellow |
| 18 | 17100 | 650 | 12043258,345 | 212,823 | Yellow |
| 19 | 21756 | 657 | 11713411,487 | 199,097 | Yellow |
| 20 | 18259 | 677 | 11418587,429 | 199,302 | Yellow |
| 21 | 9453 | 442 | 10757209,738 | 194,210 | Yellow |
| 22 | 20675 | 565 | 10658914,761 | 190,439 | Yellow |
| 23 | 10613 | 801 | 10315637,653 | 202,944 | Yellow |
| 24 | 11661 | 419 | 9709931,999 | 172,401 | Green |
| 25 | 21281 | 615 | 9532653,353 | 174,276 | Green |
| 26 | 24853 | 398 | 9392758,095 | 166,607 | Green |
| 27 | 5729 | 450 | 9209548,481 | 161,384 | Green |

**Fig. 12.4** Betweenness centrality and clustering effect in an ego-network of 25K nodes

## Betweenness Centrality in Facebook

The analysis of large ego-networks led us to another interesting consideration on the behavior of the *betweenness centrality* (BC); it goes as follows. Clearly, the more a node is central and *important*, the higher its BC. One could suppose that this measure is directly interconnected with the degree of a node, or with other measures of centrality (e.g., the Pagerank). In Fig. 12.4, we show the behavior of this metric evaluated on an ego-network of about 25,000 of nodes. The following consideration holds: the node which covers the most important position in this network (vertex "8478," in red) does not show "special" properties (e.g., its degree and its Pagerank are lower than most of the other nodes). However, it appears in more than the double of shortest paths w.r.t. the other nodes of the network. Similar considerations hold for other nodes (vertices "24221," "5851," "9453," in yellow, and "11661," "24853," in green) in this particular ranking. Intuitively, nodes with high BC represent a potential efficient way of connection among peripheral nodes.

It is known that the BC distribution follows a power law $p(g) \sim g^{-\eta}$ for scale-free networks [43]. Similarly to the degree exponent case, in general, the BC exponents increase for node and link sampling and decrease for snowball sampling as the sampling fraction gets lower. The correlation between degree and BC of nodes [12], shown in Fig. 12.10 (section "Connected Components"), could explain the same direction of changes of degree and BC exponents.

We can conclude that the study of the betweenness centrality in Facebook is fundamental for all those aspects related to discovering central nodes of the network, and that BC is a numerical property for applications (e.g., for marketing purposes, broadcasting news, etc.).

# Experimental Work

We describe some interesting experimental results as follows. To compute the community profile of a network and its node centrality measures, such as degree and betweenness, we have adopted the Stanford Network Analysis Platform (SNAP) [62], a general-purpose network analysis library.

## *Privacy Settings*

We investigated the adoption of restrictive privacy policies by users: our statistical expectation using the "Uniform" crawler was to acquire $8 \cdot \frac{2^{16}}{2^3} \simeq 65.5\text{K}$ users. Instead, the actual number of collected users was 48.1K. Because of privacy settings chosen by users, the discrepancy between the expected number of acquired users and the actual number was about 26.6%. In other words, only a quarter of Facebook users adopt privacy policies which prevent other users (except for those in their friendship network) from visiting their friend-list.

## *Degree Distribution*

A first description of the network topology of the Facebook friendship graph can be obtained from the degree distribution. According to Eq. 12.5, a relatively small number of nodes exhibit a very large number of links. An alternative approach involves the Complementary Cumulative Distribution Function (CCDF)

$$\wp(k) = \int_k^\infty P(k')dk' \sim k^{-\alpha} \sim k^{-(\gamma-1)} \tag{12.6}$$

When calculated for a complete graph, CCDF shows up as a straight line in a log-log plot, while the exponent of the power-law distribution only varies the height (not the shape) of the curve.

In Fig. 12.5 is plotted the degree distribution, as obtained from the BFS and "Uniform" sampling techniques. The limitations due to the dimensions of the cache which contains the friend-lists, upper bounded to 400, are evident. The BFS sample introduces an overestimate of the degree distribution in the left and the right part of the curves. The CCDF is shown, for the same sample, in Fig. 12.6.

## *Diameter and Clustering Coefficient*

It is well known that most real-world graphs exhibit a relatively small diameter. A graph has diameter $D$ if every pair of nodes can be connected by a path of length

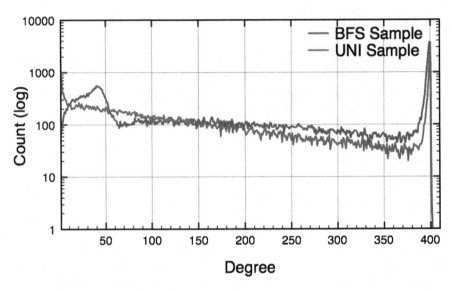

Fig. 12.5 Degree distribution

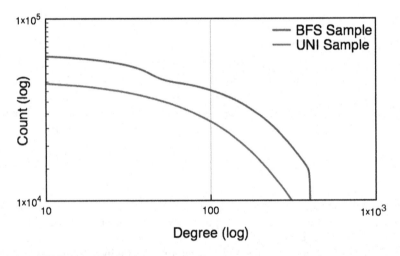

Fig. 12.6 CCDF degree distribution

of at most $D$ edges. The diameter $D$ may be affected by outliers (again, the small-world phenomenon). A robust measure of the pairwise distances between nodes in a graph is the effective diameter, which is the minimum number of links (steps/hops) within which some fraction (or quantile q, say $q = 0.9$) of all connected pairs of nodes can reach each other. The effective diameter has been found to be small for large real-world graphs, like Internet and the web, real-life and OSNs [7, 64, 68].

The hop-plot package extends the notion of diameter by plotting the number of reachable pairs $g(h)$ within $h$ hops, as a function of the number of hops $h$ [76].

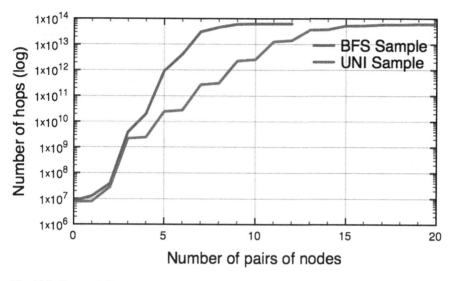

**Fig. 12.7** Hops and diameter

It gives us a sense of how quickly the neighborhoods of nodes expand with the number of hops. In Fig. 12.7, the number of hops necessary to connect any pair of nodes is plotted as a function of the number of pairs of nodes. As a consequence of the more "compact" structure of the graph, the BFS sample shows a faster convergence to the asymptotic value listed in Table 12.2.

The clustering coefficient of a node is the ratio of the number of existing links over the number of possible links between its neighbors.

Given a network $G = (V, E)$, a clustering coefficient, $C_i$, of node $i \in V$ is:

$$C_i = 2|\{(v, w)|(i, v), (i, w), (v, w) \in E\}|/k_i(k_i - 1) \qquad (12.7)$$

where $k_i$ is the degree of node $i$. It can be interpreted as the probability that any two nodes that share a common neighbor have a link between them. The clustering coefficient of a node represents how well connected its neighbors are. For any node in a tightly connected mesh network, the clustering coefficient is 1. The clustering coefficient of a network is the mean clustering coefficient of all nodes.

Often, it is insightful to examine not only the mean clustering coefficient (see section "Clustering"), but its distribution. In Fig. 12.4, it is possible to clearly identify the clustering effect of a Facebook subgraph, visually enhanced by applying several iterations of the Fruchterman-Reingold algorithm [38]. Figure 12.8 shows the average clustering coefficient plotted as a function of the node degree for the two sampling techniques. As a consequence of the more systematic approach of extraction, the distribution of the clustering coefficient of the BFS sample shows a smooth behavior.

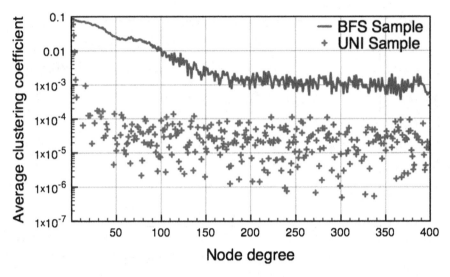

**Fig. 12.8** Clustering coefficient

**Table 12.3** "Uniform" dataset description (crawling period: 08/2011 to 20/2010)

| No. of visited users | | No. of discovered neighbors | | | | No. of edges |
|---|---|---|---|---|---|---|
| 48.1K | | 7.69M | | | | 7.84M |

| Avg. deg. | Bigg. eigenval. | Eff. diam. | Avg. clust. coef. | Coverage | Density |
|---|---|---|---|---|---|
| 326.0 | 23.63 | 16.32 | 0.0471 | 94.96% | 0.678 % |

The following considerations hold for the diameter and hops: the BFS sample may be affected by the "wavefront expansion" behavior of the visiting algorithm, while the "Uniform" sample may still be too small to represent a faithful estimate of the diameter (this hypothesis is supported by the dimension of the largest connected component which does not cover the whole graph, as discussed in the next paragraph). Different conclusions can be derived for the clustering coefficient property. It is important to observe that the average values of the two samples fluctuate in the same interval reported by recent similar studies on OSNs (i.e., [0.05, 0.18] by Wilson et al. [92], [0.05, 0.35] by Gjoka et al. [42]), thus confirming that this property is preserved by both the adopted sampling techniques.

## Connected Components

A connected component is a maximal set of nodes where for each pair of nodes there exists a path connecting them. Analogously, directed graphs show weakly and strongly connected components.

As shown in Tables 12.2 and 12.3, the largest connected components cover the 99.98% of the BFS graph and the 94.96% of the "Uniform" graph. In Fig. 12.9,

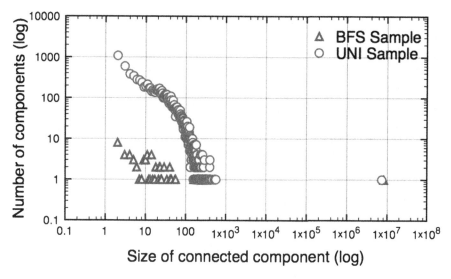

**Fig. 12.9** Connected components

the scattered points in the left part of the plot have a different meaning for each sampling techniques. In the "Uniform" case, the sampling picked up disconnected nodes. In the BFS case, disconnected nodes are meaningless, as they are due to some collisions of the hashing function during the de-duplication phase of the data-cleaning step. This interpretation is supported by their small number (29 collisions over 12.58 millions of hashed edges) involving only 0.02% of the total edges. However, the quality of the sample is not affected.

These conclusions are confirmed in Fig. 12.10, where the betweenness centrality is plotted as a function of the degree. In the right part of the plot, the betweenness centrality shows a linearly proportional behavior w.r.t. the degree. In our opinion, this implies a high degree of connectedness of the sample, since a high value of betweenness centrality is related to a high value of the degree of the nodes.

## Conclusions

The success of OSNs and the growth of their user base is of great interest to both social and computer science. Extraction and analysis of OSN data describing social networks pose both a technological challenge and an interpretation challenge. We have presented here our long-term research project on social network analysis and our two implemented systems: the ad hoc Facebook crawler and the LogAnalysis tool for analysis and visualization.

The ad hoc Facebook crawler has been developed to comply with the increasingly strict terms of Facebook end-user license, i.e., to create large, fully anonymous

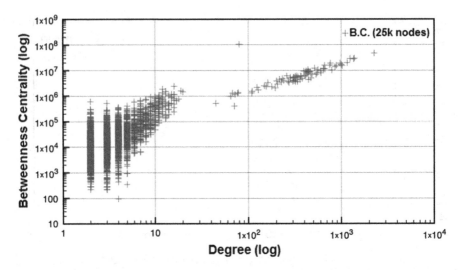

**Fig. 12.10** Betweenness centrality vs degree (on an ego-network of 25K nodes)

samples that can be employed for scientific purposes. Two different sampling techniques have been implemented in order to explore the graph of friendships of Facebook, since the BFS visiting algorithm is known to introduce a bias in case of an incomplete visit.

Analysis of such large samples was tackled using concepts and algorithms typical of the *graph theory*, namely, users were represented by nodes of a graph and relations among users were represented by edges. Our *LogAnalysis* tools support OSN analysis and give a graphical visualization of key graph theory and social network analysis concepts: degree distribution, diameter, centrality metrics, clustering coefficient computation, and eigenvalues distribution. Future developments involve the implementation of different sampling techniques (e.g., Monte Carlo Random Walks) in order to speed up the data extraction process and the evaluation of network metrics.

**Acknowledgements** We appreciated the encouragement and comments of Robert Baumgartner, Georg Gottlob, Christian Schallhart, and Domenico Ursino.

## References

1. Adamic, L., Adar, E.: Friends and neighbors on the web. Soc. Netw. **25**(3), 211–230 (2003)
2. Adamic, L., et al.: Power-law distribution of the world wide web. Science **287**(5461), 2115 (2000)
3. Adomavicius, G., Tuzhilin, A.: Toward the next generation of recommender systems: a survey of the state-of-the-art and possible extensions. IEEE Trans. Knowl. Data Eng. **17**(6), 734–749 (2005)

4. Ahn, Y., Han, S., Kwak, H., Moon, S., Jeong, H.: Analysis of topological characteristics of huge online social networking services. In: Proceedings of the 16th International Conference on the World Wide Web, pp. 835–844. ACM, Banff, AB, Canada (2007)
5. Aiello, L.M., Barrat, A., Cattuto, C., Ruffo, G., Schifanella, R.: Link creation and profile alignment in the aNobii social network. In: Proceedings of the 2nd IEEE International Conference on Social Computing, pp. 249–256. Minneapolis, MN, USA (2010)
6. Albert, R.: Diameter of the world wide web. Nature **401**(6749), 130 (1999)
7. Albert, R., Barabási, A.: Statistical mechanics of complex networks. Rev. Mod. Phys. **74**(1), 47–97 (2002)
8. Amaral, L., Scala, A., Barthélémy, M., Stanley, H.: Classes of small-world networks. Proc. Natl. Acad. Sci. **97**(21), 11149 (2000)
9. Barabási, A., Albert, R.: Emergence of scaling in random networks. Science **286**(5439), 509 (1999)
10. Barabási, A., Crandall, R.: Linked: the new science of networks. Am. J. Phys. **71**, 409 (2003)
11. Barabási, A., Jeong, H., Néda, Z., Ravasz, E., Schubert, A., Vicsek, T.: Evolution of the social network of scientific collaborations. Phy. A Stat. Mech. Appl. **311**(3–4), 590–614 (2002)
12. Barthelemy, M.: Betweenness centrality in large complex networks. Eur. Phys. J. B **38**, 163–168 (2004)
13. Batagelj, V., Doreian, P., Ferligoj, A.: An optimizational approach to regular equivalence. Soc. Netw. **14**(1–2), 121–135 (1992)
14. Blondel, V., Gajardo, A., Heymans, M., Senellart, P., van Dooren, P.: A measure of similarity between graph vertices: applications to synonym extraction and web searching. SIAM Rev. **46**(4), 647–666 (2004)
15. Blondel, V., Guillaume, J., Lambiotte, R., Lefebvre, E.: Fast unfolding of communities in large networks. J. Stat. Mech. **10**, P10008 (2008)
16. Boldi, P., Rosa, M., Santini, M., Vigna, S.: Layered label propagation: a multiresolution coordinate-free ordering for compressing social networks. In: Proceedings of the 20th International Conference on World Wide Web. ACM Press, Hyderabad, India (2011)
17. Boldi, P., Vigna, S.: The WebGraph framework I: compression techniques. In: Proceedings of the 13th International World Wide Web Conference, pp. 595–601. ACM Press, New York, NY, USA (2004)
18. Borgatti, S.P., Everett, M.G.: Models of core/periphery structures. Soc. Netw. **21**(4), 375–395 (2000)
19. Boyer, J.M., Myrvold, W.J.: On the cutting edge: simplified on planarity by edge addition. J. Graph Algorithms Appl. **8**(3), 241–273 (2004)
20. Brandes, U., Delling, D., Gaertler, M., Gorke, R., Hoefer, M., Nikoloski, Z., Wagner, D.: On modularity clustering. IEEE Trans. Knowl. Data Eng. **20**(2), 172–188 (2008)
21. Brandes, U., Eiglsperger, M., Herman, I., Himsolt, M., Marshall, M.: GraphML progress report structural layer proposal. In: Graph Drawing, pp. 109–112. Berlin, Springer (2002)
22. Catanese, S., De Meo, P., Ferrara, E., Fiumara, G.: Analyzing the facebook friendship graph. In: Proceedings of the 1st International Workshop on Mining the Future Internet, pp. 14–19. Berlin, Germany (2010)
23. Catanese, S., Fiumara, G.: A visual tool for forensic analysis of mobile phone traffic. In: Proceedings of the 2nd ACM Workshop on Multimedia in Forensics, pp. 71–76. ACM, Florence, Italy (2010)
24. Chau, D., Pandit, S., Wang, S., Faloutsos, C.: Parallel crawling for online social networks. In: Proceedings of the 16th International Conference on the World Wide Web, pp. 1283–1284. Banff, AB, Canada (2007)
25. Clauset, A., Newman, M., Moore, C.: Finding community structure in very large networks. Phys. Rev. E **70**(6), 066111 (2004)
26. Crucitti, P., Latora, V., Marchiori, M.: A topological analysis of the Italian electric power grid. Phys. A **338**, 92–97 (2004)
27. De Meo, P., Ferrara, E., Fiumara, G.: Finding similar users in facebook. In: Social Networking and Community Behavior Modeling. IGI Publisher, Hershey, Pennsylvania, USA (2011)

28. Di Battista, G., Eades, P., Tamassia, R., Tollis, I.: Algorithms for drawing graphs: an annotated bibliography. Comput. Geom. **4**(5), 235–282 (1994)
29. Di Battista, G., Eades, P., Tamassia, R., Tollis, I.: Graph Drawing: Algorithms for the Visualization of Graphs. Prentice Hall, Upper Saddle River (1998)
30. Erdős, P., Rényi, A.: On random graphs. Pub. Math. **6**(26), 290–297 (1959)
31. Erdős, P., Rényi, A.: On the evolution of random graphs. In: Publication of the Mathematical Institute of the Hungarian Academy of Sciences (1960)
32. Faloutsos, M., Faloutsos, P., Faloutsos, C.: On power-law relationships of the internet topology. In: ACM SIGCOMM Computer Communication Review, vol. 29, pp. 251–262. ACM, New York (1999)
33. Faust, K., Wasserman, S.: Centrality and prestige: a review and synthesis. J. Quant. Anthr. **4**(1985), 23–78 (1992)
34. Ferrara, E., Fiumara, G., Baumgartner, R.: Web data extraction, applications and techniques: a survey. Techinical Report (2010)
35. Fortunato, S.: Community detection in graphs. Phys. Rep. **486**, 75–174 (2010)
36. Freeman, L.: A set of measures of centrality based on betweenness. Sociometry **40**(1), 35–41 (1977)
37. Freeman, L.: Centrality in social networks conceptual clarification. Soc. Netw. **1**(3), 215–239 (1979)
38. Fruchterman, T., Reingold, E.: Graph drawing by force-directed placement. Softw. Pract. Exp. **21**(11), 1129–1164 (1991)
39. Garton, L., Haythornthwaite, C., Wellman, B.: Studying online social networks. J. Comput. Med. Commun. **3**(1), 75–105 (1997)
40. Ghosh, R., Lerman, K.: Predicting influential users in online social networks. In: Proceedings of KDD Workshop on Social Network Analysis (SNA-KDD). Washington, DC, USA (2010)
41. Girvan, M., Newman, M.E.: Community structure in social and biological networks. Proc. Nat. Acad. Sci. **99**(12), 7821–7826 (2002)
42. Gjoka, M., Kurant, M., Butts, C., Markopoulou, A.: Walking in Facebook: a case study of unbiased sampling of OSNs. In: Proceedings of the 29th Conference on Information Communications, pp. 2498–2506. IEEE, San Diego, CA, USA (2010)
43. Goh, K., Kahng, B., Kim, D.: Universal behavior of load distribution in scale-free networks. Phys. Rev. Lett. **87**(27), 278701 (2001)
44. Goh, K., Oh, E., Kahng, B., Kim, D.: Betweenness centrality correlation in social networks. Phys. Rev. E **67**(1), 17,101 (2003)
45. Goldenberg, A., Zheng, A., Fienberg, S., Airoldi, E.: A survey of statistical network models. Found. Trend Mach. Learn. **2**(2), 129–233 (2010)
46. Golub, G., Loan, C.V.: Matrix Computations. Johns Hopkins University Press, Baltimore (1996)
47. Gross, R., Acquisti, A.: Information revelation and privacy in online social networks. In: Proceedings of the 2005 Workshop on Privacy in the Electronic Society, pp. 71–80. ACM, Alexandria, VA, USA (2005)
48. Guimera, R., Amaral, L.N.: Functional cartography of complex metabolic networks. Nature **433**(7028), 895–900 (2005)
49. Guimera, R., Mossa, S., Turtschi, A., Amaral, L.: The worldwide air transportation network: anomalous centrality, community structure, and cities' global roles. Proc. Nat. Acad. Sci. **102**(22), 7794 (2005)
50. Han, J., Kamber, M.: Data Mining: Concepts and Techniques, 2nd edn. Kaufmann, San Francisco (2006)
51. Hansen, D., Smith, M., Shneiderman, B.: Analyzing Social Media Networks with NodeXL: Insights from a Connected World. Elsevier, Burlington (2010)
52. Harel, D., Koren, Y.: A fast multi-scale method for drawing large graphs. In: Proceedings of the Conference on Advanced Visual Interfaces, pp. 282–285. New York, NY, USA (2000)
53. Jeh, G., Widom, J.: SimRank: a measure of structural-context similarity. In: Proceedings of the 8th ACM SIGKDD International Conference on Knowledge Discovery and Data Mining, pp. 538–543. Edmonton, Alberta, Canada (2002)

54. Jeong, H., Tombor, B., Albert, R., Oltvai, Z., Barabási, A.: The large-scale organization of metabolic networks. Nature **407**(6804), 651–654 (2000)
55. Kim, M., Han, J.: CHRONICLE: a two-Stage density-based clustering algorithm for dynamic networks. In: Proceedings of the International Conference on Discovery Science. Lecture Notes in Computer Science, pp. 152–167. Springer (2009)
56. Kleinberg, J.: The small-world phenomenon: an algorithm perspective. In: Proceedings of the 32nd Symposium on Theory of Computing, pp. 163–170. ACM, Portland, OR, USA (2000)
57. Kleinberg, J.M.: Authoritative sources in a hyperlinked environment. J. ACM **46**(5), 604–632 (1999)
58. Kumar, R., Novak, J., Tomkins, A.: Structure and evolution of online social networks. In: Link Mining: Models, Algorithms, and Applications, pp. 337–357. Springer, New York (2010)
59. Kurant, M., Markopoulou, A., Thiran, P.: On the bias of breadth first search (bfs) and of other graph sampling techniques. In: Proceedings of the 22nd International Teletraffic Congress, pp. 1–8. Amsterdam, The Netherlands (2010)
60. Latora, V., Marchiori, M.: A measure of centrality based on network efficiency. New J. Phys. **9**, 188 (2007)
61. Leicht, E., Holme, P., Newman, M.E.J.: Vertex similarity in networks. Phys. Rev. E **73**(2), 026120 (2006)
62. Leskovec, J.: Stanford network analysis package (SNAP). URL http://snap.stanford.edu/
63. Leskovec, J., Faloutsos, C.: Sampling from large graphs. In: Proceedings of the 12th ACM SIGKDD International Conference on Knowledge Discovery and Data Mining, pp. 631–636. Philadelphia, PA, USA (2006)
64. Leskovec, J., Kleinberg, J., Faloutsos, C.: Graphs over time: densification laws, shrinking diameters and possible explanations. In: Proceedings of the 11th ACM SIGKDD International Conference on Knowledge Discovery and Data Mining, pp. 177–187. Chicago, IL, USA (2005)
65. Leskovec, J., Lang, K., Mahoney, M.: Empirical comparison of algorithms for network community detection. In: Proceedings of the 19th International Conference on the World Wide Web, pp. 631–640. ACM, Raleigh, NC, USA (2010)
66. Mathioudakis, M., Koudas, N.: Efficient identification of starters and followers in social media. In: Proceedings of the International Conference on Extending Database Technology, pp. 708–719. ACM, Saint-Petersburg, Russia (2009)
67. McCown, F., Nelson, M.: What happens when Facebook is gone? In: Proceedings of the 9th Joint Conference on Digital Libraries, pp. 251–254. ACM, Austin, TX, USA (2009)
68. Milgram, S.: The small world problem. Psychol. Today **2**(1), 60–67 (1967)
69. Mislove, A., Marcon, M., Gummadi, K., Druschel, P., Bhattacharjee, B.: Measurement and analysis of online social networks. In: Proceedings of the 7th ACM SIGCOMM Conference on Internet Measurement, pp. 29–42. ACM, San Diego, CA, USA (2007)
70. Newman, M.: Scientific collaboration networks. I. Network construction and fundamental results. Phys. Rev. E **64**(1), 16131 (2001)
71. Newman, M.: The structure and function of complex networks. SIAM Rev. **45**(2), 167 (2003)
72. Newman, M., Barabasi, A., Watts, D.: The Structure and Dynamics of Networks. Princeton University Press, Princeton/Oxford (2006)
73. Newman, M., Leicht, E.: Mixture models and exploratory analysis in networks. Proc. Nat. Acad. Sci. **104**, 9564–9569 (2007)
74. Onnela, J., Reed-Tsochas, F.: The spontaneous emergence of social influence in online systems. Proc. Nat. Acad. Sci. **107**, 18375 (2010)
75. Palla, G., Derenyi, I., Farkas, I., Vicsek, T.: Uncovering the overlapping community structure of complex networks in nature and society. Nature **435**(7043), 814–818 (2005)
76. Palmer, C., Steffan, J.: Generating network topologies that obey power laws. In: Global Telecommunications Conference, vol. 1, pp. 434–438. IEEE (2002)
77. Partow, A.: General purpose hash function algorithms. URL http://www.partow.net/programming/hashfunctions/
78. Perer, A., Shneiderman, B.: Balancing systematic and flexible exploration of social networks. IEEE Trans. Vis. Comput. Graph. **12**(5), 693–700 (2006)

79. Perer, A., Shneiderman, B.: Integrating statistics and visualization: case studies of gaining clarity during exploratory data analysis. In: Proceeding of the 26th Annual SIGCHI Conference on Human Factors in Computing Systems, pp. 265–274. ACM, Florence, Italy (2008)

80. Radicchi, F., Castellano, C., Cecconi, F., Loreto, V., Parisi, D.: Defining and identifying communities in networks. Proc. Nat. Acad. Sci. **101**(9), 2658–2663 (2004)

81. Redner, S.: How popular is your paper? An empirical study of the citation distribution. Eur. Phy. J. B **4**(2), 131–134 (1998)

82. Romero, D., Galuba, W., Asur, S., Huberman, B.: Influence and passivity in social media. In: Proceedings of the 20th International Conference Companion on World Wide Web, pp. 113–114. ACM, Hyderabad, India (2011)

83. Romero, D., Kleinberg, J.: The directed closure process in hybrid social-information networks, with an analysis of link formation on Twitter. In: Proceedings of the 4th International Conference on Weblogs and Social Media, Washington, DC, USA (2010)

84. Seidel, R.: On the all-pairs-shortest-path problem. In: Proceedings of the 24th Symposium on Theory of Computing, pp. 745–749. ACM, Victoria, BC, Canada (1992)

85. Snasel, V., Horak, Z., Abraham, A.: Understanding social networks using formal concept analysis. In: Proceedings of the Web Intelligence/IAT Workshops, pp. 390–393. IEEE, Sydney, Australia (2008)

86. Snasel, V., Horak, Z., Kocibova, J., Abraham, A.: Reducing social network dimensions using matrix factorization methods. In: International Conference on Advances in Social Network Analysis and Mining, pp. 348–351. IEEE, Athens, Greece (2009)

87. Song, X., Chi, Y., Hino, K., Tseng, B.: Identifying opinion leaders in the blogosphere. In: Proceedings of the 16th ACM Conference on Information and Knowledge Management, pp. 971–974. ACM, Lisbon, Portugal (2007)

88. Travers, J., Milgram, S.: An experimental study of the small world problem. Sociometry **32**(4), 425–443 (1969)

89. Wasserman, S., Faust, K.: Social Network Analysis: Methods and Applications. Cambridge University Press, Cambridge/New York (1994)

90. Watts, D.: Small Worlds: The Dynamics of Networks Between Order and Randomness. Princeton University Press, Princeton/Woodstock (2004)

91. Watts, D., Strogatz, S.: Collective dynamics of small-world networks. Nature **393**(6684), 440–442 (1998)

92. Wilson, C., Boe, B., Sala, A., Puttaswamy, K., Zhao, B.: User interactions in social networks and their implications. In: Proceedings of the 4th European Conference on Computer Systems, pp. 205–218. ACM, Nuremberg, Germany (2009)

93. Ye, S., Lang, J., Wu, F.: Crawling online social graphs. In: Proceedings of the 12th International Asia-Pacific Web Conference, pp. 236–242. IEEE, Busan, Korea (2010)

# Chapter 13
# Analysis of Human-Computer Interactions and Online Social Networking: A Framework

**Liguo Yu and Srini Ramaswamy**

**Abstract** Human-computer interaction plays an important role in most (if not all) computer applications. It is considered even essential for enabling social networking as dynamic Web 2.0 is becoming an important platform for communication, collaboration, information and knowledge sharing. Compared to static web pages (Web 1.0), Web 2.0 enables more intensive human-computer interactions. This chapter analyzes the relationship between human-computer interaction and social networking. A framework is outlined for representing and measuring online social networks, especially those formed through Web 2.0 applications. A case study based on this framework is performed on Wikipedia.

## Introduction

Human-computer interaction and social networking are closely related [1–4]. Before the introducing of computer networks, standalone programs are the major components of computer systems, where human-computer interaction is a pure human-computer interaction, i.e., the interaction largely happens between one human being and one computer. For example, if a user issues commands to a software program, the program will respond with some kind of results. The communication basically occurs between one human being and one computer. Because standalone programs involve few interactions between human beings, social network formation through these computer programs is rare.

L. Yu (✉)
Computer Science and Informatics, Indiana University South Bend, South Bend, IN, USA
e-mail: ligyu@iusb.edu

S. Ramaswamy
Industrial Software Systems, ABB Corporate Research Center, Bangalore, India
e-mail: srini@ieee.org

A. Abraham (ed.), *Computational Social Networks: Mining and Visualization*,
DOI 10.1007/978-1-4471-4054-2_13, © Springer-Verlag London 2012

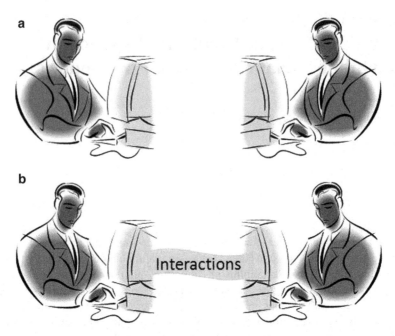

**Fig. 13.1** Interactions between human beings in (**a**) standalone programs; and (**b**) web applications

With the introducing and growth of web technologies, the computer is becoming a tool for communication, collaboration, and data/information sharing. The interaction between a human being and a computer is no longer a pure human-computer interaction. Instead, computers are largely used as the media for human-human interactions. Figure 13.1a, b illustrates the interactions occurred in standalone programs and web applications, respectively, in which, no human-human interactions occur in Fig. 13.1a while these interactions could happen in Fig. 13.1b.

If more people are involved in a web application, a social network could accordingly be formed. In that sense, computer networks (web applications) become the foundational infrastructure for social networking. These human-computer interactions serve as the media for online social networking. This is illustrated in Fig. 13.2.

Since the introducing of web technologies, online social networking has become a hot research topic [5,6]. This chapter reviews related work and analyzes web technologies and their relationship to social networking. A framework for representing and measuring online social network is outlined. Statistical studies based on this framework are performed on Wikipedia, a popular Web 2.0 site.

The remainder of the chapter is organized as follows. A review of related work is first presented. The framework is then outlined and discussed. Statistical studies are finally presented, followed by conclusions.

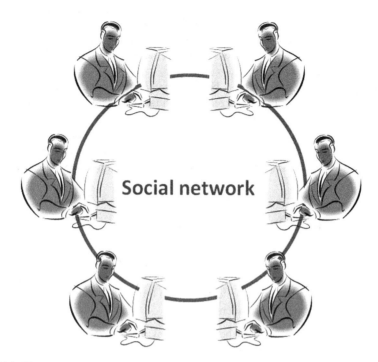

**Fig. 13.2** The social network formed through web applications

## Related Work and the Objective of This Study

Online networking has been widely studied recently, both within human-computer interaction community and outside of human-computer interaction community, such as social informatics [7–9]. One line of research is to study the properties of online social networks. For example, Arjan et al., studied the age distribution of social networks in myspace.com [10]. Zaphiris and Sarwar studied and measured the social interactions of two news groups, alt.teens and soc.senior.issues [11]. Ahn et al. [12], Liben-Nowell et al. [13], and Wilson and Nicholas [14] studied the geographical distribution of online social networks. Other research in this area includes the study of the online networking policy [15–18], and social and economical effects of online communities [19–21].

Another line of research focuses on the analysis of popular online social websites. For example, Mislove et al. examined four popular online social sites: Flickr, YouTube, LiveJournal, and Orkut [22]. They mined the publicly available user links and created the social network graph of each site. Nazir et al. developed three Facebook applications and analyzed the aggregate workload characteristics and user interaction structures [23]. They found that a small fraction of users account for the majority of activities and a small number of applications involve the majority of users. Cha et al. studied various online video systems and analyzed their popularity and statistical properties [24]. They also studied various requests, video age, aliasing and illegal content in these systems. Feng et al. studied various popular online, multiplayer, game servers [25]. Gjoka et al. [26] and Golder el al. [27] studied the properties of Facebook.

Although extensive research has been performed on popular online social networking sites, a commonly recognized and validated model to represent and study online social networks is still lacking. Different from the research described before, the objective of this study is to present a framework for representing and measuring online social networks. This framework could enable the use of statistical methods to analyze the properties and the evolution of online social networking sites.

## Framework for Online Social Networks

Online social networks are formed through computer applications, especially Web 2.0 applications, in which the key players are human beings (users). According to their relationships with online applications, two types of human beings (users) are defined. They are posters and readers.

- *Definition.* A poster is a human being who provides data/information to an online application.
- *Definition.* A reader is a human being who retrieves dada/information from an online application.

For an online video application, such as YouTube [28], a poster is the person who uploads the video clip and a reader is the person who views the video clip. For online community applications such as Facebook [29] or MySpace [30], a poster is the person who sends out a message and a reader is the person who receives that message. For a wiki application ("web pages designed to enable anyone who accesses it to contribute or modify content" [31]), such as Wikipedia [32], a poster is the person who edits an article and a reader is a person who reads the article.

Next, the terminology role is defined.

- *Definition.* A role is the function performed by a human being who participates in an online application.

There are basically two functions related to online applications: providing data (information) and receiving data (information). According to the definitions of posters and readers, a regular reader just plays one role, i.e., retrieving data (information); and a poster could play two roles: he/she not only can provide data (information) but also can retrieve data (information). This means a poster not only can view the video posted by other posters but can also view the videos posted by himself (herself).

Based on the previous discussions, it can be seen that there are no direct communications between single role players (readers), which is shown in Fig. 13.3a. The communication between a single role player (reader) and a two-role player

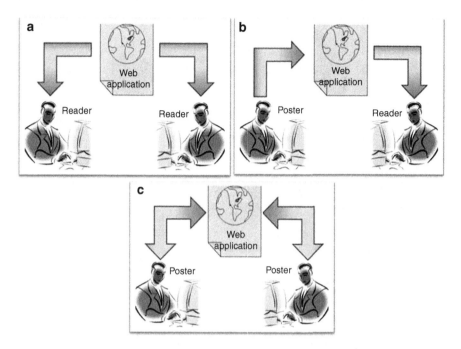

**Fig. 13.3** Information flow between (**a**) a reader and a reader; (**b**) a poster and a reader; and (**c**) a poster and a poster

(poster) has one direction, i.e., the message (information) is sent from a poster to a reader (via a web application). This is shown in Fig. 13.3b. The communication between multiple role players (posters) is bi-directional, i.e., the information could be sent back and forth from posters to posters. This is illustrated in Fig. 13.3c.

In Figure 13.3, the web applications could be in any format that allows users to participate. Besides online videos, online communities, and online knowledge base (such as Wikipedia), these web applications could also be instant messaging, newsgroup, and blogs.

Online applications not only can enable communications between two human beings, most importantly, they can also facilitate the formation of social networks that could involve hundreds, thousands, or even millions of human beings. Because different web applications might have different capabilities in facilitating human-to-human communications, we will discuss online social networks within the context of Web 1.0 and Web 2.0.

## *Web 1.0*

In Web 1.0, the web pages are static. The number of posters is much less than the number of readers. The interaction is largely one way: the information flows from the poster to the reader. The information network is asymmetric, as shown in

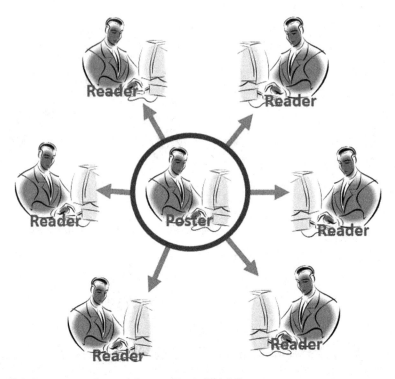

**Fig. 13.4** Pre-mature online social networking in Web 1.0

Fig. 13.4. Because the information is difficult to reach from readers to posters and from readers to readers, a large and active online social network is rare to form through Web 1.0. We call this pre-mature online social networking. The solid circle in Fig. 13.4 indicates the source of data/information; regular readers are not easy to become a poster and contribute to the data/information source.

## *Web 2.0*

In Web 2.0, the web pages are dynamic. Every reader can assume the role of a poster easily. This is represented using the dashed circle in Fig. 13.5. Two-way communications can happen between any two persons if they want to join the poster group. The social network therefore easily scales, both in the terms of size and complexity. We call this kind of social networking matured online social networking.

Because matured online social networks are more similar to real-life social networks, it is the focus of our study in this research. The online social networks that are going to be mentioned in the remaining of this chapter all refer to the matured online social network formed through Web 2.0.

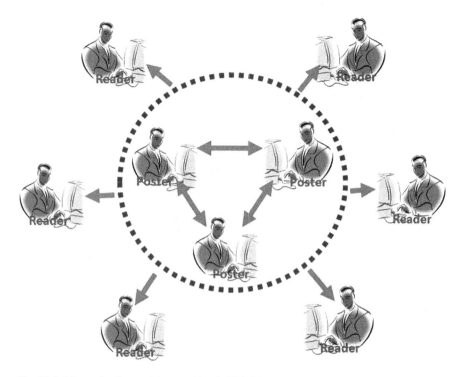

**Fig. 13.5**   Matured online social networking in Web 2.0

## Network Groups

With the evolution of online social networking, more and more people are joining the network and posting and reading various data/information. The network is becoming more and more complicated.

- *Definition.* An online network group is the composition of posters and readers who are unified by a single topic in one Web 2.0 site.

Each network group is organized though a single topic of web applications. For example, in Facebook or MySpace, the topic could be the movie star, and the group could be fans of the movie star. Similarly in YouTube, the topic could be a specific video, and the group could be the posters and the readers of that video, and in Wikipedia, the topic could be an article (or web page) and the group could be the editors and readers of that article. Figure 13.6a shows an online network group formed in one Web 2.0 site.

Because one reader/poster can participate in different groups within the same web application (Web 2.0 site), the network groups are interconnected.

- *Definition.* An online network community is the composition of online network groups that are unified through a single Web 2.0 site.

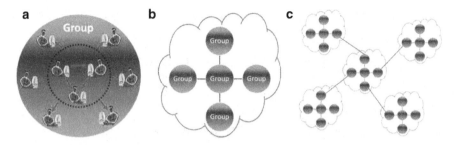

**Fig. 13.6** (a) A network group; (b) a network community; and (c) a larger social network, formed through Web 2.0 sites

Figure 13.6b shows an online network community. The connections between network groups are through posters and/or readers who are members of both groups. It is worth noting here that online social network could grow beyond one Web 2.0 site. A large network containing multiple network communities of different websites could be formed. Figure 13.6c shows a large social network composed of several network communities. The connections between network communities are through posters and/or readers who are members of different communities.

Besides readers and posters, the links (hyperlinks) can also be used to represent the interconnections between network groups and the interconnections between network communities. Accordingly, two types of links are defined.

- *Definition*. An internal link is a hyperlink embedded in one topic of a web application (site) that links to another topic of the same web application (site).
- *Definition*. An external link is a hyperlink embedded in one topic of a web application (site) that links to another topic of a different web application (site).

Internal links and external links are reasonable representations of the interconnections between network groups and the interconnections between network communities, respectively. This will be further discussed in the case study of Wikipedia presented later.

## Statistical Study of Wikipedia

In the previous section, the framework for modeling online social networks is presented and discussed. In this section, the statistical study of Wikipedia, a Web 2.0 site is presented.

### *Overview of Wikipedia*

Wikipedia is a free, multilingual online encyclopedia. It was launched in January 2001 and is currently the most popular general reference work on the Internet [33].

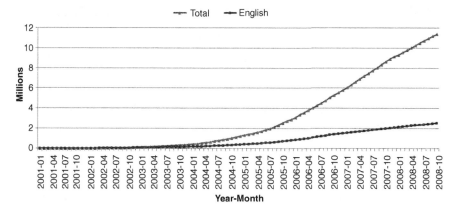

**Fig. 13.7**   The growth of the number of articles in Wikipedia (Data courtesy of [36])

Because Wikipedia is a free online encyclopedia, anyone can access any article at any time. So, everyone can become a reader. Also, because most articles in Wikipedia allow free edits by anyone and new articles can be posted by anyone, everyone can also become a poster. The communications between posters and readers and posters and posters can therefore be established through a Wikipedia article.

With more posters editing an article and more readers viewing that article, a network group could formed through that article. Also because one poster can edit multiple Wikipedia articles and one reader can view multiple Wikipedia articles, network communities are accordingly formed. Therefore, although Wikipedia does not support direct communications between posters and readers as in Facebook and MySpace, the information can be indirectly transferred from posters to readers. That is why Wikipedia is also considered as an online social networking site [34, 35].

## *Evolution of Articles (Network Groups)*

Figure 13.7 shows the growth of the number of articles in Wikipedia website. They are illustrated using both the number of English articles and the total number of articles.

Both linear regression and exponential regression are utilized to analyze these data. The results are shown in Table 13.1. It can be seen that exponential models have small values of standard error of estimates compared to linear models. This means that the growth rates of both the English articles and the total articles follow exponential models. This is also illustrated in Fig. 13.8, where exponential models better fit the observations.

**Table 13.1** Standard error of estimates of article growth

|                  | Linear model | Exponential model |
|------------------|--------------|-------------------|
| Total articles   | 1515403.04   | 1.00              |
| English articles | 292508.40    | 0.95              |

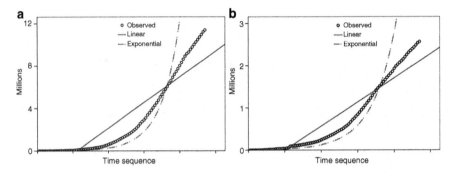

**Fig. 13.8** The observation and prediction of the growth of (**a**) total number of articles and (**b**) English articles

**Table 13.2** The number of views per article per day (Data courtesy of [36] and [37])

|           | 2003 | 2008  |
|-----------|------|-------|
| January   | 1.34 | 31.73 |
| February  | 1.39 | 33.04 |
| March     | 1.74 | 30.28 |
| April     | 2.17 | 32.07 |
| May       | 1.97 | 33.00 |
| June      | 1.80 | 33.13 |
| July      | 1.86 | 28.36 |
| August    | 2.30 | 27.60 |
| September | 4.06 | 30.25 |
| October   | 3.74 | 30.15 |

In Wikipedia, each article forms a network group, including multiple posters and multiple readers. Currently, there are over ten million network groups (article) in Wikipedia.

## *Article Views (Activity of Readers)*

The Wikipedia reader's activity can be measured using the number of article views per day. Each article view is then considered as one type of information flow from Wikipedia site to a reader. Table 13.2 shows the average views per article per day in the first 10 months of 2003 and 2008. It can be seen that for each network group (organized through an article), the reader's activity increases about 14 times: in 2003, every article receives about two views from readers per day; in 2008, this number has increased to about 30.

**Table 13.3**  The total number (in million) of article views per day (Data courtesy of [37])

|           | 2003 | 2008   |
|-----------|------|--------|
| January   | 0.18 | 295.29 |
| February  | 0.20 | 315.79 |
| March     | 0.28 | 296.45 |
| April     | 0.40 | 321.87 |
| May       | 0.39 | 338.55 |
| June      | 0.40 | 347.33 |
| July      | 0.43 | 304.26 |
| August    | 0.62 | 302.65 |
| September | 1.20 | 339.20 |
| October   | 1.20 | 343.39 |

Table 13.3 compares the total number of article views per day in the first 10 months of 2003 and 2008. It can be seen that from 2003 to 2008, on average, the number of article views per day increases about 600 times. Because article views represent readers' activity, this means Wikipedia is becoming more and more popular.

It would be interesting if we can see the growth of the number of readers of Wikipedia. Unfortunately, this cannot be directly measured. However, we can indirectly estimate this number. We define the article view requests coming from the same remote site with timeout less than or equal to 30 min as one visit (two requests coming from different sites are considered as two visits; two requests coming from the same site with timeout greater than 30 min are also considered as two visits). We find that there are about 136,000 visits per day in 2003 and 70 million visits per day in 2008. Assuming different visits are made by different users, we calculate that in 2008, on Wikipedia website, there could be about 70 million readers who have made about 300 million article views per day.

## Posters and Edits

When Wikipedia was initially launched in January 2001, there were only about ten posters. Currently (in February 2009), there are almost nine million posters (they are called Wikipedian). One activity of a poster is to edit (including post) an article. Whenever an article is edited, information is transferred from the poster to Wikipedia site.

We studied both the growth of the number of active posters (who have edited at least ten times since they joined in) and the growth of the number of edits per month from 2001 to 2006. The results show that both the number of active posters (all posters and English article posters) and the number of edits (all articles and English articles) increase exponentially, as shown in Figs. 13.9 and 13.10, respectively.

Some posters are very active in editing and posting articles; some might have never posted or edited any articles. Figure 13.11 shows the number of posters versus

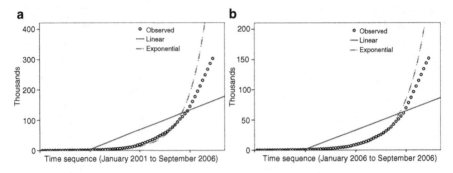

**Fig. 13.9** The observation and the prediction of the growth of (**a**) total number of active posters and (**b**) number of active English article posters (Data courtesy of [37])

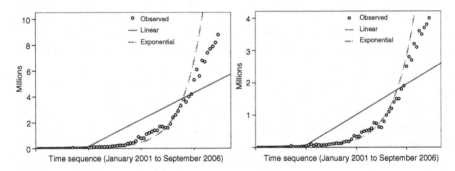

**Fig. 13.10** The observation and the prediction of the growth of the number of edits per month of (**a**) all articles; and (**b**) English articles (Data courtesy of [37])

the number of articles (in the range of 10,000–100,000) they have edited (the data is retrieved up to November 20, 2008). It can be seen that more posters have small number of edits while few posters have large number of edits.

Figure 13.12 shows the number of articles versus the number of edits (in the range of 1,000–10,000) they have been made (the data is retrieved up to May 23, 2008). It can be seen that more articles have received small number of edits while few articles have received large number of edits.

We observed that the number of articles, number of active posters, and number of edits per month all grow at exponential rates. To understand their correlations statistically, we studied their Spearman's rank correlations [40] and the coefficients are listed in Tables 13.4 and 13.5. The data is retrieved from January 2001 to September 2006, which includes 69 datasets.

In both Tables 13.4 and 13.5, all correlations are significant at the 0.001 level, i.e., strong linear correlations exist between number of articles and number of posters; number of edits and number of posters; and number of articles and number of edits. Although the statistical tests can not verify the causal relationship, it is easy to interpret the correlations: more posters mean more articles could be posted and more posters and more articles could result in more edits.

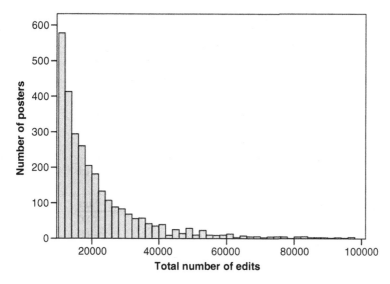

**Fig. 13.11** The number of posters versus the number of articles they have edited (Data courtesy of [38])

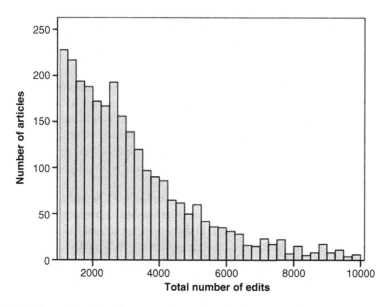

**Fig. 13.12** The number of articles versus the number of edits they have been made (Data courtesy of [39])

**Table 13.4** The Spearman's correlations among the total number of articles, total number of posters, and total number of edits (significant at the 0.001 level)

|          | Articles | Posters | Edits |
|----------|----------|---------|-------|
| Articles | –        | 0.410   | 0.404 |
| Posters  | –        | –       | 0.998 |
| Edits    | –        | –       | –     |

**Table 13.5** The Spearman's correlations among the number of English articles, number of English posters, and number of edits of English articles (significant at the 0.001 level)

|          | Articles | Posters | Edits |
|----------|----------|---------|-------|
| Articles | –        | 1.000   | 0.997 |
| Posters  | –        | –       | 0.997 |
| Edits    | –        | –       | –     |

## Network Community

As described before, each network group is organized around one article; the interconnections between network groups form the network community. The interconnections between network groups could happen between readers that access two articles and posters that edit two articles. In Wikipedia, it can also be the internal links between these two articles. This speculation is based on the following three observations: (1) Readers of one Wikipedia article quite frequently follow the internal links to read another article of Wikipedia; (2) posters of one Wikipedia article are most likely to edit another related article embedded in internal links; and (3) at least, posters of one Wikipedia article could be readers of articles of internal links, because they must have read the articles before they add the links. Therefore, in this case study, internal links are used to represent the complexity of network community of Wikipedia.

A larger network beyond a single network community (Wikipedia) could also be formed. Different network communities (websites) could be connected with readers or posters of different websites. Again, in this chapter, external links in Wikipedia articles are used to represent the connections between Wikipedia community and other online network communities (websites). This representation is based on the observation that readers of Wikipedia articles could also be the readers of another website if they follow the external links in the Wikipedia article.

We studied the evolution of the internal links and the external links in Wikipedia. Both linear model and exponential model are utilized to estimate their growth. The results are listed in Table 13.6.

Table 13.6 shows that the growth of the total number of internal links and the growth of the total number of external links are better represented as exponential

**Table 13.6** Standard error of estimates of links

|  | Linear model | Exponential model |
|---|---|---|
| Total number of internal links | 3988847.61 | 0.67 |
| Average number of internal links per article | 0.20 | 0.22 |
| Total number of external links | 766356.12 | 0.95 |
| Average number of external links per article | 0.06 | 0.58 |

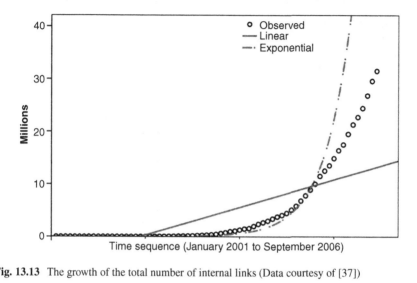

**Fig. 13.13** The growth of the total number of internal links (Data courtesy of [37])

models, while the growth of the average number of internal links per article and the growth of the average number of external links per article are better represented as linear models. The observations and the estimations using different models are also illustrated in Figs. 13.13–13.16.

We found that the total number of articles, the total number of internal links, and the total number of external links all grow at exponential rates. To understand their correlations statistically, we studied their Spearman's rank correlations, and the coefficients are listed in Table 13.7. The data is retrieved from January 2001 to September 2006, which includes 69 datasets.

It can be seen from Table 13.7 that both the number of internal links and the number of external links are linearly correlated with the number of articles. From the social network point of view, it is easy to understand their relations: both internal links and external links are embedded in Wikipedia articles, their numbers will grow with the increase of the number of articles. Therefore, we found that in Wikipedia, interconnections between network groups (represented with the internal links) and the interconnections between network communities (represented with external links) are positively correlated with the size of the network (represented with articles).

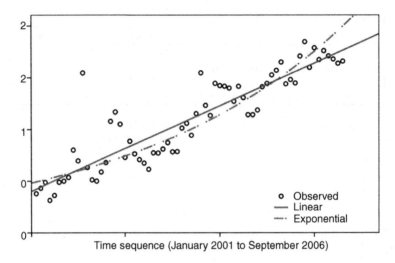

**Fig. 13.14** The growth of the average number of internal links per article (Data courtesy of [37])

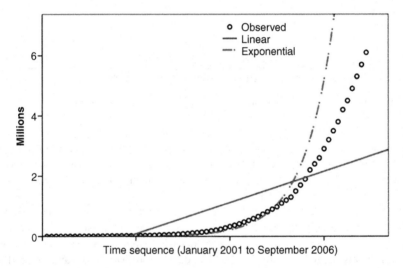

**Fig. 13.15** The growth of the total number of external links (Data courtesy of [37])

## Conclusions

In this chapter, we analyzed the relationship between human-computer interaction and online social networking. A framework is outlined for representing and measuring online social networks, especially those formed through Web 2.0 sites. We performed a case study on Wikipedia using this framework. Statistical methods were used to analyze the structures and the evolution of Wikipedia network. The major findings are listed below:

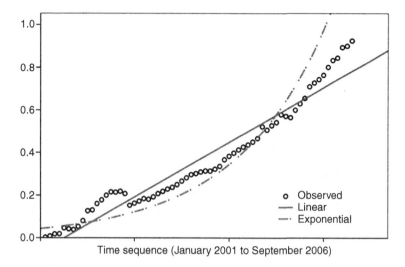

Time sequence (January 2001 to September 2006)

**Fig. 13.16** The growth of the average number of external links per article (Data courtesy of [37])

**Table 13.7** The Spearman's correlations between total number of articles and total number of internal links, total number of articles and total number of external links (significant at the 0.001 level)

|  | Number of internal links | Number of external links |
|---|---|---|
| Number of articles | 0.997 | 1.000 |

- The number of network groups (articles), number of posters, and number of edits of Wikipedia grow exponentially and they are linearly correlated.
- The number of interconnections between network groups (articles) grows exponentially and it is linearly correlated with the number of network groups (articles).
- The number of interconnections between Wikipedia and other network communities (websites) grows exponentially and it is linearly correlated with the number of network groups (articles) of Wikipedia.

Our future work will focus on the study of other Web 2.0 sites (such as Facebook, MySpace, Blogger [41]) using the framework presented in this chapter. We will compare these results with what we have found in Wikipedia in order to further validate and disseminate the framework.

# References

1. Holme, P., Edling, C.R., Liljeros, F.: Structure and time-evolution of an internet dating community. Soc. Netw. **26**(2), 155–174 (2004)
2. Boyd, D., Ellison, N.: Social network sites: definition, history, and scholarship. J. Comput. Med. Commun. **13**(1), article 11 (2007)

3. Else, L., Turkle, S.: Living online: I'll have to ask my friends. New Sci. **2569**, 48–49 (2006)
4. Urstadt, B.: Social networking is not a business. MIT Technol. Rev. July/August 2008
5. Backstrom, L., Huttenlocher, D., Kleinberg, J., Lan, X.: Group formation in large social networks: membership, growth, and evolution. In: Proceedings of the 12th ACM SIGKDD International Conference on Knowledge Discovery and Data Mining, Philadelphia, August 2006, pp. 44–54
6. Albert, R., Jeong, H., Barbsi, A.L.: The diameter of the world wide web. Nature **401**, 130–131 (1999)
7. Adamic, L.A., Buyukkokten, O., Adar, E.: A social network caught in the Web. First Monday **8**, 6 (2003)
8. Adamic, L.A.: The small world web. In: Proceedings of the 3rd European Conference on Research and Advanced Technology for Digital Libraries, Paris, September 1999, pp. 443–452
9. Zillman, M.P.: Online social networking, an internet MiniGuide Annotated Link Compilation. White paper. Available at: http://whitepapers.virtualprivatelibrary.net/Online
10. Arjan, R., Pfeil, U., Zaphiris, P.: Age differences in online social networking. In: CHI'08 Extended Abstracts on Human Factors in Computing Systems, Florence, April 2008, pp. 2739–2744
11. Zaphiris, P., Sarwar, R.: Trends, similarities, and differences in the usage of teen and senior public online newsgroups. ACM Trans. Comput. Hum. Interact. **13**(3), 403–422 (2006)
12. Ahn, Y., Han, S., Kwak, H., Moon, S., Jeong, H.: Analysis of topological characteristics of huge online social networking services. In: Proceedings of the 16th International Conference on World Wide Web, Banff, May 2007, pp. 835–844
13. Liben-Nowell, D., Novak, J., Kumar, R., Raghavan, P., Tomkins, A.: Geographic routing in social networks. Proc. Natl. Acad. Sci. **102**(33), 11623–11628 (2005)
14. Wilson, M., Nicholas, C.: Topological analysis of an online social network for older adults. In: Proceeding of the 2008 ACM Workshop on Search in Social Media, Napa Valley/California, October 2008, pp. 51–58
15. Gross, R., Acquisti, A., Heinz, H.J.: Information revelation and privacy in online social networks. In: Proceedings of the 2005 ACM Workshop on Privacy in the Electronic Society, Alexandria, November 2005, pp. 71–80
16. Krishnamurthy, B., Wills, C.E.: Characterizing privacy in online social networks. In: Proceedings of the 1st Workshop on Online Social Networks, Seattle, August 2008, pp. 37–42
17. Krishnamurthy, B., Malandrino, D., Wills, C.E.: Measuring privacy loss and the impact of privacy protection in web browsing. In: Proceedings of the 3rd Symposium on Usable Privacy and Security, Pittsburgh, July 2007, pp. 52–63
18. Krishnamurthy, B., Wills, C.E.: Generating a privacy footprint on the internet. In: Proceedings of the 6th ACM SIGCOMM Conference on Internet Measurement, Rio de Janeriro, October 2006, pp. 65–70
19. Crandall, D., Cosley, D., Huttenlocher, D., Kleinberg, J., Suri, S.: Feedback effects between similarity and social influence in online communities. In: Proceeding of the 14th ACM SIGKDD International Conference on Knowledge Discovery and Data Mining, Las Vegas, August 2008, pp. 160–168
20. Job-Sluder, K.: Local vs. global networks: network analysis of a multi-user virtual environment. In: Proceedings of the 6th International Conference on Learning Sciences, Santa Monica, June 2004, pp. 657–657
21. Tian, Y., Huang, T., Gao, W.: Quantitatively evaluating the influence of online social interactions in the community-assisted digital library. In: Proceedings of the 2nd ACM/IEEE-CS Joint Conference on Digital Libraries, Portland, July 2002, pp. 409–409
22. Mislove, A., Marcon, M., Gummadi, K.P., Druschel, P., Bhattacharjee, B.: Measurement and analysis of online social networks. In: Proceedings of the 7th ACM SIGCOMM Conference on Internet Measurement, San Diego, October 2007, pp. 29–42
23. Nazir, A., Raza, S., Chuah, C.: Unveiling facebook: a measurement study of social network based applications. In: Proceedings of the 8th ACM SIGCOMM Conference on Internet Measurement, Vouliagmeni, October 2008, pp. 43–56

24. Cha, M., Kwak, H., Rodriguez, P., Ahn, Y., Moon, S.: I tube, you tube, everybody tubes: analyzing the world's largest user generated content video system. In: Proceedings of the 7th ACM SIGCOMM Conference on Internet Measurement, San Diego, October 2007, pp. 1–14
25. Feng, W., Chang, F., Feng, W., Walpole, J.: A traffic characterization of popular on-line games. IEEE/ACM Trans. Netw. **13**(3), 488–500 (2005)
26. Gjoka, M., Sirivianos, M., Markopoulou, A., Yang, X.: Poking facebook: characterization of osn applications, In: Proceedings of the 1st Workshop on Online Social Networks, Seattle, August 2008, pp. 31–36
27. Golder, S., Wilkinson, D., Huberman, B.A.: Rhythms of social interaction: messaging within a massive online network. In: Proceedings of 3rd International Conference on Communities and Technologies, East Lansing, Michigan, USA (2007). Available at http://www.hpl.hp.com/research/idl/papers/facebook/facebook.pdf
28. http://www.youtube.com/
29. http://www.facebook.com/
30. http://www.myspace.com/
31. http://en.wikipedia.org/wiki/Wiki
32. http://wikipedia.org/
33. http://en.wikipedia.org/wiki/Wikipedia
34. http://expertvoices.nsdl.org/cornell-info204/2008/04/18/wikipedia-a-social-network/
35. http://www.trustlet.org/wiki/Wikipedia_social_network
36. http://en.wikipedia.org/wiki/Wikipedia:Multilingual_statistics
37. http://stats.wikimedia.org/EN/Sitemap.htm
38. http://en.wikipedia.org/wiki/Wikipedia:List_of_Wikipedians_by_number_of_edits
39. http://en.wikipedia.org/wiki/Most_viewed_article
40. http://en.wikipedia.org/wiki/Spearman's_rank_correlation_coefficient
41. https://www.blogger.com/start

# Chapter 14
# Implementation of Social Network Analysis for Web Cache Content Mining Visualization

**Sarina Sulaiman, Siti Mariyam Shamsuddin, and Ajith Abraham**

**Abstract** A Web cache content mining is a very important part in analyzing and filtering the internet contents. Essentially, a log data will be used to identify either to cache or not to cache Web contents in a cache server. This data contains dissimilar elements consisting of URL, size, retrieval time, number of hits and other elements for Web contents. In this chapter, we propose a new method and analyses of our cache server data using social network analysis (SNA); and make a number of statistic measurements to reveal the hidden information on E-Learning@UTM (EL) and Boston University (BU) logs dataset. The log dataset was extracted by particular queries, and it was displayed as a connected graph and clustered based on a similarity of characteristics. Later, the statistical properties of dataset network were computed, including speed and complexity. The result shows the SNA important behaviors: data localization in a separate position; and centralized data in a single position approve that the concentration of data to one node. These behaviors are driven by complexity of the dataset and network nodes structure of the chosen log dataset.

## Introduction

Social network analysis (SNA) is exploited widely in data mining to make a deep analysis on e-learning log data. Besides, Web caching can be classified through a log dataset that conceals an interesting behavior and hidden information. The Web

S. Sulaiman (✉) • S.M. Shamsuddin
Soft Computing Research Group, Faculty of Computer Science and Information Systems,
K-Economy Research Alliance, Universiti Teknologi Malaysia, 81310 Johor, Malaysia
e-mail: sarina@utm.my; mariyam@utm.my

A. Abraham
Machine Intelligence Research Labs (MIR Labs), Scientific Network for Innovation and Research
Excellence, Auburn, WA 98092, USA
e-mail: ajith.abraham@ieee.org

A. Abraham (ed.), *Computational Social Networks: Mining and Visualization*,
DOI 10.1007/978-1-4471-4054-2_14, © Springer-Verlag London 2012

cache content used in this research is a log data from E-Learning@UTM (EL) Web server that has been monitored for 2 days and Boston University (BU) client server for 7 months.

In a previous study, Grissa et al. [1] discovered that the interestingness measures (IM) cluster to assist a user to make a decision on a similar behavior of the dataset. Martinez et al. [2] proposed a combination of qualitative evaluation with social network analysis to investigate the social interaction inside classroom. The relationship inside E-Learning such as: discussing, solving doubts, sharing information and creating a product become parameters to be analyzed with SNA. They succeeded in detecting the model of collaborative design derived from activity inside a class. This research has a similar interest which is to find the vital relationship between variables inside a cache server. This relationship will bring great benefits especially on cache server performance, data size and memory management.

This chapter is organized as follows. Section "Related Studies" explains the related works on SNA, web caching, and formal concept analysis. Section "The Proposed Method" presents the proposed technique. Section "Experimental Results and Analysis" describes results analysis, and section "Discussion and Conclusion" discusses the findings and concluding remark.

## Related Studies

Popularity of social network (SN) is growing and it contains a lot of information of people's behavior all around the world. The popularity of SN becomes a concern for several researchers and has lead to numerous investigations. SN is implemented in multiple applications, including for analyzing terrorist networks, friendly command and control structures, Web content mining [3], e-learning [2, 4] and other applications. SNA assumes that relationships are important. Hidden information and relationship inside SNA attracted researchers to find out what actually happen during the communication between elements in SN. Martinez et al. [2] have chosen E-Learning as a domain problem for their research. They explored the process on exchanging information in their e-learning forum. Another work comes from Shi [5], who used SNA to identify the structures of community. His method starts with selecting data using query and create a model of semantic relation using a statistical approach: collocation, weighted dependence, and mutual information [5].

Conversely, SN is also able to be combined with some other artificial intelligence technique such as the ant colony to get a good analysis result [6]. Al-Fayoumi [6] proposed a clever ant colony metaphor that can make a cluster on the SN by using maximum clique and sub grouping criteria. The expansion of SN researches as a foundation of SNA becomes a popular technique today. SNA analyses the complication of a human system through mapping and classifying a relationship among people, groups or organizations [7].

On Web cache context, many researchers look at many ways to improve the existing caching techniques. Padmanabhan and Mogul [8] recommended a predictive model to be used as a server hint. The proposed model is equipped with a server that can create a markov model by predicting a probability of an object A that is tagged with next n requests and an object B (n is a parameter of the algorithm). The server will use the model to produce a forecast for subsequent references. The client will use the forecasted result to pre-fetch an object on a server for the object that is not in the client cache. The simulation results show that the latency is reduced up to 45%. However, the network traffic is even worse which is two times compared to the conventional solution [8]. Therefore, there is a need to provide a justification of why it is important to solve the issue on latency and network reduction simultaneously.

Bestavros et al. [9] presented a model for the speculative dissemination of World Wide Web data. Their work illustrates that reference patterns from a Web server can be used as the main source of information for pre-fetching. Their study shows that latency reduction increases until 50% despite the increment of the bandwidth utilisation. In addition, Pallis et al. [10] provided the solutions on pre-fetching by implementing a clustering method. The technique creates the cluster for pre-fetching into graph-based clustering that consists of correlated and directed clusters. This technique can be adapted in a proxy server to increase the performance. The simulation conducted on a real dataset implies that the technique can increase performance of the Web caching environment efficiently. Kroeger et al. [11] suggested that a local proxy caching can decrease latency up to 26%, while pre-fetching could decrease latency up to 57%. The combination of both methods will give better latency reduction until 60%. Furthermore, the study also describes that the algorithm on pre-fetching contributes to a reduction of latency, and it can provide double improvement on caching. However, it only happens when the latency is decreased.

Furthermore, Harding et al. [12] implemented pre-fetching on a mobile device by enhancing the feature for optimum utilisation. This feature allows users to connect to the server when it is required and few amounts of data are needed to be transferred. Fig. 14.1 shows that the majority of activities are setting up on the desktop, these will be inefficient since communication between desktop and mobile is linked through the internet. When a number of tasks and services are developed in desktop application, the mobile environment must be synchronised and customised. However, the method still has challenges in terms of an application design; user interaction, usability and mentality model. Ye et al. [13] proposed a model to manage Web caching in a multi-device that is connected to two wireless networks: MSS (mobile support station), and the neighbouring peers to form the P2P (peer to peer) network.

Based on previous works, we can conclude that SNA can be put into practice to visualize and manage the Web cache content. This is because SNA has been used widely to reveal hidden information, relationship and characteristic of dataset in graph representation for different cases.

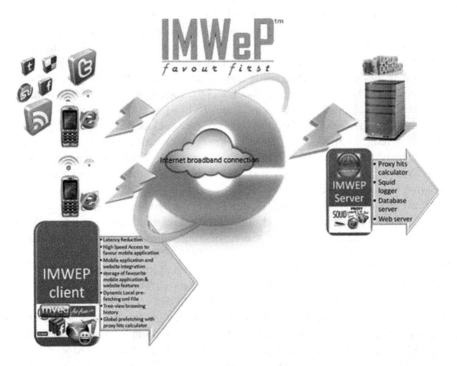

**Fig. 14.1** Architecture of Web cache server and mobile clients

## The Proposed Method

This chapter proposes an analysis of server logs data that was obtained on 13 and 14 January 2008 from one of the E-Learning@UTM (EL) servers at the Centre of Information and Communication Technology (CICT), Universiti Teknologi Malaysia (UTM) [14]. The second logs data came from a combination of 7 months (November 1994 until May 1995) of browser logs data from Boston University (BU) [15]. The investigation is intended to find a relationship between the log data variables and find a solution to increase the performance of Web cache content mining. Previously, we developed our pre-fetching technology on a mobile context and integrated it to the cache server [16, 17]. The architecture of communication between our cache server and mobile clients can be viewed in Fig. 14.1.

In Fig. 14.1, the performance of cache server is determined by the size of data transfer, relationship between elements in the cache server and also Web caching process. The proposed method is done by selecting the potential data from the main dataset and queries based on the rules generated from classification of dataset on proxy cache [18]. Next, the visualization can be perceived through a graph. Later, SNA tool will check a relationship of data and cluster the Web contents.

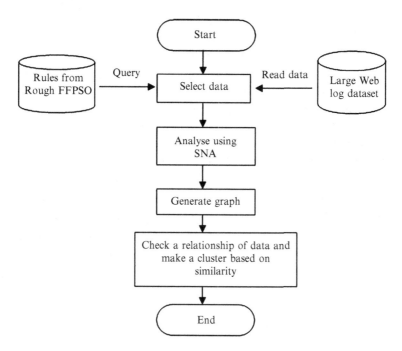

**Fig. 14.2** Methodology of the proposed method

In reality, we can learn the behavior of a Web caching process and the result can be used to enhance the cache server for future development. The process of proposed methodology is illustrated in Fig. 14.2.

## Experimental Result and Analysis

The data from large dataset is too complex and almost impossible to be analyzed with a standard PC. Therefore, as shown in the methodology Fig. 14.2, filtering procedure was used to obtain the data in small size but rich in terms of interaction. The filtered data was analysed using Organisational Risk Analyser (ORA) tool (http://www.casos.cs.cmu.edu). This tool is a statistical analysis package for analysing complex systems as Dynamic Social Networks. ORA generated a graph based on data relationship and clustered these data based on their node similarity. In this study, the node represents each element of dataset by using SNA similar to agent, resource or knowledge. The log data in Web cache server contain four main elements:

URL – Web content addresses of uniform resource locator.
SIZE – the size is expressed in bytes.

NUMBER_OF_HITS – the number of hits per data. Each complete request for Web
   content will increase the number of hits for a requested content.
CACHE – decision either to cache or not to cache the Web content.

These four elements were analyzed using SNA by checking the relationships
between URL x SIZE, URL x NUMBER_OF_HITS, while cache elements were
selected based on a particular scenario. There are several scenarios that discussed
in this chapter. The scenario is derived by selecting the data from a main dataset,
which is a very large size of data.

Each scenario contains hidden information and relationship between each element. The first and second scenario used EL dataset. At the same time, both
scenarios utilized trial and error queries to identify the nature of the relationship between Web cache contents. The third scenario with three different rules applied BU
dataset and made queries based on generated Rough FFPSO rules. Consequently,
only the first rule used the right proposed rules for BU dataset; however, the second
and third rule was queried using the proposed rules for EL dataset not for BU
dataset.

## First Scenario

The total data row for the main dataset with CACHE $= 1$ and hit number more
than zero is around two thousand records. This will affect the visualization and
analysis of the system due to the computational complexity. Hence, in this scenario
the dataset is selected using query statement:

```
SELECT * FROM [EL Dataset]
WHERE NUM_OF_HITS > 0 AND CACHE = 1 AND SIZE > 0.00269226
AND SIZE < 1;
```

After the data selection, each column needs to be associated with node class in
SNA tool:

1. URL associated as an Agent
2. SIZE associated as an Agent
3. NUM_OF_HITS as an Event
4. CACHE is not included in a process due to the cache value did not have any
   variation.

The selected data can be visualized in two modes: 2D and 3D graph. Figure 14.3
shows an interesting result in which the data is centralized in some location, and this
is similar to cluster model.

Figures 14.3 and 14.4 depict 3D visualization of the data from the first scenario
selection mode. Figure 14.3 illustrates graph positioning and zooms into one of

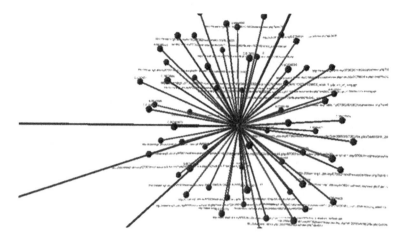

**Fig. 14.3** 3D visualization of first scenario – zoom in

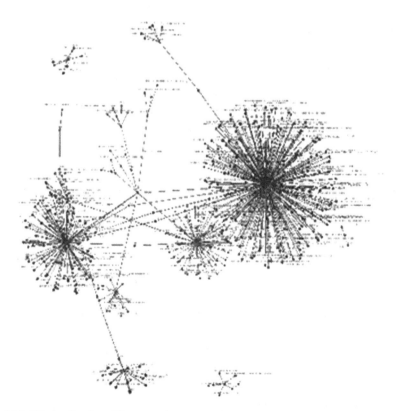

**Fig. 14.4** 3D visualization of first scenario – zoom out

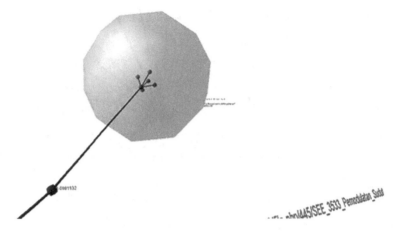

**Fig. 14.5** Clustering process on one of centralized data

the groups in dataset. This shows that the log data has a lot of similarity in one value; for example, dataset "NUM_OF_HITS" with value = 0.00175439 belongs to the numbers of rows. This similarity makes the data clustered, similar to the dataset depicted in Fig. 14.4. On the other hand, Fig. 14.5 shows the clustering process to one of the centralized data. This cluster makes the separation on the graph clear and user can easily differentiate each cluster.

The graph rendering can be monitored through networks over time. This step is useful to ensure that the 3D and 2D visualization can be generated. This step can show the duration of a transition and display phase (refer to Fig. 14.6).

Figures 14.7 and 14.8 show the graph analysis of a network level of performance measurement. Figure 14.8 focuses to detect changes in the network. The speed of agent is rising linearly according to the index of agent. The count node of agent also holds similar behavior. The node is linear increasing based on the index count node of agent. Figure 14.8 depicts that counted row between agents also rises linearly until index 2, and it changes to a steady mode after index 2. On the other hand, link count is increasing rapidly on index 4 until index 5.

## Second Scenario

The second scenario, the dataset is selected using query statement:

```
SELECT * FROM [EL Dataset]
WHERE NUM_OF_HITS > 0 AND CACHE = 1 AND SIZE > =0 AND
SIZE < = 0.00269226;
```

**Fig. 14.6** Network
monitoring

After the data selection, each column needs to be associated with node class in SNA tool:

1. URL associated as an Agent
2. SIZE associated as an Agent
3. NUM_OF_HITS as an Event
4. CACHE is not included in a process due to the cache value did not have any variation.

Total number of rows acquired from this query is 2,800 rows. These huge rows are quite hard to be visualized and analyzed. Consequently, we finally succeed to visualize this dataset and found an interesting result as shown in Figs. 14.9 and 14.10.

Figures 14.9 and 14.10 show an interesting phenomenon that happens in the second scenario. The data is pulled out to the centre of network and act like a nucleus of the dataset. It means that the dataset has a number of rows with the same "SIZE" value. Figure 14.11 illustrates this centralized effect in a 2D mode.

Figures 14.12 and 14.13 depict an analysis result of the dataset for the second scenario. Figure 14.12 shows that the values of speed for node inside the network element of this scenario dataset are very high at the beginning and drop significantly on index 2. Then, it continues to be stable until the next index. At the same time, Fig. 14.13 also shows a similar behavior where the speed of agent drops drastically when complexity starts to go up. Next, the speed of agent stays steadily on low value as long as the complexity is still in high value.

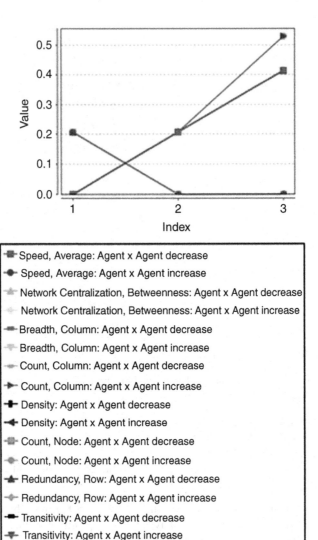

**Fig. 14.7** Over time measurement – change detection

## *Third Scenario*

The third scenario is divided into three rules. This scenario uses BU log dataset and each rule represents a particular query to filter the dataset. These rules are generated from Rough FFPSO data warehouse of intelligent Web caching on proxy cache [18, 19].

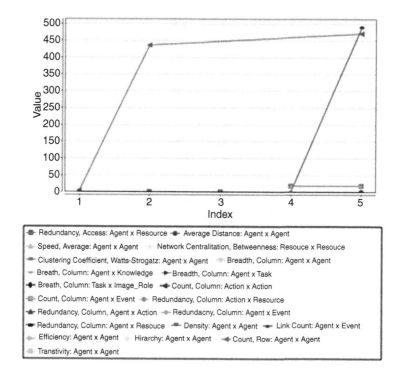

**Fig. 14.8** Over time measurement – measure value


**Rule 1: SIZE([0.00003, 0.00004)) AND NUM_OF_HITS([0.00015, 0.00045))
= > CACHE(1)**

In this rule, the selection query is made through a query as shown below:

```
SELECT * FROM [BU Dataset]
WHERE SIZE > =0.00003 AND SIZE < =0.00004 AND
NUM_OF_HITS > =0.00015 AND NUM_OF_HITS < =0.00045;
```

The visualization of this data is centralized and focused in one position as depicts in Figs. 14.14 and 14.15.

The speed of agent is steady at the beginning, and it increases rapidly starting from index 7. It reaches the climax at index 10 then starts to decrease (see Fig. 14.16).

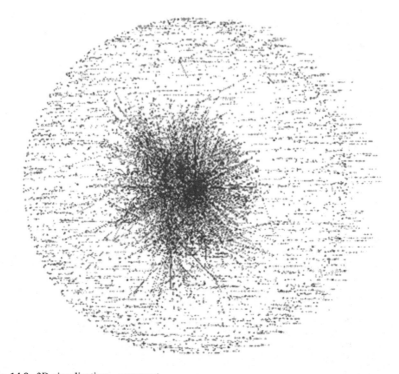

**Fig. 14.9** 3D visualization – zoom out

**Fig. 14.10** 3D visualization – zoom in

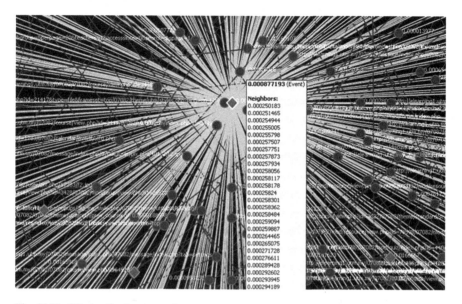

**Fig. 14.11** 2D visualization- zoom in

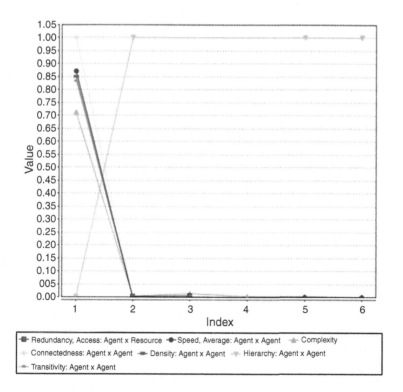

**Fig. 14.12** Over time measurement – measure value

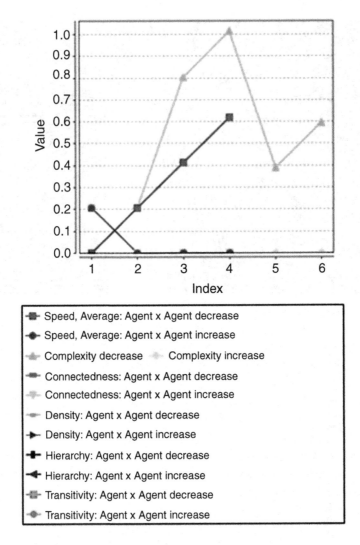

**Fig. 14.13** Over time measurement – change detection

**Rule 2: SIZE([0.00001, 0.00002)) AND NUM_OF_HITS([0.00044, 0.00132))
= > CACHE(0)**

In this rule, the selection query is made through a query as shown below:

```
SELECT * FROM [BU Dataset]
WHERE SIZE > =0.00001 AND SIZE < =0.00002 AND
NUM_OF_HITS > =0.00044 AND NUM_OF_HITS < =0.00132;
```

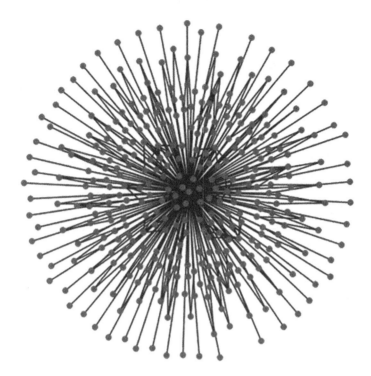

**Fig. 14.14**  Visualization of third scenario for rule 1

The second rule illustrates another interesting behavior. The BU data is centralized in two big localizations as depicted in Figs. 14.17 and 14.18.

Figure 14.19 describes the behavior of data in rule 2 and shows the increasing power in frequency 5.0. However, the power decreases in frequency between 5.0 and 7.5.

**Rule 3: SIZE([0.00006, 0.00007)) AND NUM_OF_HITS([0.00044, 0.00132)) = > CACHE(1)**

In this rule, the selection query is made through a query as stated below:

```
SELECT * FROM [BU Dataset]
WHERE SIZE > =0.00006 AND SIZE < =0.00007 AND
NUM_OF_HITS > =0.00044 and NUM_OF_HITS < =0.00132;
```

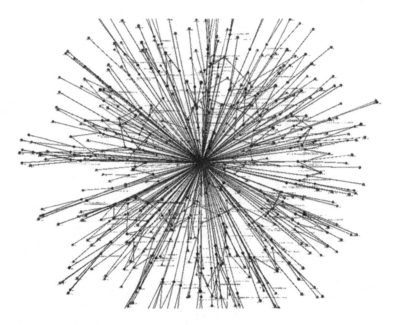

**Fig. 14.15** Visualization of third scenario rule 1 – 3D mode

The third rule has made two connected localizations and one separated localization. The separated data has shown that their data has no similarity at all other localization (see Figs. 14.20 and 14.21). Figure 14.22 is clustering mode to one of the localization in this rule 3 dataset.

Figure 14.23 describes the measurement of rule 3 dataset using change detection. Speed reaches the climax value at index 6, nevertheless starts to decrease at the next index.

Another measurement analysis that explains the performance of the graph for each scenario is as shown in Appendices (refer to Appendices 1–5). These five appendices summarize the top scoring nodes from the dataset and calculated based on (1–7) [20, 21]:

(a) Betweenness Centrality

The betweenness centrality of node $k$ in a network is defined as: across all node pairs that have a shortest path containing $k$, the percentage that pass through $k$. Individuals or organizations that are potentially influential are positioned to broker connections between groups and to bring to bear the influence of one group on

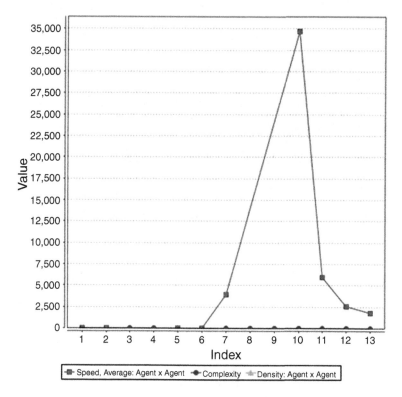

**Fig. 14.16** Over time measurement – rule1

another or serve as a gatekeeper between groups. This agent occurs on many of the shortest paths between other agents. The scientific name of this measure is betweenness centrality and it is calculated on agent by agent matrices as formulated in (14.1):

$$C_k^{\text{BET}} = \sum_i \sum_j \frac{g_{ikj}}{g_{ij}}, i \neq j \neq k \qquad (14.1)$$

where $g_{ij}$ is number of geodesic path from $i$ to $j$, while $g_{ijk}$ is number of geodesic path through node $k$.

(b) Closeness Centrality

This type of centrality calculates the average for closeness of a node to the other nodes in a network. Loosely, closeness is the inverse of the average distance in

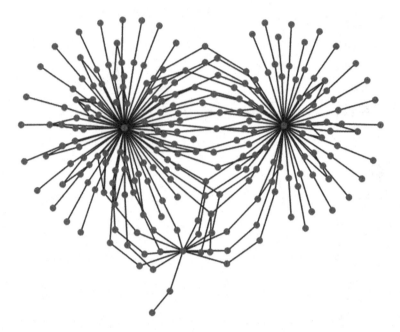

**Fig. 14.17** Visualization of third scenario for rule 2

the network between the node and all other nodes. The specific equation for this centrality as shown below in (14.2):

$$C_i^{CLO} = \sum_j dij \qquad (14.2)$$

where $d_{ij}$ is total geodesic distance from a given node to all other nodes.

(c) Eigenvector Centrality

This kind of centrality calculates the principal eigenvector of the network. A node is central to the extent that its neighbors are central. Leaders of strong cliques are individuals who or organizations who are collected to others that are themselves highly connected to each other. In other words, if we have a clique then the individual most connected to others in the clique and other cliques, is the leader of the clique. Individuals or organizations who are connected to many otherwise isolated individuals or organizations will have a much lower score in this measure then those that are connected to groups that have many connections themselves. The scientific name of this measure is eigenvector centrality, and it is calculated on agent by agent matrices as follows in (14.3):

$$\lambda v = A v \qquad (14.3)$$

**Fig. 14.18** Visualization of third scenario rule 2 – 3D Mode

where $A$ is the adjacency matrix of the graph, $\lambda$ is a constant (the eigenvalue), and $v$ is the eigenvector.

(d) Degree Centrality

The degree centrality is divided into three centralities: in-degree, out-degree and total centrality. Equation 14.4 is a basic formula to calculate the degree centrality:

$$C_d^{\text{DEG}}(v, G) \equiv |N(v)| \text{ for undirected } G \tag{14.4}$$

In the directed case, three notions of degree are generally encountered:

(e) In-degree Centrality

The in-degree centrality of a node is its normalized in-degree. For any node, e.g. an individual or a resource, the in-links are the connections that the node of interest receives from other nodes. For example, imagine an agent by knowledge matrix

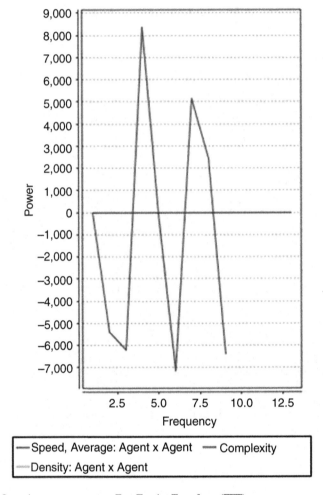

**Fig. 14.19** Over time measurement – Fast Fourier Transform (FFT)

then the number of in-links a piece of knowledge has is the number of agents that are connected to. The scientific name of this measure is in-degree and it is calculated on the agent by agent matrices as shown in (14.5):

$$\left(C_{d-}^{DEG}(v, G) \equiv |N^-(v)|\right) \tag{14.5}$$

(f) Out-degree Centrality

For any node, e.g. an individual or a resource, out-links are the connections that the node of interest sends to other nodes. For example, imagine an agent by knowledge

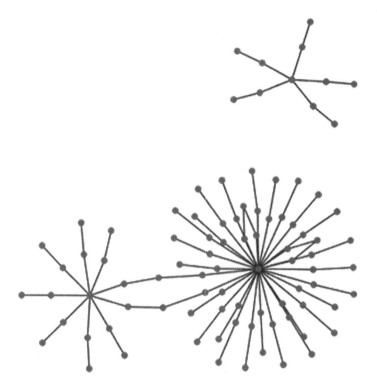

**Fig. 14.20** Visualization of third scenario for rule 3

matrix then the number of out-links an agent would have is the number of pieces of knowledge it is connected to. The scientific name of this measure is out-degree and it is calculated on the agent by agent matrices. Individuals or organizations who are high in most knowledge have more expertise or are associated with more types of knowledge than are others. If no sub-network connecting agents to knowledge exist, then this measure will not be calculated. The scientific name of this measure is out degree centrality and it is calculated on agent by knowledge matrices. Individuals or organizations who are high in "most resources" have more resources or are associated with more types of resources than are others. If no sub-network connecting agents to resources exist, then this measure will not be calculated. The scientific name of this measure is out-degree centrality and it is calculated on agent by resource matrices as formulated in (14.6):

$$\left( C_{d+}^{\mathrm{DEG}}\left(v, G\right) \equiv \left| N^{+}(v) \right| \right) \tag{14.6}$$

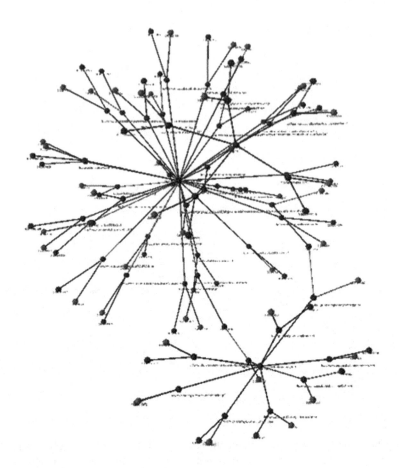

**Fig. 14.21** Visualization of third scenario rule 3 – 3D mode

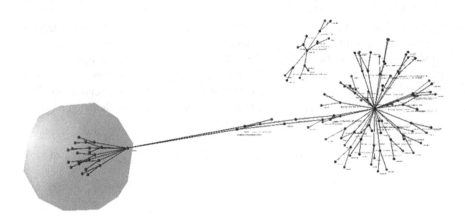

**Fig. 14.22** Visualization of third scenario rule 3 – cluster mode

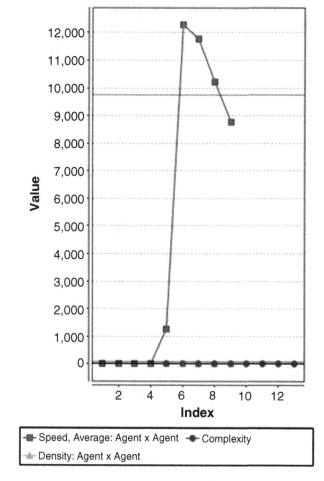

**Fig. 14.23** Over time measurement – change detection

(g) Total-degree Centrality

The total degree centrality of a node is the normalized sum of its row and column degrees. Individuals or organizations who are "in the know" are those who are linked to many others and so, by virtue of their position have access to the ideas, thoughts, beliefs of many others. Individuals who are "in the know" are identified by degree centrality in the relevant social network. Those who are ranked high on this metrics have more connections to others in the same network. The scientific name of this measure is total degree centrality and it is calculated on the agent by agent matrices. Equation 14.7 is a total between the in-degree and out-degree formula to get a calculation of the total-degree centrality:

$$\left( C_{d^t}^{DEG}(v, G) \equiv C_{d+}^{DEG}(v, G) + C_{d-}^{DEG}(v, G) \right) \tag{14.7}$$

ORA tool provides an automatic calculation of centrality measurement in their system. We used the ORA facilities to analyze our data.

## Discussion and Conclusion

This chapter proposes a new method and reveals hidden information of two different Web log dataset from two different servers using SNA. First scenario shows that the behavior of dataset is centralized in several positions and looks like they are making their own cluster. Second scenario is centralized in one position and makes network resembling a nucleus of an atom. This means that the data in the second scenario is mostly referred by other nodes inside the network. According to the measurement using the standard network analysis, the speed of second scenario drops much faster than the first scenario due to the complexity of network on dataset two which is higher than the first scenario. Alternatively, the third scenario also reveals interesting results; the first rule characteristic is centralized in one node, while in second rule it has been localized at two major locations. The third rule shows a different view than the previous rule. It is illustrated in two connected locations and one separated position. The different between expected and obtained results between each rule can probably a consequence of the exact rules for the precise dataset, as claimed in section "Experimental Result and Analysis".

This experiment reveals the capability of SNA in revealing the hidden behavior and information of Web cache data. If we use either the accurate proposed Rough FFPSO rules or trial and error queries for the right Web log dataset, we will find that a network position will be centralized. The centralization in one location demonstrates that one of the dataset is potential to be another data. This means we need to handle this data in the future in order to avoid overload access to one of the dataset.

**Acknowledgments** The first author would like to thank the Ministry of Higher Education (MOHE) for her scholarship. The authors also would like to thank Research Management Centre (RMC), Human Capital Development Unit and Soft Computing Research Group (SCRG), K-Economy Research Alliance, Universiti Teknologi Malaysia (UTM) for their overwhelming cooperation. We are sincerely thankful to Ahmad Hoirul Basori for providing helpful and excellent support to realize this research.

# Appendices

**Appendix 1**  Scenario One (Top Scoring Nodes Side by Side for Selected Measure)

| Rank | Betweenness centrality | Closeness centrality | Eigenvector centrality | In-degree centrality | Out-degree centrality | Total degree centrality |
|---|---|---|---|---|---|---|
| 1 | http://elearning1.utm.my/07082/07082/course/view.php?id=440 | http://elearning1.utm.my/07082/07082/course/view.php?id=440 | http://elearning1.utm.my/07082/07082/course/view.php?id=440 | http://elearning1.utm.my/07082/07082/course/view.php?id=440 | http://elearning1.utm.my/07082/07082/course/view.php?id=440 | http://elearning1.utm.my/07082/07082/course/view.php?id=440 |
| 2 | 0.00413256 | 0.00413256 | 0.00413256 | 0.00413256 | 0.00413256 | 0.00413256 |
| 3 | http://elearning1.utm.my/07082/mod/resource/view.php?id=91854/07082/file.php/6114/week_3/2-Intro-UTM-.ppt | http://elearning1.utm.my/07082/mod/resource/view.php?id=91854/07082/file.php/6114/week_3/2-Intro-UTM-.ppt | http://elearning1.utm.my/07082/mod/resource/view.php?id=91854/07082/file.php/6114/week_3/2-Intro-UTM-.ppt | http://elearning1.utm.my/07082/mod/resource/view.php?id=91854/07082/file.php/6114/week_3/2-Intro-UTM-.ppt | http://elearning1.utm.my/07082/mod/resource/view.php?id=91854/07082/file.php/6114/week_3/2-Intro-UTM-.ppt | http://elearning1.utm.my/07082/mod/resource/view.php?id=91854/07082/file.php/6114/week_3/2-Intro-UTM-.ppt |
| 4 | 0.0639999 | 0.0639999 | 0.0639999 | 0.0639999 | 0.0639999 | 0.0639999 |
| 5 | http://elearning1.utm.my/07082/course/category.php?id=26&perpage=20&page=3/07082/course/view.php?id=6114 | http://elearning1.utm.my/07082/course/category.php?id=26&perpage=20&page=3/07082/course/view.php?id=6114 | http://elearning1.utm.my/07082/course/category.php?id=26&perpage=20&page=3/07082/course/view.php?id=6114 | http://elearning1.utm.my/07082/course/category.php?id=26&perpage=20&page=3/07082/course/view.php?id=6114 | http://elearning1.utm.my/07082/course/category.php?id=26&perpage=20&page=3/07082/course/view.php?id=6114 | http://elearning1.utm.my/07082/course/category.php?id=26&perpage=20&page=3/07082/course/view.php?id=6114 |
| 6 | 0.00324554 | 0.00324554 | 0.00324554 | 0.00324554 | 0.00324554 | 0.00324554 |
| 7 | http://elearning1.utm.my/07082/mod/resource/view.php?id=91855/07082/file.php/6114/week_3/3-Intro-UTM.ppt | http://elearning1.utm.my/07082/mod/resource/view.php?id=91855/07082/file.php/6114/week_3/3-Intro-UTM.ppt | http://elearning1.utm.my/07082/mod/resource/view.php?id=91855/07082/file.php/6114/week_3/3-Intro-UTM.ppt | http://elearning1.utm.my/07082/mod/resource/view.php?id=91855/07082/file.php/6114/week_3/3-Intro-UTM.ppt | http://elearning1.utm.my/07082/mod/resource/view.php?id=91855/07082/file.php/6114/week_3/3-Intro-UTM.ppt | http://elearning1.utm.my/07082/mod/resource/view.php?id=91855/07082/file.php/6114/week_3/3-Intro-UTM.ppt |

(continued)

**Appendix 1** (continued)

| Rank | Betweenness centrality | Closeness centrality | Eigenvector centrality | In-degree centrality | Out-degree centrality | Total degree centrality |
|---|---|---|---|---|---|---|
| 8 | http://elearning1.utm.my/07082/file.php/6114/200708/ Tutorial-basic.doc/07082/course/view.php?id=6114 | http://elearning1.utm.my/07082/file.php/6114/200708/ Tutorial-basic.doc/07082/course/view.php?id=6114 | http://elearning1.utm.my/07082/file.php/6114/200708/ Tutorial-basic.doc/07082/course/view.php?id=6114 | http://elearning1.utm.my/07082/file.php/6114/200708/ Tutorial-basic.doc/07082/course/view.php?id=6114 | http://elearning1.utm.my/07082/file.php/6114/200708/ Tutorial-basic.doc/07082/course/view.php?id=6114 | http://elearning1.utm.my/07082/file.php/6114/200708/ Tutorial-basic.doc/07082/course/view.php?id=6114 |
| 9 | http://elearning1.utm.my/07082/mod/ resource/view.php?id=93456/07082/file.php/6114/200708/4-stereochem-UTM.ppt | http://elearning1.utm.my/07082/mod/ resource/view.php?id=93456/07082/file.php/6114/200708/4-stereochem-UTM.ppt | http://elearning1.utm.my/07082/mod/ resource/view.php?id=93456/07082/file.php/6114/200708/4-stereochem-UTM.ppt | http://elearning1.utm.my/07082/mod/ resource/view.php?id=93456/07082/file.php/6114/200708/4-stereochem-UTM.ppt | http://elearning1.utm.my/07082/mod/ resource/view.php?id=93456/07082/file.php/6114/200708/4-stereochem-UTM.ppt | http://elearning1.utm.my/07082/mod/ resource/view.php?id=93456/07082/file.php/6114/200708/4-stereochem-UTM.ppt |
| 10 | http://elearning1.utm.my/07082/mod/ resource/view.php?id=93458/07082/file.php/6114/200708/5-Bondin-VBT-UTM.ppt | http://elearning1.utm.my/07082/mod/ resource/view.php?id=93458/07082/file.php/6114/200708/5-Bondin-VBT-UTM.ppt | http://elearning1.utm.my/07082/mod/ resource/view.php?id=93458/07082/file.php/6114/200708/5-Bondin-VBT-UTM.ppt | http://elearning1.utm.my/07082/mod/ resource/view.php?id=93458/07082/file.php/6114/200708/5-Bondin-VBT-UTM.ppt | http://elearning1.utm.my/07082/mod/ resource/view.php?id=93458/07082/file.php/6114/200708/5-Bondin-VBT-UTM.ppt | http://elearning1.utm.my/07082/mod/ resource/view.php?id=93458/07082/file.php/6114/200708/5-Bondin-VBT-UTM.ppt |

**Appendix 2** Scenario Two (Top Scoring Nodes Side by Side for Selected Measure)

| Rank | Betweenness centrality | Closeness centrality | Eigenvector centrality | In-degree centrality | Out-degree centrality | Total degree centrality |
|---|---|---|---|---|---|---|
| 1 | http://elearning.utm.my/07082 | http://elearning.utm.my/07082 | http://elearning.utm.my/07082 | http://elearning.utm.my/07082 | http://elearning.utm.my/07082 | http://elearning.utm.my/07082 |
| 2 | 0.0000186767 | 0.0000186767 | 0.0000186767 | 0.0000186767 | 0.0000186767 | 0.0000186767 |
| 3 | http://elearning.utm.my/07082/ | http://elearning.utm.my/07082/ | http://elearning.utm.my/07082/ | http://elearning.utm.my/07082/ | http://elearning.utm.my/07082/ | http://elearning.utm.my/07082/ |
| 4 | http://elearning.utm.my/07082/ 0.00180896 | http://elearning.utm.my/07082/ 0.00180896 | http://elearning.utm.my/07082/ 0.00180896 | http://elearning.utm.my/07082/ 0.00180896 | http://elearning.utm.my/07082/ 0.00180896 | http://elearning.utm.my/07082/ 0.00180896 |
| 5 | http://elearning1.utm.my/07082/07082/theme/standard/styles.php?lang=en_utf8 | http://elearning1.utm.my/07082/07082/theme/standard/styles.php?lang=en_utf8 | http://elearning1.utm.my/07082/07082/theme/standard/styles.php?lang=en_utf8 | http://elearning1.utm.my/07082/07082/theme/standard/styles.php?lang=en_utf8 | http://elearning1.utm.my/07082/07082/theme/standard/styles.php?lang=en_utf8 | http://elearning1.utm.my/07082/07082/theme/standard/styles.php?lang=en_utf8 |
| 6 | 0.00269226 | 0.00269226 | 0.00269226 | 0.00269226 | 0.00269226 | 0.00269226 |
| 7 | http://elearning1.utm.my/07082/07082/theme/utm/styles.php?lang=en_utf8 | http://elearning1.utm.my/07082/07082/theme/utm/styles.php?lang=en_utf8 | http://elearning1.utm.my/07082/07082/theme/utm/styles.php?lang=en_utf8 | http://elearning1.utm.my/07082/07082/theme/utm/styles.php?lang=en_utf8 | http://elearning1.utm.my/07082/07082/theme/utm/styles.php?lang=en_utf8 | http://elearning1.utm.my/07082/07082/theme/utm/styles.php?lang=en_utf8 |
| 8 | 0.000631347 | 0.000631347 | 0.000631347 | 0.000631347 | 0.000631347 | 0.000631347 |
| 9 | http://elearning1.utm.my/07082/07082/lib/javascript-static.js | http://elearning1.utm.my/07082/07082/lib/javascript-static.js | http://elearning1.utm.my/07082/07082/lib/javascript-static.js | http://elearning1.utm.my/07082/07082/lib/javascript-static.js | http://elearning1.utm.my/07082/07082/lib/javascript-static.js | http://elearning1.utm.my/07082/07082/lib/javascript-static.js |
| 10 | 0.000404541 | 0.000404541 | 0.000404541 | 0.000404541 | 0.000404541 | 0.000404541 |

**Appendix 3** Scenario Three: First Rule (Top Scoring Nodes Side by Side for Selected Measure)

| Rank | Betweenness centrality | Closeness centrality | Eigenvector centrality | In-degree centrality | Out-degree centrality | Total degree centrality |
|---|---|---|---|---|---|---|
| 1 | http://wings.buffalo.edu/world | http://wings.buffalo.edu/world | http://wings.buffalo.edu/world | http://wings.buffalo.edu/world | http://wings.buffalo.edu/world | http://wings.buffalo.edu/world |
| 2 | 0.0000342883 | 0.0000342883 | 0.0000342883 | 0.0000342883 | 0.0000342883 | 0.0000342883 |
| 3 | 0.000300571 | 0.000300571 | 0.000300571 | 0.000300571 | 0.000300571 | 0.000300571 |
| 4 | http://mistral.enst.fr/~pioch/louvre/corp/eb/jump.gif | http://mistral.enst.fr/~pioch/louvre/corp/eb/jump.gif | http://mistral.enst.fr/~pioch/louvre/corp/eb/jump.gif | http://mistral.enst.fr/~pioch/louvre/corp/eb/jump.gif | http://mistral.enst.fr/~pioch/louvre/corp/eb/jump.gif | http://mistral.enst.fr/~pioch/louvre/corp/eb/jump.gif |
| 5 | 0.0000338095 | 0.0000338095 | 0.0000338095 | 0.0000338095 | 0.0000338095 | 0.0000338095 |
| 6 | http://cs-www.bu.edu/staff/TA/nafnaf/www/icons/redball.gif | http://cs-www.bu.edu/staff/TA/nafnaf/www/icons/redball.gif | http://cs-www.bu.edu/staff/TA/nafnaf/www/icons/redball.gif | http://cs-www.bu.edu/staff/TA/nafnaf/www/icons/redball.gif | http://cs-www.bu.edu/staff/TA/nafnaf/www/icons/redball.gif | http://cs-www.bu.edu/staff/TA/nafnaf/www/icons/redball.gif |
| 7 | 0.0000303987 | 0.0000303987 | 0.0000303987 | 0.0000303987 | 0.0000303987 | 0.0000303987 |
| 8 | http://cs-www.bu.edu/staff/TA/nafnaf/www/icons/yellowball.gif | http://cs-www.bu.edu/staff/TA/nafnaf/www/icons/yellowball.gif | http://cs-www.bu.edu/staff/TA/nafnaf/www/icons/yellowball.gif | http://cs-www.bu.edu/staff/TA/nafnaf/www/icons/yellowball.gif | http://cs-www.bu.edu/staff/TA/nafnaf/www/icons/yellowball.gif | http://cs-www.bu.edu/staff/TA/nafnaf/www/icons/yellowball.gif |
| 9 | http://zcias3.ziff.com/~pcweek/eamonn/icons/redball.gif | http://zcias3.ziff.com/~pcweek/eamonn/icons/redball.gif | http://zcias3.ziff.com/~pcweek/eamonn/icons/redball.gif | http://zcias3.ziff.com/~pcweek/eamonn/icons/redball.gif | http://zcias3.ziff.com/~pcweek/eamonn/icons/redball.gif | http://zcias3.ziff.com/~pcweek/eamonn/icons/redball.gif |
| 10 | 0.0000318348 | 0.0000318348 | 0.0000318348 | 0.0000318348 | 0.0000318348 | 0.0000318348 |

**Appendix 4** Scenario Three: Second Rule (Top Scoring Nodes Side by Side for Selected Measure)

| Rank | Betweenness centrality | Closeness centrality | Eigenvector centrality | In-degree centrality | Out-degree centrality | Total degree centrality |
|---|---|---|---|---|---|---|
| 1 | http://www-penninfo.upenn.edu:1962/penninfo-srv.upenn.edu/9000/11584.html | http://www-penninfo.upenn.edu:1962/penninfo-srv.upenn.edu/9000/11584.html | http://www-penninfo.upenn.edu:1962/penninfo-srv.upenn.edu/9000/11584.html | http://www-penninfo.upenn.edu:1962/penninfo-srv.upenn.edu/9000/11584.html | http://www-penninfo.upenn.edu:1962/penninfo-srv.upenn.edu/9000/11584.html | http://www-penninfo.upenn.edu:1962/penninfo-srv.upenn.edu/9000/11584.html |
| 2 | 0.0000136435 | 0.0000136435 | 0.0000136435 | 0.0000136435 | 0.0000136435 | 0.0000136435 |
| 3 | 0.000901713 | 0.000901713 | 0.000901713 | 0.000901713 | 0.000901713 | 0.000901713 |
| 4 | http://cs-www.bu.edu/faculty/heddaya/CS103/syllabus.html | http://cs-www.bu.edu/faculty/heddaya/CS103/syllabus.html | http://cs-www.bu.edu/faculty/heddaya/CS103/syllabus.html | http://cs-www.bu.edu/faculty/heddaya/CS103/syllabus.html | http://cs-www.bu.edu/faculty/heddaya/CS103/syllabus.html | http://cs-www.bu.edu/faculty/heddaya/CS103/syllabus.html |
| 5 | 0.0000172937 | 0.0000172937 | 0.0000172937 | 0.0000172937 | 0.0000172937 | 0.0000172937 |
| 6 | gopher://gopher.enews.com:2100/11/newsletter/bw/Current%20Issue | gopher://gopher.enews.com:2100/11/newsletter/bw/Current%20Issue | gopher://gopher.enews.com:2100/11/newsletter/bw/Current%20Issue | gopher://gopher.enews.com:2100/11/newsletter/bw/Current%20Issue | gopher://gopher.enews.com:2100/11/newsletter/bw/Current%20Issue | gopher://gopher.enews.com:2100/11/newsletter/bw/Current%20Issue |
| 7 | 0.0000187897 | 0.0000187897 | 0.0000187897 | 0.0000187897 | 0.0000187897 | 0.0000187897 |
| 8 | 0.000601142 | 0.000601142 | 0.000601142 | 0.000601142 | 0.000601142 | 0.000601142 |
| 9 | gopher://gopher.enews.com:2100/11/magazines/alphabetic/gl/games/Current%20Issue | gopher://gopher.enews.com:2100/11/magazines/alphabetic/gl/games/Current%20Issue | gopher://gopher.enews.com:2100/11/magazines/alphabetic/gl/games/Current%20Issue | gopher://gopher.enews.com:2100/11/magazines/alphabetic/gl/games/Current%20Issue | gopher://gopher.enews.com:2100/11/magazines/alphabetic/gl/games/Current%20Issue | gopher://gopher.enews.com:2100/11/magazines/alphabetic/gl/games/Current%20Issue |
| 10 | 0.0000147206 | 0.0000147206 | 0.0000147206 | 0.0000147206 | 0.0000147206 | 0.0000147206 |

**Appendix 5** Scenario Three: Third Rule (Top Scoring Nodes Side by Side for Selected Measure)

| Rank | Betweenness centrality | Closeness centrality | Eigenvector centrality | In-degree centrality | Out-degree centrality | Total degree centrality |
|---|---|---|---|---|---|---|
| 1 | http://multivac.ludd.luth.se/pub/sounds/songs/bach/ | http://multivac.ludd.luth.se/pub/sounds/songs/bach/ | http://multivac.ludd.luth.se/pub/sounds/songs/bach/ | http://multivac.ludd.luth.se/pub/sounds/songs/bach/ | http://multivac.ludd.luth.se/pub/sounds/songs/bach/ | http://multivac.ludd.luth.se/pub/sounds/songs/bach/ |
| 2 | 0.00006726 | 0.00006726 | 0.00006726 | 0.00006726 | 0.00006726 | 0.00006726 |
| 3 | 0.000601142 | 0.000601142 | 0.000601142 | 0.000601142 | 0.000601142 | 0.000601142 |
| 4 | http://www.ccs.neu.edu/home/thigpen/ROM/ROM.html | http://www.ccs.neu.edu/home/thigpen/ROM/ROM.html | http://www.ccs.neu.edu/home/thigpen/ROM/ROM.html | http://www.ccs.neu.edu/home/thigpen/ROM/ROM.html | http://www.ccs.neu.edu/home/thigpen/ROM/ROM.html | http://www.ccs.neu.edu/home/thigpen/ROM/ROM.html |
| 5 | 0.0000619941 | 0.0000619941 | 0.0000619941 | 0.0000619941 | 0.0000619941 | 0.0000619941 |
| 6 | 0.00120228 | 0.00120228 | 0.00120228 | 0.00120228 | 0.00120228 | 0.00120228 |
| 7 | http://metaverse.com/ | http://metaverse.com/ | http://metaverse.com/ | http://metaverse.com/ | http://metaverse.com/ | http://metaverse.com/ |
| 8 | 0.0000667215 | 0.0000667215 | 0.0000667215 | 0.0000667215 | 0.0000667215 | 0.0000667215 |
| 9 | http://www.ibm.com/images/solutions_icon1.gif | http://www.ibm.com/images/solutions_icon1.gif | http://www.ibm.com/images/solutions_icon1.gif | http://www.ibm.com/images/solutions_icon1.gif | http://www.ibm.com/images/solutions_icon1.gif | http://www.ibm.com/images/solutions_icon1.gif |
| 10 | 0.0000647468 | 0.0000647468 | 0.0000647468 | 0.0000647468 | 0.0000647468 | 0.0000647468 |

# References

1. Grissa, D., Guillaume, S., Nguifo, E. M.: Combining clustering techniques and formal concept analysis to characterize interestingness measures. CoRR abs/1008.3629 (2010)
2. Martinez, A., Dimitriadis, Y., Rubia, B., Gomez, E., Fuente, P.D.L.: Combining qualitative evaluation and social network analysis for the study of classroom social interactions. Comput. Educ. **41**, 353–368 (2003)
3. Kudelka, M., Snasel, V., Horak, Z., Hassanien, A.E., Abraham, A.: Web communities defined by web page content. In: Computational Social Networks: Tools, Perspectives and Analysis, pp. 349–370. Springer, London (2010). ISBN 978-1-84882-228-3
4. Erlin, A., Yusof, N., Abdul, R.A.: Overview on agent application to support collaborative learning interaction. J. US-China Educ. Rev. **5**(38), 52–60 (2008). ISSN 1548-6613, USA
5. Shi, X.: Social Network Analysis of Web Search Engine Query Logs. Technical Report, University of Michigan, School of Information (2007)
6. Al-Fayoumi Jr., M., Banerjee, S., Mahanti, P.K.: Analysis of social network using clever ant colony metaphor. World Acad. Sci. Eng. Technol. J. **53**, 970–974 (2009)
7. Sammantha, L., Magsino, R.: Applications of Social Network Analysis for Building Community Disaster Resilience: Workshop Summary. National Academies Press, Washington, DC (2009). ISBN 0-309-14095-1
8. Padmanabhan, V.N., Mogul, J.C.: Using predictive pre-fetching to improve world wide web latency. Comput. Commun. Rev. **26**, 22–36. In: ACM, SIGCOMM'96, July 1996
9. Bestavros, A., Cunha, C.: A pre-fetching protocol using client speculation for the WWW. Technical Report TR-95-011, Boston University, Department of Computer Science, Boston, MA, Apr 1995
10. Pallis, G., Vakali, A., Pokorny, J.: A clustering-based approach for short-term prefetching on a web cache environment. Comput. Electr. Eng. J. **34**(4), 309–323 (2008)
11. Kroeger, T.M., Long, D.E., Mogul, J.C.: Exploring the bounds of web latency reduction from caching and prefetching. In: USENIX Symposium on Internet Technologies and Systems (USITS), Monterey, CA, 8–11 Dec 1997
12. Harding, M., Storz O., Davies, N., Friday, A.: Planning ahead: techniques for simplifying mobile service use. In: Proceedings of the 10th workshop on Mobile Computing Systems and Applications, Santa Cruz, CA, pp. 1–6, 23–24 Feb 2009
13. Ye, F., Li, Q., Chen, E.: Benefit based cache data placement and update for mobile peer to peer networks. World Wide Web J. **14**(3), 243–259 (2008)
14. Sulaiman, S., Shamsuddin, S.M., Forkan, F., Abraham, A., Sulaiman, S.: Intelligent web caching for e-learning log data. In: Third Asia International Conference on Modelling and Simulation, AMS 2009, pp. 136–1410. IEEE Computer Society Press, Washington, DC (2009)
15. Sulaiman, S., Shamsuddin, S.M., Forkan, F., Abraham, A.: Autonomous SPY: intelligent web proxy caching detection using neurocomputing and particle swarm optimization. In: Proceeding of the 6th International Symposium on Mechatronics and its Applications (ISMA09), Sharjah, UAE, pp. 1–6. IEEE Press, Washington, DC, ISBN: 978-1-4244-3480-0 (2009)
16. Sulaiman, S., Shamsuddin, S.M., Abraham, A., Sulaiman, S.: Intelligent mobile web prefetching using XML technology. In: Proceedings of the Sixth International Conference on Next Generation Web Services Practices (NWeSP 2010), India, pp. 129–134. IEEE Press, Washington, DC, ISBN:978-1-4244-7818-7 (2010)
17. Sulaiman, S., Shamsuddin, S.M., Abraham, A.: Rough neuro-PSO web caching and XML prefetching for accessing Facebook from mobile environment. In: Proceedings of the 8th International Conference on Computer Information Systems and Industrial Management (CISIM 2009), pp. 884–889. IEEE Press, Washington, DC, ISBN: 978-1-4244-5612-3 (2009)
18. Sulaiman, S., Shamsuddin, S.M., Abraham, A.: Rough Web Caching, Rough Set Theory: A True Landmark in Data Analysis, Studies in Computational Intelligence, pp. 187–211. Springer, Berlin (2009). ISBN 978-3-540-89920-4

19. Sulaiman, S., Shamsuddin, S.M., Abraham, A.: Data warehousing for rough web caching and prefetching. In: Proceedings of the IEEE International Conference on Granular Computing (IEEE GrC 2010), San Jose, pp. 443–448. IEEE Computer Society, Washington, DC, ISBN 978-0-7695-4161-7 (2010)
20. Borgatti, S.P., Everett, M.G.: A graph-theoretic perspective on centrality. Soc. Netw. **28**(4), 466–484 (2006)
21. Butts, C.T.: Social network analysis with SNA. J. Stat. Softw. **24**(6), 1–51 (2008)

# Index